Aboriginal and Treaty Rights in Canada

Edited by Michael Asch

Aboriginal and Treaty Rights in Canada: Essays on Law, Equality, and Respect for Difference

UBC PRESS / VANCOUVER

Published in association with the Centre for Constitutional Studies, University of Alberta

Printed in Canada on acid-free paper ∞

ISBN 0-7748-0580-3 (hardcover)
ISBN 0-7748-0581-1 (paperback)

Canadian Cataloguing in Publication Data
Aboriginal and treaty rights in Canada

Includes bibliographical references and index.
ISBN 0-7748-0580-3 (bound)
ISBN 0-7748-0581-1 (pbk)

1. Native peoples – Canada – Legal status, laws, etc.* 2. Native peoples – Canada
– Land tenure.* 3. Native land transfers – Canada.* 4. Native peoples – Canada –
Claims.* 5. Native peoples – Canada – Government relations.* I. Asch, Michael.
E92.A23 1997   323.1'197071   C96-910882-6

Publication of this book has been made possible by a special project grant gener-
ously provided by the Alberta Law Foundation.

UBC Press gratefully acknowledges the ongoing support to its publishing
program from the Canada Council, the Province of British Columbia Cultural
Services Branch, and the Department of Communications of the Government of
Canada.

UBC Press
University of British Columbia
6344 Memorial Road
Vancouver, BC V6T 1Z2
(604) 822-3259
Fax: 1-800-668-0821
E-mail: orders@ubcpress.ubc.ca
http://www.ubcpress.ubc.ca

Contents

Acknowledgments

I wish to thank Larry Chartrand, Kate Sutherland, and Sharon Venne for their advice in working through issues to be addressed in the book, the Alberta Law Foundation for providing material support to the project, and the people at UBC Press for their cooperation in seeing the book come to completion. To Shirleen Smith, David Schneiderman, Joyce Green, and Margaret Asch, I offer a heartfelt 'thank you' for the contributions you have made and the support it has provided for me throughout this project.

Introduction

Michael Asch

Law has two contrasting faces.[1] On one face, the rule of law represents a crucial means whereby the dominant rules and values in a society are applied and enforced. On the other, law represents a place where, sometimes, those rules and values are challenged and new ways of understanding may emerge. Such is the case with Aboriginal rights law. It is axiomatic that, since Confederation, Canadian law has represented a fundamental means whereby the values and institutions derived from the culture of the settlers, immigrants, colonists, and their descendants were to be imposed upon Indigenous peoples. At the same time, there have been moments when these institutions and values have been successfully challenged through the application of the rule of law.

One central moment of challenge was the 1973 decision by the Supreme Court of Canada in the *Calder*[2] case. That decision established that, notwithstanding either the course of Canadian history as understood by the descendants of the settlers, immigrants, and colonists or legal precedent derived from British colonial law, the Canadian state was required to recognize the self-evident yet hitherto ignored fact that Aboriginal peoples lived in societies prior to the arrival of Europeans and that, as a consequence, there was a likelihood that their institutions, tenures, and rights to government remained in place despite the presumption of Canadian sovereignty. It was a singular moment and it did not go unnoticed by the governing politicians or by the legal community. Indeed, such is the power of law that this decision set in motion a course that, ultimately, led governments to move from a position where Aboriginal rights were deemed not to exist to a place where both Aboriginal and treaty rights were recognized and affirmed in the 1982 Canadian Constitution Act.

As the legal and constitutional events that followed ratification of the Constitution attest, at one level the ramifications of the process initiated by *Calder* are still in play. Yet at the same time it has become clear that the law, as understood and implemented by both courts and legislatures, has pulled back from the challenge to forge new ways of understanding relations between Aboriginal peoples and Canada as first articulated in *Calder* and later expressed in the affirmation and recognition of Aboriginal and treaty rights in the Constitution Act of 1982. Instead, courts and legislatures have returned to a reliance on modes of understanding that find their firm footing in the legacy of the British colonial legal system.

In this book, the authors are drawn to address the following question: What are some steps whereby law could take up the challenge issued by Justice Hall in *Calder*[3] to approach legal interpretation and assessment 'in the light of present-day research and knowledge' and re-imagine a legal regime that was founded on the presumed equality of peoples and respect for difference – concepts that are in keeping with contemporary Canadian institutions and values?

The book begins with three papers that outline general themes that, were they adopted as interpretive frames by the politicians and judges, could promote the ideals articulated in *Calder*. J. Edward Chamberlin, in an essay entitled 'Culture and Anarchy in Indian Country,' challenges the legal reading and current mainstream political view of historic treaties. Using evidence gleaned from the treaty-making process and from mid-nineteenth-century British culture as exemplified in the work of Matthew Arnold, Chamberlin advances the proposition that, at the time historic treaties were negotiated in the Canadian west, Canadian and British authorities, as well as the leadership of the First Nations, recognized that each belonged to a separate polity. Therefore, the objective of making a treaty on both sides was to replace the anarchy that generally results when two polities occupy the same space without agreement with a system of predictable and lawful relations based on a mutual meeting of the minds. As Chamberlin states: 'on *both* sides [treaties] were about culture and anarchy – about establishing social, political, and economic cultures within which diversity would still flourish, and between which there were some common standards.' This respect for separable identities that infused treaty-making needs to be reflected in the manner in which we understand the treaties today. To this end, Chamberlin finds that, in deciphering the 'grammar of assent' in the present day, it is essential to refer to the oral understanding of the treaties, for these 'spoken texts' are 'the texts upon which both the political authority and the cultural integrity of both sides depend, bulwarks against the anarchy of relativist political (which is to say, legal) interpretations and the chaos of cultural pluralism.'

If Chamberlin urges a fully contextualized historical approach to understanding in order to circumvent the revisionism of presentist interpretations, Bell and Asch assert the importance of applying contemporary social science and legal understandings to the interpretation of historical fact. In their paper 'Challenging Assumptions: The Impact of Precedent in Aboriginal Rights Litigation,' they assert that, to understand Aboriginal rights issues appropriately, jurisprudence must turn away from the asymmetrical ethnocentrism of historic precedent and towards the stance of cultural relativism characteristic of contemporary thought. Using evidence derived from contemporary anthropological theory and accepted techniques of legal reasoning, the authors indicate how the judicial system can adopt an approach that better reflects contemporary knowledge about the nature of human social groups. This approach thereby shifts the burden of proof to those who would deny contemporary understandings about the nature of social life. While the viewpoints found in the two papers may appear contradictory, in fact they are complementary, for in some basic respects the reasoning that derives from Arnold and mid-nineteenth century British thought dovetails with more contemporary thought on an essential element: that there is a need to acknowledge difference and to premise interaction on the presumption that the culturally different Other is autonomous. Where they differ, and this is significant, is that in contemporary thought, unlike in nineteenth-century thought, one accepts the presumption that both parties are of equal cultural status.

For many, a crucial aspect of developing a justice system that eschews ethnocentrism and promotes cultural equality is the inclusion of 'Aboriginal traditions' in the judicial process. While in its proper context such an appeal has merit, Emma LaRocque, in her paper, 'Re-examining Culturally Appropriate Models in Criminal Justice Applications,' cautions us to be careful. First, this appeal has often resulted, particularly with respect to concepts of justice and the role of women in Aboriginal societies, in 'a growing complex of reinvented "traditions" which have become extremely popular even while lacking historical or anthropological contextualization.' These reinvented traditions have sometimes created a description of an Aboriginal culture that is distorted in the extreme, at times transforming it into a form that is 'more Christian and patriarchal in origin than it is either Aboriginal or therapeutic.' Second, the appeal to tradition is sometimes inappropriate to current circumstances. As she says, 'while restoring social harmony between parties in a dispute may have made sense in a small hunting society (note: except in cases of serious crime and violence), such an overriding goal today may not make any sense at all.' Furthermore, because Aboriginal people live in the contemporary world, 'we have many worlds from which to draw with respect to ideals of human rights or healing' and therefore do not have to rely solely on 'tradition.' She concludes that 'it is possible to construct new models that accommodate real human multidimensional lives.' In order to best ensure this goal is achieved, LaRocque suggests that, when they are to be incorporated, 'traditions can and must be used in a contemporary context in such a way as to bring meaning to our young people, justice and equality to women, and safety and human rights protection to everyone.'

The next three articles focus on particular legal issues that relate directly to Aboriginal and treaty rights questions. In 'The Impact of Treaty 9 on Natural Resource Development in Northern Ontario,' Patrick Macklem indicates how a close reading of contextual information can address the constitutional relationship between governments, third party interests, and treaty rights in a new light, even where the written version of a treaty may still be considered authoritative. Noting the Supreme Court of Canada's view that the analysis of treaties needs to incorporate Aboriginal understandings, Macklem re-examines a number of original sources regarding Treaty 9. On this basis, he asserts that 'Aboriginal people viewed [the treaty] as a means of protecting their traditional ways of life, especially hunting, trapping, and fishing, from non-Aboriginal incursion' and through negotiations ensured that there was agreement on this point. He then uses this understanding to analyze the distribution of rights where provincial and third party activities come into conflict with treaty provisions respecting Aboriginal rights. He argues that, even if the written treaty provisions where the Aboriginal parties cede and surrender lands are accepted as legitimate, those parties are protected from the unilateral actions of Ontario, for 'governments and third parties cannot undertake economic development in the [Treaty 9] area which would infringe treaty rights without specific legislative authority to do so,' and the terms of the treaty do not authorize provincial infringement of treaty rights. He concludes that 'such legislation would have to be federal' and could only occur in the most limited of circumstances, for, following from *Sparrow*, it would have to be justified on the basis that 'there are no other viable alternatives for meeting that objective.'

In his paper 'The Meaning of Aboriginal Title,' Kent McNeil examines the value of 'Aboriginal title' as a legal construct in the resolution of Aboriginal land title questions. Focusing in particular on how the courts have defined the *sui generis* aspect of that title as well as its nature and content, McNeil concludes that the legal concept of Aboriginal title has been applied in a way that restricts its impact even when it has been successfully established in court. Because the term has been defined in such a restricted way, notwithstanding that various courts recommend negotiated settlements, he asks, 'What incentive is there for governments to reach agreements which give effect to the "aspirations of the aboriginal peoples" after the courts have reduced the already limited bargaining power of those peoples by embracing a narrow definition of their Aboriginal rights?' For him, the alternative is to understand that, while Aboriginal title may be unique or *sui generis* in its origin, it is more appropriate to define the rights associated with such title on the basis of original 'possession, not on the specific uses to which the land is put.' As he states, 'This approach accords with common law principles, avoids discrimination, and provides the Aboriginal peoples with the opportunity to develop their lands in ways that meet the contemporary needs of their communities.'

In 'Wampum at Niagara: The Royal Proclamation, Canadian Legal History, and Self-Government,' John Borrows addresses the prevalent legal interpretation of the Royal Proclamation of 1763, which is one of the cornerstone documents used in recent jurisprudence. In particular, he challenges the view that the Royal Proclamation is best understood as a unilateral statement by the British monarch to assert sovereignty over a vast area of North America, which indirectly recognizes Aboriginal title by setting out the means of extinguishing title. Instead, he reads the Royal Proclamation in light of the active part played by First Nations in its genesis and in the context of other relevant historical documents, in particular the Treaty of Niagara of 1764, which was ratified by over 2,000 chiefs who attended negotiations with the Crown. The terms of the 1764 treaty established a relationship based on peace, friendship, respect, and mutual non-interference between the British and First Nations; and Borrows concludes that these terms represent the context within which the full impact of the Royal Proclamation of the previous year must be understood. Given this reading, Borrows questions the appropriateness of juridical interpretations of the Royal Proclamation which assert that it is an instrument to enable unilateral diminishment of Aboriginal rights by the Crown. Rather, he suggests that the full legal consequence of the Royal Proclamation is to bind the Crown to ensure that the Aboriginal and treaty rights of the First Nations, including their right to govern themselves, are not undermined.

The two final papers in the collection focus on the implications to the fundamental political relationship between Indigenous peoples and Canada, were the legal and political system to adopt the principles of equality and respect for difference as interpreted with reference to history and contemporary values. Sharon Venne, in 'Understanding Treaty 6: An Indigenous Perspective,' asserts that the written version of that treaty does not accurately reflect the terms of agreement between the parties. In order to ascertain this original understanding, Venne relies on the oral tradition and on the cultural rules of Cree society. She suggests that 'each nation in treaty negotiations delegated certain members of their citizenry to negotiate the treaty, and empowered them to make a certain kind of agreement with negotiators from the other nation.' By delegating this responsibility to men, the Cree ensured that cession of their lands would not occur, for in Cree culture, 'Because of [women's] spiritual connection with the Creator and Mother Earth, it is the women who own the land.' 'Man can use the land, protect and guard it, but not own it. Women can pass on authority of use to the man, but not the life of the earth.' Furthermore, she argues that this was appropriate in the circumstances, for the chiefs could only agree to share the land *as requested by the treaty commissioner*. Following this reasoning and applying certain decisions in international law, Venne concludes: 'Only agreements entered into with the Indigenous peoples of the territory can give any legitimacy to the use and occupancy of the lands. Canada must recognize the position of the traditional governments that entered into treaty with the British Crown. To discount the legitimate governments of Indigenous peoples is to discount Canada's own legitimacy.'

Asch and Zlotkin, in 'Affirming Aboriginal Title: A New Basis for Comprehensive Claims Negotiations,' address how the acceptance of the proposition that Indigenous peoples still hold underlying title might affect the Canadian polity and, by extension, Canadian jurisprudence. Their examination focuses in particular on policy matters related to a long-standing point of friction between First Nations and Canada: the requirement in federal policy that Indigenous peoples 'extinguish' their title in order to obtain a settlement of outstanding land questions. The authors assert that the government should abandon its extinguishment policy because it is 'harmful and counterproductive ... to our understanding of what the purpose of such settlements needs to be if we are to build a new relationship between Aboriginal peoples and Canada.' Instead, they argue that the recognition and affirmation of Aboriginal title provides the best avenue to develop a better relationship and assist in defining a new role for Aboriginal nations within Canada, one that will benefit not only Aboriginal peoples but also Canada itself. In analyzing policy on underlying title, Asch and Zlotkin conclude that current legal and political thinking relies on British colonial legal precedents based on ethnocentric and racist values which are generally rejected by Canadians today. A reappraisal of the issue in light of this fact leads the authors to assert that Aboriginal peoples hold a better claim to underlying title than does Canada. Further, they find that, due to the essential difference between certain Aboriginal and western philosophies on the relationship between a people, their land, and the Creator, acceptance of this assertion will enable Canada to move discussion away from a focus on title and towards a discussion of political relationship that is based on sharing and mutual accommodation. They conclude that acceptance of the perspective on title advanced in their paper will not only facilitate claims settlements, but will also strengthen the legitimacy of Canadian title by joining it, through negotiated relationships with First Nations, 'with roots going back to time immemorial.'

Collectively, the essays in this volume confirm by means of specific examples that, despite the progress that has occurred, Canadian law as reflected in jurisprudence and legislation has reinforced rather than challenged traditional ways of framing Aboriginal and treaty rights. The essays reveal the ethnocentric biases that derive when, as Justice Hall stated in *Calder*,[4] the legal system acts by adopting rather than 'disregarding ancient concepts formulated when understanding of the customs and cultures of our original people was rudimentary and incomplete and when they were thought to be wholly without cohesion, laws, or culture, in effect a sub-human species.' At the same time, the essays do not merely bemoan the present situation and request future legislative or constitutional change to address these issues. Rather, they offer concrete proposals for changes in substantive, process, and conceptual matters as well as new ways to apply sound judgement, which, if implemented, would provide immediate redress for the specific and systemic biases that now exist.

The collection shows that, despite Canada's constitutional recognition and affirmation of 'existing aboriginal and treaty rights,' change to the way these rights are understood is sorely needed. The essays offer food for thought on how such a reconfiguration could be realized in a way that promotes rather than denies equality of peoples and respect for difference.

Aboriginal and Treaty Rights in Canada

1

Culture and Anarchy in Indian Country

J. Edward Chamberlin

In 1867, by coincidence the year of Canadian confederation, Matthew Arnold delivered the last of his lectures as Professor of Poetry at Oxford. It was called 'Culture and its Enemies,' and was published later that year in one of the widely read journals for which England was becoming famous, the *Cornhill Magazine*. In the following months, Arnold added five more essays, this time under the title 'Anarchy and Authority.' Then in 1869, he brought them and their titles together in a book. It was probably the most influential of the many influential books to come from the generation of Victorian sages that included Thomas Carlyle, John Stuart Mill, John Henry Newman, John Ruskin, and Oscar Wilde; and it has gone beyond even such an illustrious gathering to become one of the most important books written in English in the nineteenth century. It was called, of course, *Culture and Anarchy*.

In language that still resonates in contemporary public policy, Arnold spoke of the importance of 'getting to know, on all the matters which most concern us, the best which has been thought and said in the world,'[1] and of the urgent need to create a society in which the 'coarsely tempered natures' of the 'barbarians and philistines' would be imbued with the 'sweetness and light' of a truly cultivated, civilized community. He celebrated the authority of what he called 'touchstones,' written texts that embodied the grace and power that inspire civilized conduct. In place of the venerable power of spiritual texts, he proposed a secular canon of (mostly European) cultural touchstones.

Arnold was not sitting on some elegant English verandah when he wrote *Culture and Anarchy*, though its breathtaking confidence might remind us that he was living on an island. But Great Britain was anything but insular, and its future was certainly not safe and secure. Arnold's country was in the midst of a deadly serious economic depression, in which differences of region and class and race were writ large; and it had just embarked on major democratic reforms (epitomized by the Reform Bill of 1867, which dramatically extended the franchise) that were dividing an already deeply divided country. He – and many others – felt the menace of mid-nineteenth-century European revolution, and the disorderly forces of social, economic, and political change that seemed to be sweeping his world.

He was in the midst of it all. He wrote with passionate dismay about the stresses and strains that were threatening to break up his badly fractured nation, one that had been infamously characterized as really 'two nations' by its sometime prime minister, Benjamin Disraeli (in the title of one of his novels, *Sybil, or the Two Nations*). And Arnold wrote in ways that tried to redefine the categories of rich and poor, or (in the geography of England) of south and north, that Disraeli emphasized. Instead, he proposed a set of dichotomies – between order and chaos, civilians and barbarians, those with culture and those without – that shaped discussion well into the twentieth century. No debate about cultural relativity and no discussion of national identity in the past hundred years has been able to ignore Arnold's formulation. Like Adam Smith in *The Wealth of Nations*, published just about a hundred years earlier in 1776, Arnold's *Culture and Anarchy* defined the choices for the coming generations.

And in Arnold's persuasive account, they *were* choices. The spectre of anarchy that haunted him was both social and spiritual, both individual and collective. It was embodied in an excessive materialism – what he scornfully referred to in one of the chapter titles of *Culture and Anarchy* as 'Doing As One Likes' – and, most profoundly, in the subversive pluralism to which he felt his society had surrendered. This pluralism, for Arnold, meant the disintegration of a sense of shared, permanent values, and a corresponding collapse of cultural standards. The collapse of civil society was bound to follow.

Arnold's apocalyptic vision was immensely compelling both to his contemporaries, preoccupied with troubles at home and abroad, and to succeeding generations of Europeans and European migrants devastated by world wars, widespread economic depression, and demographic changes unknown since the last great period of cultural and territorial paranoia, the Middle Ages. In the Americas, too, the period of the late nineteenth and early twentieth century witnessed disruptions on a scale that seemed to rival those great precontact shifts of climate and culture that overwhelmed the Dorset, and brought the Navaho to the Southwest. It was a vision that was given grim voice by William Butler Yeats, contemplating the disintegration of Europe, the bloody revolution in Russia, and the civil war in Ireland with caustic despair: 'Things fall apart; the centre cannot hold; / Mere anarchy is loosed upon the world, / The blood-dimmed tide is loosed, and everywhere / The ceremony of innocence is drowned.'[2] In the face of this kind of nightmare, Arnold had a simple dream – a dream of a common culture, celebrating common meanings and values, with ceremonies that confirmed a common purpose.

It was not just a European's dream; and we misunderstand the encounter between natives and newcomers in the Americas if we think that it was. Certainly on the western plains, at precisely the same time Arnold was pronouncing on culture and anarchy, the Aboriginal peoples were doing exactly the same thing. Like Arnold and many of their newcomer neighbours, they shaped their politics and their statecraft around this core belief in the importance of maintaining a community, and a continuity, of cultural values. They were deeply suspicious of any convenient pluralism, and they believed, no less than Arnold did, that culture must maintain an orderly balance between the stabilities of convention and the energies of change, or else anarchy will take hold.

What makes *Culture and Anarchy* especially interesting, in relation to late-nineteenth-century circumstances in what was then referred to as the Canadian Northwest, is that it elaborates a theory of traditions – that is, a theory about the ways in which peoples pass on things of meaning and value in oral and written texts, and in doing so, maintain cultural habits and the necessary coherences and continuities of a civil society. Traditions, of course, are implicit in all societies; but in Arnold's time – which is to say, in the time of the so-called numbered treaties in Canada – their importance had just been given explicit recognition in Europe in another very widely read book, Henry Maine's *Ancient Law*. It was first published in 1859; and within a decade, and until at least the end of the century, Henry Maine, John Stuart Mill, and Thomas Hobbes were lumped together as *the* modern political philosophers. Maine argued that law and order, like art and culture, depend upon a sense of tradition. For him, this was by no means true only for European societies. It was true for all societies – many of his examples were drawn from the ancient tribal villages of India – and it had obvious implications for British colonial practice, and for those who inherited it in Canada.

One aspect of Maine's argument was especially important, and it had to do with the relationship between tradition and authority. Traditions accommodate *change* – resistance and innovation, as well as appropriation, are their stock-in-trade. But they do not easily tolerate *competition*. Authority, on the other hand, thrives on competition and is often quite comfortable with contingent power relationships, provided only that the boundaries are clearly established. Traditions, for their part, always want the field to themselves, though they accept – indeed sometimes even encourage – periodic changes in boundaries. That is why many post-

Renaissance European societies could strictly separate the *traditions* of church and state at the same time as they continued to acknowledge contingencies of secular and sacred *authority* within each tradition.

Many Aboriginal societies, during much the same period, developed no less peculiar contingencies of authority involving carefully (or to an outsider, confusingly) delineated boundaries – just as the boundaries established by Europeans were alternately confusing and comical to Aboriginal observers – while maintaining traditions in which, while there were no boundaries at all between the material and the spiritual (which also confused the Europeans), there were strict boundaries between cultural communities. For Aboriginal communities in the Americas, therefore, just as for Matthew Arnold, the contingencies of authority were always negotiable. Traditions, on the other hand, could *never* be contingent, and therefore could never be negotiated. Coherence and continuity were absolutes within traditions; and they were threatened more by pluralism than by power. And so the challenge for these Aboriginal communities in negotiating the treaties was to trade some power for protection against cultural pluralism.

In this, though it is obscured by current (and convincing) claims of fraud and bad faith, they had essentially the same ambition as the Queen's negotiators. The history of the treaties is the history of a clash not so much between Aboriginal and non-Aboriginal traditions as between the domains (and the rhetorics) of tradition and authority, and between the dynamics of cultural pluralism and political power. The prominence given to military and political leaders in the process masks its deeper significance as a negotiation of the conditions for maintaining cultural integrity. So long as we construe the treaty process as an exercise in power-broking and the orderly and ostensibly lawful transfer of authority, we will miss the fundamental issue, the one that Ahtahkakoop and Mawedopenais no less than Arnold realized: that the cultural *traditions* of their people, their ways of passing on things of meaning and value in their lives, were more important – and more durable – than the sometime circumstances of the day. They were also non-negotiable. Authority, on the other hand, was always open to negotiation. If alliances could ensure the provision of new supplies, including new knowledge and resources, and possibly new delegations of responsibility, then these alliances should be pursued, but only in those ways that would also ensure the independence of a defining core of traditions. When Aboriginal people agreed to give up a measure of 'sovereignty,' and to accept some measures towards 'subsistence,' or some 'power' to ensure 'survival,' they did so in the same spirit as Arnold's England had done over the preceding centuries when it entered into treaties with France and Spain, giving up and gaining authority over this or that. Nothing of importance was lost in the exchange – no sense of racial or cultural difference, for example, or of language. Replacing the English language with the French language, now – Matthew Arnold would have fiercely resisted *that* ... and for precisely the reasons Aboriginal people resisted the subversion of their languages and of the traditions these languages sustained. The treaties are silent on such matters not because they were unimportant but because compromise on them was inconceivable. They were inviolate, and non-negotiable. Traditions of hunting and gathering, though no less important, were signalled because the Canadians apparently needed to be reminded that these were part of *tradition* rather than of authority, and were therefore also not up for negotiation.

Aboriginal peoples had lived side by side with other peoples for centuries, making all sorts of arrangements to get through the season, or the territory, or the dispute. But even with the inevitable assimilation of neighbouring linguistic forms and functions, they had kept their distinctive languages – and with them, their distinctive cultures and traditions. One of the pernicious habits in contemporary thought is to forget this, out of enthusiasm for a homogenized chronicle of Aboriginal victimization. Another is to read late-twentieth-century non-Aboriginal enthusiasms for pluralism back into the nineteenth century, or into Aboriginal cultures. For all his provincialism, Matthew Arnold makes useful reading for those who would understand what was going on in treaty time.

There are few areas of human community in which tradition is more important and involves a more complex confusion of the secular and the sacred, than land. Even the most superficial reading of the Old Testament confirms this with regard to the Judeo-Christian heritage; and Aboriginal societies provide abundant evidence of this too. The texts and ceremonies – the traditions – according to which land is passed on often constitute a society's self-definition; and they also determine the ways in which land conveys authority from one person to another, and from one generation to the next.

By conveyed, of course, I mean both carried across and communicated. And this is where we get into another area of serious misunderstanding with regard to the treaties and the venerable oral traditions of most Aboriginal societies, traditions in which *inter alia* land is accorded meaning and value, and its stewardship assigned. This misunderstanding is most apparent in the accounts routinely given of oral traditions by societies where written texts are privileged. Because the critical discourse about such matters has been so relentlessly determined by these habits of privilege, a cluster of misconceptions about oral traditions has very wide currency. For the past several hundred years, culminating in the nineteenth century in Europe, the absence of written traditions has been an insignia of otherness, a defining part of the convenient European (and sometimes Asian) classification of peoples into primitive 'them' and civilized 'us.' The stereotypes that have accompanied these classifications are fairly well chronicled, though mostly in ways that entrench the very geography of margins and centres that the chroniclers claim to abhor. Some of the stupider statements that have been made about oral traditions – ruthlessly discounting or ridiculously exaggerating them – have long since been laid to rest. But there remains a persistent habit of reducing oral texts to the status of secondary documents rather than accepting their primary authority.

More than that, orality has often been considered according to a model that presumes literacy to be a step further along the evolutionary scale. For the likes of the modernist Marshall McLuhan, his student the medievalist Walter Ong, and his classicist colleague Eric Havelock, the printed word embodied a new, more advanced form of thinking and feeling. As McLuhan outlined his argument in *The Gutenberg Galaxy,* printing played a 'crucial role in staying the return to the Africa within us,'[3] a return to the heart of darkness. McLuhan, who knew very little about oral traditions, relied for much of his authority on the work of one J.C. Carothers, who wrote books with titles like *The African Mind in Health and Disease.* And while we may think we have moved beyond McLuhan in our understanding of orality, in fact we have not moved much at all. The words we use to classify those who do not conform to our notions of literacy – that is, to our notions of a writing system that is more or less visible speech (one which does not accommodate, for instance, the reading necessary for the pictographic and petroglyphic forms of ancient Aboriginal cultures, north and south; Iroquoian condolence canes and wampum belts; the carvings of Haida totem poles and Kwaguilth masks; or the knotted and coloured strings of Peruvian *quipu*) – are illuminating in this regard: illiterate, nonliterate, preliterate. All of them carry negative baggage; indeed, they are linked in much current social, economic, and political discourse with disease and poverty, often in a way that implies a causal relationship, as in a recent article in the *Globe and Mail* (pointed out by David R. Olson in his book *The World on Paper*) asserting that 'malnutrition, ill-health and illiteracy form a triple scourge for developing nations,' and that the illiterate are doomed to 'lives of poverty and hopelessness' because they are 'deprived of the fundamental tools to forge a better life.'[4] So it is too with a term such as prehistory. And although that prefix might seem the least offensive, it assumes an evolutionary model that assigns those whose history or literature does not fit into our written models an 'early' stage of development. When such people 'grow up,' goes the logic, they will know how to read; and when writing arrives, history begins. And in fact the *Globe and Mail* remark, typical as it is, is not far removed from comments such as Edward Gibbon's, written in 1776 at the beginning of modern European historical discourse, that 'we may safely pronounce that, without some species of writing, no people has ever preserved the faithful annals of their history, ever made any considerable progress in the abstract sciences, or even possessed, in any degree of perfection, the useful and agreeable arts of life.'[5] If recent court cases are any indication, Gibbon is still alive and well here in Canada.

There are some understandable reasons for this continuing narrow-mindedness, of course. Oral traditions, like all traditions of secular and sacred expression, are closely involved in the conditions of their language; and in the case of many Aboriginal peoples, and peoples living in the African diasporas of the world that are the legacy of slavery, this includes the conditions of dispossession and dislocation which they have experienced. In this scenario, their oral traditions are taken as reflections not so much of their primitive condition as of their degenerate state, to which we respond these days less with colonial superiority (though there is still a fair measure of it) than with postcolonial indignation. And yet this is ultimately misleading too, for it reinforces a pernicious tendency to see language in exclusively instrumental terms – as a pure (or impure) medium of communication in which the best language is the most transparent. But long before Marshall McLuhan, people understood that much language is ostentatiously opaque, drawing attention to itself for its own sake. This is as true of written as it is of oral texts, of course, but oral texts have suffered in a special way from our tendency to look through or around or behind them, rather than to look at them in and for themselves. This becomes a special hazard where the texts are performative, and where the conditions (including the witnessing) of such performances involve an assumption that the knowledge they convey is *revealed* through the *experience* of the text rather than *expressed* as a *communication*.

Recent studies in what has become known as speech act theory – in which what are referred to as the 'illocutionary' rather than the 'locutionary' functions of language (what language *does* rather than what it *is*) are primary – have emphasized a set of necessary conditions for all speech acts, of all sorts. They are remarkably pertinent to our consideration of the treaties, for they underline how easily we can ignore in one set of circumstances what we take for granted in every other. These are the conditions as outlined by the originator of contemporary speech act theory, J.L. Austin, in a series of lectures given at Harvard in 1955 under the title 'How to Do Things with Words': 'there must exist an accepted conventional

PROcedure having a certain conventional effect, that procedure to include the utterance of certain words by certain persons in certain circumstances.'[6] As the commentator Sandy Petrey has noted, 'the repeated "conventional" and the redundant "accepted" all designate the same necessity for communal agreement. As its etymology specifies – *convenire* means to come together, to convene – a convention exists by virtue of transindividual ratification. Part of what's accepted in any convention is that more than one person is doing the acceptance.'[7] This, of course, is central to an understanding of the 'comings together' of the treaties as oral texts, where the tradition vested authority in the occasion as well as in the orator – that is, the audience generated the meaning and value of the text just as much as the speaker did.

Our eighteenth- and nineteenth-century European disciplines of discursive analysis reinforce many of our misunderstandings of oral traditions, and therefore of treaties. For treaties are in many ways our central constitutional conventions. Their words constitute – they bring into being – the communities they describe. They enact rather than represent the reality they envisage; and they embody ceremonies and texts that in the first years of Canadian independence were, in an important sense, home-made, uniquely committed to that interrelated sense of place and people by means of which communities create themselves – in this case, a place that was both homeland and frontier, and people who were both natives and newcomers. The treaties were grounded in a sense of place as the British North America Act never was; and they aspired, however imperfectly (and imperially), to elucidate a new accommodation of the traditions of the founding peoples, Aboriginal and European. They were deliberate attempts to balance a pluralism of *authorities* with an independence of *traditions*. In this regard, while they reflected the different authorities of Aboriginal and settler sovereignties, they maintained the strict separation of the traditions (including the oral and written discourses) of each – a fact which has ironically contributed to the misunderstandings that now plague us. Finally, the treaties affirmed their status as constitutional documents in the face of menacingly uncivilizing forces (of hunger and disease, for instance), forces recognized clearly by Aboriginal elders learned in the wisdom of ancient civilizations, civilizations far older than many of those from which the European settlers claimed descent.

In order to recognize all of this, we need to revisit not just the history of the treaties but the hermeneutics of reading *and* listening that should inform their interpretation and evaluation. We need to learn how to listen; or more precisely, to recognize that it doesn't come naturally. Listening is a learned, and a learned, skill. It comes easier to some, Aboriginal as well as non-Aboriginal, but it does *not* come naturally. Nor is it the same across different traditions, listening to which may be as different as reading English and Chinese and Arabic. Many of us in the academy, I think, arrogantly assume that it does, and that it is, and that we know how. Some of us, in some of our lives and through some of our learning, may have become literate in oral traditions, and have learned to listen. But it's time we stopped taking this for granted. Few of us would suggest that reading is the same thing as seeing. And yet we routinely operate as though listening were the same thing as hearing. I don't mean in our everyday affairs, though it is undoubtedly true there; but in the ways in which we respond to the stories and songs of people for whom speech is much more important than writing, people whose traditions of imaginative and historical and philosophical expression are oral rather than scribal. Such people *can* read of course – no society would last long without a sophisticated ability to read the weather and the land and the water and the movement of fish and game – but their forms of expression require a differently (though no less sternly) schooled skill in listening.

And it's time we stopped assuming that all traditions are the same, and that we can listen to them all in the same way. We need to return our attention to the forum, the frame, and the focus of oral traditions. I have heard Aboriginal as well as non-Aboriginal people mock oral traditions that are not theirs – the oral tradition of someone such as Saddam Hussein, for example, celebrating 'the mother of all battles.' However much we may wish to make fun of Saddam Hussein, the rhetorical convention he uses in such a statement goes back thousands of years. I have heard Aboriginal as well as non-Aboriginal people scoff at Muhammad Ali, insulting his opponents and entertaining his audiences in a venerable tradition of taunting and boasting – 'I'll fly like a butterfly, sting like a bee' – that is part of his African heritage, and of European oral tradition too. (In fact, he sounds exactly like one of Homer's heroes, or like any number of trickster figures in the great storytelling traditions of many Aboriginal peoples.) Perhaps we *do* have something to learn from Justice McEachern, judge of the British Columbia Supreme Court, claiming that he had a tin ear, that he didn't know how to listen, when Mary Johnson sang her *ada'ox* in court in the *Delgamuukw* case. Or more generally, perhaps we need to pay more attention to three fundamental issues: the diversity not just of Aboriginal cultures but of the form and function of their oral traditions; the importance of representing this diversity in genuinely Aboriginal discourses, undistorted by the pressures of either colonial *or* anticolonial polemic; and the debilitating effect of historical studies that homogenize Aboriginal experiences, exoticize Aboriginal traditions, and plagiarize Aboriginal voices.

There is something else, too, the flip side of this. We need to remember that the same words, even when used with apparent confidence by different people, can sometimes be understood in significantly different ways. Two terms that have been at the centre of the discussion over the past couple of decades – subsistence and sovereignty – exemplify this. Both, of course, are English words; but both seem to have found a place in Aboriginal communities. The terms are related, like fresh air and freedom to breathe. But at the same time they seem to come from the opposite ends of the political, social, and economic spectrum. They go in and out of fashion in Canada, though they are in currency in the United States and in Australia right now. And yet there remains a significant gap between Aboriginal and non-Aboriginal understandings of these terms, and indeed between the different understandings *within* each of these communities.

Sovereignty, for example, is understood on the one hand as underwriting political and constitutional power. In the case of the Americas, this power was historically realized by both European and Aboriginal nations in the circumstances of contact, including contact *before* Columbus *between* Aboriginal nations, and between them and the African, Asian, and European travellers who came across the oceans in the preceding millennia. It was then qualified after European settlement by peace treaties and land cession agreements – what someone once called, quoting St. Augustine, 'fair thievish purchases.' On the other hand, sovereignty is affirmed as the inviolable expression of a people's collective identity, transcending the particulars of time and place and the irrelevant polemic of treaties. It does not need anyone else's validation, Aboriginal or non-Aboriginal; and it is inextinguishable, like an individual's conscience. There is a shuttling between the absolute and the relative with regard to the notions of sovereignty, often as much for rhetorical persuasion as out of high principle. In instrumental terms, it is often deemed a relative concept, leaving room for contingent sovereignties (which have had a long history in Europe since the Middle Ages). In non-instrumental terms, especially when it takes on a spiritual dimension, sovereignty becomes an absolute. The misunderstandings which result from different uses of this term need much wider attention than they are getting; and they need attention well beyond the political arena, for they are part of people's attitude to everything from fish and forests to education and health. (The various uses of the Maori words *kawanatanga* [which roughly means governance] and *rangatiratanga* [roughly again, chieftainship] in the Waitangi Treaty in New Zealand to deal with questions of sovereignty highlights this from another perspective.) The positive side of all this is that such conceptual and ideological contradictions can themselves provide a set of political and constitutional checks and balances, which might be no less complex, and no less important, than the dynamics of, say, individual and collective rights upon which European political systems have developed for centuries. The consequent negotiation between meanings and values can be a constructive and continuing part of the *process* of reaching community consensus. The negative side is that these differences, especially when poorly articulated in the images and arguments of popular as well as political culture, encourage a frustrated – and for many young people, often deadly – kind of fatalism.

The same dilemma is even more obvious with the word subsistence. It is alternatively a diminishing term, the minimum necessary for survival; and a term used routinely by Aboriginal peoples to refer to all that is essential to their well-being, including their attachment (spiritual as well as material) to their homeland. This latter conception is not properly acknowledged, indeed often is not even recognized, by an instrumental understanding of the term, which is common in many non-Aboriginal societies, where relentlessly utilitarian habits often inhibit a fuller appreciation of what is meant when Aboriginal people talk about subsistence – that is, about shaping their lives according to patterns of sufficiency rather than of surplus.

Let me give an example, this time within a specifically constitutional frame of reference, of this kind of discrepancy between what I have called instrumental and non-instrumental understandings. In a book called *Community and the Politics of Place,* Daniel Kemmis begins by comparing the preambles to the constitutions of the state of Montana and the United States. They both begin with the words 'we the people'; and the preamble to the United States Constitution then proceeds immediately to identify the specific purposes of government of which the constitution is to be the instrument. Montana's preamble, however, before getting down to the instrumental details, has this to say: 'We the people of Montana, grateful to God for the quiet beauty of our state, the grandeur of its mountains, the vastness of its rolling plain' and then goes about ordaining and establishing the constitution. Kemmis remarks as follows: 'Why did the authors of this constitution pause to express their gratitude for the Montana landscape? It would be possible to argue that they were simply being long-winded in a document which should be lean and concise. But it could also be argued that [they] said not a word more than they had to say, and that [what] they had to say ... [was] that the way they felt about the place they inhabited was an important part of what they meant when they said "we the people."'[8] That is, it may be that they recognized that the political culture of a place cannot be something apart from the place itself. The community which develops and depends upon that culture is also, in a fundamental way, a part of that place; and the ways in which a 'people' become 'public,' the ways in which they constitute themselves as a people, are determined by deep convictions about that participation in place, and the culture which is nourished by it. These convictions, like these cultures, obviously differ. But we need to be very careful with regard to the treaties, for example, that we listen attentively to – and learn to take seriously – the language of the texts, and not discount what we may initially take to be their decorative flourishes; that we do all we can to recover the language of the oral texts in particular; and that we not turn over their interpretation and evaluation to the relentlessly instrumental habits of lawyers and politicians (on either side).

This kind of interdependence between places and peoples, this kind of conviction about the connections between spiritual and material subsistence (which is ultimately indistinguishable from a conviction about the connection between material and spiritual sovereignty), and this kind of respect for language, is implicit in comments by Aboriginal peoples about both subsistence and sovereignty. To construe either subsistence or sovereignty, or the set of relationships between them, in purely instrumental terms is to miss the mark by a mile.

Treaties, therefore, might best be understood as saying not a word more than they had to say. The trouble is, we have only a partial text, the written text, whose rhetoric is almost comically inclined to various legal excesses, including redundancies and repetitions, which are nonetheless taken seriously by the courts and legislatures. We need to match this with the character of Aboriginal rhetoric, and with a correspondingly scrupulous attention to its intention and effect.

And so to the treaties. When Canada came into being, a d then came into its western territories, it did so with Arnold's map of *Culture and Anarchy* laid out before it, and troubles everywhere. The topography included the recent chaos in the United States, which had just completed one civil war in the South and seemed to be ready to begin a series of foreign wars with Aboriginal peoples in the West. The vast majority of settler Canadians were imbued with a commitment to authority which came out of their mainly European (and mostly non-revolutionary) traditions of law and order, and with a consensus about the importance of shared meanings and values which came out of their sense of what a civil society was all about. The architects of Canadian confederation were determined to demonstrate their faith in the country's future by establishing a common culture that was based on something other than the revolutionary rhetoric of the American Declaration of Independence – whose phrases about 'life, liberty and (especially) the pursuit of happiness' sounded almost as hokey to them as 'the mother of all battles' does to some of us. The authority of the monarchy, along with the celebration of the Victorian virtues of industry and thrift, seemed one good antidote to republican indulgence, extravagance, and anarchy; and a rhetoric of obedience and duty a wise part of the national discourse.

The treaties were about many things. But most of all, on *both* sides, they were about culture and anarchy – about establishing social, political, and economic cultures within which diversity would still flourish, and between which there were some common standards. We make a serious mistake if we interpret this simply as imperial arrogance on the part of European settlers. There was a good deal of that, to be sure; but it was almost certainly more than matched at the time by assumptions of social, cultural, political, and in some cases military superiority by Aboriginal leaders. To be sure, the economic situation required a more complex and conditional approach by Aboriginal peoples; but coming to treat with each other, both sides undoubtedly brought their own ambitions as well as their own anxieties.

And there were anxieties aplenty. The new Euro-Canadians were outnumbered, and sometimes outclassed as well by the great leaders of the tribal nations, men and women of considerable stature and statecraft refined through generations of dealing with other strangers and settlers – Aboriginal ones. The Europeans were often gifted, occasionally greedy, sometimes wise and generous of spirit; but they were more likely to be amateurs (though there had been a class of professionals in the British colonial service, some of whom remained with the new Canadian civil service. The discouraging of local arrangements in Indian affairs also helped maintain standards of probity and professionalism). On the other hand, the Aboriginal people were outmanoeuvred – at least in the timing of some of the treaties – and of course they were outsiders to the European ceremonies and texts. But they had their own texts and ceremonies; and they too saw them in terms of a dichotomy of culture and anarchy. Arnold's argument about the importance of establishing a common cultural ground must have had its persuasive counterpart in Aboriginal communities. Listening to the language that has come down to us from Aboriginal leaders at the time, it seems clear that they were just as preoccupied as Arnold with the battle between culture and anarchy – they were, after all, not in some hinterland, but in their own metropolis – and just as aware as any Canadian treaty commissioner of the need to articulate a sense of common purpose, if possible in a common discourse. And so both sides used their respective rhetorics, proclaiming a time of peace and prosperity in terms that were ostentatiously spiritual as well as material. Both sides, too, while they spoke within a deliberate calculus of losses and gains, were inspired by an overriding sense of possibility, even with the challenges they saw before them. For both, anarchy was not the opposite of culture but what William Blake would have called its 'spectre,' a fallen or lapsed version of culture that comes into being when the institutions and ceremonies of society are no longer informed by a civilized and civilizing imagination.

But that said, there was still a fundamental difference between Aboriginal and non-Aboriginal approaches, one that we often forget. Perhaps the best way of understanding it is by reference to our contemporary scene, where the clash between local nationalism and a kind of international cosmopolitanism is agonizingly apparent – as the urgent and awkward nationalisms of Eastern Europe or the Middle East or Russia or Africa or wherever are castigated by the urbane cosmopolitan emissaries of the world for their benightedness and backwardness, their regression to tribalistic filiations that inhibit full participation in the wider community of international, postnational affiliations. And yet those urbane cosmopolites who condemn the rough nationalists are usually secure in their own identity as national subjects. The conclusion is not that the cosmopolitan ideal is mere self-serving casuistry (though it often is just that), but that there are, and have always been, possibilities for combining both national identity and cosmopolitan mobility. Like the cosmopolitans of the late twentieth century, the Aboriginal peoples of the nineteenth century, confident in their nationalism and sophisticated in their internationalism, *assumed* this. The settlers did not, or at least (since they carried with them a whole set of imagery of a native homeland elsewhere, a mother- or fatherland) did not assume it for others.

We deeply discredit Aboriginal participation in the process if we see it as powerless, victimized, defrauded. The fault lies mostly in what followed the treaties, and in our pernicious habits of crediting written texts more than oral. To the extent that we misunderstand the oral traditions of which these treaties are a central part, we extend that fault line. In 1991, in the aftermath of the Oka crisis, the Canadian government established a Royal Commission on Aboriginal Peoples to look into the situation of Native peoples in the country. One of the commission's first initiatives was to sponsor a widely based program of research projects, most of them to be designed and developed in concert with Native communities. This immediately presented a challenge, for Native communities have become deeply (and rightly) suspicious of research activities. And so there was discussion of how to approach the communities, and how to persuade them of the seriousness of the commission's commitment to genuinely cooperative research. I had been asked, on behalf of the commission, to ensure that each research project was grounded in a consciousness of historical circumstances, and to develop a broadly based Aboriginal history project that would be centred in the oral traditions of the various tribal communities. So I was sitting in on many of these discussions. The good will of the commission staff, many of whom were also Aboriginal, was undeniable. But I remember listening to them talk about how to convince the tribal communities that they were serious about a new kind of research, one that would involve them at every stage, and more importantly, one that would reflect their oral traditions. 'We'll meet with them,' it was agreed, 'and we'll tell them what we're going to do. We'll give them our word.' Then, in the face of suggestions that many tribal communities had long since learned to distrust the word of outsiders, Aboriginal or non-Aboriginal, one of the leaders of the discussion went to the bottom line, as it were, and said, 'Then we'll take minutes. We'll put it on paper.' I mention this not to discredit the royal commission, but to emphasize that even within that well-informed (and largely Aboriginal) group, the prejudice against oral traditions continued to shape thought and behaviour.

We compound all these habits of mind with our habit of reading the treaties as though they were written contracts. In this, our stubborn reliance on only one set of texts, the written texts, becomes much more than a legal disability. It masks the extent to which the treaties, on both sides, were about culture and anarchy; and the extent to which the paraphrases on both sides – and the written texts are certainly just that – represented an Arnoldian discourse of authority and tradition. To the extent that they were contractual, the treaties *enacted* rather more than they enunciated a social contract. The complementary oral and written discourses of the treaties should reflect this enacting character, though even this can be distorted by the attitude of each side towards the treaties, oral or written, as monolithic, semi-sacred texts. They are surely not. And yet, like texts such as the Declaration of Independence, they have immense authority as representations of occasions on which both sides 'declared' – the presumption of orality is hardly incidental here – the meanings and values upon which they were establishing a new order.

In what way were the treaties about culture and anarchy? Well, first and last by being *story*lines. They were, again on both sides, attempts to provide what one of Arnold's contemporaries, John Henry Newman, used to call a 'grammar of assent,' a way of saying yes. This is where I think we often get bound up – on both Aboriginal and non-Aboriginal sides – by our biases, and by recent historical methodologies that encourage us to interpret the treaties in purely instrumental terms. There were such terms, to be sure, and they undoubtedly provided a meeting ground. Both sides needed something out of the process. But both sides also needed a way of *talking about* each other that was not cast in the melodrama of villains and victims, or of enemies. The enemy was anarchy and chaos, the absence of cultural centres and ceremonies. Each side had differing senses of where chaos intervened, of where anarchy threatened. For some Aboriginal peoples, it was in the breaking up of tribal houses and clans, the fracturing of the structures of collective origin and purpose. For others, it was the encroachment on tribal territory, the stewardship of which ensured not just the economic and political but the spiritual well-being of the community. For still others, it was in the turning of land into property – a disorderly act the character of which can best be caught by the (in our terms ironically) misnamed European and Russian political anarchists of the 1930s, who believed that 'all property is theft.'

But even when we remember that the treaties embodied storylines, we often forget something else. We should in fact remember this easily, for in the Aboriginal versions, the Aboriginal texts of the treaties, *the stories needed to be told.* And retold. Retelling, of course, is a central constituent of all stories. Stories take on their character – their meaning – in the *re*telling as much as in the telling; and this reflects the way in which it is not the presentation of events but the presentation of words that is important, providing the surest check against the anarchy of falsifying or forgetting.

There are a couple of ways in which this works. First of all, such retellings are not primarily instrumental. The stories, including the stories that are the treaties, are retold for their own sake, not for the sake of proving this or that to someone else. Nor are such stories exclusively inscribed in either the history *or* the antihistory of colonialism. They are *sui generis*, their details lined up against the homogenizing and essentializing tendencies of any stories that claim to represent 'Aboriginal history' in the abstract. Furthermore, they take their authority not so much from the experience of Aboriginal peoples as from the expression of Aboriginal *voices*. The distinction between direct speech and narration, like that between showing and telling, is crucial here; for the heart of the treaties is in the *telling*, not the *showing*.

This goes against some of our instincts, especially of those of us who are dedicated to written texts. 'Show, don't tell,' we say to aspiring writers. But perhaps we can see the point better if we recall that speech is always action as well as representation ... language in action. And so were the treaties language in action. Furthermore, as performative texts, they required certain conditions, the sort I referred to above as constituting the conventions of speech acts. Some of these conventions included material objects and forms of writing on the Aboriginal side, from the regalia that were part of the formalities of the Prairie treaties to the writing both with and without words that constituted the wampum belts and strings of the Iroquois.

Sometimes we have difficulty with this for the simple reason that we don't have very good texts, or we reconstitute superficial contexts, for the treaties. The referential precision of the written versions, for which we have ostensibly accurate texts (though they are often read in anachronistic ways), is not matched by any correspondingly accurate version of the essentially non-referential, but no less rigidly determined and determining, impacts and implications of the spoken texts. And the interpretive contexts that have up to now been used to display both spoken and written texts – as a point of reference for constitutional debates, or comprehensive claims, or fiduciary irresponsibility – have a relentlessly instrumental and ruthlessly reductive character about them. Treaties are seen as a means to an end, a way of proving something, a testimony on someone else's terms.

Perhaps it might be worth taking a few minutes to examine some of these contextual interpretations. Many of the commentaries ignore the fact that the situation on the western plains at the time of the numbered treaties had precedents in the political, economic, and military history of British jurisdiction over Indian affairs in British North America. And this history embodied some essential principles, referred to often in the decades after Confederation. These treaty principles – and the practices which flowed from them – had two features that endeared them to the Canadian government: they had a clear purpose, and they worked.

They had been expressed in statements and exemplified in statecraft with Aboriginal peoples during the long period of imperial authority and British settlement in North America. (Exactly the same is true, in many respects, of Aboriginal statements and statecraft during the treaty process, which reflected in both structural and substantive terms long-standing principles and practices refined over centuries of dealings with other Aboriginal peoples. This is abundantly clear from traditional historical accounts, and although it is not my purpose to outline this here, it is worth emphasizing.) From the seventeenth through the nineteenth centuries, the British government developed a policy to regulate transactions with Indian people in North America. This policy promoted continuous expansion of economic activity and settlement into the traditional territories of the Indian people. It recognized Indian people's continuing rights within their territory, and it required that these be dealt with by an agreement negotiated between the imperial authority and the Indian tribal leadership – the Aboriginal authority – before settlement would be allowed in that territory. The essence of the policy was the acquisition of Indian territory for purposes of colonization, and the protection of the Indian people from unrestricted and uncontrolled settlement.

The chief architect of this policy was William Johnson, who was first appointed an Indian agent in 1744 in what is now New York state, and who established the basic principles which governed British Indian policy for the next hundred years. In fact, for most of that time a member of the Johnson family was in charge of Indian affairs in British North America, for on Sir William's death in 1774, he was succeeded by Colonel Guy Johnson, his nephew and son-in-law; and then in 1782, responsibility for the Indian Department in British North America was turned over to Sir John Johnson, Sir William's son, who was in charge until he died in 1830. These were the custodians of order, of centralized colonial culture, against the anarchy of the dog's breakfast of local arrangements that did eventually transpire after the American Revolution.

Sir William saw good relations with the Indian tribes as a matter of expedience, indeed at times a matter of necessity, and the policy he implemented reflected that view. In a letter to the Earl of Shelburne written in 1767, he described the policy:

> Now as the Indians who possess these countries are by numbers considerable, by inclination warlike and by disposition covetous (which last has been increased from the customs in which the French have bred them), I find on all hands that they will never be content without possessing the frontier, unless we settle limits with them, and make it worth their while, and without which should they make peace to-morrow they would break the same the first opportunity ... I know that many mistakes arise here from erroneous accounts formerly made of Indians; they have been represented as calling themselves subjects, although the very word would have startled them, had it been ever pronounced by any interpreter. They desire to be considered as Allies and Friends, and such we may make them at a reasonable expense and thereby occupy our outposts, and carry on a trade in safety.[9]

Johnson knew that any misrepresentation of the Aboriginal people as subaltern was both very dubious and very dangerous. Call the Indians subjects, he warned, and you had better have an army behind you. And although he represented it in self-interested terms, he acknowledged the importance of the *process* of maintaining alliances and friendships. These are not casual terms. They reverberate in eighteenth-century public and private discourse with an implication of interrelated obligations, and an acknowledgment of independent attitudes and ambitions. They also resonate with a sense of mutual interest, of common cause, of the culture of friendships and alliances versus the anarchy of distrust and disrespect.

One of the most important accounts of the British Indian policy which Johnson put in place was written in 1912 by Duncan Campbell Scott, in a series of three articles published in the collection of essays by notable scholars entitled *Canada and Its Provinces*, edited by Adam Shortt and Arthur G. Doughty, and published between 1913 and 1914. Scott's account is close enough to the period of the treaty negotiations to be informed by an understanding of their language and logic, and yet sufficiently distant to have a perspective on the attitudes and ambitions. It is also very well-informed from a government perspective. Scott wrote his essays after serving as a civil servant in the Department of Indian Affairs for two decades, in a career which by 1912 had included responsibilities as a treaty commissioner (in the summers of 1905 and 1906) during negotiations on Treaty 9 with the Ojibwa and Cree of northern Ontario. Furthermore, he was on the eve of taking up the position of deputy superintendent-general of Indian affairs in 1913, and this exercise in identifying the roots and tracing the development of British policy with regard to the Aboriginal peoples of North America was a kind of preparation for his new position, a position in which he played a magisterial (and in the opinion of some, an alternately mischievous and malicious) role in Indian affairs in Canada for the next twenty years until his retirement in 1932.

The single most important fact about Scott's account is that he took seriously the language in which British Indian policy had been routinely expressed. He assumed that it meant something, and that it determined the ways in which successive administrations undertook their responsibilities. Furthermore, Scott insisted that the principles which had from early days shaped British Indian policy continued to inform the responsibilities of the Canadian government after Confederation. As he described it,

William Johnson was appointed Indian agent by Governor George Clinton in 1744. From that date to the present there runs through the Indian administration a living and developing theory of government ... The year 1830 may be fixed as the limit of the first regime in Indian affairs. Before that date a purely military administration prevailed, the duty of the government being restricted to maintaining the loyalty of the Indian nations to the crown, with almost the sole object of preventing their hostility and of conserving their assistance as allies. About 1830 the government, with the disappearance of the anxieties of the first period, began to perceive the larger humane duties which had arisen with the gradual settlement and pacification of the country. The civilization of the Indian became the ideal ... When the Dominion in 1867 gathered up and assumed the responsibilities of the colonial governments to the Indians of the provinces this policy was not changed, but a great expansion in its current occurred, and the development of the new western territories largely increased the burden.[10]

The development of the new western territories, and in particular the acquisition of Rupert's Land, brought back what Scott called 'the anxieties of the first period'; and the duty of the government was taken to be to combine the principles (of colonization) which prevailed in the earlier period of military concern with those (of civilization) which evolved in more settled times. Culture and anarchy writ on a large canvas. A western canvas.

We may lament the logic, but maintaining the complementary principles of protection and advancement, or of colonization of the new land and civilization of its Aboriginal inhabitants, was in many ways the defining characteristic of British and then Canadian Indian administration. There were tensions and choices and a balancing of priorities, but there was never a sense that these principles could not coexist, though to be sure in different ways in different times and places. This was the challenge: to assess the circumstances, and apply the principles accordingly.

'In the early days,' in Scott's words, 'the Indians were either feared as foes or valued as allies.'[11] When word reached London in August 1763 of the conspiracy of Indian nations which the Ottawa chief Pontiac was organizing, the imperial government felt the need to affirm its authority in North America, and particularly in the valley of the Ohio River, which had been one of the theatres of war between the British and the French in the widespread conflict between European powers known as the Seven Years War. Britain took possession of the entire area east of the Mississippi by the Treaty of Paris in 1763, and as Pontiac began stirring up trouble, Britain moved by way of the Proclamation to ensure peaceful coexistence between the British Crown and the Aboriginal peoples by establishing all of the lands west of the Alleghenies as Indian territory. In doing so, Britain reaffirmed its commitment to a set of principles that would provide a framework for developing alliances with Indian tribes, alliances that would profit imperial interests by protecting tribal interests.

It is important to realize that the British government at this time would not have seen the political interests of any nation, whether Old World or New World, whether led by a Philip or a Louis or a Pontiac or a Tecumseh, as distinct from what we would call its social or economic, or its military interests. These interests were collective, and they were inseparable. This was embodied much later by the Canadian government in the Indian Act, the central logic of which presumed that individual Indian interests were located in a fusion of the Indian band as a political unit and Indian land as the basis of its social and economic identity.

The language we might now use to separate social and economic and political interests was simply not developed in the sixteenth, seventeenth, or eighteenth centuries. There was not yet a social science of economics.

The word 'economy' was used mainly in domestic or theological terms until the late eighteenth century; the word 'social' had a correspondingly narrow reference; and the word 'class' did not take on its present meaning until 1772. Consider how arbitrary it would seem to us to separate the political autonomy of a nation from its military authority, except in terms of authority delegated through formal alliances. Whenever political and military *are* separated in an independent nation, we usually get something like a military coup to bring them back together. It would have seemed equally absurd to those charged with responsibility for British affairs in North America to separate economic and social from political interests; and it would have seemed likely that if they were separated, there would be a war to bring them back together. The British would have naturally assumed that other nations, Indian nations for instance, thought likewise. And they would have assumed that separating these interests would invite trouble. Experience with contingent authorities, coming out of a couple of centuries of European continental warfare, was limited. There was much to learn from Aboriginal leaders. Some, such as William Johnson, learned their lesson well.

So the British government in 1763 put together advice from colonial officials such as Johnson to form a major statement of political and administrative principles, the Royal Proclamation. It was the product of imperial wisdom in London as well, and it was followed over the next twenty years by several Additional Instructions to colonial governors. To use Johnson's phrasing, the Proclamation of 1763 'settled limits' with 'the Indians who possess these countries,' and 'made it worth their while' to accept these limits. It expressed the essence of British Indian policy, and established procedures for ensuring stability in relations between settlers and Indians in British North America. Justice and reasonableness were appealed to in the preamble to the Proclamation, but it was clear that its preoccupations were elsewhere – with questions of imperial interest and colonial stability.

Colonial security was the key to imperial success, so it is not surprising to see in the Proclamation a primary concern with peace and stability. The Indian tribes were perceived as potential trouble in British North America. Either tribal interests were friendly to British interests, according to this logic; or they were opposed. The British knew the costs of such opposition; and they were therefore determined to make allies rather than enemies of the Indian tribes, and to appeal to what they thought would satisfy tribal interests.

The Royal Proclamation required that certain formalities be observed in dealings between Indian tribes and the imperial government, and that these formalities convey the understandings upon which the economic and social and political transactions between imperial and Indian interests were founded. These transactions had developed early in the seventeenth century, with what Scott describes as 'treaties and agreements [that] had defined the civil relation of the aborigines and the ruler. It was the British policy to acknowledge the Indian title to his vast and idle domain, and to treat for it with much gravity, as if with a sovereign power.'[12] Recognizing the tribe as a political entity was the key to this process. Again, the language used was sometimes different from ours, for until the early nineteenth century there was not a 'science' of politics to develop this language and articulate what we now understand as a logic of political interests. The practice of entering into treaty with Indian tribes flowed from the recognition of the tribe as a political entity. The strategy was to deal with the Indians together – and where necessary to move them out of the way together.

We tend to associate Scott and his predecessors in nineteenth-century British/Indian affairs with inflexibility of mind. But they were much more flexible than we realize. Some observers, especially in the United States, were outraged by what they saw as the anomalous character of the relationships which had developed under British policy. The American president Andrew Jackson remarked in the 1830s that 'treaties with the Indians are an absurdity not to be reconciled with the principles of government.'[13] Others, such as the very well informed American Lewis Cass, were more resigned to the practical realities of the situation, as he indicated in an article in the *North American Review*, also in the 1830s: 'The Indians themselves are an anomaly upon the face of the earth; and the relations, which have been established between them and the nations of Christendom, are equally anomalous. Their interest is regulated by practical principles, arising out of peculiar circumstances.'[14] To be sure, the Indian tribes *were* anomalous. There was nothing else quite like them in British colonial experience, which in British terms meant 'anywhere.' But they were also convenient. Furthermore, as the British (who seldom put themselves at the mercy of tidy ideology) had recognized, the Indians – organized into tribes, with a strong sense of territorial affiliation – were facts of life in North America, like the geography and the climate. Unexpected at first, and sometimes menacing, but *there*, immutably, undeniably there.

So were the British, there to stay. And to the Aboriginal peoples, this was obvious. To them also, the settlers must have seemed no less 'an anomaly upon the face of the earth'; and the relations with them accordingly 'regulated by practical principles, arising out of peculiar circumstances.' The comments conveyed in Aboriginal oral traditions about the settlers underline this time and again. They also remind us that Aboriginal peoples had much more experience than the settlers in dealing with such anomalies, and in reaching accommodations that preserved the cultural integrity of their tribal communities as a sure line of defence not so much against a range of cultural appropriations, which they might well (based on thousands of years of experience) have considered inevitable, as against the anarchy of cultural pluralism.

Given these two facts of British North American life, the existence of Indian tribes was an advantage, for as political units with whom the British could deal the tribes provided a convenient structure for the management of Aboriginal interests, and thereby of British interests. If Indian tribes had not been there, the British might have had to invent them (as the Canadian government did in a sense invent their institutional successors, the Indian Act bands). The quite different British response to the interests of the aborigines in Australia is due in no small measure to the fact that the aborigines there were not organized into tribes. As a consequence, they were deemed to have no collective political interests that the British need bother about (leaving them instead to the vagaries of humanitarian concern for individuals). Also, they were no military threat.

On the Aboriginal side in the Americas, there was clearly some anxiety (especially among the nations with a distinguished military history) about the military power of the British and the new Canadian government, just as there must have been anxiety about the military adventurism of the American army; and there was a widely shared sense of the need to make alliances for economic reasons. There was also a deep fear of the possibility of a breakdown of law and order – Aboriginal law and order as well as the newer, settler sort – if some arrangements were not put in place to maintain traditions and confirm authorities. The treaties were the framework for this, dealing with anxieties on both sides about culture and anarchy.

The anomalous character of the treaty arrangements, with their acknowledgment of the independent yet contingent character of Aboriginal political interests, should not obscure the fact that the Canadian negotiators were comfortable with these arrangements. Here we come to an apparent contradiction which bothers us much more than it bothered those charged with responsibility for the equitable dealings between the British and Canadian Crown and the Aboriginal peoples in North America.

Indian treaties and the Indian tribes were political, military, economic, and social conveniences, at least in the sense in which we have described it above. Another convenience was the presumption that the tribes would eventually disappear, and the treaties be part of some distant past, like Indian wars. But this presumption, widespread though it was at various times in the nineteenth century, was *never* thought to exempt the British and Canadian government from the responsibility of protecting tribal

interests while they still existed. Indeed, one of the things which was routinely said to distinguish British from American policy was its faithfulness
to the responsibilities which it had assumed in its dealings with the Indian
tribes, and its consistent application of the principles that informed these
dealings. The *ideal* of *advancement* – complete assimilation of Indians into
the settler society – which had wide currency for about a hundred years
from the 1850s to the 1950s, did not obliterate the *reality* of Indian tribes,
nor the responsibility of the government to fulfil its duty – enthusiastical-
ly undertaken and explicitly expressed – to *protect* the interests of these
tribes. To take an analogy that is close to the maternalistic logic of Indian
advancement, one's duty to children as a parent or guardian does not
cease to exist *because* they will grow up and no longer be children, but
ceases when they grow up. When the Indian tribes cease to exist, so will
the government's duty: this was the presumption of Indian policy in
Canada in the late nineteenth and early twentieth centuries. It should be
added that this evolutionary model did not really have a hold in the seventeenth and eighteenth centuries; but it does now, affecting our attitudes
to everything from literacy to economic development, and deeply influencing the ways in which we interpret the treaties. And among Aboriginal
peoples, for most of whom it has a particularly grotesque character, the
need to constantly argue against it often skews their commentaries.

The idea of individual Aboriginal identity was from the beginning associated with collective identity, an association which is enshrined in the earliest legislative definition in British North America in 1850 of Indian status
as contingent upon membership in a band or tribe. The system of reserves
under the Canadian Indian Act, with Indian interest represented as a collective interest in land, indicates how much the Canadian government
has followed policy lines that flowed from the principle inherited from the
British regime of respecting collective Indian interests embodied in the
band or tribe. Even in a period when both Duncan Campbell Scott and the
government he served were very impatient with the slow progress of
Indians towards acceptance of the virtues of individual responsibility and
private property, and therefore towards full assimilation with the mainstream society, Scott could still write that 'there is nothing repugnant to ...
the exercise of useful citizenship in the idea of a highly civilized Indian
community living upon lands which its members cannot sell.' This statement was made in the context of Scott's affirmation that 'the happiest
future for the Indian race is absorption into the general population, and
this is the object of the policy of our government.'[15]

As we shall see in a moment, the idea of enfranchisement was developed to provide a distinctly British mechanism allowing Indians to grow

up, as it were, and their collective affiliations to lapse. But I suggest that enfranchisement ultimately *confirmed* rather than contradicted the reality of Indian bands or tribes as autonomous, albeit anomalous, political entities, with their own separate and distinct political interests.

The Aboriginal peoples of the country were used to living in a changing world, and to making alliances from time to time to cut their losses, as well as to consolidate gains. One distinctive feature in the first (1845) report of a commission (set up in 1842) to examine Indian affairs (with an eye to finding ways of reducing expenditures) was that it emphasized the importance attached by the Indian tribes to the Royal Proclamation, and to the special relationship with the British Crown and the protection of tribal interests which it prescribed. Again, this legacy was reiterated by Scott; and much later, in evidence given before the Special Joint Committee of the Senate and the House of Commons looking into revisions to the Indian Act in 1946 by T.L.R. MacInnes, the secretary of the Indian Branch (which was, following a 1936 reorganization, the successor to the Department of Indian Affairs in a new Department of Mines and Resources). Referring by way of contrast to a recent report on American Indian policy, MacInnes celebrated what he felt to be a record of consistent adherence to the principles of British policy:

> The main conclusion I would like to put before this committee from the viewpoint of the department, is that all the Indians in Canada are treated as though they were under treaty, whether they are actually under treaty or not. The treaty idea, from the proclamation of 1763, has been the underlying basis of Indian policy, with this primary consideration, that Indians who have lands for their own use, that those lands should be inalienable, except by mutual consent of the Indians and the government; and that the Indians on those lands should be protected by the government, as a government responsibility, from trespass, exploitation or molestation of any kind.
>
> Then, from that basic idea of protected lands or areas, there follow the other services necessary to provide Indians with proper life on those reserves, sometimes specified in treaties and sometimes not, but always recognized, nevertheless, such as education, with a school system, a special school system for Indians, health services, social services and protection, generally ...
>
> Now, as I mentioned before, that treaty system has formed the basis of policy, the distinctive Anglo-approach to the Indian problem.[16]

With this policy came a complication, however. Indians were recognized as separate peoples through the treaty process, and the British

Crown accepted a responsibility to protect their separate interests. But the assumption was that as they advanced, again with the help of the British Crown, at some point Indians would assimilate with British (later Canadian) society, and be fully integrated into its political as well as its economic and social structure. One question was how to provide for a formal recognition of this change in status. The answer, which was first proposed in 1857 in an Act to Encourage the Gradual Civilization of the Indian Tribes (and followed a recommendation from the 1842 commission), was called 'enfranchisement.' Enfranchisement was a part of the strategy to ensure coherence and continuity in the settlement of the country. Even more, it reflected a determination to protect against the kind of pluralism that Arnold identified as inimical to a civil society. But there was a fundamental irony in the enfranchisement provisions, for though their purpose was to facilitate assimilation, the principle and procedures of enfranchisement provide conclusive evidence of the sovereign political status of Indian tribes, and by implication the fundamentally political character of those tribal interests which the Canadian government undertook to protect.

Let me open up this issue of enfranchisement a bit, for it involves, among other things, another problem of language. The notion of citizenship as we understand it, involving certain rights and duties in relation to the state, was not a term in general currency in the eighteenth and nineteenth centuries. The word 'citizen' referred to a wide range of conditions, from being resident of a town or city (as distinct from a rural dweller or a peasant, say) to being a member of the community of civilized people, a 'citizen of the world.' On the other hand, the more recent idea of allegiance to a particular nation-state or political unit usually included a sense that this allegiance was material, or functional, with regard to the social, economic, and political operations of the state, and therefore involved specific responsibilities on both sides; and a sense that it was also spiritual, involving an attachment which had to do with individual identity and collective purpose, the kind of thing that nineteenth-century nationalisms relied on for their extraordinary hold on the imaginations of their 'citizens.'

Enfranchisement, using this later terminology, was about citizenship. Specifically it was about achieving British (and in due course Canadian) citizenship. It was also, therefore, about Indian citizenship. For what the notion of enfranchisement affirmed was that an Indian must give up tribal allegiance, which is to say being an Indian, in order to be accepted as British or Canadian. Put simply, the 1857 Act confirmed that what we might for convenience call 'dual citizenship' was not acceptable in British North America. Indian citizenship, however, certainly was. The idea of

Indian tribal citizenship, and therefore of Indian tribal government, was implicit in the enfranchisement provisions. So was the same deep distrust of pluralism, whether of cultural traditions or citizenship, that informed Matthew Arnold's arguments.

As with other applicants for British or Canadian citizenship, Indians had both to desire it and to deserve it. There was considerable frustration among those responsible for enfranchisement that even those who 'deserved' it, according to the always arbitrary measures for such things, did not seem to desire it. Some observers saw this as further proof that they did not deserve it. Others simply redoubled their recruitment efforts. (Unlike children, who gained citizenship upon reaching a certain age without a competency test, a probationary period was effectively pre-scribed for Indians.)

It was the case, of course, that Indians were assumed to be insufficient-ly instructed in the civil order of British and Canadian society. There was no sense that Indians were insufficiently instructed in the order of their own society. Indeed, quite the opposite. It became clear that Indians were much more thoroughly imbued with tribal values than the British and Canadian proponents of Indian advancement assumed. And these values, as the process of enfranchisement confirmed, were both political and cul-tural, for enfranchisement confirmed the shift of political allegiance (as distinct from exclusively military allegiance, for example) from the Indian tribe to the British (and after 1867, the Canadian) government. As of 1869, even band consent was specifically required for the enfranchisement of any individual member of a band. It was part of a strategy to diminish the anxiety of bands about the reduction of their land base; but it was indeed consistent with, and served to confirm, the autonomous political order of which tribal citizenship was a symbol.

It was certainly true that many British and Canadian citizens deemed tribal values to be primitive and those who held such values by definition to be either undeveloped or degenerate (both models had some currency). But the fact that European settlers thought Indians inferior did not mean that they thought they had no political affiliations or cultural traditions. The Europeans had been long accustomed to accepting the political authority and cultural difference of people whom they thought inferior, most notably the tribal nations in west Africa, from whom they began buying slaves in the middle of the sixteenth century. The Spanish, who were sticklers for such things, based their notion of a 'just title' to the slaves they bought and sold on a logic of local sovereignty that gave the tribal chiefs the right to sell them. With the Indians of North America, the situation was even clearer; and the precedent set by early British dealings with the Iroquois nations was carried over to later dealings with other Indian tribes, and informed the theory behind the enfranchisement provisions.

This legacy of British Indian policy had another dimension, of course, a product of the sense of responsibility to advance as well as protect Indians. To be sure, there was a contradiction involved. Indians were treated as collectively competent, certainly competent enough to negotiate international treaties, but as individually incompetent, in that they needed to be civilized. Parliament dealt with the first, making treaties or sending troops, or establishing policy along lines roughly consistent with the British policy of dealing with Indians as collectively capable of entering into international alliances; and the Department of Indian Affairs dealt with the second (under legislation passed by Parliament, to be sure) along lines that assumed the incapacity of individual Indians and generated administrative arrangements that made this fiction seem like fact. Indeed, much of the legislation, like its administration, created categories that simply confirmed these assumptions, as (to take a contemporary nineteenth-century British analogy) the Vagrancy Acts did when they criminalized previously non-criminal behaviour, such as hanging around the dockyard without a job, which was typical of Irish immigrants. The Irish were therefore turned by legislation into criminals, as the Indians were into incompetents.

This second dimension, in which Indians were represented as either degenerate or undeveloped, was the basis for the humanitarian side of British policy towards Indians. It was based on notions both of racial superiority and of the necessary conditions for progress – which among other things included a measure of social and economic and political complexity (which was not often recognized in Aboriginal societies, though it was certainly there), as well as some obvious things such as a belief in Christianity and private property and agriculture and a settled way of life.

But no matter how much attention was paid to the advancement of individual Indians, the cornerstone of British Indian policy was collectively held Indian land. This was why protection continued to be the fundamental of Indian policy; and why treaties continued to be the central instrument. Land represented power; and its regulated transfer, as far as the settlers were concerned, guaranteed stability. Settlers wanted land. And especially during the eighteenth and nineteenth centuries, land was central to British political ideology about the relationship between the individual and the state, and among individuals. In fact during the 1860s and 1870s, the period of the Rupert's Land transfer and the early numbered treaties, questions about the nature of land as property and about whether the ability to buy and sell land was a central tenet of civilized society were being debated throughout Great Britain, and the pages of the notable journals of the period were filled with speculation about the issue. John Stuart Mill had written extensively about this in his work on political economy; and the Irish Land Bill of 1870 provided a focus for discussion. It is not inconsequential that in the midst of this, the British government should be reaffirming a policy regarding Indian tribal interest in North America which recognized some significantly different principles of political and civil order, and of relationship to land. Again, the fact that these were anomalous is not nearly as important as the fact that they were acknowledged. And what exactly was the nature of this acknowledgement? Quite simple. Maintaining the political integrity of Aboriginal tribes meant maintaining a land base, however diminished it might be. And even allowing for their differing attitudes towards land, the same kind of logic clearly informed the Aboriginal perspective. That is, they *had* an attitude towards land, and this attitude was an inseparable part of their attitude towards political and cultural integrity as well as economic and social prosperity. If we do not understand the arbitrariness, the political and cultural artifice, of the British frame, we are unlikely to acknowledge, much less to appreciate, the Aboriginal frame – no less arbitrary, of course, but also no less grounded in a long-standing theory and practice designed to ensure the continuing ascendancy of culture over anarchy.

I mentioned earlier that the treaties were storylines. They dealt with the menace of anarchy by advocating cultural meanings. They were – and they still are – ceremonies of belief as much as chronicles of events. The stories that sustain cultures are typically about place as much as they are about people. If the place is gone – if the land has been alienated – then these stories run the risk of becoming merely nostalgic, and losing their power to maintain order and balance in the community. Contrary to some common non-Aboriginal misconceptions, Aboriginal stories about the land, insofar as they have a continuing hold on the imaginations (and therefore on the identity) of the community, are never nostalgic. They may occasionally be elegiac – but that is an entirely different thing.

Perhaps an analogy might be helpful, this time from Australia, where the late anthropologist W.E.H. Stanner talked about how

> no English words are good enough to give a sense of the links between an aboriginal group and its homeland. Our word 'home,' warm and suggestive though it be, does not match the aboriginal word that may mean 'camp,' 'hearth,' 'country,' 'everlasting home,' 'totem place,' 'life source,' 'spirit centre,' and much else all in one. Our word 'land' is too spare and

meagre. We can scarcely use it except with economic overtones unless we happen to be poets. The aboriginal would speak of 'earth' and use the word in a richly symbolic way to mean his 'shoulder' or his 'side.' I have seen an aboriginal embrace the earth he walked on. To put our words 'home' and 'land' together into 'homeland' is a little better but not much. A different tradition leaves us tongueless and earless towards this other world of meaning and significance. When we took what we call 'land' we took what to them meant hearth, home, the source and locus of life, and everlastingness of spirit. At the same time it left each local band bereft of an essential constant that made their plan and code of living intelligible. Particular pieces of territory, each a homeland, formed part of a set of constants without which no affiliation of any person, no link in the whole network of relationship, no part of the complex structure of social groups any longer had all its coordinates.

Stanner described the consequences as 'a kind of vertigo in living':

They had no stable base of life; every personal affiliation was lamed; every group structure was put out of kilter; no social network had a point of fixture left. There was no more terrible part of our ... story than the herding together of broken tribes, under authority, and yoked by new regulations, into settlements and institutions as substitute homes. The word 'vertigo' is of course metaphor, but I do not think it misleading. In New Guinea some of the cargocultists used to speak of 'head-he-go-round-men' and 'belly-don't-know-men.' They were referring to a kind of spinning nausea into which they were flung by a world which seemed to have gone off its bearings. I think that something like that may well have affected many of the homeless aborigines.[17]

That's what the treaties were about. Making sure the centre held. Keeping the world on its bearings by maintaining an understanding of the difference between Aboriginal and non-Aboriginal traditions, and a corresponding acceptance of the untranslatable as well as the translatable senses of home, and of the boundaries regulating authority in homelands that were also frontiers.

The 1860s in the West was a contentious time. The settler expansionists were frustrated at the slow progress of western settlement, and blamed imperial self-interest and the Hudson's Bay Company for conspiring to limit new opportunities for settlement and development. The Aboriginal people were frustrated at the changes that were overwhelming their territories, many of them seemingly outside anyone's control. For the settlers, there was a constant threat of war, and constant reminders of how precarious the hold of British settlement was on the western plains, especially given Indian antagonism and American imperialism. Furthermore, this unease was reinforced by the anxieties of an imperial government preoccupied with troubles – in India, Ireland, the West Indies, among other places – and on the lookout for ways to avoid uprisings. The prospects for colonization were surrounded by difficulties. For Aboriginal people, the catastrophic decline of buffalo stock during this decade – analogous in many ways to the recent disastrous decline of cod stocks on the East Coast and surprising to almost everybody – and the contentious relationships between the Metis and the Indians created a new sense of urgency, and a frustration and fear on the Indian side to match that of the settlers.

For the Canadian government, the menace of conflict was everywhere. By the early 1870s, events such as the Battle of Oldman River (1870) and the so-called Cypress Hills Massacre (1873) had underlined the anxieties of those who looked to the West as the new frontier for settlement, and who looked to the south at the United States for a model of what not to let happen. As Doug Owram notes in his book on the Expansionist Movement,

> by the 1870s a good many Canadians were convinced that the history of American Indian policy was, as the Toronto *Globe* once said, 'a dark record of broken pledges, undisguised oppression and triumphant cruelty.' Canadians felt that the United States was practising a policy of extermination towards the Indian and that the government of the United States, rather than the Indian, must assume major responsibility for the violence which had disfigured the frontier.
>
> In contrast, Canadians believed that their approach to the Indian, inherited from the British, was both just and practical. As such it gave them further evidence that the British rather than the American model was best suited for the development of the frontier.[18]

The comparison was intensified a few years later with the publication in 1881 of Helen Hunt Jackson's *A Century of Dishonour*, with its chronicle of what the author called a record 'of broken faith, of violated treaties, and of inhuman deeds of violence.' And also of Indian wars. Jackson's book was referred to during the debates in the House of Commons in 1886 which followed the Riel Rebellion; and when one member of the House (M.C. Cameron) made a sustained and documented attack on the policies and practices of the Department of Indian Affairs, his comparisons to the American situation were denounced by the government as among his most incendiary utterances.

The argument that the principles that had governed the British Crown in its dealings with Aboriginal peoples provided the best guide to peaceful and prosperous colonization and settlement of the western Prairies was widely accepted, and widely repeated. The treaties signed after 1871 were seen as the tangible expression of those principles. In his book *The Canadian Prairies: A History*, Gerald Friesen outlines the situation: 'The violence of the decade after 1865 only made plain what everyone already knew, that the inhabitants of the western interior required new political and judicial arrangements to replace the now irrelevant authority of the Hudson's Bay Company. One of the most pressing issues was the Indian claim to sovereignty. This had not concerned the fur companies, but had been of sufficient concern to Lord Selkirk that he had negotiated a treaty with five Cree and Ojibwa chiefs in July 1817.'[19]

Those charged with responsibility for opening up the West for settlement and bringing it into the union accepted their duty along lines described by Friesen, confirming the account of Scott and others from the turn of the century: 'The Canadian authorities did not lack for guidance in their deliberations. The basis of Canadian Indian policy had been set out over a century earlier in the British proclamation of 1763, which provided the rules for the administration of the former territories of New France, and in the administrative practices of Sir William Johnson, superintendent of Indian affairs.'[20]

The instructions to Adams G. Archibald, appointed lieutenant governor of the Northwest Territories in 1870, were precisely along these lines. His instructions open in language that could have been lifted right out of the eighteenth century when the Johnsons were in charge: 'You will with as little delay as possible open communication with the Indian bands occupying the country lying between Lake Superior and the Province of Manitoba, with a view to the establishment of such friendly relations as may make the route from Thunder Bay to Fort Garry secure at all seasons of the year, and facilitate the settlement of such portions of the country as it may be practicable to improve.'[21]

In the following year, Adams and Wemyss Simpson negotiated with the Ojibwas the first of the numbered treaties. Friesen describes these as

a means of cementing a relationship between peoples and setting out the rules by which that relationship would be governed. Though often scorned today as an empty form imposed by a conqueror on the conquered, the treaties of the 1870s should not be dismissed so quickly. The Indians had much less autonomy in the negotiations than would have been the case twenty-five years earlier, but they still negotiated as firmly as they could, won concessions where possible, and produced a settlement that had positive as well as negative features for their group. The Europeans entered the negotiations with limited financial resources to pay for concessions, little military power to enforce their will, and a great deal of nervousness as to what the Indians would accept. Thus the necessity of a treaty was more than a mere formality in the view of the Canadian government. The Indians were a sufficiently powerful military force in the early 1870s to evoke fears in official circles and, if nothing more, to threaten immigration prospects for a generation. The fact that there were 25-35,000 Indians in the western interior in 1870, and another 10,000 metis, and fewer than 2,000 Europeans or Canadians reinforced the government's concern.[22]

In the years after Confederation, the policy direction was coming from Ottawa, where familiarity with the Indians of Ontario and Quebec set the standards and, more specifically, the goals of advancement and assimilation. But the action was in the West, where alliances with the Indian tribes were urgently needed to establish conditions for peaceful settlement and protection of the interests of the Indian tribes. In only six years, between 1871 and 1877, seven treaties were signed, the western interior opened for settlement, and an Indian Act incorporating many assumptions based on experience in central and eastern Canada was passed (in 1876). By the 1880s, the differences between the situation in the West and in Ontario, Quebec, and the Maritimes were becoming apparent, so that, for example, the enfranchisement provisions of the 1880 Indian Act did not apply outside the four original provinces unless Cabinet issued a special proclamation. Similarly, the legislative provisions for Indian self-government, which bore little relationship to what the western tribes would have recognized as autonomy, were designed with the settled bands of central and eastern Canada in mind.

The other point of reference was the United States, and there is much to be learned about the motive and meaning of Canadian Indian policy and its commitment to the British tradition by looking at what was happening south of the border. That was certainly what those in what had been British North America were doing, especially in the West. Treaties were in trouble in the United States in the years after the Civil War. Many Americans felt that they were absurd concessions to the primitive fiction of Indian sovereignty, and had no place in a modern society. In 1871, for a variety of reasons which included a long-standing dispute between the Senate (which, along with the president, ratified treaties) and the House of Representatives (which was routinely called upon to appropriate funds for treaty arrangements it had no hand in making), the United States government passed an amendment to its Indian Appropriations Act to the effect that while existing treaty commitments would be honoured, 'hereafter no Indian nation or tribe within the territory of the United States shall be acknowledged or recognized as an independent nation, tribe or power with whom the United States may contract by treaty.'

This created a new anomaly (since the constitutional basis upon which the federal government of the United States dealt with Indians had to do either with its treaty-making power, or with its responsibility for regulating trade) and, in the eyes of many Canadians, a new example of the troubles Americans created for themselves by their inconsistent application of those principles upon which the British had prided themselves in their dealings with Aboriginal peoples. And so the Canadian government proceeded with treaty-making in 1871 at precisely the time that the United States government rejected this long-standing principle. It is clear that the Canadian government was ostentatiously acknowledging the sovereign political and cultural status of Indian nations, since that is precisely what the Americans were ostentatiously rejecting. At least in the opinion of Canadians and the Aboriginal peoples with whom they entered into treaty, the Americans were encouraging chaos. The logic of the treaties, as well as what Gerald Friesen refers to as their liturgy (which included such material expressions as annual salaries for the chief and subordinate officers of a tribe, and the issue to the chief of 'suitable' clothing and a medal) reinforced the extent to which they were an attempt to maintain the principles articulated in Matthew Arnold's *Culture and Anarchy.*

They also reinforced something else – a commitment to what might be (and was then) called 'keeping your word.' For the Canadians, treaties depended on that commitment, which (in the rhetoric of the time) distinguished those of British descent from their American neighbours, who had proved first in their rebellion and over and over again since then just how un-British they really were. For Aboriginal peoples, failing to keep your word was the quintessentially uncivil, and uncivilized, act. And although they must have had doubts about some of the behaviour of the Canadians, they had to assume that they were more or less civilized.

Keeping your word. Your *spoken* word. That's where the difference between Canadian and American practice was located; and that's where the Canadian breach of trust, the barbarism, took place. Not simply in breaking the promises, but in putting them on paper (and thereby opening them to convenient rather than conventional interpretations). The oral versions, the spoken texts, of the treaties are fundamentally important not just because they are original – though they certainly are – but because they are the texts upon which both the political authority and the cultural integrity of *both* sides ultimately depend, bulwarks against the anarchy of relativist political (which is to say, legal) interpretations and the chaos of cultural pluralism.

2
Challenging Assumptions: The Impact of Precedent in Aboriginal Rights Litigation

Catherine Bell and Michael Asch

Introduction

The concept of Aboriginal rights is in the process of evolution. The recognition and affirmation of Aboriginal rights in section 35 of the Constitution Act, 1982 acted as a catalyst for the reconceptualization of these rights in legal and political discourse.[1] However, judicial consideration of rights claims remains beholden to the past. Although the recognition of contemporary theories of equality has chipped away at certain aspects of dated decisions, precedent has played a pivotal role in judicial reasoning, preventing meaningful recognition of the rights claimed. Of particular concern is the uncritical acceptance of legal principles based on discriminatory assumptions about the nature of Aboriginal societies. This, combined with the sanctified legal rationales for anchoring present decisions in the past, renders judges who wish to remain true to the discipline of legal reasoning formidable and unyielding. However, close examination of the role of precedent reveals that it is not necessary to perpetuate the status quo in order to be faithful to the discipline of law. Rather, numerous mechanisms are available which allow a judge to respond to changing social values within the confines of traditional legal analysis.

In order to illustrate the importance of precedent and how it can be used to promote and prevent change, this paper focuses on recent claims by First Nations to ownership of, and jurisdiction over, traditional lands. In particular we emphasize the *Delgamuukw* and *Hamlet of Baker Lake* decisions.[2] It is our contention that if the court is to be an effective forum for the realization of Aboriginal autonomy, a significant change in legal thought must occur. We argue that this will only take place if the court critically analyzes the relevance of Aboriginal title cases as the main source of legal principles to guide contemporary judicial decision-making on Aboriginal rights matters. We begin with an overview of the role of precedent in the art of legal reasoning and how the doctrine of *stare decisis* can be used to promote stability or change depending primarily on the characterization of issues and rules of relevance adopted by a particular judge. This is followed by a discussion of the detrimental impact that legal principles and presumptions derived from dated Aboriginal title precedent have had on Aboriginal claims for ownership and jurisdiction. Recognizing that application of Aboriginal title precedent need not perpetuate the status quo, we raise arguments that support distinguishing Aboriginal title precedent. We limit ourselves to two central arguments, namely, the questionable informational value of precedent informed by dated, ethnocentric legal theory; and the substantial change in anthropological theory upon which some of the most influential decisions are based. Central to our analysis is the assertion that the court must draw on a broader interpretive framework to fully understand the meaning of Aboriginal title precedent. We conclude that the argument 'we are bound by previous decisions' is a position of convenience adopted by a court reluctant to embrace meaningful change and diversity in Canadian law.

The Role of Precedent in Judicial Reasoning

Although *stare decisis* is only one method of argument utilized in contemporary legal reasoning, its importance can not be understated as it is 'often as persuasive as it is pervasive.'[3] According to the doctrine of *stare decisis* lower courts must follow like decisions of higher courts within the same judicial hierarchy to the extent that they apply to the case before them. Present decisions are justified by looking to decisions of the past. A 'pure argument from precedent depends only on the results of [previous] decisions, and not the validity of reasons supporting those results.'[4] Utilized this way, the doctrine serves to limit a decisionmaker's flexibility, prevents judges from doing 'what they might subjectively think (or feel) might be the right or just thing to do in a particular case' and promotes the myth of legal objectivity.[5]

The authority for the doctrine of *stare decisis* is long-term practice by the judiciary. Continuity, fairness, certainty, and predictability are the rationale for this doctrine, which is viewed as crucial in maintaining a tradition of legal objectivity. The concept of fairness reflects a formal notion of equality that all people should stand equally before the law. In the context of *stare decisis,* this is manifested in the notion that like cases should be decided alike. 'To fail to treat similar cases similarly, it is argued, is arbitrary, and consequently unjust and unfair.'[6] The concepts of continuity, certainty, and predictability presume the ability to apply an existing rule of law deductively. This is viewed as desirable because through the process of logical deduction people can anticipate the future, plan their lives with some certainty, and avoid the potential chaos created by unexpected change.

However, it may be argued that the doctrine of *stare decisis* need not operate as a constraint on judicial reasoning, particularly in emerging areas of law such as Aboriginal self-government. Although the doctrine promotes uniformity, a court can remain true to what it perceives to be the objective discipline of legal reasoning by utilizing mechanisms already built into the doctrine of *stare decisis*. Indeed these mechanisms have been used throughout the evolution of the common law to develop, expand, and change the common law in response to the changing circumstances, priorities, and social mores of Canadian society. The common law evolves not only when precedent is followed but also when it is distinguished. It is not precedent itself that binds, but judicial interpretation of the past and its relevance to the present. The hard question is not whether like cases should be decided alike but 'what we mean by "alike."'[7] The determination of 'likeness' lies with the present decisionmaker. The characterization of material facts in past and present decisions, and the identification of the rationale and principles of law of a previous decision are all central to the determination of relevance. There are always factual distinctions between the precedent case and others, allowing a judge to narrow the principle or reasons to the facts of the precedent case. The principle and reasons may be interpreted narrowly to eliminate inconsistencies between the precedent case and other cases. They may also be broadened to incorporate what a judge perceives to be similar facts or legal issues. However, the principles and reasons in their modified form must be 'a possible basis for the original decision.'[8] Viewed in this way, the doctrine of *stare decisis* 'does not *constrain* the present decision, and the present decision maker violates no norm by disregarding it.'[9]

Interpretation and distinguishment are the mechanisms which allow a judge to respond to changing social values within the confines of traditional legal analysis. Indeed the practice of distinguishing precedents has been recognized by Chief Justice Dickson of the Supreme Court of Canada (as he then was) as one which preserves formal adherence to the doctrine of *stare decisis* and at the same time allows a court to escape 'the folly of perpetuating to eternity, principles unsuited to modern circumstances.'[10] Adopting interpretive strategies, a judge chooses one precedent in favour of another, appearing to find, rather than create law. The appearance of finding is important because it deflects charges of result-oriented reasoning and judicial legislation. It also absolves judges of personal responsibility for what they decide. M.R. Cohen explains it this way: 'To speak of finding the law seems to connote that law exists before the decision, and thus tends to minimize the importance of the judicial contribution to the law or the *arbitrium judicium* and the factors that determine it.'[11]

Such discreet creativity can be contrasted to decisions where new law is created in absence of relevant precedent or an appellate court expressly overrules a lower court decision. Interpretation of a previous decision may lead to the conclusion that there are no relevant binding precedents or persuasive precedents. A persuasive precedent is one which is viewed as not binding the court but as having some pertinence to the outcome of a decision. Cases that traditionally fall into this category are decisions from foreign jurisdictions (such as the United States), lower level courts, and courts of coordinate jurisdiction. Also, courts may find a case is dissimilar in some aspects and similar in others, so that some comments or the reasoning of the decision may be treated as persuasive. In the absence of binding and persuasive precedent, the court must build its legal argument on other sources of law such as legislation, the Constitution, and public policy. However, legal analysis which does not draw on arguments of precedent is rare at all levels in the judicial hierarchy. Many judges regard the creation of new law in the absence of relevant precedent as the task of legislators and believe judges should leave such matters to them.

The ability to overrule is a built-in mechanism of checks and balances in recognition of a lower court's interpretive powers. This power is most often invoked when an appellate court finds that the decision of a lower court is based on an erroneous interpretation of the law. In such cases the appellate court will also clarify the law so that lower courts in the future can apply the law correctly. The Supreme Court of Canada is also able to overrule its own decisions and Canadian decisions of the Privy Council.[12] However, in the interests of certainty and predictability in the law, such action is limited to exceptional circumstances where compelling reasons for change can be shown.[13] The ability to depart from their own past decisions remains controversial among intermediate appellate courts.[14]

Courts are also open to questioning the informational value of dated decisions due to ideologies influencing decisionmakers of the past or to changing socio-economic circumstances. For example in *R. v. Simon*, Chief Justice Dickson (as he then was) drew a distinction between language and substance in rejecting counsel's argument that the case of *R. v. Syliboy* applied to the facts before him.[15] Noting that the language used by Justice Patterson in 1928 'reflects the biases and prejudices of another era in our history,' he selected numerous precedents to illustrate that Patterson's findings on the legal incapacity of Indians to enter treaties have been rejected and should not be adopted by the Supreme Court.[16]

Changes in ideology may motivate a particular interpretation, but are rarely expressed as the basis to distinguish or overrule a previous decision.

Reluctance to expressly distinguish or overrule a decision for this reason may be due to various factors. Some judges perceive the discipline of law as a highly structured discipline of logical deduction and mechanical interpretation of legal rules. This perception of legal reasoning discourages clear and unequivocal assessment of the ideology informing the interpretive process as a legitimate basis to distinguish or overrule. Inherent in this approach is a concern for maintaining the illusion of legal objectivity and certainty. However, as argued above, the central role of judicial interpretation in legal reasoning allows for as much uncertainty and unpredictability as it does certainty. Justice Holmes explains the problem as follows: 'Perhaps one of the reasons why judges do not like to discuss questions of public policy, or to put a decision in terms upon their views as lawmakers, is that the moment you leave the path of merely logical deduction you lose the illusion of certainty which makes legal reasoning seem like mathematics. But certainty is only an illusion, nevertheless.'[17]

Despite reluctance to admit the significant influence of factors that lie outside the pure discipline of legal analysis, it is clear that such influences have resulted in significant change where a judge has chosen to yield to them. Again in the words of Justice Holmes, 'the result of the often proclaimed judicial aversion to deal with such considerations is simply to leave the ground and foundation of judgements inarticulate and often unconscious.'[18] Put more harshly, in such cases the written decision reflects result-oriented censored reasoning which on the surface adheres to deductive legal reasoning, but in essence is driven by considerations of public policy. As an illustration of this point consider the decision of the Privy Council in *Edwards* v. *A.G. Can.*[19] In this decision the Privy Council interpreted the word 'persons' in section 24 of the Constitution Act, 1867, to include women and in doing so recognized their legal right to participate in Canadian government. Prior to this decision, Anglo-Canadian law accepted as factual the idea of difference between men and women, thereby denying women many legal rights historically attributed to men.[20] There was no existing precedent recognizing women's rights to take part in public life, and indeed analogous precedent emphasizing the theory of difference supported the status quo of exclusion. Defining the issue narrowly as interpretation of the word 'persons,' Lord Sankey reviewed the precedents relied on by the Supreme Court of Canada and concluded they were not relevant. Freed from past decisions, he adopted a liberal interpretation of the word 'persons' and stated that the onus of proof in this case should be on those who deny the inclusion of women. Although Lord Sankey does not clearly articulate the reasons for his refusal to apply past precedent, he states at the beginning of his opinion that 'the exclusion of women from all public office is a relic of days more barbarous than ours,' suggesting that his logic is motivated by a different ideology on the role of women than that articulated in past decisions.[21] His interpretation of precedent allowed him to reach a conclusion compatible with his views on the past discriminatory treatment of women.

Accepting the central role of interpretation in the application of precedent it becomes clear that 'the truths of the common law are ... a function of the values of the judge who discovers them.'[22] The real question is not can a judge change existing law and remain true to the discipline of legal reasoning, but 'when will the tendency toward stability prevail?'[23] By adopting a philosophy of judicial constraint and reaching predictable results, a judge adds little to the substantive evolution of the law. Thus, the tendency towards stability or change will be influenced by the area of law being considered. For example, changes to the Canadian Constitution in 1982 articulating the rights and freedoms of Canadian citizens have highlighted the court's role in judicial review of government action and the creation of a new body of constitutional law. In the words of Dale Gibson, 'the demanding task of putting legal flesh on the Charter's bones is the sole responsibility of judicial law-makers.'[24] This area of law can be contrasted to the common law of real property in which judges are prone to adopt a philosophy of judicial constraint in keeping with the predominant and 'cautious view that the categories of property rights should be carefully controlled.'[25] The rationale behind the reluctance to reform land law is linked to the acceptance of property as a central commodity of exchange and fear of chaos in the marketplace if rights in land are confused and unpredictable.

The level of court may also influence the extent of judicial activism, as lower courts tend to approach change with caution, leaving fundamental questioning to the appellate levels. Confronted with vast amounts of litigation, lower courts opt for the philosophy of judicial constraint for reasons of efficiency and timeliness. Manipulation of precedent, in particular distinguishing precedent which has historically been treated as binding or persuasive, is time-consuming. If insufficient attention has been paid to interpretive issues, some comfort lies in the fact that there exists an appellate court for the correction of errors. At the intermediate appellate level, courts are more willing to consider change, but stability often prevails if change brought about by a decision could have a significant social, political, or economic impact, is difficult to enforce, or has the potential to proliferate litigation. It is not surprising then that the most significant changes occur at the highest level. However, this is problematic, as lower courts are often the courts of last resort. Many litigants can not afford to have their issues addressed by appellate courts. Further, the interpretation of evidence and conclusions relating to factual issues will not be reversed on appeal unless an appellate court can demonstrate that failure to appreciate evidence is based on misapprehension of some legal principle,[26] or the trial judge has made a palpable or overriding error, such as failure to support findings with clear and adequate reasons based on the evidence before her.[27] Indeed the presumption of appellate courts is that they should not intervene on questions of fact because the trial judge is in the best position to deal with these issues. As the nature of common law is such that law is developed in relation to facts and the consequences to be drawn from them, the reluctance of appellate courts to review facts in many cases will render the trial division the court of last resort. Therefore, it is at this level that judges must be encouraged to take a more critical approach to analysis of existing precedent for timely and responsive change to occur.

For many judges, the discipline of legal reasoning also translates into a clear division of roles between the courts and legislatures. A distinction is drawn between law and public policy. The role of the court is to declare the common law as it presently exists and, where appropriate, to extend existing principles of common law to address situations not previously encountered.[28] The creation of new law due to changes in public policy, morality, or other ideological influences is for elected representatives. However, drawing clear lines between the institutional function of the court and the legislatures is artificial and impractical. It is artificial in the sense that judges are constantly creating new law when they adopt interpretive techniques, they just don't like to admit it. Dale Gibson suggests there are several reasons why judges are reluctant to openly adopt the role of judicial legislators: 'The most extreme rationale is that if members of the public became aware that unelected judges were making laws [rather than declaring existing common law], they might insist on introducing democracy to the process by requiring judges to be elected to office.'[29] This, combined with the likelihood of increased public criticism as judicial activism becomes common knowledge, could undermine the perceived impartiality of the courts. Judges are also concerned with maintaining the myth of consistency and certainty in the law, thereby limiting their admissions of creativity to 'situations where existing law is manifestly incomplete or unsatisfactory.'[30] From a practical perspective, Gibson points out that the legislators have not got time to set the agenda for all legal reform. Further, they do not have the incentive or expertise to do so.[31] Finally, in his opinion 'there is one area of law – constitutional law – where the legislatures have no role to play at all.'[32] The whole point of constitutional law is to act as a check on government action.

Judicial Constraint and the Doctrine of Aboriginal Rights

Emerging judicial opinion on Aboriginal self-government has adopted Canadian law on Aboriginal title as a primary source for relevant precedent. An examination of recent judicial consideration of Aboriginal political rights reveals the unlikelihood of any meaningful recognition of Aboriginal autonomy if this pattern continues. The characterization of Aboriginal political autonomy being 'like' an Aboriginal title claim has created the potential for the wholesale application of principles developed within this stream of law without the need for critical analysis or consideration of alternative precedent. Despite the existence of mechanisms to distinguish and reinterpret these decisions, Canadian courts challenged to recognize new rights remain openly deferential to the past. The result has been judicial denial of the contemporary existence of an inherent right to government and legislative power. This approach is particularly appealing to a lower court or a judge with an emotional and intellectual commitment to the status quo as it allows one to empathize with the discriminatory treatment of Aboriginal people and at the same time declare helpless bondage to fundamental principles firmly established in the common law.

Principles and Presumptions

Ironically, one of the cases most frequently cited in the development of Canadian Aboriginal rights law is a United States decision, *Johnston* v. *McIntosh*.[33] In this decision Justice Marshall 'invented a body of law which was virtually without precedent.'[34] Although Marshall stayed within the realm of English property law by recognizing that Aboriginal peoples acquired a right of occupancy arising from actual possession, the theory of rights informing his analysis was based on misinterpretations and creation of international law doctrines relating to territorial acquisition. One of the most criticized areas of analysis is his application of the doctrine of discovery to support Crown title in, and acquisition of sovereignty over, occupied lands. In his opinion the Crown's title and sovereign powers necessarily diminished Indian rights to sovereignty and Indian people's power to alienate their lands. According to Justice Marshall 'absolute ultimate title [was] considered [in international law] as acquired by discovery, subject only to the Indian title of occupancy, which title the discoverers possessed the exclusive right of acquiring.'[35] Settlement on Indian lands and conquest were considered legitimate methods to acquire the Indian interest.

The theory informing this analysis is that Aboriginal lands could be considered vacant and subject to discovery because of the method of Aboriginal land use and the superiority of English institutions. Cultivation and settlement was labour worthy of reward, but roaming the land like 'savages' was not.[36] Although Marshall states that he is not willing to entertain 'the controversy, whether agriculturalists, merchants and manufacturers, have a right, on abstract principles, to expel hunters from the territories they possess,'[37] his acceptance of European superiority clearly influences his reasoning as evidenced by the following quotes:

> On the discovery of this immense continent, the great nations of Europe were eager to appropriate to themselves so much of it as they could respectively acquire. Its vast extent offered ample field to the ambition and enterprise of all; and the character and religion of its inhabitants afforded by apology for considering them as people over whom the superior genius of Europe might claim ascendency.[38]
>
> But the tribes of Indians inhabiting this country were fierce savages, whose occupation was war, and whose subsistence was drawn chiefly from the forest. To leave them in possession of their country, was to leave the country a wilderness; to govern them as a distinct people was impossible, because they were as brave and high-spirited as they were fierce, and were ready to repel by arms every attempt on their independence.[39]

Subsequent decisions by Marshall's court limit the doctrine of discovery and clarify that the only legitimate method to acquire title to occupied lands is through purchase or cession. The leading decision on this point is *Worcester* v. *Georgia*.[40] In *Worcester* v. *Georgia*, Marshall accepts that the Crown somehow acquired sovereignty but argues that the principle of discovery did not affect the right of those already in possession.[41] He concludes, rather, that, in accord with international opinion, title to occupied lands could only be acquired through cession. Furthermore, in his opinion Indians did not automatically cease to be sovereign and self-governing nations upon entering treaties nor were those rights necessarily diminished upon discovery. Rather, powers of government both internal and external to Indian territory continued, unless they were surrendered by treaty, overruled by congressional enactments, or limited in their exercise by reasonable state regulation. This theory of continuance, often referred to as the doctrine of residual sovereignty, is the basis for the authority of Indian Nations in the United States to enact and enforce their own laws within their own territories. Although substantial restraints have been placed on the contemporary exercise of Aboriginal government, particularly in the areas of criminal law, the underlying legal theory is recognition of a pre-existing inherent right to sovereign jurisdiction and a continuing right to tribal government within Indian territories.

It is now commonly accepted by legal academics that one cannot look to discovery as an explanation for the legitimate acquisition of territorial sovereignty by the Crown. However, despite Marshall's reasoning in *Worcester* and substantial academic commentary, Canadian courts still cite *Johnston* v. *McIntosh* to support the legal presumption of Crown sovereignty. Indeed, *Johnston* v. *McIntosh* has been hailed as 'the *locus classicus* of principles governing Aboriginal title.'[42] Others, unwilling to explore the legitimacy of Crown sovereignty in fact or law simply presume that at some point Crown sovereignty was effectively asserted. In the words of Brian Slattery:

> Canadian law treats the question of when and how the Crown gained sovereignty over Canadian territories in a somewhat artificial and self-serving manner. To state a complex matter simply, the courts apparently feel bound to defer the official territorial claims advanced by the Crown, without inquiring into the facts supporting them or their validity in international law. This judicial posture of deference is designed to leave the executive with a relatively free hand in matters of foreign policy. So a Canadian court will ordinarily recognize historical claims officially advanced by the Crown to American territories as effective to confer sovereignty for domestic purposes.[43]

Another important legacy of *Johnston* v. *McIntosh* is that Marshall's conclusions on the effects of discovery have been adopted as fundamental principles in Canadian Aboriginal rights law. The effects of the doctrine of discovery on judicial analysis can be summarized in the following judicial presumptions:

(1) Sovereignty and legislative power is vested in the British Crown.
(2) Ownership of Aboriginal lands accompanies sovereignty over Aboriginal territory.
(3) Aboriginal peoples have an interest in land arising from original occupation that is less than full ownership.
(4) The British Crown obtained the sole right to acquire the Aboriginal interest.
(5) Aboriginal sovereignty was necessarily diminished.

In the context of Aboriginal title litigation, the refusal to challenge these presumptions meant that judges became engaged in exercises to clarify the nature and source of Aboriginal title accepting that: (a) the Crown owned the land and had sovereign jurisdiction and (b) some form of interest in land less than ownership could arise from Aboriginal occupation. For example, citing *Johnston* v. *McIntosh* as the 'classic and definitive judgement' on point, Lord Watson, sixty-five years later, in the *St. Catherine's*

Milling case, described the Indian right of occupancy as 'a *personal* and usufructuary right dependent on the goodwill of the Sovereign.'[44] He also stated that Indian possession 'such as it was, can only be ascribed to the ... Royal Proclamation in favour of all Indian tribes then living under the sovereignty and protection of the British Crown.'[45] This description of Aboriginal title by the Privy Council implied that Aboriginal title was contingent on Crown grant or recognition. 'Indian title was something like a mere license to use the land, which the Crown could unilaterally revoke at any time by executive act.'[46] Classifying the interest as personal removed the protection traditionally accorded to proprietary interests, namely, the need for surrender to the Crown or specific legislation enacted by a competent legislative authority to effectively terminate the interests.[47]

Subsequent Canadian decisions debated back and forth the personal and proprietary nature of Indian title, but failed to carefully analyze the legitimate acquisition and legal nature of the Crown's interest. The next major development was eighty-five years later in the *Calder* case. In this case the Supreme Court of Canada rejected the notion that Aboriginal title was contingent on Crown recognition. In the words of Justice Judson, Aboriginal title arose from the fact that 'when settlers came, the Indians were there, organized in societies and occupying land as their forefathers had done for centuries.'[48] The idea that Aboriginal rights have a source independent of Crown recognition is now firmly entrenched in Canadian law as the inherent rights theory.[49] However, *Calder* also affirmed Crown sovereignty and its presumptive effects. In particular, the Supreme Court upheld the notion that with Crown sovereignty comes the power to terminate Aboriginal interests and alter the common law. A fundamental doctrine of constitutional law is applied, namely, that common law rights can be altered by a competent legislature. The legal debate in the decision was whether the intent to do so must be clear and plain.

The most recent description of Aboriginal title articulated in the *Guerin* case is that it is a *sui generis*, or unique right, to which the courts have almost 'inevitably found themselves applying a somewhat inappropriate property law.'[50] The characterization of the legal nature of Aboriginal title as *sui generis* provided Canadian courts with the opportunity to explore beyond the confines of English property law to determine the scope and content of Aboriginal title and its relationship with the Crown's interest. The recognition of the uniqueness of Aboriginal title was a clearly articulated, interpretive tool which could be invoked to distinguish previous precedent which did not fully appreciate the restraints imposed by the language and concepts of English and Canadian common law. For example, focusing on the uniqueness of Aboriginal title, a court could abandon the law of real property as relevant to its inquiry and look to the property systems of the Aboriginal claimants to define the scope and content of their rights. However, with the exception of a few notable dissenting opinions,[51] the concept of *sui generis* has simply been invoked in legal reasoning to deny classification of Aboriginal title as fee simple ownership with all the rights flowing therefrom.[52] For example, the concept is used to justify a lesser variety of title: occupancy and use. The concept of *sui generis* has also been applied to treaties and other Aboriginal rights claims. As we will discuss shortly, in the context of claims to government, it has significant potential to act as a catalyst for change.

The presumption of Crown ownership has resulted in Canadian courts placing the onus on Aboriginal claimants to prove that they and their ancestral societies occupied a specific territory at the time Crown sovereignty was asserted. In addition they must show they occupied the territory to the exclusion of other Aboriginal societies. These proofs make sense to Canadian judges because they are familiar tests associated with possessory title in English law. Because of the corollary presumption that Aboriginal title is a unique interest that falls short of ownership, Aboriginal litigants also have the burden of proving the scope of rights that flow from occupancy. The content of the rights is determined by an assessment of 'traditional activities recognized by the aboriginal society as integral to its distinctive culture.'[53] As discussed below, parallel burdens of proof appear to be developing in the context of self-government litigation.

The potential impact of the above principles, presumptions, and interpretive mechanisms on the law of self-government is revealed in the trial and Court of Appeal judgments in *Delgamuukw*, the first case to analyze issues of Aboriginal jurisdiction and government after the rendering of the *Guerin* and *Sparrow* decisions by the Supreme Court. At trial, Justice McEachern referred to *St. Catherine's* and *Johnston* v. *McIntosh* to conclude that 'discovery and occupation of the lands of this continent by European nations, or occupation and settlement, gave rise to a right of sovereignty.'[54] Equating the plaintiffs' claim to jurisdiction as a claim to sovereignty, he points to *St. Catherine's* and *Sparrow* as conclusive authority against the plaintiffs' claims for ownership and sovereign jurisdiction.[55] Having reached this conclusion he engages in a factual analysis of whether the plaintiffs exercised sovereign jurisdiction prior to and at the date Crown sovereignty was asserted in the contested area, and a legal analysis of whether Aboriginal jurisdiction survived the advent of Crown sovereignty.

As in the case of Aboriginal title where proof of occupation does not give rise to the presumption of a full bundle of ownership rights in favour of Aboriginal claimants, proof of occupation by an ancestral society does not give rise to a presumption that the society had legal, political, and other institutions attributed to all societies. McEachern places the burden for proving institutions of government on the Aboriginal plaintiffs. They must prove their ancestral organization in societies, the nature of their institutions, and the existence of the particular institutional rights claimed (e.g., law-making powers) to rebut the presumption that English institutions were automatically received in a lawless and politically barren land. The philosophy that informed the requirement of proofs to rebut Crown ownership also lies at the heart of McEachern's self-government analysis. In short, this philosophy is one that presumes vacancy in the case of land and a vacuum in the case of institutions because aboriginal societies 'are so low on the scale of social organization that their usages and conceptions of rights and duties are not to be reconciled with institutions of the legal ideas of civilized society.'[56]

The tradition of moulding Aboriginal interests into familiar categories of English law and measuring their enforceability by English standards also prevails in McEachern's analysis. Carrying forward the tradition of judicial constraint, he too refuses to give significant meaning to the concept of *sui generis*, as illustrated in the following quote: 'It became obvious during the course of the trial that what the Gitksan and Wet'suwet'en witnesses describe as law is a really most uncertain and highly flexible set of customs which are frequently not followed by the Indians themselves ... In my judgement, these rules are so flexible and uncertain that they cannot be classified as law.'[57] Elsewhere he considers the existence of a legislative institution as essential to the existence of government and concludes: 'I do not suggest the Indians have not always participated in feasting practices, and I accept that it has played, and still plays, a crucial role in the social organization of these people. I am not persuaded that the feast has ever operated as a legislative institution in the regulation of land. There are simply too many instances of prominent chiefs who have conducted themselves other than in accordance with the land law system for which the plaintiffs contend.'[58]

Ironically, McEachern imposes standards for the clarity and enforceability of Aboriginal laws in a more rigorous fashion than they are normally applied to English and Canadian legal institutions. As our analysis of *stare decisis* and Aboriginal title precedent has shown, the common law as it is developed by Canadian courts has an inherent capacity to be flexible and uncertain. And of course, many of our laws are not followed or enforced. Further, McEachern's search for familiar institutions, such as legislative institutions, completely ignores the unique nature of Aboriginal rights. The concept of *sui generis* suggests that Aboriginal customs, traditions, and practices are the appropriate source to determine the binding nature and enforceability of Aboriginal laws. However, as in the context of Aboriginal title, McEachern follows judicial tradition and fails to take advantage of this interpretive tool for the benefit of the Aboriginal plaintiffs.

Drawing on Aboriginal title precedent, McEachern argues that 'aboriginal rights exist at the pleasure of the Crown and may be extinguished when the intention of the Crown is clear and plain.'[59] Further, he argues that 'the aboriginal system, to the extent that it constituted aboriginal jurisdiction or sovereignty, or ownership apart from occupation for residence and use, gave way to a new form of colonial government which the law recognizes to the exclusion of other systems.'[60] If he is wrong in this conclusion, he adds that any residual aboriginal or other legislative jurisdiction that might have survived the colonial period was clearly and plainly extinguished by the enactment of the British North America Act, 1867.[61] The result in his opinion is that 'self-government is possible only with the agreement of both levels of government [federal and provincial] under appropriate, lawful legislation.'[62] The majority of the Court of Appeal did not question the analytical tools adopted by McEachern to measure self-government, and upheld his findings of fact.

Reinterpreting Precedent and Adopting New Rules of Relevance

The application of Aboriginal title precedent, including *Johnston* v. *McIntosh*, need not result in denial of the existence of an Aboriginal right to government. The key to recognition or denial of the original right rests in the legal rule of relevance or organizing principle that the judge adopts as the basis for case manipulation. Consideration of the dissenting opinion of Justice Lambert in the *Delgamuukw* appeal illustrates this point. His decision also illustrates how techniques of judicial interpretation, discussed earlier in this paper, can be invoked to create a substantially different outcome.

According to Lambert all Aboriginal rights are best understood not by drawing analogies to English law, but by evidence of customs, practices, and traditions of Aboriginal peoples that are an integral part of their distinctive culture. He cites *Guerin* and *Sparrow* to support his analysis. Further, his reasoning illustrates that Aboriginal rights are not understood by limiting the legal frame of reference to American precedents on the effects of discovery, English common law, or Canadian Aboriginal title cases. Rather, applying contemporary academic analysis he concludes that the appropriate rule of relevance to identify and analyze precedent is unique customary rights and the doctrine of continuity.

The doctrine of continuity accepts that the Crown at some point, in some way, acquired sovereignty. However, it also accepts that the assertion of Crown sovereignty alone did not necessarily vest ownership in the Crown nor did it automatically terminate existing Indigenous practices, customs, and traditions. Sovereignty essentially gave the Crown the power to make just laws and acquire Aboriginal lands. Accordingly, Aboriginal 'customary' rights continue except insofar as they are 'inconsistent with the concept of sovereignty itself, or inconsistent with laws clearly made applicable to the whole territory and all of its inhabitants, or with principles of fundamental justice.'[63] Aboriginal rights implicitly extinguished because of inconsistency with the concept of sovereignty would include the right to make war and impose Aboriginal customs on settlers subject to British law. Within this legal organizing principle, Crown sovereignty can coexist in law with a right of Aboriginal peoples to own and govern their territories.

The doctrine of continuity finds its precedent origins in *Campbell* v. *Hall*, an early English case dealing with conquered lands.[64] Some might argue the case is not applicable because Canada was never conquered. However, Lambert argues that the case is relevant and the doctrine applies to all occupied territories regardless of the mode of acquisition. To support this position he argues that the early cases drew a distinction between conquered, ceded, and settled colonies because of a notion that certain societies were so primitive ⁺heir land could be treated as uninhabited or *terra nullius*. Citing *Mabo* v. *Queensland*, a recent decision rendered by the Australian High Court, he argues it is no longer acceptable to treat lands occupied by Indigenous peoples as *terra nullius*.[65] Therefore, laws which applied to inhabited lands should also apply to lands occupied by Aboriginal peoples.

Accepting the doctrine of continuity as the proper organizing principle, Lambert interprets Canadian precedent to fit this doctrine and profiles commonwealth decisions that have historically been given attention in passing by Canadian courts. The importance of this expansive interpretation of relevant precedent cannot be underestimated as it allows Lambert to remain true to the discipline of legal reasoning by appearing to find the law in previous decisions. At the same time he is able to effectively deal with principles and presumptions which plague Canadian law. For example, as a result of adopting the doctrine of continuity as the main rule of relevance for identifying precedent, *Johnston* v. *McIntosh* is interpreted as supporting the fundamental proposition that 'rights of Indians in the lands they traditionally occupied prior to European colonization both predated and survived the claims of sovereignty made by ... European nations.'[66] Comments on discovery and its effect do not enter the analysis. *St. Catherine's*, he argues, relates only to the Royal Proclamation of 1763 and does not treat Aboriginal title as *sui generis*. He defines *sui generis* as 'in a class or category of its own.'[67] Thus he argues 'the solution to further problems in relation to aboriginal title should be sought in a deeper understanding of the nature of the aboriginal title itself, in aboriginal terms, and not in attributing consequences under common law on the basis that those consequences flow from the common law classification for tenure purposes of the aboriginal title or right as either proprietary or personal.'[68]

Another example of reinterpretation based on new rules of relevance is found in his treatment of the *Baker Lake* case. Although Lambert maintains that the onus is on Aboriginal plaintiffs to prove their rights, he rejects aspects of *Baker Lake* which he feels are not based on the customs, practices, and traditions of Aboriginal peoples. For example, he expressly disagrees with the notion that Aboriginal societies must occupy the land claimed to the exclusion of other societies. Citing American authority he argues: 'If the right that is asserted ... is a right to occupation that is shared by two or three separate organized societies of indigenous people, who shared such occupancy at the time of sovereignty and earlier, and who, in each of their societies, recognized or controlled the exercise of shared rights by their own societies, then I do not see why there should not be an aboriginal right to shared occupancy.'[69]

He also interprets the test articulated in *Baker Lake* as supporting the position that Aboriginal societies need not prove occupation since time immemorial. In his interpretation, the need to establish occupation at the date sovereignty was asserted does not necessarily incorporate the time immemorial test.[70] In his opinion 'there is nothing in that principle about Aboriginal occupation, possession, use and enjoyment having to have been in place for a long, long time, a very long time, or even a long time.'[71]

Lambert also argues that the trial judge in *Delgamuukw* is wrong in suggesting that Aboriginal rights are those that have been carried on for a lengthy period of time free of European influence. Aboriginal rights are rooted in presovereign exercise but must be permitted to maintain contemporary relevance. Their recognition at common law is not dependant on immemorial Aboriginal practice but on the doctrine of continuity. However, he admits, endurability may be powerful evidence of existence at the date sovereignty was asserted. On this point he states: 'The long-time user test seems in my opinion to depict aboriginal societies as societies frozen in their development. In *Sparrow*, however, the frozen rights theory was rejected and in *Guerin*, in *Calder*, and in *Amodu Tijani* we have been warned against the dangers of cultural perceptions in considering aboriginal rights. The long-time user test embodies a static view of aboriginal culture. I do not believe those societies have been static or frozen ... Once it is recognized that aboriginal societies were societies capable of change, the notion that there is an "aboriginal" use which can be discovered only on the basis of evidence of long-time user must be rejected.'[72]

Lambert applies this same analysis to self-government. Drawing on the concept of *sui generis* customary rights, he argues:

> I conclude that the trial judge was in error when he concluded that the claim to 'jurisdiction must fail because the nature of aboriginal self-government and self-regulation was such that it does not produce a set of binding and enforceable "laws."' Aboriginal rights of self-government do not rest on 'Laws.' They rest on customs, traditions and practices of the aboriginal people to the extent that those customs, traditions and practices formed and form an integral part of their distinctive culture ... In my opinion, the trial judge erred in imposing standards from the common law on aboriginal rights of self-government and self-regulation. The Aboriginal rights of self-government and self-regulation are *sui generis*, just as aboriginal title is *sui generis*.[73]

Lambert later states it is wrong to conclude there are no Aboriginal rights of self-government because customs are flexible and open to more than one interpretation. Similar examples can be found in common law. This may just mean that 'the law is not well or universally understood.'[74]

Although Lambert's analysis provides a useful model of how existing precedent can be interpreted to support a broader definition of Aboriginal rights, it can only take Aboriginal plaintiffs so far, as Lambert takes away with one hand what he gives with the other. He too operates on the presumption that the Crown's assertion of sovereignty is legitimate and that the sovereign has the power to terminate Aboriginal rights through actions which demonstrate a clear and plain intention to bring about extinguishment. Administrative or executive action authorized by legislation (adverse dominion) may also extinguish rights. In his words 'the intention to extinguish must be clear and plain; it must be the intention of the Sovereign Power; it must be legislatively brought about; and, if it is implicit, the implication must not simply be probable, it must be necessary.'[75] These concepts apply 'just as straightforwardly to the extinguishment of aboriginal rights of self-government and self-regulation as they do to the extinguishment of aboriginal title.'[76]

Construing the claim for jurisdiction as a claim for 'a right to exercise control over themselves as a community, and over their own land and institutions in that community,' Lambert sees no inconsistency with the plaintiffs' claim to jurisdiction and the concept of Crown sovereignty.[77] He argues it is a misconception to construe the claim as a claim to sovereignty, noting that the plaintiffs are seeking to regulate their 'conduct towards each other and ... towards others' not the 'conduct of others towards them.'[78] The claim is characterized as a claim to self-government or self-regulation. Accepting the concept of Crown sovereignty, the key question for Lambert is whether the colonial government or Parliament clearly and plainly extinguished the right of Aboriginal peoples to govern themselves. Lambert agrees with the majority that Aboriginal government did not automatically cease with the establishment of colonial governments, and colonial proclamations or ordinances designed to open up British Columbia for settlement do not evidence a clear and plain intent to extinguish. Further, in his opinion provincial laws of general application cannot operate to extinguish Aboriginal government because Aboriginal rights lay at the core of Indianness.[79] Only federal law can extinguish these rights. Federal laws with the clear and plain intent to extinguish were not referred to on appeal. As a result the appropriate remedy was to declare the existence of the right of self-regulations and the referral of outstanding matters, such as the scope of the right, back to the British Columbia Supreme Court.

Distinguishing Aboriginal Title Precedent

We have illustrated that application of Aboriginal title precedent can have a detrimental impact on the realization of Aboriginal autonomy. Although this precedent can be reinterpreted in a way to favour Aboriginal claimants, the tradition of judicial constraint inherent in title claims suggests that the proactive approach will continue to be favoured by a minority. Further, one has to question the utility of judicial manipulation of precedent when the ultimate issue of Crown power is not challenged and the precedent itself is informed by an ideology which conflicts with contemporary concepts of culture. In the words of Mr. Justice Brennan of the Australian High Court, 'a common law doctrine founded on unjust discrimination in the enjoyment of civil and political rights demands reconsideration.'[80]

It is our view that common law precedent is founded on assumptions that require reconsideration and ultimately a reversal of logic. A key reason for this view is that the conceptual framework regarding the nature of culture as applied in law is founded on principles that are both incorrect and ethnocentric. It is therefore necessary to distinguish or reverse this precedent to level the field, especially where First Nations are asserting claims for ownership and jurisdiction. We will illustrate this point by reference to the *Baker Lake* case and how the definition of culture outlined there was both incorrect and formed a precedent framework inherently biased against First Nation litigants.

Culture Precedent

One of the most serious impediments to the use of the domestic courts as a vehicle to resolve Aboriginal rights issues, and especially those that relate to Aboriginal ownership and jurisdiction, is the framework they use to interpret Aboriginal culture. This framework, as we have discussed elsewhere,[81] relies on precedents which contain an approach to the analysis of culture which is out of date, biased, and ethnocentric. As a result, Aboriginal plaintiffs are required to carry a burden of proof with respect to establishing fact which is absurd, and for this reason, among others, the legal system places them at a tremendous disadvantage in litigation.[82] We have suggested elsewhere that the courts revise their framework to take into account more contemporary understandings of Aboriginal culture. Here, we will provide more detail on the need for change and what changes may be required. We begin with a description of how the courts now frame their interpretation of the culture of Aboriginal peoples.

The leading precedent used in Canadian courts to determine the extent of Aboriginal rights concerning ownership and jurisdiction is *Baker Lake*.[83] In it, Mr. Justice Mahoney develops a 'test' to be used in the determination of the rights of Aboriginal peoples which has been applied to the resolution of issues respecting ownership and jurisdiction of lands. This test contains four elements. These are:[84]

(1) that they and their ancestors were members of an organized society
(2) that the organized society occupied the specific territory over which they assert the Aboriginal title
(3) that the occupation was to the exclusion of other organized societies
(4) that the occupation was an established fact at the time sovereignty was asserted by England.

Of these elements, the one most critical to the development of the current legal framework for understanding Aboriginal culture is the first. On a naive reading of that clause, it would seem to make common sense. After all, if the courts wish to affirm a collective right, they would certainly wish to differentiate between an organized society and a collection of individuals who could show no relationship to each other. However, that is not the reading given to this element either by Justice Mahoney or by Justice McEachern, who used *Baker Lake* in his framing of Aboriginal culture in *Delgamuukw*. Rather, in the 'legal' reading of this clause, the objective is to differentiate between those societies which were sufficiently organized in order for their descendants to successfully assert a cause with respect to ownership and jurisdiction, and those societies which were too primitive at the time of contact for their descendants to successfully make such an assertion.

In reading the decisions of the trial judges in both *Baker Lake* and *Delgamuukw*, it is clear that the judges' interpretation of the meaning of 'an organized society' derives from their reliance on a 1919 decision of the Privy Council in *Re Southern Rhodesia* to provide precedent.[85] In particular, their decisions rely on the following description provided by the Privy Council in that case:

> The estimation of the rights of aboriginal tribes is always inherently difficult. Some tribes are so low in the scale of social organization that their usages and conceptions of rights and duties are not to be reconciled with the institutions or legal ideas of civilized society. Such a gulf cannot be bridged. It would be idle to impute such people some shadow of the rights known to our law and then to transmute it into the substance of transferable rights of property as we know them. In the present case it would make each and every person by a fictional inheritance a landed proprietor 'richer than all his tribe.' On the other hand, there are indigenous peoples whose legal conceptions, though differently developed, are hardly less precise than our own. When once they have been studied and understood they are no less enforceable than rights arising under English law. Between the two there is a wide tract of much ethnological interest, but the position of the natives of Southern Rhodesia within it is very uncertain; clearly they approximate rather to the lower than to the higher limit.[86]

This statement gives authority to the view that there may be societies too primitive at the time of first contact with Europeans to have contained the elements of ownership and jurisdiction of land at a level of sufficient 'reconcilability' (read 'civilization') for their descendants to be successful in asserting such rights in a court action. It therefore invites and, indeed, requires that a judge in each instance must evaluate whether an Aboriginal society meets this standard.

The idea that judges need to differentiate between cultures where rights are to be recognized and those where they are not, did not originate with the Privy Council in *Re Southern Rhodesia* but derives from legal precedents which go back at least as far as *Calvin's Case* which was decided in 1608. At that time, the crucial differentiation was whether the society was or was not Christian. As the judge said there:

> And upon this ground there is a diversity between a conquest of a kingdom of a Christian King, and the conquest of a kingdom of an infidel; for if a King come to a Christian kingdom by conquest, seeing that he hath

vitoe et necis potestatem, he may at his pleasure alter and change the laws of that kingdom: but until he doth make an alteration of those laws the ancient laws of that kingdom remain. But if a Christian King should conquer a kingdom of an infidel, and bring them under his subjection, there *ipso facto* the laws of the infidels are abrogated, for that they be not only against Christianity, but against the law of God and of nature.[87]

Broadly speaking, the terms for differentiation were altered in the nineteenth century to emphasize a distinction between cultures that had an agricultural base and those which relied on hunting. As Tucker said in 1803:

Plantations or colonies, in distinct countries, are either such where the lands are claimed by right of occupancy only, by finding them desert and uncultivated, and peopling them from the mother country; or where, when already cultivated, they have been either gained, by conquest, or ceded to us by treaties. And both these rights are founded upon the law of nature, or at least upon that of nations. But there is a difference between these two species of colonies, with respect to the laws by which they are bound. For it hath been held, that if an uninhabited country be discovered and planted by English subjects, all the English laws then in being, which are the birthright of every subject, are immediately there in force ... But conquered or ceded countries, that have already laws of their own, the king may indeed alter and change those laws; but, till he does actually change them, the ancient laws of the country remain.[88]

In short, the Privy Council in *Re Southern Rhodesia* maintained the precedent that a differentiation must be made between those societies where rights would be recognized and those where they would not. All they did was to change the comparative form to one based on an evolutionary framework.

The evolutionary framework adopted by the Privy Council fell within the contemporary view of the nature of culture as it was understood in the late nineteenth and early twentieth centuries. This view of culture presumed the existence of a universal 'scale of social organization.' It further presumed that such a scale could be used to measure whether the social organization of an Aboriginal culture with respect to 'usages and conceptions of rights and duties' were merely 'differently developed' but 'hardly less precise than our own' or 'so low' in that scale that their practices could not be 'reconciled' with 'civilized society.'[89] In sum, in relying on *Re Southern Rhodesia* as precedent, the courts have uncritically adopted the framework for understanding the nature of culture as it existed at the time of that decision.

The Impact of *Re Southern Rhodesia* on *Baker Lake* and *Delgamuukw*

As stated above, *Re Southern Rhodesia* became incorporated into Canadian domestic law as the leading precedent with respect to tests for Aboriginal title through the 'Reasons for Judgement' of Justice Mahoney in the 1979 *Baker Lake* case,[90] which in turn has become the leading precedent for other similar cases. *Baker Lake*, a decision of the Federal Court of Canada, Trial Division, substantively concerned a request by the Inuit of Baker Lake to obtain an injunction to stop the exploration activities of certain mining interests. The basis for the request was their view that these mining activities adversely effected their Aboriginal right to occupy the land specifically for the purpose of fishing and hunting, especially for caribou. As the case was brought prior to the passage of the Constitution Act, 1982, and the recognition of 'existing Aboriginal Rights' in the Canadian constitution, the application arose out of a common law right which, it was presumed, had not been extinguished through competent legislation.

Regarding the substance, Justice Mahoney denied the injunction on the grounds that the mining activities were not interfering sufficiently at that time with an Aboriginal right to occupy the land to hunt caribou. Therefore, the practical consequences of the decision were hardly effective in addressing the concerns which brought the Inuit to court. At the same time, Mahoney did conclude that the Inuit still possessed a common law right to occupy their lands for the purpose of fishing and hunting, particularly for caribou, and that they might therefore have grounds in future to bring an action on that basis.

What is of particular moment for this paper is the basis upon which Mahoney incorporated *Re Southern Rhodesia* in his 'Reasons for Judgement' and the consequences this has had for the way in which subsequent Canadian courts characterize and interpret Aboriginal cultures for the purpose of establishing their jurisdictional and ownership rights. According to Mahoney, 'proof that the Plaintiffs and their ancestors were members of an organized society is required by the authorities.'[91] In his view, the rationale for the requirement derives in Canadian law on the basis of two passages from different judgments in *Calder*. The first is the phrase 'organized in societies' used by Mr. Justice Judson to describe Aboriginal cultures at the time the 'settlers came.'[92] The second is the passage from the American decision *Worcester* v. *Georgia*: 'having institutions of their own, and governing themselves by their own laws' in the judgment by Mr. Justice Hall regarding Aboriginal cultures at the same period.[93] He then asserts that Canadian law on the topic is linked to precedent in English law, for he asserts that 'the rationale of the requirement [the need to prove that an Aboriginal culture was 'organized in societies' at the time the settlers came] is to be found in the following dicta of the Privy Council in *Re Southern Rhodesia.*'[94] He then cites the passage which incorporates the now discredited ideas about the evolution of social organization.[95]

Following the traditional precedents, Mahoney does not question if the relevant passage from a decision of the Privy Council remains factually or conceptually appropriate to the social science of the 1970s. Rather, he accepts it as correct on its face. He then concludes by incorporating the reasoning in *Re Southern Rhodesia* with that found in *Amodu Tijani*, a Privy Council decision of 1921, to make the following generalized statement about the nature of Aboriginal culture and how to reconcile it with the common law:

> It is apparent that the relative sophistication of the organization of any society will be a function of the needs of its members, the demands they make of it. While the existence of an organized society is a prerequisite to the existence of an aboriginal title, there appears no valid reason to demand proof of the existence of a society more elaborately structured than is necessary to demonstrate that there existed among the aborigines a recognition of the claimed rights, sufficiently defined to permit their recognition by the common law upon its advent in the territory. The thrust of all the authorities is not that the common law necessarily deprives aborigines of their enjoyment of the land in any particular but, rather, that it can give effect only to those incidents of that enjoyment that were, themselves, given effect by the regime that prevailed before.[96]

Turning to the specific findings in *Baker Lake*, Mahoney defines the Aboriginal culture of the Inuit as follows: 'The fact is that the aboriginal Inuit had an organized society. It was not a society with very elaborate institutions but it was a society organized to exploit the resources available on the barrens and essential to sustain human life there. *That was about all they could do: hunt and fish and survive'* (emphasis ours).[97] On this basis Mahoney concludes that he can support the Aboriginal rights claims asserted by the Inuit because 'the aboriginal title asserted here encompasses only the right to hunt and fish as their ancestors did.'[98] With respect to other aspects of their social organization, Mahoney asserts that, in principle, the Inuit may have had their own laws. He suggests that in such a case these would have survived even after the establishment of the Hudson's Bay Company Charter.[99] At the same time, Mahoney describes the jurisdictional aspect of Aboriginal Inuit culture in very minimal terms: 'The band itself had no political hierarchy; that existed only at the camp level. Major decisions all involved the hunt, conducted at the camp level and were made by the oldest hunters. Neither individuals, camps or bands claimed or recognized exclusive rights over a particular territory.'[100]

Describing the Inuit as 'nomadic,' he continues: '[The Inuit] associated dialectic differences with particular geographic areas and the people who lived there, but, to them, Inuit were Inuit and they plainly had no conception that the people who lived in a particular area and spoke the dialect associated with it constituted any sort of a tribe or political subdivision within the larger body of Inuit, "the people."'[101] He concludes his discussion of Aboriginal Inuit culture with respect to ownership and jurisdiction with the following: 'The absence of political structures like tribes was an inevitable consequence of the *modus vivendi* dictated by the Inuit's physical environment.'[102]

In short, Mahoney implies that Aboriginal Inuit culture lacked any sophistication with respect to ownership and jurisdiction. Therefore, it probably existed only at the (presumed) 'low end of the scale of social organization.' As a consequence, it is reasonable to hypothesize that, had the Inuit application been based on their jurisdiction and ownership of land, it would have been rejected by Mahoney on the grounds that the legal claim exceeded the limits of their Aboriginal social organization as defined by precedent.

Although yet to be directly considered by the Supreme Court, the reasoning of Justice Mahoney of the Federal Court, Trial Division, has been adopted without close scrutiny by trial and appellate courts with the same conviction as would be given to a binding superior court decision. Emphasizing the *sui generis* nature of Aboriginal rights and the ideology informing the analysis, a court could distinguish or overrule aspects of Mahoney's tests, given the level of court and the fact that the decision predated *Guerin*. Instead however, Canadian courts continue to force Aboriginal rights into a 'mold familiar to English law, while at the same time disregarding factors peculiar to its origin.'[103]

The conceptual framework found in *Re Southern Rhodesia* and *Baker Lake* to deal with questions of Aboriginal ownership and jurisdiction over land and people is central to the legal reasoning found in the *Delgamuukw* judgments both at trial and at the British Columbia Appeals Court. For example, Justice McEachern rests his argument about sovereignty and jurisdiction on the premise that there was a 'jurisdictional vacuum' in the period prior to the assertion of sovereignty by the Crown, a premise that presumes that the Gitksan and Wet'suwet'en were so low in the scale of social organization that such a vacuum could exist. He also follows the reasoning of the Supreme Court in *Sparrow*, which states that 'there was from the outset never any doubt that sovereignty and legislative power and indeed the underlying title to such lands vested in the Crown.'[104] As has been argued elsewhere, this statement clearly rests on the premise that Canada (including British Columbia) was a *terra nullius* (or uninhabited land) prior to the assertion of sovereignty by Great Britain[105] and hence on the logical premises of *Re Southern Rhodesia*.

At the appeals level, the judgments of Justices Macfarlane, Wallace, and Lambert, regardless of the differences in their ultimate disposition of the case, all rely on the reasoning found in the *Baker Lake* and *Re Southern Rhodesia* precedents. Macfarlane says: 'I think the trial judge was correct in applying the test derived from Baker Lake.'[106] Wallace concludes that the common law 'requires' claimants to establish precisely those matters, such as 'being members of an organized society,' which are found in *Baker Lake*.[107] Lambert says: 'Mr. Justice Mahoney, in my opinion, correctly concluded that there must be an organized society in occupation of specific territory, though the occupation may be nomadic, at the time of the assertion of British sovereignty.'[108] Indeed, Lambert whose substantive decision is most supportive of the plaintiffs' views, nonetheless suggests that, following *Re Southern Rhodesia*, it is possible, in principle, to find a society where 'the people were so primitive that they could not be regarded as an organized self-regulating society.'[109]

Again following the logic of the three precedents that dealt with the subject, the justices agreed that the Gitksan and Wet'suwet'en lived in 'organized societies' before the assertion of British sovereignty and that these societies had some form of 'ownership' and 'jurisdiction' over at least some of its claimed territory as well as its population.[110] Justices Macfarlane (with Taggart concurring) and Wallace, basing their findings on a comparison with forms found in the English common law, suggested that the term 'ownership' might better be understood as a right to occupy and use the land rather than as a property right.[111] Justice Lambert, basing his view of ownership on the *sui generis* characterization of an Aboriginal right rather than on a common law definition, held that it was comparable to a property right;[112] a view also held by Justice Hutcheon.[113] However, neither Lambert or Hutcheon were willing to characterize the full extent of that right both Aboriginally and as against existing property rights. Rather, they called for a retrial to make these determinations.[114]

They did disagree at points as to the presumed level of social organization. Justice Lambert, following a more contemporary line of reasoning and clearly wishing to demonstrate that the Aboriginal institutions were 'different' rather than 'inferior to' non-Aboriginal ones, asserted that the Gitksan and Wet'suwet'en had a form of jurisdiction Aboriginally that was comparable to Canadian concepts.[115] In support of this view, he provided a discussion of ways in which the 'feast' performed certain legislative and judicial functions.[116] He characterized the jurisdiction of these functions as 'self-government and self-regulation relating to their organized society, its members, its institutions and its interests.'[117] Ultimately, both he and Hutcheon reasoned that at least some rights of 'self-regulation' survived the assertion of British sovereignty.[118] In contrast, Macfarlane (with Taggart concurring)[119] and Wallace,[120] while agreeing that the plaintiffs had a form of jurisdiction, did not find that these rights survived the assertion of British sovereignty.[121] Justice Wallace proved the most cautious about accepting that the plaintiffs had jurisdiction. In a discussion that seems to adhere to the tenets of *Re Southern Rhodesia* most faithfully, he followed the explicit logic of these precedents, reasoning that 'the Indians exercised jurisdiction in the territory *to the extent made possible by their social organization*' (emphasis ours).[122]

While none followed precisely the specifics outlined by the trial judge, the three judgments which dealt with the issues (Macfarlane, Wallace, and Lambert) all agreed with his finding that Canada had ultimately acquired sovereignty in British Columbia. However, as the discussion above indicates, they disagreed as to whether or not this assertion had completely nullified whatever Gitksan and Wet'suwet'en ownership and jurisdiction existed in the time before the acquisition of sovereignty by Britain. At least six substantive reasons were raised in the three judgments to explain how the Crown acquired sovereignty over the plaintiffs and their lands.[123]

Of these, two relate to the form of reasoning found in *Re Southern Rhodesia* and *Baker Lake*. The first is the 'ontological argument' which states that the British obtained sovereignty over the plaintiffs through asserting their own jurisdiction notwithstanding the existing sovereignty and jurisdiction of the plaintiffs. It is a form of reasoning that *implies* that the territory of the plaintiffs was a *terra nullius*, but never actually defines them as being 'too low on the scale of social organization' to have recognized law.[124] The second argument which follows these precedents states directly that the ownership and jurisdiction of the Gitksan and Wet'suwet'en did not survive the assertion of British sovereignty precisely because their social organization was deemed to be too low for it to be recognized by the colonizing power. Mr. Justice Wallace explains that the 'native immunity from English law under the imperial regime [in Africa and Asia] do[es] not describe the legal situation which has prevailed in British Columbia since 1846.'[125]

In support of this view Wallace cites a number of court cases from colonial Africa and India, including one in which the people of India are described as living in a 'highly civilized country, under the Government of a powerful Mohammedan ruler.'[126] From this evidence he concludes: 'In sum, while the native law systems which continued in certain parts of the British Empire may have retained the capacity to create new rights and customs which were justiciable in the courts, and binding upon all inhabitants in those colonies, this was not the case in British Columbia.'[127] Such reasoning by Wallace seems clearly related to the proposition found in *Re Southern Rhodesia* that there are 'tribes' whose social systems are so primitive that their rights cannot be reconciled with those of 'civilized society,' and that the Gitksan and Wet'suwet'en are among them.

As *Delgamuukw* attests, the Canadian judiciary still rely on *Re Southern Rhodesia* and *Baker Lake* as precedents with regard to assessing Aboriginal culture and, particularly, rights respecting ownership and jurisdiction. As a consequence, the Canadian judiciary continue to use an analytical framework which was developed by the social sciences in the nineteenth century.

Anthropology and the 'Legal Theory of Culture'

Clearly, the precedents discussed here have been applied consistently. The difficulty is that the framework used for understanding culture, while it was reasonable at the time it was first asserted in *Re Southern Rhodesia*, is now considered to be inappropriate, biased, and frankly wrong. This conclusion is not of recent vintage. It goes back in anthropological theory at least to the 1920s when the functionalists, and especially Radcliffe-Brown and Malinowski, showed the inappropriateness of an analytical framework based on an evolutionary theory. As Malinowski said in his 1922 opus, *Argonauts of the Western Pacific*, a book that defined the radical departure from the earlier evolutionary perspective: 'In each culture, we find different institutions in which man pursues his life-interest, different customs by which he satisfies his aspirations, different codes of law and morality which reward his virtues or punish his defections. To study the institutions, customs, and codes or to study the behaviour and mentality without the subjective desire of feeling what these people live, of realising the substance of their happiness – is, in my opinion, to miss the greatest reward which we can hope to obtain from the study of man.'[128] He also had occasion to confront the evolutionary logic of the *Re Southern Rhodesia* precedent directly. As he stated: 'Hence the Judicial Committee plainly regard the question of native land tenure as both beyond the scope of practicable inquiry and below the dignity of legal recognition. On the contrary, I maintain that there is no people "so low in the scale of social organization" but have a perfectly well-defined system of land tenure. It is absurd to say that such a system "cannot be reconciled with the institutions or legal ideas of civilized society." To reconcile the two is precisely the task of Colonial statesmanship.'[129] In short, in the period just after the *Re Southern Rhodesia* decision, the evolutionary paradigm upon which the precedents adopted in contemporary Canadian law are based came under sustained criticism. Indeed, the work of anthropologists during this period so clearly demonstrated the weaknesses of existing evolutionary theory as well as the methodological and theoretical superiority of more contemporary approaches that, 'by 1932, the evolutionary bundle had fallen to pieces.'[130] The change brought about by these scholars was 'fundamental'[131] in that all subsequent anthropological method and theory-building have approached data collection and analysis in a manner that is radically different from that which was employed when evolutionism was dominant.

Today, there is a stark contrast between the scientific understanding of culture and the presumptions about culture used by Canadian courts in Aboriginal rights litigation. As exemplified by the discussion in this paper, law believes in the validity of the following four postulates regarding the nature of human groups and societies. For the purpose of this discussion, we will define them as forming a core set of postulates for a 'legal theory of culture.' These are:

(1) The legal theory of culture allows for the possibility that human beings may live in groups and yet not live in society.[132]
(2) The legal theory of culture allows for the possibility that societies can exist that are not 'organized' or that may be 'organized' only with respect to some aspects of social life.[133]
(3) The legal theory of culture allows for the possibility that organized societies exist that do not have jurisdiction over their members and their territory.[134]
(4) The legal theory of culture allows for the possibility that organized societies exist where there is no 'ownership,' particularly with respect to land.[135]

Following upon their reliance on these four postulates, the Canadian courts accept the possibility that the Aboriginal litigants who are seeking judicial recognition for 'ownership and jurisdiction' based on Aboriginal rights may be descendants of a group of human beings who, before the assertion of British sovereignty, did not live in a society, or lived in a society that was either not organized or only partly organized, or lived in an organized society which did not incorporate institutions that might be considered equivalent to 'jurisdiction' and/or 'ownership.' Therefore, litigation places a heavy burden of proof on the Aboriginal party. As we will show, reliance on precedent informed by these postulates and the conclusions that flow from them is not justifiable in light of contemporary knowledge about culture. Therefore, the burden of proof upon the Aboriginal party becomes absurd and virtually impossible to meet.

In order to facilitate an abbreviated discussion and yet ensure that the conclusions reached are held widely in the field, we have chosen to direct our attention specifically to two introductory texts in the field of anthropology. These books, *Culture, People, Nature* by Dr. Marvin Harris[136] and *An Introduction to Social Anthropology* by Dr. Lucy Mair,[137] were written by leading figures in the discipline. However, the approaches they espouse represent contrasting poles within it.[138] Therefore, agreement between them is a likely signal of convergence among the members of the discipline as a whole. We will further limit the discussion by directing attention specifically to the four propositions listed above, which we will rephrase in the form of questions and then investigate in terms of how contemporary anthropological theory responds to them. While our conclusion will be detailed below, suffice it to say that the responses derived from the discipline of anthropology will be virtually the converse of those derived from the 'legal theory of culture.'

(1) Is it possible that human beings may live in groups and yet not live in society?
The proposition that all human beings live in society is so well established that the texts do not expend much effort to explain it. Dr. Mair states quite simply that 'we all live as members of society.'[139] Dr. Harris provides some discussion to indicate that anthropological research into earlier forms of the human species as well as other primates has established that *Homo sapiens* (our species) have always lived in a system based upon cultural attributes (p. 78) and that culture itself is a basic 'characteristic of a societal group.'[140] Therefore, notwithstanding the postulate of the 'legal theory of human groups and society,' it is not possible for human beings to live in groups and yet not live in a society. Rather, it is a certainty that all human beings living today, as well as for tens of thousands of years, have lived in a society.

(2) Is it possible that societies can exist that are not 'organized' or are 'organized' only with respect to some aspects of social life?
Anthropological research has established conclusively that all societies are organized, and are organized with respect to all aspects of social life. Indeed, the notion that a society could exist that was not organized is virtually a contradiction in terms, for the definition of society itself assumes organization. As Dr. Harris states: 'society means an organized group of people who share a habitat and who depend on each other for survival and well-being. Each human society has an overall culture.'[141] Dr. Mair's view, although phrased differently, is identical in meaning. As she states: 'we think of the society ... as an orderly arrangement of parts, and that our

business [as anthropologists] is to detect and explain this order. It consists in relationships between persons which are regulated by a common body of recognized rights and obligations.'[142]

Therefore, again notwithstanding the postulate of the 'legal theory of human groups and society,' it is not possible for a society to exist that is not organized. Rather, all societies are organized with respect to all aspects of social life. Therefore, it is the job of the person undertaking an analysis of a society to determine not *if* it is organized, but *how* it is organized.

(3) Is it possible that organized societies exist that do not have jurisdiction over their members and their territory?

Both Harris and Mair discuss this proposition in more detail than they do the previous two questions. Each concludes, for similar reasons based on the study of many different cultures and societies, that no society exists that does not have jurisdiction over its members and its territory. With regard to the existence of a political system, Dr. Mair says: 'The political system ... is what supports the system of rights and obligations that any society must have if it is to be a society at all (since a society *is* a body of people linked together by mutually recognized rights and obligations)' (emphasis hers).[143] Later in the book she states categorically that: 'An earlier chapter discussed the question whether any society could be said to lack a political system, and answered it in the negative.'[144] Dr. Harris also states: 'Anthropologists agree that every human society has provisions for behaviour and thoughts related to making a living from the environment, raising children, organizing the exchanges of goods and labor, living in domestic groups and larger communities, and the creative, expressive, playful, aesthetic, moral, and intellectual aspects of human life.'[145]

One of the universal attributes of society that arises out of 'living in domestic and larger communities' is the existence of a political system. This system will always include, among other institutions, means of mobilizing public opinion, resolving disputes, and designating leaders.[146] However, the forms that institutions such as leadership might take can range from the very informal to the highly formal.[147]

Both scholars also agree that every society has the institution of law and the means to enforce sanctions against its members. As Dr. Mair states, 'every society has some rules of a kind that we would not hesitate to call laws when they apply to ourselves.'[148] She then proceeds to describe in some detail the various ways in which legal matters such as dispute resolution and judicial processes are dealt with.[149] Harris provides an extended discussion on the subject of law. He begins by explaining that law is necessary in all societies because 'people in every society have conflicting interests. Even in band-level societies, old and young, sick and healthy, men and women do not want the same thing at the same time. Moreover, in every society people want things that others possess and are reluctant to give away. Every culture, therefore, must have structural provisions for resolving conflicts of interest in an orderly fashion and for preventing conflicts from escalating into disruptive confrontations.'[150]

He then explains that the differences between societies lie in the kinds of conflicts that develop and the ways in which these are resolved.[151] He concludes that, merely because some societies (such as village societies, or many hunting and gathering societies) 'have no written law codes and no formal law courts; no lawyers, bailiffs, judges, district attorneys, juries or court clears; and no patrol cars, paddy wagons, jails or penitentiaries';[152] this does not mean they have no law. The lack of these specific forms is not explained by a presumption that these societies are lower in the scale of social organization. Rather, as Harris suggests, the differences are best attributed to differences in the structures and the requirements of different cultures. Thus, for example, with respect to hunting and other societies, he states: 'The basic reasons for the difference are (1) the small size of simple band and simple village societies, (2) the central importance of domestic groups and kinship in their social organization, and (3) the absence of marked inequalities in access to technology and resources.'[153]

There is no discussion by the authors specifically directed to jurisdiction over, rather than ownership of, territory. Much of the discussion with respect to jurisdiction is found in sections that address ownership in what appears to be a property sense. In our view, this may be due to the fact that anthropologists tend to conflate land ownership in a property sense with dominion over a territory. Nonetheless, there is enough information to suggest that anthropologists agree that all societies have provisions for jurisdiction over their territory. For example, Dr. Mair states: 'the fact that the band think of themselves as all being kin does not preclude their believing that they have joint rights over a territory, and in fact this *is* what they believe; they may allow outsiders into their territory, but they claim it as their own and nobody else's.'[154] On the same point of land ownership, Harris accepts that members of the societies he discusses always perceive that they have jurisdiction over certain territories and that jurisdiction includes the right to withhold permission to use these lands. Finally, there is no discussion in either Harris or Mair to suggest that members of a society ever believe that they do not have jurisdiction over their territories with respect to the rights of people who do not live within that society. This view was reinforced most clearly by Chief Daniel Sonfrere, a key witness in *Paulette* v. *R.* Mr. Sutton, the attorney for the applicants, asked Chief Sonfrere: 'If a number of white people came into your area without your permission, how would you feel about that, your hunting and trapping area?'[155] In response, Chief Sonfrere stated: 'If such a thing is going to occur, they should consult with me, and I will consult with my people and there will be a decision made in such a thing, but they should never barge in like that.'[156]

In sum then, the evidence from anthropology strongly confirms the view that all societies possess institutions with respect to jurisdiction over their members and their territory. The form that jurisdiction takes will differ between societies, for it depends on the kind of society it is and the demands made upon it by the way of life of its members.

(4) Is it possible that organized societies exist where there is no 'ownership,' particularly with respect to land?

The topic of ownership, especially of land in Indigenous societies, has engendered much discussion, debate, and controversy in anthropology.[157] It is a topic we have discussed elsewhere,[158] and it is explored at some length in the texts by Harris and Mair. Ultimately, we believe anthropologists would agree that *individual* ownership of land does not exist in all societies. However, this does not mean that ownership of land does not exist, nor that the concepts of land ownership in Indigenous societies cannot be reconciled with concepts of individual ownership of land derived from Canadian law.

Anthropologists have found that individual ownership of property exists in all societies. Mair says: 'Ideas about property in movable objects do not differ much from one part of the world to another,'[159] whereas Harris states: 'Many material objects of band-level societies[160] are effectively controlled ('owned') by specific individuals.' Anthropologists have also found that some form of land ownership[161] exists in every society.[162] One question anthropological research focuses on is determining the landholding individual or group within a society. In some cases, as Harris suggests, the society as a whole might best be considered the owner.[163] Often ownership is vested in smaller units than the society as a whole, such as lineages or residence groups.[164] Indeed, even in instances where Harris might find it most appropriate to consider the society as a whole the land owner, he suggests that the members of the society *conceptualize* ownership of land as vested in smaller units: he states that among the !Kung, who live in a 'simple' hunting-gathering society, 'waterholes and hunting-and-gathering territories are emically[165] "owned" by the residential core of particular bands.'[166]

Therefore, it can be concluded that *individual* ownership exists in all societies and that *ownership of land* exists in all societies. Ownership of land itself, however, may not necessarily be vested in individuals, but is often vested either in the society as a whole or in units other than individuals within it. While there are societies where land is held collectively by units such as lineages, Mair suggests that it is still the case that rights of access are held by individuals, some of whom may not be members of the landholding group for other purposes:[167] 'Literally understood the phrase ["communally owned"] is perhaps correct; but if it is taken to imply that individuals have no rights at all in specific areas, it is wholly misleading. It might be more helpful to think of rights in land as being divided into rights of *use* and rights of *administration*.'[168]

While ownership of land is universal, according to the findings of anthropologists concepts such as 'the individual ownership of land' are held by only certain kinds of society and culture. As Mair suggests: 'rules relating to land are different where it is not a saleable commodity from what we find in wholly commercialized societies.'[169] She elaborates on this point in the first edition of her text where she says: 'People who do not grow crops for sale do not think of land as a resource which must be turned to maximum advantage, so that if you have rights over land which you are not using yourself you should seek to make a profit by charging someone else a rent for the use of it. Hence there is no such demand for the unrestricted control over an area of land – individual title – as arises on the one hand from people who want to be landlords collecting rent, and on the other from people who want to be free from dependence on landlords.'[170]

Harris makes a similar point, albeit more obliquely. He suggests that many societies exist where 'equality of access to technology and natural resources means that food and other forms of wealth cannot be withheld by a wealthy few while others endure shortages and hardships.'[171] In such societies, Harris's approach infers, individual ownership of land would not likely be present.

Anthropological research, then, provides conclusive evidence that the concept of individual ownership can be applied to all societies as can the concept that land is 'owned.' What is not universal is the application of the concept of 'individual ownership' to land. Rather, ownership may be held by the society as a whole or a smaller collectivity within it, such as a lineage. Individual ownership of land is restricted to certain kinds of societies. Given that both individual ownership and the ownership of land exist in all societies, it is therefore reasonable to presume that individual ownership of land will be found only when the economy of a society contains certain features.[172]

Thus, anthropological evidence suggests there are certain features of land ownership as defined in Canadian law, such as individual ownership and the right to alienate land through sale, which are not universal. However, there are other crucial attributes, such as the designation of a legitimate owner of a parcel of land and rights to administer and use that land, which are found in all societies. Therefore, notwithstanding the postulate of the 'legal theory of culture,' all societies incorporate at least some crucial features of landholding that are reconcilable with the concept of 'land ownership' as defined in Canadian law.

In sum, notwithstanding the 'high authority' given to the words of the Privy Council in *Re Southern Rhodesia* and despite the general application of the approach and the test developed in *Baker Lake* in litigation regarding Aboriginal rights, the factual premises upon which these authorities base their legal doctrines are simply wrong. It is not possible, despite the words of the Privy Council, Mahoney, McEachern, and the other justices, to presume that human beings can live in groups but not live in society; that societies can exist that are not organized or are only partly organized; or that a society can exist that does not incorporate jurisdiction over territory as well as its members, or contain elements of tenure reconcilable to the ownership of land.

Conclusion

Reliance on precedent is fundamental to the process of legal reasoning and to the presumption that this reasoning is based on logic rather than whim, on law rather than policy. It is a time-honoured legal principle which has much relevance to jurisprudence. It is not our intent to eviscerate it. Still, as the *Persons*[173] case, as well as *Brown* v. *Board of Education*[174] in the United States attest, there comes a time when it is necessary to reassess precedent in light of more contemporary knowledge. Now is the time to undertake this reassessment with respect to Aboriginal title litigation and in particular the use of an outmoded and biased theory of culture to interpret the facts of Aboriginal society that are contained in the leading precedents of *Re Southern Rhodesia* and *Baker Lake*. It is a view anticipated by Mr. Justice Hall (as he was then) when he stated in *Calder* that the courts must not base the interpretation of fact on a conceptual framework that arose in a period when Aboriginal people 'were thought to be without cohesion, laws, or culture, in effect a subhuman species.'[175] If this dictum applies anywhere, surely, as the evidence provided here indicates, it applies to the methods of interpretation of fact found in *Re Southern Rhodesia* and *Baker Lake*. Hall's words provide sage advice, and we merely recommend that it be followed.

We have other, practical reasons for recommending a reappraisal of the way these precedents are used. Their approach to interpretation of fact is not merely wrong, it also produces severe structural biases against Aboriginal litigants which place them at a significant disadvantage. Under the current system, the courts presume that, prior to the assertion of

British sovereignty, Aboriginal people may have lived in groups that are not societies; that these societies may not have been organized at all; and that they may not have had institutions respecting ownership and jurisdiction. Failure to establish a factual basis for a burden of proof to counter these presumptions means failure to establish a factual premise upon which to found continued recognition of rights within the Canadian legal system. Thus, the approach requires that Aboriginal litigants search back through written records and oral traditions to a time over a century or more ago, in order to provide specific factual evidence which accurately describes the existence and operation of their institutions. Any approach that requires such detail, even about institutions as central and enduring as those regarding jurisdiction and ownership, is stringent in the extreme. It requires much expenditure of time and money. Also, as the *Delgamuukw* trial attests, it requires an inordinate number of court days to enter and defend this evidence. Given that the burden of proof lies with the Aboriginal party, the cost requirements in both time and money rest differentially upon them.

To require such a stringent burden of proof might indeed be reasonable could such facts truly be in doubt. Yet, notwithstanding what the courts have stated, the facts are never in doubt. The fact is, because they are human beings, Aboriginal people at the time of the assertion of British sovereignty did live in societies that were organized and had institutions respecting land ownership as well as jurisdiction over members and territory. Therefore, the burden of proof ought to be reversed so that those who would assert that any litigants did not live in society would have to provide factual evidence to support such a contention.

Another concern is that the present system invites judgments that are biased against Aboriginal litigants. This concern arises largely because the precedents infer the possibility that the ancestral societies of the litigants were inferior in some respect to the society out of which the Canadian legal system developed, as, for example, when a judgment asserts that the Aboriginal party has failed to prove that it had institutions equivalent to those of 'civilized' society or that it was a society which could only 'hunt and fish and survive.' However, the need to establish the facts for such a proof creates prejudice against an Aboriginal party, even when a judgment explicitly confirms that the Aboriginal litigant has proved 'equivalence,' for it assumes that 'Canadian' society is 'civilized' without requiring any proof and also suggests that the 'civilized' nature of the Aboriginal society was in doubt.

Finally, the current approach is problematic in that it enables judgments to focus unduly on the assessment of the 'presumed' factual questions about the nature of Aboriginal culture rather than on questions of law. An examination of the judgments from the *Delgamuukw* and *Baker Lake* cases indicates that the trial judges expended much effort and space in their judgments on the establishment of fact about Aboriginal society prior to the assertion of sovereignty by Britain. Given the amount of training that judges receive in the analysis of non-Western cultures as compared to their training in law, and given that the matters they are reviewing critically are often facts that ought to have been admitted in evidence as self-evident, the effort expended in judgments on cultural analysis rather than legal analysis is often profoundly wasteful of judicial time and expertise.

Rather than the current approach, then, we recommend that the judicial system adopt an approach that better reflects contemporary knowledge about the nature of human social groups. This approach would mean adopting the proposition that all human beings, including those who lived in North America prior to the assertion of sovereignty by Britain, live in societies and that societies are always organized with respect to all aspects of their social life including, specifically, the ownership of land and jurisdiction over territory and society members.

One clear implication of adopting this view of society, as we have stated previously,[176] is that the burden of proof would be placed on those parties at litigation who would challenge this premise in a specific instance. While there might be grounds upon which to discharge such a burden, the challenge would require the introduction of very specific facts regarding the particular circumstances of a case. It could not be discharged successfully, as it is under the current system, on the basis of vague generalizations based on invalid premises regarding the nature of society.

A second implication of adopting this view of society is that it would deflect litigation away from the interminable preoccupation with the specific factual details about the society of Aboriginal litigants at the time prior to the assertion of sovereignty by Britain. It would shift the focus, instead, onto the primary issues of fact and law. Under the current system, judges are able to avoid critical legal issues by determining, improperly, that a society did not have ownership and jurisdiction in a form that could survive the assertion of sovereignty by Britain. Accepting contemporary propositions about the nature of culture would enable the courts to refocus their attention to the essential legal question: Given that, at the time Britain asserted sovereignty, all societies in North America had institutions including those regarding land ownership and jurisdiction in forms reconcilable to Canadian and English legal norms, how did Britain and later Canada legitimately acquire ownership and jurisdiction over Aboriginal peoples and their lands?

In making this recommendation, we realize the importance of following established precedent to the appropriate functioning of our legal system.

However, it is possible and sometimes even necessary for the legal system to shift away from established precedent when the premises upon which it is based have proven to be no longer tenable. We suggest that this is the situation with respect to *Re Southern Rhodesia* and *Baker Lake*. In making this statement, we are advocating the adoption of the sage view advanced by Justice Hall in the *Calder* decision. We note as well that a similar view was advanced over two centuries ago when Lord Mansfield, on behalf of the Court of King's Bench in *Campbell* v. *Hall*, specifically repudiated the differentiation between Christians and pagans that was used as the rationale for the determination of rights of people in conquered countries first advanced in *Calvin's Case*. Here, Lord Mansfield stated: 'the laws of a conquered country continue in force until they are altered by the conqueror: the absurd exception as to pagans, mentioned in *Calvin's Case*, shows the universality and antiquity of the maxim. For that distinction could not exist before the Christian area; and in all probability arose from the mad enthusiasm of the Crusades.'[177]

While we do not believe the notion of conquest provides an apt characterization of the facts regarding the assertion of sovereignty by Britain over Indigenous people and their lands,[178] we believe that Lord Mansfield's dictum regarding the interpretation of fact in *Calvin's Case* provides solid evidence for the assertion that precedent itself should not survive when it no longer provides an appropriate instrument on which the judicial system can rely for determining legal rights fairly.

Aboriginal rights litigation over the past two decades has revealed a critical flaw in the system of legal reasoning. It is now clear that the precedential base upon which facts about Aboriginal cultures are understood is founded upon notions about culture that are both incorrect and highly prejudicial to the Aboriginal party. Given these circumstances, it is impossible to presume that the system of judicial reasoning is any more fair or balanced or reflective of contemporary societal values than it was with respect to women before the *Persons*[179] case, or would be with respect to blacks in the United States were the reasoning in *Dred Scott*[180] adopted by contemporary courts. In such a situation, it is necessary for a judicial system that wishes to ensure fairness, balance, and a level field in litigation to reappraise the precedents it uses in assessing evidence. As we have indicated in this paper, such a necessity exists with respect to Aboriginal litigation, and it is possible, in principle, for the judicial system to make such reforms. Given that the foundations of precedent and legal reasoning regarding the nature of culture in contemporary Aboriginal rights litigation are so obviously invalid and inappropriate, it is our view that the need to reform this area of jurisprudence is compelling and past due.

3
Re-examining Culturally Appropriate Models in Criminal Justice Applications

Emma LaRocque

In the winter of 1993, the *Winnipeg Free Press* reported on the first Aboriginal community to exercise justice presumably based on 'tradition' by forming a 'healing circle' to 'pass sentence on the crimes of their neighbours.' The crime was committed by a couple from Hollow Water, Manitoba, a reserve 160 kilometres northeast of Winnipeg. This couple had raped their two daughters numerous times. For these unspeakable acts the Hollow Water community of 450 'sentenced' the couple to three years of supervised probation 'during which time the couple must continue healing under the guidance of the circle members.'

I received so many telephone calls from Native women across Canada, women expressing horror and outrage at the Hollow Water 'sentence,' that I decided to follow up on some cautionary questions and issues I had raised about the Hollow Water Project in a previous article on 'Violence in Aboriginal Communities' (1993).[1] There are a number of unsettling ramifications that come with the Hollow Water model with respect to victims of violence in Native communities. Involved are numerous complex issues, many necessarily beyond the scope of this paper. The Hollow Water incident is very important in the consideration of not only culturally appropriate models but also of gender issues, especially in view of Aboriginal self-government aspirations.

At the outset I wish to emphasize that my academic field is history and literature, not criminology or social work. As a contemporary Native woman I do, however, have social and ethical concerns in the area of justice, women, and governance. One cannot look at the Hollow Water model without raising a lot of questions.

This paper will examine assumptions of 'tradition' upon which Aboriginally controlled justice systems seem to be based. By 'traditions' I am referring largely to ideas, theories, and assumptions relevant to this discussion, not to spirituality or associated rituals. Also, I am not in any way suggesting that traditions are no longer extant in Aboriginal lives, nor that Aboriginal peoples cannot 'borrow' other traditions. The concern is the misuse of 'traditions.' Because these 'traditional' perspectives on 'culturally appropriate' justice models as practised on victims of violence may be having drastic effects on the victims and therefore on the Native community, they must be questioned and re-evaluated.

The emphasis is to raise ethical issues; to provoke thought and re-examination of popular premises concerning notions of culture, healing, and sexual offender-victim mediation programs; and to open up discussion on freedom of expression and contemporary human rights within the Aboriginal community, especially on issues of concern to women and on culturally appropriate programs/governance.

Aboriginal people have called for the right to control their own justice systems as part of the package for self-government. The 1991 Aboriginal Justice Inquiry of Manitoba (AJI) reported that 'there is widespread interest in and growing support for distinct Aboriginal justice systems.'[2] Accordingly, the AJI recommended that 'the federal and provincial governments recognize the right of Aboriginal people to establish their own justice systems as part of their inherent right to self-government.'[3] Further, the AJI recommended that 'Aboriginal traditions and customs be the basis upon which Aboriginal laws and Aboriginal justice systems are built.'[4] Other major Native organizations also subscribe to this, as do a number of high-profile white professionals.

Terms such as 'traditional' or 'culturally appropriate' appear as a matter of course in discussions on Aboriginal governance, or for that matter, on any community-oriented programs related to justice, violence, women, and 'healing.' As a recent federal discussion report on family violence prevention puts it: 'The issue of cultural appropriateness is now accepted as central to creating effective services for Aboriginal individuals, families and communities.'[5] Native peoples have fought long and hard for cultural recognition. Within this often politically charged atmosphere, a considerable number of 'traditions' and 'values' have been recalled. The result has been a growing complex of reinvented 'traditions' which have become extremely popular even while lacking historical or anthropological contextualization. This is particularly true with respect to notions of justice and the role of women in Aboriginal societies, past and present. In effect, much of what is unquestionably thought to be tradition is actually syncretized fragments of Native and Western traditions which have become highly politicized because they have been created from the context of colonization.[6]

Of some fascination to me has been the mushrooming of 'charting' out these traditional perspectives. In the last decade or so, charts comparing supposed Native and white values have become popular in various work-shops attempting to deal with Native/white relations. Such charts are pre-sented to non-Native professionals such as social workers, teachers, police, and medical personnel, who work with (or at) Native peoples or Native organizations, and usually the goal is to sensitize them to cross-cultural dynamics. It is from such workshops that notions of culturally appropri-ate programs have arisen. What was always obvious to Native peoples seems to have finally become apparent to non-Natives: that there is a need to develop services, programs, and organizations that are appropriate to the people on the receiving end of such programs. Clearly, such a realiza-tion is long past due, and the issue of real cultural differences does merit a much larger discussion than this paper can address. One cannot empha-size enough the need for Aboriginal peoples and cultures to be taken seri-ously, given the long history of their devaluation.

However – and the point to this paper – there are profound problems to restricting the discussion on cultural appropriateness to typologies and charts. While one may appreciate the need for sorting out and making meaningful Native cultural values when applying them to life and pro-grams, few, whether Native presenters or non-Native audiences, seem to realize that charting out supposed differences evolves from and leads back to stereotypes – stereotypes founded, justified, and perpetuated by the colonial process. Among other things, 'typologizing' Aboriginal cultures results in gross generalizations, draws on stereotypes, reduces Aboriginal cultures to a pitiable handful of 'traits,' and by oversimplifying, ends up infantilizing the very cultures Aboriginal peoples are trying to build up in the eyes of the colonizers.[7] Further, reducing and fitting cultural expres-sions into charted, boxed-in modules falls prey to simplistic, rigid, formu-laic, and doctrinaire 'solutions' to very complex issues and problems.

Of particular interest to this writer is an article by Len Sawatsky called 'Self-Determination and the Criminal Justice System.'[8] I believe the chart under the section on 'Aboriginal Views of Justice' is an accurate reflection of prevailing beliefs about Aboriginal traditions as practised in justice deci-sions. Indeed, as Sawatsky explains in a footnote, 'the articulation of the aboriginal justice paradigm is the author's and has been informed and guided by the assistance of elders and leaders of First Nations in Manitoba and B.C.'[9]

The 'traditional' perspective and Aboriginal justice (or health, or 'heal-ing') paradigms have, of course, been enunciated by other writers and political organizations, for example, Maggie Hodgson in *The Spirit Weeps* (1988), the *Report of the Aboriginal Justice Inquiry of Manitoba*, and selections from the Royal Commission on Aboriginal Peoples collection, *The Path To Healing*. The most current typological module can be seen in a draft document from Health and Welfare Canada Family Violence Prevention Division prepared by Robert Hart.[10] Hart uses popularized workshop notions regarding Native 'traditions and values' which are very similar to Sawatsky's, which is an indication that trait-listing has become deeply embedded in current social thinking on Native cultures. However, I will refer primarily to the Sawatsky chart as an example and springboard for analysis because of how neatly it exemplifies the prevailing notions, beliefs, and positions of culturally appropriate paradigms.

Sawatsky sets out a chart which compares a supposed Aboriginal justice paradigm with the supposed European-originated Canadian criminal justice system. Predictably, his typology is fraught with stereotypes, generalizations, oversimplifications, and reductionism. On examining it, we will see what risks it poses to victims of violence in Native communities. Since this type of thinking is 'all the rage,' we must scrutinize and challenge it.

The following is Sawatsky's chart comparing supposed Aboriginal and Euro-Canadian 'justice paradigms.'[11]

Chart 3.1

	European/Retributive	Aboriginal
1	Crime defined as violation of the state	No word for crime but recognition of injury, harm, conflicts and disputes
2	Focus on establishing blame, guilt, on the past (did he/she do it?)	Focus on identifying the conflict, on establishing accountability, on the current situation (what can we do?)
3	Adversarial relationships and process are normative	Consensus of elders/chiefs to advise on steps to take towards establishing harmony
4	Imposition of pain to punish and deter/prevent	Holding parties in conflict accountable to each other in context of family, community and Mother Earth
5	Justice defined by intent and by process, right rules	Justice defined by social harmony and needs being met, judged according to community solidarity and survival

6 Interpersonal, conflictual nature of crime obscured, repressed: conflict seen as individual vs. state

Interpersonal conflict acknowledged in the context of responsibility to family, community and Mother Earth

7 One social injury replaced by another

Focus on repair of social injury and restoration of social equilibrium and healing

8 Community on sideline, represented abstractly by state

Community as facilitator, role of the elder respected

9 Encouragement of competitive individualistic values

Encouragement of spirituality, self-esteem and collective identity

10 Action directed from state to offender:
– victim ignored
– offender passive

Recognition of victim's needs and offender accountability but in the context of wisdom and insight exercised by elders

11 Offender accountability defined as taking punishment

Offender accountability defined as willingness to take steps to restore peace and harmony with self, victim, families, community, and the Great Spirit

12 Offence defined in purely legal terms, devoid of moral, social, economic or political dimensions

Offence understood in whole context – morally, socially, economically, politically and in relation to the land

13 'Debt' owed to state and society in abstract

Offender is held accountable to the victim, victim's family and community

14 No encouragement or opportunity to express remorse or forgiveness

Encouragement for apology, forgiveness and healing with a view to making peace

15 Dependence upon proxy professionals

Direct involvement of participants to the dispute under guidance of elders

Generally, Sawatsky dismisses the mainstream justice system as 'adversarial and retributive' and having negative consequences for everyone. At no point does he provide substantiation for his claim that a retributive system is necessarily negative for the victim. His focus and emphasis are on how bad the system is for the offender: he hardly notices the victim.

On the Aboriginal side of the column, Sawatsky waxes romantic as to what constitutes an Aboriginal view of justice. Of the fifteen presumably Aboriginal traits, fourteen are debatable. Most troublesome is the key claim that the collectivity is more important than individual rights, with the implication that the 'healing' of the offender is more important than the well-being of the victim. Underlying these claims are layers of other generalizing notions such as the universalization of an individual's criminal behaviour as simply the product of 'two-sided conflict,' and the idea that Native people's overriding objective is communal 'harmony,' no matter what the nature of the crime.[12]

Based on such generalizations and typologies, Aboriginal mediation programs generally operate in the following way: the 'offender' is also seen as a 'victim,' and his 'needs' must also be met for 'healing' to occur.[13] To achieve this, both victim and abuser are brought together to share their 'pain.' Often, the focus is on the 'pain' of the attacker. The basis for this process is the 'restoration of harmony' in the community, and it is the community that determines the 'punishment' for the offender. However, punishment has meant virtually nothing, particularly in cases of sexual assault. Both the Canadian and Native systems of 'justice' have been disturbingly, if not wantonly, lenient.[14] Leniency has been justified on the premise that (1) it is good for the community (social harmony), (2) it is good for the family (unity), (3) it is good for the victim ('forgiveness' is 'healing'), and (4) it is good for the offender (rehabilitation).

If such notions are carried to their logical limit, contradictions and illogical conclusions result. Discrepancies between theory and practice have gone unchallenged, and sorting them out is more difficult than unravelling a tightly twisted rope. The disturbing trend in these trait-listing programs is that their orientation is always to the advantage of the offender. What is of additional concern is the single-mindedness with which they are being practised.

There is an argument for 'social harmony' in which individuals are expected to submit to the collective good. Interestingly, this dictum is most often applied to cases of particular concern to women, namely, violence, and the Constitution.[15] With respect to violence, the argument for community is transparently a case of favouring one individual (offender) over another (victim), elevating the offender's interests to 'collective rights' while reducing the victim's interests to 'individual rights.' It remains a puzzle how offenders, more than victims, have come to represent 'collective rights.' Besides disregarding all contemporary discourse on justice and ethics, the premise that individual rights should be sacrificed for the supposed good of the community has no substantiation. It is as if individuals are not part of the collective good, as if the only way to ensure 'collective' rights is to subvert individual ones, or at least those of certain individuals. However, it cannot be good for the collective to disregard individual rights or well-being.

Accompanying the collective good theory is the related tenet that everything should be done to avoid incarceration and to maintain the family unit.[16] As the recent Health and Welfare discussion report on family violence prevention outlines: culturally appropriate Native programs would make an 'effort to keep abusers in the community while protecting the victim(s)/survivors(s).' Hart does caution that keeping abusers at home in small and isolated communities is a particular concern.[17]

Such sweeping cultural program proposals are deeply troubling because, among other things, they completely fail to discriminate between issues.[18] Whether an offender is incarcerated or not, he should be removed from the community of the individual or family he has attacked, not only in the interests of justice, but also for the safety of the victim(s) and, it follows, for the well-being of the family (community). Hart's cautionary remarks above sound hollow given what we know about sexual offender patterns.

We know that keeping child molesters and rapists in the same vicinity as victims puts victims at greater risk,[19] and studies on sexual abuse also strongly indicate it is psychologically destructive for victims to be subjected to their attacker's presence.[20] This is exacerbated in small communities, and, it must be emphasized, most Native communities are small, with a national average of about 350 people per reserve. In short, it is a total contradiction to keep abusers at home while at the same time claiming to protect victims and survivors! In the Hollow Water decision, for example, it is difficult to believe that the victims were in any condition to be a part of decisions in the 'healing circle.' What could they do or say in such a small community?

While concern for the victim's healing saturates culturally appropriate rhetoric,[21] it has simply not been established that forcing mediation on victims is either helpful to the victim or 'rehabilitating' for the attacker. Further, studies suggest that emphasis on 'forgiveness' adds stress and guilt to victims of sexual assault, something that victims can do without.[22]

Concerning the argument that everything should be done to maintain family 'unity,' in terms of sexual abuse, *statistics show that homes and families are the least safe.*[25] Ethically, it is questionable how anyone can argue that everything should be done to save family units. In modern times, families can be chosen; victims do not have to feel responsible for maintaining biological units that act most unfamilial! While the emphasis on family and community cohesion may remain an ideal, we cannot and should not, given the history of residential schools and the 'sixties scoop' of Native children, put community members' rights and safety at risk in response to a historical injustice.[24] The net effect, thus far, has been consistent disregard for victims and community safety, with no apparent rehabilitation of offenders. This is not how precolonial First Nations practised justice or community well-being.

Another disturbing trend is the tendency to whitewash and 'soften' the impact and individual responsibility of criminal behaviour by manipulating words and phrases. For example, we do not have rapists, we have 'sexual offenders'; we do not have wife batterers, we have 'family violence'; we do not have child molesters, we have 'incest'; and so forth. Such play with phraseology has a mitigating, even neutralizing, effect on the gravity of sexual assault.

Similarly, Sawatsky reduces 'crime' to a 'two-sided conflict.' He writes as item 4 of his chart: 'Holding parties in conflict accountable to each other in context of family, community and Mother Earth.' What exactly is the assumption here? Is it not that victims are to be held equally 'accountable?' Obviously, there are instances when 'conflict' is two-sided (e.g., a fist fight between equals), but surely, in the context of today, crimes such as child neglect, sexual assaults, wife battering, stealing, drunk driving, vandalizing, terrorizing, drug trafficking, child prostitution, and so on, cannot be seen or treated as 'two-sided conflict.' Why should victims of these type of acts be made 'accountable,' which is to say, responsible? Aboriginal or any other justice systems must acknowledge that individuals commit crime (colonization or no colonization), sometimes heinous crime, and must be held solely responsible. At the very least, Native victims of Native crime should not be held accountable. Simple common sense would be an asset in these cultural models. Furthermore, it is historically incorrect to claim that all Aboriginal cultures believed all conflict was always and necessarily two-sided.

Sawatsky claims that Aboriginal languages do not have a word for crime, but such a claim should be contextualized. In Cree one of the words closest to crime is 'My-yen-kewin,' which means 'doing something wrong or bad,' with the connotation of wilfulness.[25] Whether or not Aboriginal peoples have the Euro-originated word 'crime' in their lexicons, they definitely have recognized wrongdoing. To claim otherwise is to suggest they were bereft of notions of justice and morality. In fact, traditional societies had well-developed notions of crime and justice, with uncompromising mechanisms for controlling errant behaviour.

When comparing current mediation and community programs such as Hollow Water with historical examples of how Aboriginal peoples addressed wrongdoing, we will see that, contrary to popular stereotypes, original peoples held exacting notions of crime and punishment, and valued individuality as well.

Traditional Regard for Individuals and Justice

In anthropological fact individuals were highly regarded in Native societies, and their safety and dignity was, as a rule, not sacrificed for the collectivity. The vision quest with its emphasis on individual dreams, the daring culture of the coup among the Plains, the competitive haranguing traditions of important leaders in the potlatch system, and the independent Metis are among the many examples of individuality expressed within Aboriginal cultures.[26]

Generally, much was done to compensate injury done to individuals; in cases of murder, death of the guilty one was sought. Other crimes were treated with various degrees of punishment including torture, shunning, public banishment, ridicule, or some form of required repayment. Often, families or clans of victims made the move towards justice.

Offender mediation processes such as 'healing circles' were not usually pursued. Indeed, there is much evidence to the contrary; many Aboriginal societies lived with the biblical dictum: An eye for an eye. Traditionally, there was swift justice for transgressions such as murder, physical or psychic assault, theft, or personal injury, indicating that 'healing' was not the means of dealing with criminals. For example, lineage kinsmen were morally obligated to secure captives on behalf of bereaved Iroquois women who could then adopt or consign the captive to torture to replace a murdered kin.[27]

While punishment for enemy offenders was generally more severe and less conciliatory than punishment for offenders within family, kinship, clan, or societal systems, various punitive measures were taken against community offenders, irrespective of the organization and size of the Aboriginal group.[28] Even small hunting societies, such as the Ojibway of northern Manitoba, had effective social control mechanisms; for serious crimes such as murder or injury to persons, an offender could expect to be punished by illness, death, or psychic manipulation.[29]

Most anthropological and historical sources consulted for this paper simply did not comment on sexual assault.[30] This makes sense because early anthropology consisted of white men talking to Native men for any cultural information.[31] It can be surmised that neither the white interviewers (often with Victorian sensibilities) nor the Native informants (with strict sexual taboos) would feel comfortable in broaching the subject. However, there is strong indication that for a variety of cultural reasons, sexual assaults were not tolerated and therefore were not committed to any great degree.[32] Contrary to popular myths, even women taken in captivity were not sexually molested.[33] Further, for First Nations along the Atlantic seaboard, often referred to by American historians as New England Indians, *rape was punishable by death*.[34] As American ethnohistorian James Axtell explains: 'Since murder was a crime to be revenged by the victim's family in its own way and time, rape was the only capital offense punished by the tribe as a whole.'[35]

In some Native cultures, punishment against sexual offenders consisted of ostracism, spiritual consequences (i.e., psychic manipulation resulting in illness or death), or family 'revenge.'[36] All original cultures exercised strict mores and taboos to regulate sexual relations.

The Hollow Water sentencing must be re-evaluated in light of real traditional justice. The decision to merely 'supervise' two adults who had committed horrific crimes poses, or at least should pose, many disturbing questions with respect to certain uses of 'traditions' such as 'healing circles' within Aboriginally controlled justice systems. Frankly, it is difficult to comprehend the Hollow Water decision given the mind-boggling nature of the crime.

It may be instructive to review the reporter's description of what the crime was. Headlined 'Hollow Water sex offenders sentenced by reserve members,' the 11 December 1993 *Winnipeg Free Press* story described the crimes as follows:

> The 38-year-old man pleaded guilty to three counts of incest against his two daughters and three additional counts of sexual assault.
>
> The incidents began in 1986, when the daughters were 12 and 13 years old, and continued until last year. The man committed numerous acts of forced sexual intercourse and other sexual offenses with his daughters. He also pleaded guilty to two more sexual assaults involving a 14-year-old female cousin last year.
>
> His 34-year-old wife pleaded guilty to two counts of sexual assault against her daughters. The circle heard that on nine occasions the woman held the girls down while the man sexually assaulted them.

An obvious question should occur to everyone here: Upon whose 'tradition' is the Hollow Water decision based? Clearly, no one considered those Aboriginal traditions that punished sexual offenders with severity. If programs are claiming to apply traditional measures, then they should.

But traditional justice is unrecognizable here, as in most other mediation and healing circle programs.

Origins of Current Notions and Practices

If Hollow Water and other mediation programs are not exactly practising traditional methods of justice, the question must be asked: Have they, in fact, fallen prey to contemporary, white, leftist/liberal, Christian, and even New Age notions of 'healing,' 'forgiveness,' and offender 'rehabilitation'?

Most of the culturally appropriate programs being promoted as alternatives to the existing justice system rely on assertions of 'healing' and 'forgiveness.' For example, in a tone reminiscent of a pacifist church pamphlet, Sawatsky claims Aboriginal justice entails 'encouragement for apology, forgiveness and healing with a view to making peace' (item 14 on his chart). Sawatsky goes on to claim: 'From an aboriginal perspective, victims need to meet the offender face to face, receive personal restitution and be directly involved in a fair settlement.'[37] This is a highly questionable assertion from any perspective. As established above, there is no anthropological basis for asserting it is Native tradition for victims to either 'forgive' or meet 'offenders.' It is, however, traditional to pursue 'healing' in the form of justice. A 'fair settlement' would mean the victims or their families would seek some form of justice in kind, not rehabilitation as such. There is every indication in human history that the ancients had learned there is no healing without justice.

But whether in ancient or modern times, in the case of rape, how can any victim want to meet his or her attacker, and how can one believe that rape is restitutional? (It should be noted that most of the models under discussion here have been formulated by men). And in the case of child molestation, are not children too young to be subjected to their attackers? And can children be expected to comprehend their experience in terms of mediation settings? These are just some of the questions that need to be pursued.

Pressuring victims to 'forgive' is more Christian and patriarchal in origin than it is either Aboriginal or therapeutic. If notions of forgiveness and healing originate in Christian doctrines, the emphasis on collectivity resembles misconstrued socialist ideals and romanticized Noble Savage images. For example, Sawatsky's characterization of Aboriginal 'justice defined by social harmony and needs being met, judged according to community solidarity and survival' (item 5 on the chart) sounds more like an eclectic combination of a leftist political speech and primitivist fantasy than original Aboriginal teachings.

It is true that most Aboriginal cultures were built on egalitarian ideals, but it does not follow that individual rights were disregarded. There is nothing traditional about subverting individual well-being or rights to the collectivity, but its popularity in Aboriginal agendas is a reflection of our continuing colonization.

In recent times, mediation programs have been promoted by various political interests, church organizations, and an overloaded criminal justice system; they have been adopted and adapted largely by Aboriginal and other minority groups. It is understandable why these groups would be anxious for alternatives to the racist record of existing justice (and other) systems, and there is nothing inherently wrong with Natives' use of other traditions. The problem is not in the borrowing but in the confusion surrounding cultural and traditional values and their applications, particularly as they relate to the oppression of women and other victims of violence. Mediation programs do present untenable options for the oppressed (i.e., victims of violence) because the pendulum has swung way too far to the advantage of the oppressors (i.e., offenders) within Native communities. And 'culturally appropriate' definitions and applications are paving the way for a pattern of abandoning the oppressed to the oppressed.[38]

While in many non-violent crimes such as theft, fraud, embezzlement, and so forth, mediation programs may be more constructive for all parties concerned than the existing justice criminal options, they may be devastating in cases of sexual assault and other forms of aggravated violence against persons. For a more thorough discussion on the need to differentiate between offenders and victims, between types of crimes and the nature and extent of harm and therefore types of alternative programs, see my recommendations in 'Violence in Aboriginal Communities' included in the Royal Commission on Aboriginal Peoples' *Path To Healing (1993).*[39]

Sexual offence cannot be reduced to a 'two-sided conflict' nor trivialized to an issue of 'healing.' It is a particularly noxious violation against human dignity and must be treated accordingly. It has long been established that victims of child sexual abuse and/or rape experience lifelong suffering such as flashbacks, nightmares, poor health, low self-esteem, isolation, fear, anger, depression, and suicide, all symptoms of post-traumatic stress syndrome.[40]

Given that there is a wealth of documentation on the severity of harm to victims; given that no one has established that rehabilitating rapists is possible or even definable; and given that no one has established that subordinating victim rights to the collective is healing either for the victim or the community, one must further explore why 'culturally appropriate' advocates persist with their lines of defence.

Political Factors in the Defence of Offenders

I believe there are a number of significant political factors that help explain the persistence of 'culturally appropriate' rhetoric, factors that can only be briefly introduced here. As colonized peoples, Natives have been forced to use whatever arsenal is at their disposal in response to relentless political pressure – pressure that amounts to sociological and cultural warfare – from Canadian governments, especially on issues of land rights and identity. Native peoples have been forced to make their case for Aboriginal (land) rights on the basis of cultural differences, when it should simply be on the basis of inherent rights that flow from aboriginality.[41] Justices have made appalling decisions on the basis of what they perceive as Native culture, whether it concerns sexual assault or land rights.[42] Native leaders, faced with convoluted, self-serving, and shrewd legal arguments, have had to scramble for proof of cultural differences.

The issue of 'individual' versus 'collective' rights is a perfect example of Natives resorting to a cultural framework when boxed in by Western liberal democratic traditions that are associated with individualism. Perhaps unavoidably, Native leaders have had to overemphasize collective rights to make the point that such rights are even culturally feasible. However, the fact that Native cultures were egalitarian in organization does not mean Native peoples acted on some instinct akin to a buffalo herd with no regard for the well-being of individuals! Native people have had to emphasize collective rights on the issue of land, but it must be remembered that the framework around which Aboriginal rights are pursued originates in European theory and law.[43] Further, Native 'collectivity' was in many ways invented through the creation of reserves and a legalized collective identity via the Indian Act. Obviously, there is much more to consider on the matter of land rights and the Aboriginal collective.[44] It is more my purpose here to show how parties in conflict utilize these colonially derived notions with the stamp of 'tradition' in the service of political interests.

Political interests are at work in the well-known dispute between the Assembly of First Nations (AFN) and the Native Women's Association of Canada (NWAC). In the area of Native women's rights, the AFN tactic has been to accuse NWAC of being under the influence of white feminists (who, in turn, are often accused of espousing individual rights as if they exist apart from society), of being interested more in their individual (i.e., selfish?) rights as opposed to some generalized Native communal well-being.[45] This has resulted in dismissing Native women's issues by pitting women against 'their own people,' and putting them in an untenable position of having to choose between gender and culture – as if gender rights were never, or should never be, an issue within Native families, homes, and traditions.

Another reason why Native peoples have clung to the defence of being culturally different lies in the racist myth of European 'civilization' confronting Native 'savagery.'[46] In response to the Euro-Canadian theft of

Aboriginal history and of the ground upon which Aboriginal cultures are based, contemporary Native peoples have been trying to prove they do have cultures – and often morally better ones at that – hence the romanticization evident in most culturally appropriate models, as well as the reluctance to critique them.

There is such hunger within the Native community for an identity separate from the Canadian mainstream that a number of issues have become hopelessly entangled. Take, for instance, the notion of forgiving and healing the offender. It seems that spirituality has become a precondition of being accepted as Native, and spirituality, or 'following traditional teachings,' entails having to 'forgive.' What arises from this belief is the confused expectation that Native victims must forgive the offender in order to qualify as being truly Native. As a Native woman expressed it in a letter to me:

> There isn't a whole lot out there for training specifically in the field of sexual assault support.
>
> Our community is looking at using the Hollow Water project for our offenders. I feel the same way you do about the project and I am having a hard time relaying these feelings to some of the other committee members ... I guess I am having a hard time with this because I am a survivor of sexual assault and I do want to know more about the surrounding support in the community for survivors. I am also getting tired of being told that I am to try to forgive or even the suggestion that I confront the offender because that is the 'native way.' I feel that with being told this all the time that my feelings of just being human are being ignored because I am native.
>
> I would like to know how you suggest to these people that I am human before I am native?
>
> I also feel that it is my right to heal myself and not to try to look at healing of the offender too. Why must I feel the need to heal the offender as a native person? I try to make it clear that for some survivors this might do more harm than good. I want to be recognized as a native person, but I am getting confused on what it means to be native in the healing process.[47]

That Native people, particularly youth, are profoundly hungry for an identity distinct from mainstream Canadian society is to be expected, given the disorienting consequences of dispossession, and should be addressed. Nevertheless, victims of violence should not be put in situations as described above.

I have long been concerned with the contradictions, confusion, and abuses inherent in 'cultural difference' arguments.[48] Besides the tendency of reducing pan-Indianized cultural values to a handful of 'traits,' as already noted, problems of racism from the outside and gender domination on the inside have been routinely whitewashed under the rubric of cultural differences.

Of the arguments in defence of offenders, the 'culturalization' of rape remains to be examined, and is perhaps the most distressing. Drawing on notions of community, as well as social and personal history (males as victims of colonization and/or sexual abuse) to mitigate sentencing, Native and non-Native advocates of Aboriginal justice have turned to distorted 'cultural explanations.' But these contain glaring discrepancies, not the least of which is claiming that colonization has devastated Native persons and cultures while in the same breath, drawing upon Native traditions as if they exist in whole, for models which on one hand support offenders and on the other, undermine victims.

In the guise of cultural sensitivity, non-Native judges and lawyers have, as a rule, sympathized with Native rapists and child molesters on cultural grounds, as if they have any critical basis for deciphering cultural knowledge. In her study of sexual assault cases involving Native males against Native females, Margo Nightingale[49] has found that assorted defence arguments have been used, whichever is most efficacious. Either the Native men were ignorant of Canadian law, or the men were drunk, or they came from terrible socio-economic conditions, and so forth. In an Inuit case, a judge went so far as to suggest that when Inuit girls reach puberty, sexual intercourse is expected.[50] Note the racist implications here: that Native men are so culturally primitive, depraved, or deprived they cannot be held responsible for any act; that Inuit men are unable to make a cultural distinction between rape and sexual intercourse ... or is it that the judge himself is unable to make the distinction?

Typically, the emphasis has been on the harm done by colonial forces to men, without due regard to the damage done to women, not only by colonial forces but also by the sexually violent offender. There is no question that colonization has wreaked havoc in the lives of men, but colonial oppression is not equally experienced within Native communities; it has a different impact on Native women than on Native men. Women continue to bear the greatest brunt of social disintegration while being alienated from decolonization efforts. As one analyst has put it: 'In the Aboriginal struggle to achieve a measure of self-determination, the rights of Aboriginal women have been submerged.'[51]

For instance, to fend off racism in victim services, Native women have called for 'culturally appropriate' measures, but this has been retooled into a vehicle for the justification of sexual offenders. 'Culturally appropriate sensitivity' has resulted largely in disregarding Aboriginal women's experiences, perspectives, and human rights. But as I have pointed out in a previous work, when cultural justifications are used on behalf of the sexually violent, 'we are seeing a gross distortion of the notion of culture and of Native peoples. Men assault, cultures do not ... Rape in any culture and by any standards is warfare against women. And the degree to which any community tolerates sexual violence is an indication of concurrence in this warfare against women ... and if there is any culture which condones the oppression of women, it should be confronted to change. Further, would one entertain using "racial differences" as an explanation for sexual assaults? Is it any less racist to resort to "cultural" ones?'[52] Besides using cultural explanations in the service of offenders, there are other problems with the 'cultural differences' argument. One of the most persistent and frustrating stereotypes about Native cultures is their relegation to the past, which has led to the false dichotomization of many contemporary issues. Making individual rights antithetical to collective rights, confusing spirituality with healing, and identity are among the problems deriving from the ossification of tradition.[53] Further, freezing Native culture in the past makes it virtually impossible for Native people to engage in contemporary rights debates such as freedom of religion, speech, personal choice, citizenship, or women's rights.

When Native women turn to contemporary analysis to explicate their double oppression, they are often accused of using 'white' instead of Native traditions – clearly an instance of the double standard, since white traditions are heavily borrowed for culturally appropriate programs. When Aboriginal women demand justice in a contemporary context, they are accused of betraying 'solidarity,' putting them, in effect, in an absolutely no-win situation between justice and community. Clearly, 'tradition,' 'culture,' and 'history' are political handles with many twists that result in the continued oppression and silencing of women.

The strident insistence by the Native leadership on our cultural differences has pushed Aboriginal people to the extreme margins. We have given the message that we are so fathomlessly different as to be hardly human.[54] We are supposedly so different as to be exempt from the Canadian Charter of Rights and Freedoms, as if our history of oppression has made us somehow immune to ordinary human evils, as if we do not require basic human rights that other Canadian citizens expect. As evidenced by statistics and court decisions regarding Native sexual violence, 'otherness' can be carried to rather chilling extents by both communities. It is ironic that today as we struggle to decolonize, we ourselves are turning to the stereotypes that have segregated and defined us as inferior in the first place.

Role of Tradition in a Contemporary World

This paper has questioned and challenged popular notions and myths about the use of Aboriginal 'traditions' in justice issues. Whatever one decides about the truth or importance of traditions, it remains questionable whether, or to what extent, 'traditional' (albeit relaxed) means of defining and controlling crime can be applied to our complex, colonized, contemporary communities. While restoring social harmony between parties in dispute may have made sense in a small hunting society (note: except in cases of serious crime and violence), such an overriding goal today may not make any sense at all.

The point remains that we live in a contemporary world, whether in a rural or urban setting. This means we have many worlds from which to draw with respect to ideals of human rights or healing. If we do not like non-Native Canadian models – for example, the Canadian Charter of Rights and Freedoms – we can turn to international charters and models. In other words, Native peoples do not have only things of the past for our resources. On the issue of justice for victims of violence, we have numerous sources and resources for discussion, models, and therapy.

The Hollow Water healing circle, for example, could have ruled quite differently and still remained true to 'tradition' and 'healing' while drawing on contemporary measures. If the offending couple were viewed as too sick to be put in prison, then on the basis of contemporary knowledge about the need to protect victims from further exposure to their attackers, they could have been involuntarily placed into an alternative institution. Such a centre should allow Native practices, elders, and other Native experts to be part of therapeutic treatment. The Canadian government must provide rehabilitation centres for sexual offenders, but centres that protect victims and restrict offender movement until such time as offenders prove themselves worthy of societal engagement. And their movements should be monitored with all the modern technology available today. These centres should have access to a combination of historical, sociological, and cultural education and consciousness-raising on the nature and devastating effects of colonization and sexual violence, as well as the most modern kinds of therapies possible.

The point is, decisions and models other than the existing 'retributive' or, much more frequently, *wanton* types[55] can be possible in an Aboriginally controlled justice system, particularly in cases of sexual assault. I am not arguing that Native peoples cannot or should not control their programs, but it is possible to construct new models that accommodate real, multidimensional human lives. Traditions can be and must be used in a contemporary context in such a way as to bring meaning to our young people, justice and equality to women, and safety and human rights protection to everyone.

Nevertheless, tradition cannot necessarily or always be of value or relevance in our times. 'Healing,' for instance, cannot be the sole means of dealing with the sexually violent in our midst. There comes a time when, for ethical and moral considerations, a people must confront or change their own traditions. There is no need to wait for external forces to make us change. And we must never assume that our historical oppression has somehow made us extraordinarily moral. If there is one thing we can learn from history, it is that human beings do not become better people, that is, more morally sensitive, just because they have been oppressed. Morality is an ongoing dialogue, it is not innate. Our traditions and cultures cannot be immutable. For this reason, we must be vigilant in our suppositions and behaviours as to what constitutes the good, the bad, and the moral. Even seemingly 'good' notions such as 'family' or 'forgiveness' need to be re-examined; there are things human beings, human families, do that are so dehumanizing and destructive that the only word and concept we can use to describe them is 'evil.'

It may be ethically wrong to 'forgive' evil. Are we to forgive the conquistadors? The Nazis? Isn't rape and child molestation evil in that it is as calculating, debasing, and devastating as cultural genocide? Should not rape and child molestation be considered a form of holocaust experienced at a group level, and do they not warrant political consideration? That women and children are assaulted on an individual basis should not detract us from the fact that, altogether, untold millions have been and continue to be attacked. Moreover, survivors of sexual attacks suffer much the same consequences as survivors of warfare and other terrors. Given such established knowledge, it is truly mystifying how human societies continue to tolerate and 'forgive' rapists and child molesters. As international human societies we seem to have evolved enough to consider genocide 'unforgivable'; clearly, we need to evolve further to see that sexual assault should also be considered unforgivable.

As Native peoples we are caught within the burdens and contradictions of colonial history, but nonetheless, we cannot use colonization or culture to excuse violence; we are challenged to meet our responsibilities in a manner that is consistent with international human rights standards.[56] I would like to think our traditions and cultures do not contravene such standards.

Gross tolerance of sexual assault is neither traditional, nor a culturally viable option today (or any day!). We cannot rest with some idea that we have reached the ultimate solutions in the existing mediation programs. In the hasty quest for something different than what has been, we seem to have increased the risk of abandoning victims of violence. And in the drive for self-determination, we risk using victims of assault as test cases for alternative models.

Many Native communities are undergoing dramatic social upheaval and disintegration, an upheaval well-documented by sociological, anecdotal, and governmental studies.[57] If Native communities are not willing to take an uncompromising stand against violence, particularly sexual violence, there may not be functioning Native communities in the future. Studies show that, as young people and women have more access to urban centres, they will run from abusive or desperate environments.

Freedom of Expression

I am aware of the depth of emotion the Hollow Water sentencing generated. I have received many calls from concerned people expressing the view that Hollow Water is a travesty of justice and a cruel disregard for human dignity. In particular, Native women expressed shock, disgust, and outrage. Many said that if Hollow Water is any example of things to come with respect to 'culturally appropriate' applications of justice to women, they would fear to live under Aboriginal self-governments. One Native woman who was in law school considered challenging the decision under the Canadian Charter of Rights and Freedoms. Even white journalists urged me to make a statement and told me they were not politically free to question the Hollow Water decision. All those Native women who called asked to remain anonymous because they too did not feel free to publicly challenge Hollow Water. I have not felt free either.

What have we come to in our community? It is this fear of free expression that has provided the impetus for me to write this paper. It appears that culturally appropriate applications are increasingly becoming rigid and doctrinaire, leading to the alienation of valuable community members. Such a path is more Western in tradition than it is Native, for as has been amply indicated already, the best of Native traditions place high regard on freedom, democracy, justice, and gender inclusiveness.

My observations and research indicate that there are a substantial number of Native organizations, communities, and individuals that have concerns about gender equality, violence, constitutional protection, and Aboriginally controlled systems. These concerned people include northern Native chiefs, incarcerated Native women, Native women's organizations, and Native women analysts.[58] There are indications that women have felt uncertain about their role in Aboriginal self-government. In 1991 NWAC went to court arguing against its exclusion from constitutional talks. As Gail Stacey-Moore, speaker for NWAC has put it:

Why should Aboriginal women have less protection for their human, civil, political, legal and sexual equality rights than other Canadians? Why should Aboriginal women be burdened with fighting in every Aboriginal community for protections enjoyed by other Canadians? ... Why are we so worried as women? Because we have never discussed Self-Government in our communities ... We are living in chaos in our communities ... We have a disproportionately high rate of child sexual abuse and incest. We have wife battering, gang rapes, drug and alcohol abuse ... The development of programs, services, and policies for handling domestic violence has been placed in the hands of men. Has it resulted in a reduction of this kind of violence? Is a woman or a child safe in their own home in an Aboriginal community? The statistics show this is not the case.[59]

Clearly, the extent of community support for all these programs that have gone unchallenged in courts, healing circles, umbrella Native organizations, and white males' intellectual writing is in question.

Joyce Green, a Native doctoral student in political science at the University of Alberta, has produced a number of incisive and thoughtful works on the issue of Native women's rights within decolonizing, male-dominated, Native organizations.[60] In an article discussing NWAC's participant status in the Charlottetown Accord constitutional negotiations, Green borrows Mary Daly's terminology in referring to the 'male-stream' tactic of undermining Native women's efforts with accusations of 'feminism.' While noting the existing differences between Aboriginal and white women's concerns, she recognizes that 'the analysis of inequitable relations between men and women has much in common with the feminism of other Canadian women, and provides a basis for solidarity between women's organizations.'[61] Concerning the alienating effects on Native women of being branded 'feminist,' Green writes:

Aboriginal feminists take great risks and display real courage in continuing their activism. This intimidation is shared by all feminists who find themselves targets of ridicule, marginalization, and other sanctions including physical assault. However, it is a more profound threat for Aboriginal women because the attackers deny the validity of their [the women's] analysis as authentically Aboriginal. It is a painful thing to be labelled as a dupe of the colonizing society for undertaking to name and change women's experience ...

No one speaking for NWAC, NAC, or the National Metis Women of Canada is opposed to constitutional affirmation of the inherent right of Aboriginal peoples to their own governmental powers. But the women's organizations do not accept that a choice must be made between justice for Aboriginal societies vis-à-vis the dominant society and justice between Aboriginal women and men ... So far Aboriginal organizations have been unwilling to be internally critical, to tolerate any criticism or to accept responsibility for discriminatory behaviour and politics ... the problem of sexism persists ... While male leaders speak 'for their people,' dissident women's voices are silenced.[62]

With respect to the exclusion of Native women's experiences (and analyses, I might add) in white intellectual works, Diane Bell, a critical anthropologist, has pointed out that while mainstream historians and anthropologists have begun to 'develop more and more sophisticated models of colonial relations ... they have, for the most part, paid scant attention to the different impact of colonial practices on men and women.' This has created 'a niche for the consolidation of male power ... the most consistent outcome [of which] appears to be that while men assume the political spokesperson role, the women run the welfare structures.'[63]

Bell notes that her analysis can be resisted with the argument that 'foregrounding gender is divisive, irrelevant, a middle-class feminist plot' or that 'racism is more fundamental than sexism.' Such arguments, 'raised in the name of self-determination,' Bell counters, 'serve to mask the power which the new elites enjoy in decision-making, in negotiations, in their interactions with the instrument of the state. Not surprisingly, a feminist analysis is threatening both to the colonizer and to the colonized.'[64]

Speaking directly to the exclusion of women's analyses, Joyce Green states: 'So much of women's experience has been classified as non-data. So much of women's analysis *as women* has been ignored by the academy and by the activists. The consequence is male-gendered theoretical and epistemological development that is presented as authentic reflection on the *human* condition ... But knowledge is dynamic, and there is nothing preventing the incorporation of new female and aboriginal ways of knowing.'[65]

Summary Comments

One can only agree that Aboriginal peoples have been despicably treated by the Canadian criminal justice system (and society), and that a 'paradigm shift' (Sawatsky) or a structural revolution is required to address the complex systemic problems involved. While one cannot argue against the ideal of humane principles and outcomes in the area of justice, one must argue against disregarding victim interests in the name of 'restoring harmony' in the Native community. Some violations are so noxious, fundamental, and irreparable that 'harmony' is not only impossible to restore, it should not even be the overriding objective. We have to build programs around those who contribute to the fabric of our communities rather than those who destroy. In order to redress the wrongs of an ineffective, racist, dominant system, Aboriginal communities should not feel compelled to replace them with disregard for innocent people's rights. Nor should Aboriginal communities disregard women's perspectives while utilizing charts, models, and analyses produced by white (usually) males.

If Aboriginal self-government or any other community-based organizing model is to be created under the healthiest of circumstances, everyone must be free to examine issues in a context of freedom, honesty, creativity, caring, and gender equality. It is incumbent upon Aboriginally controlled, 'culturally appropriate' justice (and other) systems to value and protect the contemporary human rights of all individuals. Everyone must be safe from personal violence and political interference. Integrity is required with respect to the uses of 'tradition.' We must continually examine community beliefs and/or practices; otherwise, individuals in our communities will become even more vulnerable to political suppression. If people are silenced, they will abandon their homes and seek refuge in the mainstream society. How ironic it would be, after 500 years of having to protect ourselves from the prejudices of mainstream Canada, that we would have to run there for protection. Then colonization will have won.

4

The Impact of Treaty 9 on Natural Resource Development in Northern Ontario

Patrick Macklem[1]

Introduction

Faced with heightened domestic and international demand for natural resources, government and industry in the twenty-first century likely will increase natural resource exploration and development activity in northern Ontario.[2] To date, little has been written on the extent to which treaties between the Crown and Aboriginal peoples restrict such activity by non-Aboriginal governments and third parties.[3] In this paper I examine the nature, scope, and status of Treaty 9, one of eleven numbered treaties negotiated between the federal government and Aboriginal peoples between 1871 and 1921. My aim is to provide insight into the extent to which Treaty 9 constrains natural resource exploration and development activity by the Crown and third parties on lands subject to its terms.[4]

Although a more detailed description of its terms will be offered in part 1, Treaty 9 covers lands in northern Ontario that lie north of the Robinson-Superior and Robinson-Huron Treaties of 1850 and that abut the Quebec border to the east, the territory covered by Treaty 3 to the west, and Hudson Bay and James Bay to the north. Treaty 9 was negotiated and signed in 1905 and 1906 by Commissioners Duncan Campbell Scott and Samuel Stewart, representatives of the federal government, Commissioner Daniel McMartin, representative of the Province of Ontario, and numerous Aboriginal leaders of Cree and Ojibwa peoples living in the area. Treaty-signing ceremonies occurred at Osnaburgh, Fort Hope, Marten Falls, Fort Albany, Moose Factory, New Brunswick House, and New Post in the summer of 1905, and at Abitibi, Matachewan, Mattagami, Long Lake, and Flying Post in the summer of 1906. The written text of the treaty contains a series of promises made by the federal government in return for the apparent agreement of Aboriginal people to surrender certain rights, initially to 130,000 square miles of ancestral lands, and relocate to reserves totalling 524 square miles. In 1929-30, adhesions were made to Treaty 9 extending its coverage over an additional 128,000 square miles to Ontario's present border with Manitoba. Signing ceremonies occurred at Trout Lake in 1929, and Windigo River, Fort Severn, and Winisk in 1930. Treaty 9 currently covers more than two-thirds of present-day Ontario.[5]

As will be seen, an examination of the nature, scope, and status of Treaty 9 raises complex questions regarding the relationship between oral and written understandings of the treaty's terms. It also raises more general questions concerning the constitutional status of treaty rights and the extent to which treaty rights trump governmental and third party activity. In this light, Treaty 9 serves as a vehicle to explore the relationship between constitutional rights and economic and political power. I hope that this paper will assist in the more general task of determining the constitutional relationship between treaty rights and government and third party power in Canada.

Part 1 of the paper summarizes a number of key principles established by the Supreme Court of Canada regarding the interpretation of treaties between the Crown and Aboriginal peoples. Part 2 describes events leading up to the negotiation of Treaty 9, and identifies federal, provincial, and Aboriginal interests structuring negotiations. Part 3 explores the terms of the treaty itself, including Aboriginal and non-Aboriginal understandings of its land surrender clause and its provision for hunting, trapping, and fishing rights. Part 4 examines the constitutional underpinnings of legislative action decreeing or authorizing economic activity by the Crown or third parties on lands covered by the treaty, whereas part 5 examines the extent to which the treaty itself authorizes Crown or third party natural resource development and economic activity. Finally, in part 6, I examine the effect of constitutional recognition and affirmation of existing treaty rights by section 35(1) of the Constitution Act, 1982, on natural resource exploration and development initiatives by government and third parties.

(1) General Principles of Treaty Interpretation

Recent jurisprudence by the Supreme Court of Canada requires that treaties entered into by the Crown and Aboriginal peoples are to be interpreted in a manner befitting their unique status and importance in Canadian law. In *Nowegijick* v. *The Queen* for example, Justice Dickson (as he then was), for a unanimous Court, stated that 'treaties and statutes relating to Indians should be liberally construed, and doubtful expressions resolved in favour of the Indians.'[6] Guiding Justice Dickson's views on the subject was the nineteenth-century judgment of the United States Supreme Court in *Jones* v. *Meehan*, in which it was declared that 'Indian treaties must be construed, not according to the technical meaning of their words, but in the sense in which they would naturally be understood by the Indians.'[7] More recently, in *R.* v. *Badger,* Justice Cory, for a majority of the Supreme Court of Canada, stated that treaties are 'sacred,' and that 'any limitations which restrict the rights of Indians under treaties must be narrowly construed.'[8]

In this vein, while the Court has held that extrinsic evidence should not be used as an aid to interpreting a treaty in the absence of ambiguity or where the result would be to alter its terms by adding or subtracting words from the written agreement,[9] it has also held that written terms alone often will 'not suffice to determine the legal nature of the document.'[10] The Court has further indicated that the judiciary should not automatically interpret written terms of a treaty by reference to non-Aboriginal understandings.[11] Extrinsic evidence of the parties' intent to enter into a treaty and of facts closely associated with the signing of the treaty are to be examined to determine its legal effect.[12] This general approach has been affirmed by the Supreme Court of Canada in several recent cases involving the interpretation of treaty rights and statutes aimed at Aboriginal peoples.[13]

In *Simon* v. *The Queen,*[14] for example, at issue was the extent to which the Treaty of 1752 between the British Crown and the Micmac nation recognized a right to hunt so as to preclude the application of provincial legislation. Chief Justice Dickson held that 'Indian treaties should be given a fair, large and liberal construction in favour of the Indians.'[15] As a result, he called for an interpretation of the right to hunt contained in the treaty that would be 'sensitive to the evolution of changes in normal hunting practices,' and which 'ensures that the treaty will be an effective source of hunting rights.'[16] He added that 'the right to hunt to be effective must embody those activities reasonably incidental to the act of hunting itself.'[17]

The Court has also addressed the extent to which treaty rights can be exercised on lands put to use by the Crown and third parties. In *R.* v. *Sioui,*[18] for example, at issue was whether members of the Huron Band on the Lorette Indian reserve in Quebec could claim protection from provincial legislation by virtue of a treaty entered into by the Huron nation and the British Crown in 1760. The treaty guaranteed 'the free Exercise of [the Hurons'] religion, [and] their Customs.'[19] Justice Lamer (as he then was) reaffirmed the general principles articulated in *Jones* v. *Meehan* and *Simon* v. *The Queen,* and called for 'a just, broad and liberal interpretation.'[20] In his view, this entailed an examination of 'the historical context and perception each party might have as to the nature of the undertaking contained in the document under consideration' and 'the intention of the parties ... at the time it was concluded.'[21] Despite the fact that there was no mention made in the treaty of the territory over which the rights may be exercised, Justice Lamer concluded that 'the rights guaranteed ... could be exercised over the entire territory frequented by the Hurons at the time [of signing], so long as the carrying on of the customs and rites is not incompatible with the particular use made by the Crown of [the] territory.'[22]

Similarly, in *R. v. Badger*, the Court held that treaty rights to hunt for food could be exercised on private property. Stating that at the time the treaty was negotiated, Aboriginal signatories 'would not have understood the concept of private and exclusive property ownership separate from actual land use,' Justice Cory held that treaty rights could be exercised on privately owned land unless such land is being put to a 'visible, incompatible' use.[23] Thus, an Aboriginal person can exercise a Treaty 8 right to hunt on uncleared, privately owned property, but not on privately owned land that displays evidence that crops have been recently harvested.

The interpretive approach called for by the Supreme Court of Canada suggests an emphasis on Aboriginal understandings of the terms of a treaty. Treaty terms are to be interpreted in a manner sensitive to Aboriginal expectations. The Court has signalled that there is more to a treaty than its written text: 'treaties, as written documents, recorded an agreement that had already been reached orally and they did not always record the full extent of the agreement.'[24] Where a treaty right admits of more than one interpretation, the Court will look to extrinsic evidence, and ambiguities are to be resolved in favour of Aboriginal interests.[25] Depending on the meaning of the terms of Treaty 9, Crown and third party economic development on lands contemplated by the treaty may affect treaty rights to land and water, and to hunt, trap, and fish. The remainder of this paper addresses the scope of land, water, hunting, trapping, and fishing treaty rights of Aboriginal peoples currently living within the scope of Treaty 9, in view of the interpretive approach called for by the Supreme Court of Canada and in light of available archival and published historical documentation. At a general level, it also examines whether the Province of Ontario and third parties can claim legal authority under Treaty 9 to engage in natural resource exploration and development on treaty lands.

(2) The Historical Background to Treaty 9

Aboriginal Petitions for a Treaty

At the turn of the century, Aboriginal people living in northern Ontario began to urge that the federal government address their concerns. Aboriginal requests for a treaty provide some indication of the expectations of

Aboriginal people surrounding present-day treaty rights and obligations. As early as 1884, Chief Louis Espagnol, chief of a subgroup of the Eshkemanetigon or Spanish River Band on Lake Huron and not ultimately a signatory to Treaty 9, wrote James Phipps, visiting superintendent of Indian affairs for Manitoulin Island and Lake Huron, stating that 'the trappers have stolen all our beaver, so there is nothing left for them to hunt and they are too old to go anywhere else ... there are also about twenty old sick women, invalids and orphans who are very badly off and they all join me in asking you to help us.'[26]

In 1899, Aboriginal people from the area subsequently covered by Treaty 9 met with J.A. Macrae, inspector of Indian agencies and reserves, and Duncan Campbell Scott, an accountant for Indian Affairs at the time, to discuss the possibility of a treaty with the federal government. According to Macrae, they sought to safeguard their ways of life: 'These Indians had come from considerable distances and asked what the Government proposed to do about the rights of Indians residing between James Bay and the Great Lakes who had not been treated with by the Honorable Mr. Robinson (in 1850), saying that they heard that railroads were projected through their country, and that already miners, prospectors, and surveyors were beginning to pass through it [in] such largely increased numbers that the game was disturbed, interference with their means of livelihood had commenced, and their rights were being trespassed upon.'[27]

Similarly, Aboriginal people living at the head of the Albany River near Lake Joseph and Osnaburgh petitioned the Crown in 1901 to meet with them to determine rights to the land. The written document spoke of the fact that 'for the last two or three years exploration for minerals has been carried on in the country contiguous to Lake St. Joseph – and an occasional party has penetrated to the Lake itself, and the Waters of the Albany River have been descended as far as the Eabamet Lake in the prosecution of the search.'[28] The petitioners requested a treaty with the federal government, given that 'white men are already building upon land which we desire to retain.'[29]

In 1902, William Nichols, acting Indian agent at Sault Ste. Marie, visited and met with Aboriginal people living near Biscotasing, Chapleau, and Missinabae. Nichols reported: 'Many of these on account of bush fires [and] the encroachment of prospectors and fishermen find their hunting and trapping greatly interfered with and are in many cases reduced to sore straights during the winter season and are largely dependent upon the Hudson's Bay posts for means of subsistence.'[30]

Not all Aboriginal peoples were in favour of a treaty with the Crown, as is evidenced by internal correspondence between Hudson's Bay officials in 1902: 'Whatever is done in the matter by the Department the sooner the better. The Osnaburg Indians are anxious for it. There may be some little difficulty with the Fort Hope Indians now but it may not be insurmountable. They were alright last year. Unless they have changed their minds the Indians as far as the Attawapiskat River northward from the Albany were inclined to accept it. The R[oman] C[atholic] Attawapiskat Indians are led by Kachang who is not anxious for government control.'[31] In the view of James Morrison, 'a band's interest in treaty relations with the government was, by 1901, generally proportional to its proximity to the railway line and the newcomers who were arriving with it.'[32]

In short, petitions made by Aboriginal people living in northern Ontario at the turn of the century indicate that Aboriginal leaders generally desired to enter into treaty with the Crown to offset social and economic damage that had befallen their people. Railway construction, surveying activity, and an unprecedented rise in hunting, trapping, and fishing by non-Aboriginal people had increased Aboriginal dependence upon Hudson's Bay posts and made it increasingly difficult for Aboriginal people to maintain their traditional ways of life. Agreement was sought with the federal government to provide protection for Aboriginal hunting, trapping, and fishing on ancestral lands in the face of economic and railway development. Financial aid was also sought to alleviate the economic suffering caused primarily by the depletion of game and fish. The petitions illustrate a desire on the part of Aboriginal peoples to maintain traditional ways of life in the face of economic development and increased settlement.

Railway Construction and Economic Development

In fact, the construction of the railway is seen by historians to be the major factor in causing Aboriginal people to seek relief from the Crown. The ensuing influx of non-Aboriginal settlers, traders, and hunters strained the ability of Aboriginal people to continue their traditional ways of life in northern Ontario. This fact was acknowledged not only by Aboriginal spokespersons, as the quote from Chief Espagnol indicates,[33] but also by government officials. As Visiting Superintendent of Indian Affairs James Phipps stated in 1885, 'construction of the Canadian Pacific Railway has opened up the country in the neighbourhood of Lake Pogamasing to White Trappers who deprive the Indians of the Beaver (which they carefully preserved, never taking all, but leaving some to increase) and as the Whites kill and destroy all they can, the consequence will be that no Beaver will be left in that section of country.'[34]

Similarly, E.B. Borron, a stipendiary magistrate at the time, wrote the following in relation to the Brunswick Lake Indian Band:

No treaties have yet been concluded with the Indians in this territory for the surrender of their claims. To do so with the natives on or near the coast of James Bay may perhaps be premature and uncalled for by circumstances. But as regards the Missinaibi and other Indians whose case I have promised the chiefs of the former band to represent there can be no reasonable doubt on this subject. The Canadian Pacific Railway for upwards of a hundred miles passes through their hunting grounds, and will unquestionably lead, sooner or later, to the destruction of the larger game, the fur-bearing animals, and to some extent also of the fish, on which they are solely and entirely dependent for a living. These Indians are simply hunters and trappers, and not one in twenty grows even so much as a potatoe. They have no other resource to fall back upon. The completion of the railway renders their hunting grounds easily accessible at all seasons of the year. Hence it may be expected that white hunters and trappers from other parts of Ontario and Quebec will pour into this territory. It is probable also that a large number of Indians belonging to bands south of the height of land, whose own hunting grounds have been depleted of game and fur-bearing animals, will also trespass on the hunting grounds of these northern or height of land Indians. Nor can it be doubted that railway employees, squatters and lumbermen will engage in hunting and trapping for profit and amusement. Thus there are too many and strong grounds for fearing that these poor Indians will soon be deprived, in a great measure, of their only means of subsistence.[35]

John Long described railway construction and economic development in the region in the following terms:

A railway to James Bay was now underway. W.A. Charlton and Charles T. Harvey had proposed such a route in 1897 – a short cut to the Klondike! When Ontario's 'great Clay Belt' was discovered around the turn of the twentieth century, Ontario Premier George Ross announced his government's plans to build a railroad from North Bay to Temiskaming. The Temiskaming and Northern Ontario Railway (T. & N.O. was sometimes deciphered as 'Time No Object') was chartered in 1902, reached Cochrane in 1908, and Moosonee in 1932. On its way north, the railroad paid some unexpected – but welcome – dividends: gold was discovered at Cobalt in 1905, at Kirkland Lake, and in the Timmins/Porcupine region.[36]

The influx of non-Aboriginal traders was so great and so threatening to Aboriginal ways of life that several government officials began to discuss the feasibility of a law against trapping by white people.[37] E.B. Borron, for example, argued for a law that would 'strictly prohibit both white men and other Indians from hunting, fishing or trapping on "unsurrendered territory" north of the height of land; or, at all events, without a special license to do so from the proper authority.'[38] It should be noted that Borron viewed such a proposal as an alternative to the negotiation of a treaty,[39] implying that he was of the view that a treaty would at least protect aboriginal hunting, fishing, and trapping on ancestral land from outside interference.[40] In addition to railway construction and an unprecedented rise in non-Aboriginal hunting, trapping, and trading, significant surveying activity for mineral excavation began to occur in earnest around the turn of the century.[41]

Federal Interests in Treaty Negotiations
There is historical evidence to suggest that the federal government's underlying reason for negotiating Treaty 9 had less to do with ameliorating the negative effects of settlement, exploration, and development on the Aboriginal population in the north, and more to do with facilitating the completion of the railway. In 1901, the federal government announced plans to build a new transcontinental railway, this time from Roberval, Quebec, through Moose Factory and on to Port Simpson, British Columbia.[42] The 1904-5 annual report of the Department of Indian Affairs referred to railway construction as 'the immediate cause' of federal action on Aboriginal requests:

> This measure [treaty negotiations] was adopted in pursuance of the old established policy of keeping sufficiently in advance of settlement to avert the danger of complications or, worse still, conflict with the aboriginal claimants of the soil.
>
> The immediate cause in this instance was the projected passage of the new transcontinental railway through their territory, and the increasing influx of prospectors which seemed to have ripened the time for acceding to the requests in this direction which the Indians had been urging upon the government for some years past.[43]

Similarly, in a letter from Frank Pedley, deputy superintendent of Indian affairs, to Clifford Sifton, superintendent-general of Indian affairs, Pedley wrote that 'the strong reason by which this Government is actuated in the making of the treaty is the old and well-established rule that a way must be smoothed for exploration, location of railway lines and construction, by extinction of the Indian title.'[44]

When the draft terms of Treaty 9 were sent to the Province of Ontario for its concurrence, the federal government indicated that 'it is the fixed policy of this Government to pave the way for exploration, location and construction of railway lines by the extinction of all aboriginal rights in the territory to be exploited.'[45] A similar sentiment was expressed to Sir Wilfrid Laurier by Pedley: 'When the matter was first taken up, the Indians themselves approached the Government and requested to be informed when their aboriginal rights would be extinguished. Later it became evident that the treaty had become a necessity owing to the activity in railway operations on the part of the Province of Ontario, and general exploration on the part of the Dominion. The project of a new transcontinental railway made it obligatory that prompt action should be taken.'[46] Pedley urged Laurier to obtain the Province of Ontario's agreement, stating that 'it is not conducive to good Government to any longer delay the making of this treaty as the influx of white men naturally causes uneasiness amongst Indians and leads to extravagant demands.'[47]

The federal government's responses to petitions by Aboriginal peoples indicate that it viewed a treaty in the area to be worthwhile. The completion of the transcontinental railway through Moose Factory was seen as a priority in the region. Acting primarily out of a desire to facilitate economic development and railway construction, the federal government was anxious to enter into negotiations with Aboriginal people. As will be seen, Ontario's interests were less clear-cut.

Provincial Interests in Treaty Negotiations

In order to understand the Province of Ontario's interests surrounding the negotiation of Treaty 9, reference must be made to the *Ontario Boundaries Case*[48] and the *St. Catherine's Milling* decision.[49] The combined effect of the *Ontario Boundaries Case* and the *St. Catherine's Milling* decision was to settle a boundary and land dispute between Ontario and the federal government. The Privy Council in the *Ontario Boundaries Case* decided in Ontario's favour and held that the limit of the province extended west to a line drawn due north from the northwest corner of the Lake of the Woods and north to the English River, Lac Seul, Lake St. Joseph, and the headwaters of the Albany River. In the *St. Catherine's Milling* decision, the Privy Council rejected the federal government's claim that, by Treaty 3, it owned the natural resources of the lands within the limits of that treaty. Perhaps bolstered by its successes in the courts, the Province of Ontario continued to dispute federal claims to the area, including the status of reserve lands created by Treaty 3.

Finally, the two governments reached an agreement and settled their differences. Legislation was passed by both Canada[50] and Ontario[51] in 1891 entitled An Act for the Settlement of Certain Questions Between the Governments of Canada and Ontario Respecting Indian Lands. In 1894, the two governments agreed to the following term: 'that any future treaties with the Indians in respect of territory in Ontario to which they have not before the passing of the said statutes surrendered their claim aforesaid, shall be deemed to require the concurrence of Ontario.'[52] Given that much of Ontario was already covered by treaty, the above clause was likely aimed at the lands recently included within the boundaries of Ontario by virtue of the *Ontario Boundaries Case* and the Canada (Ontario Boundary) Act, 1889,[53] and which subsequently were to become the subject of Treaty 9.[54]

In July 1902, the federal government reiterated its agreement to consult with Ontario in matters surrounding the negotiation of treaties with Aboriginal peoples living in the province, this time with specific reference to the location of reserves. In an agreement between counsel for Ontario and Canada, both intervening in *Ontario Mining Co.* v. *Seybold*[55] before the Privy Council, it was stated:

> As to all Treaty Indian reserves in Ontario (including those covered by the Northwest Angle Treaty [Treaty 3], which are or shall be duly established pursuant to the statutory agreement of one thousand eight hundred and ninety-four), and which have been or shall be duly surrendered by the Indians to sell or lease for their benefit, Ontario agrees to confirm the titles heretofore made by the Dominion and that the Dominion shall have full power and authority to sell or lease and convey title in the fee simple or for any lesser estate ... The question as to whether other reserves in Ontario include precious metals to depend on the instruments and circumstances and law affecting each case respectively.[56]

A framework of understanding duly established, the federal government kept the Province of Ontario informed of its plans concerning the negotiation of Treaty 9, though the exchange of information between the two levels of government was minimal, and Ontario was not very enthusiastic about the whole affair. The province was notified early on of the federal government's intention to enter into negotiations with the Aboriginal population. The Osnaburgh petition to enter into a treaty was passed by Clifford Sifton, superintendent-general of Indian affairs to Ontario Indian Commissioner J.A. McKenna for comment, who suggested that Ontario should not be party to the treaty, insofar as Indian affairs were a federal responsibility, but called for an informal 'understanding' between the two levels of government.[57] McKenna also raised the possibility that extinguishment of Aboriginal title take the form of an adhesion to the 1850 Robinson-Huron Treaty.

Apart from the initial correspondence between Sifton and McKenna, there was little subsequent correspondence between the two levels of government until well after the federal government had finalized its intentions with respect to the proposed negotiations. In a 1904 letter to the Ontario commissioner of Crown lands, the deputy superintendent-general of Indian affairs, Frank Pedley, outlined the nature of the proposed treaty as finalized by federal officials:

> It is proposed to offer the Indians a maximum annuity of $4.00 a head and a gratuity at the first payment of the same amount once and for all. It is further proposed to set apart reserves of sufficient area in localities chosen by the Indians with special regard for their needs, which reserves should be held in trust by this Department, free of any claims of the Province for timber upon, or base or precious metals in, upon or under the soil. These Reserves should be surveyed and confirmed by the Ontario Government within one year after selection by the Indians or at any time after the expiry of one year upon the request of this Department. It is proposed to provide the ordinary educational facilities afforded by day schools to be established upon Reserves. It is contended that as the entire area of the land will, by this treaty, remain with the Province free for all Indian claims, the financial responsibility, as well as the provisions of reserves, should rest with the Province of Ontario.[58]

Subsequent correspondence between the federal government and Ontario attempted to delineate the nature and extent of Ontario's participation called for by the above agreements. Not surprisingly, Ontario resisted the imposition of any financial responsibility on the province.[59] The federal government attempted to persuade the province that it was on the verge of obtaining a bargain: 'The terms laid down upon which the treaty might be based are the maximum terms which would, in any event, be offered to the Indians. They are in effect the same as those fixed by the Robinson treaty, and the Government interested might be considered fortunate to cancel the Indian title at this time by considerations which were thought adequate in the year 1850.'[60]

Ontario and the federal government finally agreed on the terms of the proposed treaty in the summer of 1905, after Ontario delayed responding for almost a year. On 8 May 1905, Pedley again wrote to the commissioner of Crown lands urging the province to agree to the proposed terms 'before the Indians come into closer contact with white people, as they are apt to be easily influenced to make extra demands.'[61] Ontario responded on 1 June 1905, agreeing to the terms of the treaty but requesting two changes.

First, Ontario asked that one of the commissioners on the negotiating team be a provincial appointee. Second, it requested that the Aboriginal peoples not be permitted to choose the location of reserve lands but that this be the responsibility of the commissioners.[62] The federal government agreed to the first request but altered the second so that the text of the proposed treaty would contain the following clause addressing reserve lands: 'the location of the said reserves having been arranged between His Majesty's Commissioners and the Chiefs and Headmen as described in the schedule of Reserves hereunto attached.'[63]

In response to the above, the provincial treasurer suggested several further changes to the draft, including greater definition of provincial liability and a clause stipulating that no site suitable for the development of water power exceeding 500 H.P. was to be included within the boundaries of any reserve.[64] Three days later the federal government indicated their acceptance of the proposed changes. With respect to the proposed restriction on the location of reserves, Pedley reported to the superintendent-general of Indian affairs that it was 'not desirable to have Indians located near large centres of population which usually grow up around large falls where water power can be readily utilized for commercial purposes.'[65] An agreement was formally signed between the Province of Ontario and the federal government on 3 July 1905, and two federal commissioners, Duncan Campbell Scott and Samuel Stewart, and one provincial commissioner, Daniel McMartin, were appointed to negotiate the treaty.[66]

In the years following the negotiation of Treaty 9, Ontario appeared to veto requests for reserve lands located on or near locations suitable for water power development. The Mattagami Band requested a location near Kenogamissi Falls, but Ontario 'wouldn't allow that.'[67] Several years later, Ontario granted a power company the right to dam the falls to supply electricity to Timmins. In the process, the company flooded part of the reserve lands allotted to the Mattagami Band.[68] In following years, other hydroelectric generating stations would be constructed on the Abitibi and Mattagami Rivers: at Iroquois Falls in 1914, at Island Falls in 1921, at Smoky Falls in 1928, at Abitibi Canyon in 1936, at La Cave Rapids in 1952, at Otter Rapids in 1961, and at Little Long Rapids in 1963.[69] At least two pulp mills began production by 1930: the Iroquois Falls pulp mill in 1914, followed by the pulp mill at Smooth Rock Falls.

(3) The Terms of the Treaty

According to the written text of Treaty 9, the Aboriginal signatories agreed to 'cede, release, surrender and yield up to the Government of the Dominion of Canada, for His Majesty the King and His successors forever, all their rights, titles and privileges' to the land covered by the treaty's terms.[70] The written text also provided that the Aboriginal signatories agreed to 'conduct and behave themselves as good loyal subjects of His

Majesty the King' and 'in all respects, obey and abide by the law.'[71] In return, each Aboriginal person under the treaty was to receive eight dollars for 1905 and four dollars for each year following, and each chief was to receive a flag and a copy of the treaty itself. The federal government also promised to pay the salaries of school teachers, and to provide adequate educational facilities and equipment.

More importantly for present purposes, Treaty 9 recognizes that Aboriginal people affected by the treaty have the 'right to pursue their usual vocations of hunting, trapping, and fishing throughout the tract surrendered.'[72] By the written terms of the treaty, these rights to hunt, trap, and fish on ancestral lands are subject to two qualifications. First, hunting, trapping, and fishing rights are 'subject to such regulations as may from time to time be made by the Government of the Country, acting under the authority of His Majesty.'[73] Second, hunting, trapping, and fishing rights do not extend to tracts of land 'as may be required or taken up from time to time for settlement, mining, lumbering, trading and other purposes.'[74] With respect to the creation of reserves, the government undertook to put aside reserves for the bands represented at the signing, leaving the location to be arranged between the treaty commissioners and the relevant Aboriginal spokespersons. As stated, the treaty also provided that no sites suitable for the development of water power exceeding 500 H.P. were to be included within the boundaries of any reserve. Aboriginal people were also prohibited from selling or otherwise alienating reserve lands to any body or person other than the federal government.

The following extract from the treaty commissioners' final report to the superintendent-general of Indian affairs captures the views of the commissioners as to the meaning and effect of the terms of Treaty 9:

> Cession was taken of the tract described in the treaty, comprising about 90,000 square miles, and, in addition, by the adhesion of certain Indians whose hunting grounds lie in a northerly direction from the Albany river, which may be roughly described as territory lying between that river and a line drawn from the northeast angle of Treaty No. 3, along the height of land separating the waters which flow into Hudson Bay by the Severn and Winisk from those which flow into James Bay by the Albany and Attawapiskat, comprising about 40,000 square miles. Gratuity was paid altogether to 1,617 Indians, representing a total population, when all the absentees are paid and allowance made for names not on the list, of 2,500 approximately. Throughout all the negotiations we carefully guarded against making any promises over and above those written into the treaty which might afterwards cause embarrassment to the governments concerned. No outside promises were made, and the Indians cannot, and we

confidently believe do not, expect any other concessions than those set forth in the document to which they gave their adherence. It was gratifying throughout to be met by these Indians with such a show of cordiality and trust, and to be able fully to satisfy what they believed to be their claims upon the governments of this country. The treatment of the reserve question, which in this treaty was most important, will, it is hoped, meet with approval. For the most part the reserves were selected by the commissioners after conference with the Indians. They have been selected in situations which are especially advantageous to their owners, and where they will not in any way interfere with railway development or the future commercial interests of the country. While it is doubtful whether the Indians will ever engage in agriculture, these reserves, being of a reasonable size, will give a secure and permanent interest in the land which the indeterminate possession of a large tract could never carry. No valuable water-powers are included in the allotments. The area set apart is, approximately, 374 square miles in the Northwest Territories and 150 square miles in the Province of Ontario. When the vast quantity of waste and, at present, unproductive land, surrendered is considered, these allotments must, we think, be pronounced most reasonable.[75]

Despite the clarity of the views of the treaty commissioners as to the scope and effect of Treaty 9, many of its terms are in fact highly ambiguous and admit of numerous potential interpretations. The agreement to 'cede, release, surrender and yield up to the Government of the Dominion of Canada, for His Majesty the King and His successors forever, all ... rights, titles and privileges whatsoever' at first glance suggests that Aboriginal signatories relinquished all their Aboriginal rights to the Crown. To what extent should the wording of this clause determine the treaty's legal effect? The treaty also recognizes continued rights to hunt, trap, and fish. What is the relationship between recognized hunting, trapping, and fishing rights and the provision to 'cede, release, surrender and yield up rights to the land'? Moreover, beyond the two qualifications placed upon their exercise, Treaty 9 does not define in any way the nature of hunting, trapping, or fishing rights. Are those rights created by the treaty or does the treaty simply retain prior Aboriginal rights? If the latter, then Aboriginal signatories did not in fact relinquish all of their land rights to the Crown, and retained continued hunting, trapping, and fishing rights as incidents of a modified version of Aboriginal title recognized by the terms of the treaty. The scope of hunting, trapping, and fishing rights is equally ambiguous. Does the recognition of a right to fish entail some control over the use to which water can be put? Does a right to fish, for example, include a right to engage in the activity of fishing or more broadly a right to regulate fishing or a right to an undisturbed supply of fish? Do the rights to hunt and trap include some protection against non-Aboriginal activity that threatens the effective enjoyment of those rights? Does the treaty contemplate any rights to water either on or off reserve lands?

Moreover, nowhere in the treaty is there any description of the extent of the discretion accorded to the 'Government of the Country' to regulate the exercise of hunting, trapping, and fishing rights. To whom does the phrase 'Government of the Country' apply? To what types of governmental action does it refer? Nor is there any clarification of the ambiguities contained in the second qualification placed upon the exercise of hunting, trapping, and fishing rights, namely, that those rights do not extend to tracts of land 'as may be required or taken up from time to time for settlement, mining, lumbering, trading and other purposes.' By what means are lands to be 'taken up for settlement' or other purposes? It is also unclear what 'other purposes' can serve to restrict the exercise of hunting, trapping, and fishing rights. Moreover, to what extent can activity occur on lands taken up for listed or unlisted purposes? The scope of hunting, trapping, and fishing rights, as well as the qualifications placed on the exercise of such rights, admit of numerous interpretations. In light of the aforementioned jurisprudence of the Supreme Court of Canada on the legal principles of treaty interpretation, resort ought to be made to Aboriginal understandings of the treaty and relevant case law in order to clarify the treaty's terms.

There are two useful sources of Aboriginal understandings and expectations of Treaty 9. First, the numerous petitions made by Aboriginal people to the government for a treaty around the turn of the century, described earlier,[76] illustrate the reasons why Aboriginal people felt it desirable to enter into a treaty with the federal government. As stated, Aboriginal leaders desired to enter into a treaty with the Crown in order to offset the social and economic damage that had befallen their people as a result of railway construction and increased settlement. Some form of protection was sought in relation to continued Aboriginal hunting, trapping, and fishing on ancestral lands in the face of economic and railway development and competition by non-Aboriginal hunting, trapping, and fishing. Financial aid was also requested to offset some of the economic hardships faced by Aboriginal peoples in the area. In short, the petitions illustrate that the Aboriginal people wanted to maintain traditional ways of life in the face of economic development and increased settlement. Second, discussed below, there are a number of documented accounts of Aboriginal understandings of the terms and effect of Treaty 9 at the time of signing.

Aboriginal Understandings of the Treaty

Duncan Campbell Scott, the chief negotiator for the federal government, described his sense of the understanding of the Aboriginal population at Osnaburgh of Treaty 9 in the following terms: 'They were to make certain promises and we were to make certain promises, but our purpose and our reasons were alike unknowable. What could they grasp of the pronouncement on the Indian tenure which had been delivered by the law lords of the Crown, what of the elaborate negotiations between a dominion and a province which had made the treaty possible, what of the sense of traditional policy which brooded over the whole? Nothing. So there was no basis for argument.'[77] According to Commissioner Scott, when he listed the benefits that would accrue to the Aboriginal people at Osnaburgh, the first stop of the treaty party, Chief Missabay 'express[ed] the fear that, if they signed the treaty, they would be compelled to reside upon the reserve to be set apart for them, and would be deprived of the fishing and hunting privileges which they now enjoy.'[78] According to documents appended to Treaty 9, the commissioners assured Chief Missabay that 'their fears in regard to both of these matters were groundless, as their present manner of making their livelihood would be in no way interfered with.'[79] Duncan Campbell Scott wrote later that Chief Missabay was informed that his people 'were not expected to give up their hunting-grounds, that they might hunt and fish throughout all the country just as they had done in the past, but they were to be good subjects of the King, their great father, whose messengers we were.'[80] The next morning, after consulting with his people, the Chief signed the treaty, and 'advised the young men to listen well to what the white men had to say and to follow their advice and not to exalt their own opinions above those of men who knew the world and had brought them such benefits.'[81] The Aboriginal people at Osnaburgh then recorded with the commissioners where they wanted their reserve.

By contrast, at Fort Hope, Chief Moonias had to be reassured that he and his people were giving up something in return for the benefits promised. According to Scott, 'he had his suspicions maybe that there was something concealed in a bargain where all the benefits seemed to be on one side. "Ever since I was a little boy," he said, "I have to pay well for everything, even if it was only a few pins or a bit of braid, and now you come with money and I have to give nothing in exchange." He was mighty pleased when he understood that he was giving something that his great father the King would value highly.'[82] The Fort Hope people were also reassured 'that hunting and fishing, in which occupations they were not to be interfered with, should for many years prove lucrative sources of revenue.'[83] A similar process of description, questions, and explanations was followed at each stop of the treaty party.

According to Morrison,

it would be difficult to argue that the treaty had not been negotiated. After all, the Indian people were given the chance for questions and discussion, even if they didn't always take advantage of it. The commissioners themselves, on their return to Ottawa at the end of August 1906, certainly had no doubts about what they'd accomplished. They reported that they had taken a cession of that part of Ontario described in the treaty (about 90,000 square miles) as well as of another 40,000 or so square miles in the Northwest Territories; and it gave them great pleasure to refer to the 'evident desire of the Indians at all points visited to display their loyalty to the government by the reception given to the commissioners and also by the recognition of the benefits conferred upon them by the Treaty.'[84]

Morrison concludes, however, that what the Aboriginal people believed was that they were being guaranteed the right to continue to hunt and fish as before. In his view, had they known that the treaty permitted Ontario to allow the exploitation of timber and mineral resources, and non-Aboriginal hunting and fishing on surrendered lands, 'most of the Albany River bands would probably have refused to participate. On the other hand, the bands on James Bay, as well as those closest to the railway line, might well have signed the treaty anyway – both because they would have felt they had no real alternative, and because ... the commissioners were very successful at promoting the tangible benefits of adherence to the treaty.'[85] Morrison refers to the testimony of an eyewitness to the negotiations at the Mattagami post, who, seventy years later, recalled the commissioners promising the Aboriginal people that they could hunt on surrendered lands as before. 'If there was any clause in the Treaty that was put in there against that, the Indians didn't understand it, and I know that quite well, because they didn't understand half of what was going on anyway.'[86] Morrison also refers to an interview given by James Wesley, who attended the signing ceremony at Fort Albany as a young boy. According to Wesley, the Aboriginal people at Fort Albany were told not to worry, 'because there will not be any legislation governing trapping, hunting animals and hunting birds and fishing if you are in favour of the Treaty.'[87] In the words of Wesley,

Duncan came down from the Albany River and the people were told one day ahead of time that there would be a meeting ... [Duncan said:] 'I am here under the British Government to tell you people if you are interested in a proposal from the British Government for you to give up your land for the government to look after. And if you are in favour of the idea give us your land. You will be given $8.00 a year when you have given us your land. We will also give $8.00 to all the people that are born from you. And also you will be visited by the doctor yearly and he will administer medicine and without charge to you people. Do not be afraid because there will not be any legislation governing trapping, hunting animals and hunting birds and fishing if you are in favour of the Treaty. If something happens to you as to sickness or need of help the Government will help you, all the people from Albany, Attawapiskat, Winisk, Fort Severn will have this help. This will be all for now; I will give you one hour to think it over. If you do not accept this treaty, the government will do whatever it wants with you. Where we have come from, all the Indians have agreed to sign treaty; if you don't you will find it hard for yourselves.'[88]

A similar sentiment was expressed by an anonymous member of the Fort Hope Band:

When the government came here, the people already knew that other treaties were signed. But you have to remember they still didn't know much about what was happening. Here was the government promising all kinds of things, like a reserve and annuity payments, and all the people had to do was promise their allegiance to the King.

But of course they didn't know the full implications, and there's little doubt about that. They didn't know they were signing away all their land for a reserve the government would control anyway, and they certainly didn't know the annuity payment, which was worth a lot of money then, would be worth nothing today.[89]

Similarly, John Fletcher of Moose Factory testified before the 1978 Royal Commission on the Northern Environment that during the negotiations at Moose Factory the commissioners promised that hunting rights would 'never be taken away' and that the Aboriginal 'way of life' would not change.[90]

In 1987, John Long began to interview and record elders who had knowledge and memories of the negotiations at Fort Albany in 1905:

The elders sat around a table, the purpose of the meeting was explained briefly in Cree, and they were encouraged to speak in Cree without interruption (except to switch tapes). In all, some twelve hours of narrative were recorded from twenty-nine elders, and each received a gift of cigarettes or groceries. It can be reported ... that the leaders at Kashechewan know which 'signatories' could read and write in the Cree syllabics, even though they made the mark of an 'X' on the treaty ... Marius Spence of Fort Albany explained why all the Xs looked the same: an official from the treaty party held the pen and made the mark, with Indian leaders merely touching the top of the pen ...

Comparing the treaty document with what little we know of Cree oral tradition ... it is not clear whether the Indians understood that there was a land surrender; they expected that they would share the resources (Moose Factory and Kashechewan) and act as custodian (Moose Factory); they would also retain their right to hunt, their way of life and culture (Moose Factory).[91]

Long argues that the written text of the treaty conflicts with Aboriginal oral agreements and understandings of the negotiations.

The records of the oral agreement conflict with the text of the signed treaty on several points. The written treaty is a complex legal document; with the oral agreement some simple facts were stated and the idea of a parental relationship was encouraged. In the treaty document, there is a surrender of 99 percent of the Indians' lands, while the oral agreement at Osnaburg states that hunting grounds are not surrendered and at Fort Hope only the useless land is lost; there is no evidence that the Indians consented to a 'surrender' – any land transfer might more properly be called an acquisition by the Crown. The signed treaty states that harvesting (hunting, fishing, trapping) is subject to regulation by Canada; at Osnaburg and Fort Hope the oral agreement guarantees no interference. The government's treaty grants privileges; the Indians' treaty grants rights.[92]

Long's last point should not be overlooked. He is of the view that some Aboriginal signatories may have been aware that they would have to obey Canadian law. Duncan Campbell Scott has stated that, in negotiations with the Ojibwa at Fort Hope, he informed them that 'by signing the treaty they pledged themselves not to interfere with white men who might come into the country surveying, prospecting, hunting or in other occupations; that they must respect the laws of the land in every particular.'[93] One can only speculate as to what Aboriginal signatories thought when he referred to 'the laws of the land,' yet even assuming that they understood the reference to be to Canadian law, Long makes the simple point that 'they probably never imagined that those laws could override the treaty promises.'[94]

Hunting, Trapping, and Fishing Rights

As stated,[95] Treaty 9 recognizes that Aboriginal people have the 'right to pursue their usual vocations of hunting, trapping, and fishing throughout the tract surrendered.' The previous survey indicates that Aboriginal signatories to the treaty were unanimous in their understanding that the treaty permitted their people to continue to hunt, trap, and fish over surrendered lands as they had done in the past. When the treaty is seen against the backdrop of the petitions made to governmental officials surrounding the turn of the century, it is clear that Aboriginal people viewed it as a means of protecting their traditional ways of life, especially hunting, trapping, and fishing, from non-Aboriginal incursion. In fact, the evidence suggests that this objective was the main, if not the only, reason for entering into the treaty. To reiterate Morrison, the interest of Aboriginal peoples in entering into a treaty with the Crown was directly proportionate to their proximity to non-Aboriginal economic development and increased settlement.[96]

The evidence also suggests that a guarantee of continued hunting, trapping, and fishing rights was a precondition for at least some of the Aboriginal signatories; some would not have signed the document had they been told that it did not contain such a guarantee. Morrison is of the view that other bands, such as the bands on James Bay, may well have signed in any event.[97] Assuming this to be the case, however, the important question for analysis is not whether the James Bay bands would have signed Treaty 9 had they been told that it would not protect hunting, trapping, and fishing rights, but instead whether the parties understood the treaty to guarantee those rights. If such a guarantee was understood, then the treaty ought to be interpreted in light of such an understanding. More specifically, the right to hunt, trap, and fish on ancestral lands ought to be viewed as a guarantee from the Crown that entitled Aboriginal peoples, subject to the effect of the two qualifications contained in the treaty's text, to continue their ways of life on ancestral lands despite non-Aboriginal settlement and economic development. The evidence strongly indicates this to be the case, and there is no evidence to suggest that any of the parties were of a contrary view.

An expansive interpretation of the right to hunt, trap, and fish would be consonant with the legal principles of treaty interpretation outlined previously. As previously stated, the Supreme Court of Canada in *Simon* called for an interpretation of the right to hunt which ensured that the treaty was an 'effective source of hunting rights.'[98] For Treaty 9 to be an effective source of hunting, trapping and fishing rights, those rights ought to be interpreted as including not only the right to engage in the activities of hunting, fishing, and trapping but also, as in the case of *Simon*, the right to engage in activities 'reasonably incidental' to the activities themselves.[99] Moreover, when one begins to examine the reasons for protecting rights to hunt, fish, and trap, it becomes clear that what Aboriginal people were seeking to protect was their traditional ways of life from non-Aboriginal erosion. Hunting, trapping, and fishing were and are critical components of an Aboriginal economy threatened by non-Aboriginal incursion. Hunting, trapping, and fishing rights in Treaty 9 thus represent an attempt to protect Aboriginal economic, social, and commercial practices from the side-effects of railway construction and, more generally, non-Aboriginal economic development.[100] As such, they ought to be viewed as not only conferring the right to engage in the activity listed by the terms of the treaty but also including the right to expect that such activity will continue to be successful, measured by reference to the fruits of past practice.[101]

The above approach also entails a recognition of a right approximating a treaty right to water,[102] a fact acknowledged by the Department of Indian Affairs with respect to water flowing through reserve land as early as 1920: 'I am satisfied that the Courts in construing the treaties between the Crown and the Indians under which reserves were set apart would follow the view taken by the American Courts that there must be implied in such treaties an implied undertaking by the Crown to conserve for the use of the Indians the right to take for domestic, agricultural purposes all such water as may be necessary, both now and in the future development of the reserve from the waters which either traverse or are the boundaries of reserves.'[103] American jurisprudence to which the above quote refers supports the conclusion that Aboriginal peoples have, by virtue of treaties establishing reserves in exchange for the surrender of ancestral lands, not only rights to an uninterrupted flow of water through reserve land[104] but also rights to water to sustain hunting and fishing rights.[105] Treaty rights to water to support hunting and fishing rights were described by Justice Fletcher in *United States* v. *Adair* in the following terms:

> The right to water reserved to further the Tribe's hunting and fishing purposes is unusual in that it is basically non-consumptive. See 1 R. Clark, Waters and Water Law s. 55.2, at 578-81 (1967). The holder of such a right is not entitled to withdraw water from the stream for agricultural, industrial, or other consumptive uses (absent independent consumptive rights). Rather, the entitlement consists of the right to prevent other appropriators from deleting the streams' waters below a protected level in any area where the non-consumptive right applies ... In this respect, the water right reserved for the Tribe to hunt and fish has no corollary in the common law of appropriations.[106]

Richard Bartlett further explains the difference between treaty water rights, which apply to water flowing through reserve land and may extend to waters beyond reserve land depending upon the terms of the treaty at issue, and riparian rights to water, a version of which attach to waters flowing through reserve land.

> Water rights derived from treaty are in addition to riparian rights – those rights to water which were recognized by the common law as a natural incident to the right to the soil itself. They are 'natural' rights derived from possession of land adjacent to water. They do not depend upon any express or presumed grant. The riparian land owner 'has the right to have [the water] come to him in its natural state, in flow, quantity and quality, and go from him without obstruction.' Riparian rights entail the right to the natural flow of the water – that it should run as it has been accustomed to run. Treaty water rights are substantially broader than those derived from Indian ownership of riparian rights to land. But riparian rights do pose a formidable constraint upon upstream uses. Hydroelectric generation which depletes the water supply, alters the flow or affects water quality will breach the rights of Indian riparian landowners. Riparian rights suffice to protect the traditional and domestic uses of water by Indian people.[107]

There has been little Canadian jurisprudence on treaty rights to water, although the judgment of the British Columbia Court of Appeal in *Saanichton Marine Ltd.* v. *Claxton*[108] offers some guidance on the subject. In *Saanichton Marine*, at issue was whether the Saanich people of Vancouver Island could rely on a treaty negotiated in 1852 with the governor of British Columbia to bar the construction of a marina in Saanichton Bay. The treaty provided that the Saanich people 'are at liberty ... to carry on [their] fisheries as formerly.' Justice Hinkson for a unanimous Court held that 'the right granted to the Indians by treaty is unique in the sense that it is difficult to describe it within the framework of traditional legal terminology. While the right does not amount to a proprietary interest in the sea bed nor a contractual right to a fishing ground, it does protect the Indians against infringement of their right to carry on the fishery, as they have done for centuries, in the shelter of Saanichton Bay.'[109] Moreover, Hinkson held that 'the right granted by the treaty is broader than the words of the treaty may on their face indicate.' Applying Chief Justice Dickson's judgment in *Simon*,[110] he concluded that 'the right to carry on the fishery encompasses other rights which are incidental to the right granted by the treaty,' that 'the effect of the treaty is to afford to the Indians an independent source of protection of their right to carry on their fisheries as formerly,' and that it included as well 'the right to travel to and from the fishery.'[111] In the result, Hinkson upheld a permanent injunction against the construction of the marine. *Saanichton Marine* is an indication that the judiciary is willing to interpret a treaty right to fish in an expansive fashion, as approximating a right to water.

The Relationship Between Treaty Rights and the
Land Surrender Provision

The fact that Aboriginal signatories generally viewed Treaty 9 as a means of protecting their traditional economies, and in particular their rights to hunt, trap, and fish throughout the treaty area, has important implications for the meaning to be given to the treaty's land-surrender provision. Aboriginal signatories no doubt realized that reserves would be set aside for their exclusive occupation and use, but they were also concerned that their use of the rest of the lands covered by the treaty not be curtailed. In light of the many assurances made to them by the treaty commissioners that they would not be confined to the reserves and that their traditional pursuits on other lands would not be interfered with, could they have understood the treaty to involve an absolute surrender to the Crown of their rights to those lands? It seems highly unlikely. On the contrary, the record indicates that the Aboriginal signatories understood that the government wanted some of those lands for settlement and other purposes, subject always to the guarantee that the Aboriginal use which their economies required would be preserved and protected. In other words, the historical record supports the conclusion that Aboriginal signatories thought that treaty lands outside of their reserves would be shared.

In this light, reference to *Re Paulette's Application* is instructive.[112] In *Re Paulette*, Justice Morrow held that notwithstanding language in Treaties 8 and 11 similar to the land-surrender provision in Treaty 9, there existed sufficient doubt whether Aboriginal title had been extinguished, and hinted that 'the treaties were mere "peace" treaties and did not effectively terminate Indian title – certainly to the extent that it covered what is normally referred to as surface rights – the use of the land for hunting, trapping and fishing.'[113]

When the land-surrender provision contained in the text of Treaty 9 is read in light of the treaty's guarantee of hunting, trapping, and fishing rights, one is driven to the same conclusion as that reached by Justice Morrow in *Re Paulette*. Properly understood, the guarantee of hunting, trapping, and fishing rights involves much more than a licence to use Crown lands for those pursuits until they are 'taken up' for purposes authorized by the treaty. From the perspective of Aboriginal people in the area, the most important aspect of Aboriginal title appears to have been retained. Aboriginal signatories may have thought that they were giving up some of their rights, such as exclusive rights to open mines and engage in lumbering, but they did not view the treaty as surrendering the right to use the lands for their traditional pursuits. Hunting, trapping, and fishing rights form part of the bundle of Aboriginal title enjoyed by Aboriginal people in the area under consideration, and, in the words of Justice Cory in *Badger*, have been 'recognized in a somewhat limited form by the treaty.'[114]

At common law, at least some rights associated with Aboriginal title presumably are exclusive.[115] Exclusivity would entail that non-Aboriginal hunting, trapping, and fishing could not occur on surrendered lands without Aboriginal consent. Since some non-Aboriginal use apparently was acceptable to the Aboriginal signatories, however, a more modest interpretation is that some non-Aboriginal hunting, trapping, and fishing activity was contemplated by Aboriginal people. Even if this is the case, Aboriginal hunting, trapping, and fishing rights recognized in Treaty 9 entail that Aboriginal hunting, trapping, and fishing would at least enjoy priority over non-Aboriginal hunting, trapping, and fishing in the event of conflict. Otherwise, Aboriginal people would have no greater rights than the general public, which would render the treaty guarantee meaningless.

Given the aforementioned scope of treaty rights, more relevant for present purposes is the fact that natural resource exploration and development activity by the Crown or third parties, in some cases at least, will infringe Treaty 9 rights to hunting, trapping, and fishing. It therefore becomes necessary to discuss whether and to what extent the Crown or a third party can engage in such activity. The next two parts of this paper address the extent to which the government of Ontario has the constitutional authority to pass legislation authorizing or decreeing natural resource exploration and development activity on lands covered by Treaty 9, and the extent to which the terms of the treaty themselves allow for such activity to occur.

(4) Treaty Rights and the Distribution of Legislative Authority

Prior to 1982, Canadian law did not view Aboriginal treaty rights as binding upon the exercise of legislative authority. At best, they were viewed as contractual rights against the Crown, enforceable against Crown inaction, but subject to the overarching legislative authority of Parliament and the provinces.[116] Each level of government was entitled to pass laws regulating treaty rights, so long as such legislation was a valid exercise of legislative authority. Parliament was entitled to pass legislation regulating the exercise of treaty rights, for example, if it could be shown that the pith and substance of the law in question fell within the legislative authority of Parliament. Section 91(24) of the Constitution Act, 1867, confers on Parliament legislative jurisdiction over 'Indians, and Lands reserved for the Indians,'[117] which has been held as authorizing Parliament to pass laws directly in relation to Aboriginal peoples; in addition, Parliament was also entitled to pass laws pursuant to other heads of power listed in section 91 that have the effect of regulating Aboriginal and treaty rights.[118]

By contrast, under the Constitution Act, 1867, a province is not entitled to pass legislation directly in relation to Aboriginal people; legislation to this effect would be in pith and substance legislation in relation to 'Indians, and Lands reserved for the Indians' and therefore *ultra vires*.[119] As stated by the Court in *Badger*, 'the regulation of hunting rights would ordinarily come within the jurisdiction of the Federal government and not the Province.'[120] Generally speaking, however, a province prior to 1982 was entitled to pass legislation with a valid provincial purpose that has the effect of applying to Aboriginal peoples, so long as such legislation does not invade federal jurisdiction. A provincial law will intrude on federal jurisdiction over 'Indians, and Lands reserved for the Indians' if it does not have a uniform territorial operation, i.e., where it is not a law of 'general application,'[121] or where it 'impairs the status or capacity' of Aboriginal peoples.[122] 'Status' and 'capacity' have been interpreted as referring to legal status under federal law, namely, 'Indian status ... [or] rights so closely connected with Indian status that they should be regarded as necessary incidents of status such for instance as registrability, membership in a band, the right to participate in the election of chiefs and band councils, reserve privileges, etc.'[123]

Whether provincial laws of general application that affect the exercise of treaty rights necessarily intrude on federal jurisdiction is an open question. On the one hand, general principles of constitutional interpretation would suggest that so long as the law in question has a valid provincial purpose, it can affect the exercise of treaty rights.[124] On the other hand, earlier jurisprudence has held that provincial legislation that affects hunting rights guaranteed by treaty is automatically *ultra vires* a province, regardless of purpose.[125]

Regardless of the above ambiguity, Parliament, by virtue of section 88 of the Indian Act,[126] has incorporated provincial laws of general application that intrude upon 'the essence of federal exclusive power under section 91(24)' of the Constitution Act, 1867, except to the extent that they conflict with treaty rights.[127] Under the basic constitutional principle that federal law is paramount over conflicting provincial legislation,[128] section 88 of the Indian Act has the effect of shielding treaty rights from the operation of provincial law.[129] Although treaty rights are subject to the overarching legislative authority of the Canadian state, such legislative authority is subject to the principles governing its distribution between Parliament and the provinces, and Parliament has decreed in section 88 that treaty rights are to be immune from provincial law.[130]

Any provincial law relied on as authorization for economic development either by the Crown or by a third party is subject to the constitutional principles mentioned above. That is, any provincial legislation authorizing or decreeing economic activity must not conflict with rights accorded to Aboriginal people by virtue of Treaty 9. Governmental or third party initiatives undertaken pursuant to *intra vires* provincial legislation that threaten Aboriginal hunting, trapping, and fishing rights, and activity reasonably incidental to their continued existence on surrendered ancestral lands must find authorization from Treaty 9 itself. Otherwise, section 88 of the Indian Act provides that treaty rights are to prevail in the event they conflict with provincial laws of general application.[131] Accordingly, the next part is devoted to an analysis of the two qualifications placed on hunting, trapping, and fishing rights contained in Treaty 9. The impact of section 35(1) of the Constitution Act, 1982, on Treaty 9 rights is discussed in part 6.

(5) Treaty Limitations on Hunting, Trapping, and Fishing Rights

As stated, there are two qualifications placed on hunting, trapping, and fishing rights by the terms of Treaty 9 itself. First, hunting, trapping, and fishing rights are 'subject to such regulations as may from time to time be made by the Government of the Country, acting under the authority of His Majesty.' It is extremely doubtful that the Province of Ontario or a third party can rely on this qualification in support of provincial legislative or regulatory initiatives decreeing or authorizing economic activity which interferes with the exercise of hunting, trapping, and fishing rights. Courts have interpreted this proviso as applying only to regulations made by the federal government. In *R.* v. *Batisse*,[132] for example, Justice Bernstein stated:

> Forgetting for the moment the promises and assurances made to the Indians to entice them into the treaty, it seems to me that the ordinary rules of construction and interpretation indicate that the 'Government of the country' refers exclusively to the federal Government. It must be remembered that this treaty was negotiated in 1905, some 38 years after Confederation. The term 'the government' obviously refers to only one body. Had the words used been '*a* government' then the meaning would have been different. Furthermore, I have not been directed to any authority, historical or otherwise, where any Province after Confederation was referred to as a 'country.' In 1905 the only *Government of the country* was

the federal Government and this distinction between federal and provincial authorities was well known to all (including the Indians). Indeed, the very fact that the federal Government was referred to in two other non-identical terms confirms my view that the drafters of the treaty were not very careful with the technical terms used throughout the document. If the makers of the treaty intended to delegate authority to regulate the Indian hunting and fishing rights to the Government of the Province of Ontario, they would have specifically said so. I note, for example, that in the Agreement between the provincial and federal Government (to which the treaty specifically) referred, there was no hesitation in using the term 'the government of the province of Ontario' when referring to that body ...

The Indians who signed Treaty No. 9 were very concerned about their continuing right to hunt and fish over the ceded lands. The Reports of the Commissioners suggest that several of the signatories would not have executed the treaty unless they were assured of those rights. It cannot be said, therefore, that the proviso concerning those rights was included as an afterthought or as somehow incidental to the other terms. Indeed that particular term of the agreement was, in all likelihood, considered by the Indians to be the main form of consideration flowing to them. That being the case, it would be unreasonable to assume that either the federal Government or the Indians believed for a moment that those ancient rights could be unilaterally taken away by a third party. The Courts must not assume that His Majesty's Commissioners were attempting to trick or fool the Indians into signing an agreement under false pretences. Indians have, in general, assumed that their status is protected by the federal Government. If there is any ambiguity in the term 'the government of the country' (and I do not believe there is) then, in my view, such ambiguity should be resolved in favour of the Indian. I feel that this principle dictates that the term be interpreted as meaning the federal Government, which after all, has the constitutional duty to protect the rights and privileges of the Indians in Canada.[133]

Similarly, in *Cheechoo* v. *R.*,[134] Justice Maranger of the Ontario District Court, in reaching the same conclusion as Justice Bernstein in *R.* v. *Batisse*, stated that it was significant that Treaty 9 was made with the agreement of the federal government and the Province of Ontario. In his view, it would be 'logical to infer that any rights given to the province with respect to Treaty No. 9 would be recorded in that agreement.'[135] Since there was no explicit authorization for the province to limit or interfere with hunting, trapping, and fishing rights in the treaty itself, Justice Maranger was of the view that it should not be interpreted so as to authorize the application of provincial conservation legislation. This conclusion conforms with the Supreme Court of Canada's decision in *Badger* to the extent that the Court in *Badger* viewed provincial regulatory authority as flowing not from Treaty 8 but from a Natural Resources Transfer Agreement of 1930 applicable to the territory in question and not applicable to lands located in Ontario.[136]

The second qualification in Treaty 9 is the fact that hunting, trapping, and fishing rights do not extend to tracts of land 'as may be required or taken up from time to time for settlement, mining, lumbering, trading and other purposes.' It will be recalled that the written text of the treaty provides that Aboriginal signatories agreed to 'cede, release, surrender and yield up to the Government of the Dominion of Canada, for His Majesty the King and His successors forever, all their rights, titles and privileges' to the land covered by the terms of the treaty. Assuming but not deciding that Treaty 9 did extinguish some aspects of Aboriginal title to the land in question, namely, those aspects excluded from the treaty's recognition of continued hunting, trapping, and fishing rights, the effect of the surrender would have been to vest the province with at least partial title to the surrendered land.[137] This is due to the fact that section 109 of the Constitution Act, 1867, provides that all lands belonging to the province at the time of Confederation continue to belong to the province.[138]

Having at least partial title to the surrendered lands, by virtue of the combination of Treaty 9 and section 109 of the Constitution Act, 1867, would the province be in a position, either directly or by delegation to public or private entities, to engage in economic activity on such lands that conforms to the purposes listed in the terms of the treaty? As stated, the province's proprietary interest would not entitle the provincial legislature to pass laws regulating the exercise of hunting, trapping, and fishing rights, a matter held by the judiciary to be exclusively assigned by the treaty to the government of Canada. Would the province, however, be entitled to restrict the area over which such rights could be claimed by asserting its proprietary interest in accordance with the qualification contained in the treaty that hunting, trapping, and fishing rights do not extend to tracts of land 'as may be required or taken up from time to time for settlement, mining, lumbering, trading and other purposes'? In other words, do rights to hunt, fish, and trap over surrendered land automatically cease once land is 'taken up' for one or more of the purposes listed in the treaty?

An answer to this question may depend on whether the purpose is one that is actually listed in the treaty, or whether it falls under the phrase 'other purposes.' Hydroelectric power, for example, is not expressly listed as a purpose justifying geographic encroachment on hunting, trapping, and fishing rights. However, one interpretation of the treaty could be that hydroelectric activity falls within the general reference to 'other purposes' for which surrendered lands may be used for non-Aboriginal purposes, and that hydroelectric activity can therefore occur on surrendered lands without regard to continued hunting, trapping, and fishing rights.

Such an interpretation, however, would be antithetical to recent Supreme Court of Canada jurisprudence on the legal principles of treaty interpretation. As previously stated, the Court has held that 'treaties ... relating to Indians should be liberally construed and doubtful expressions resolved in favour of the Indians.'[139] The words, 'other purposes,' in Treaty 9 admit of several interpretations, ranging from an open-ended grant of discretion to governmental authorities and other non-Aboriginal parties to engage in commercial and other forms of development on lands otherwise reserved for Aboriginal hunting, trapping, and fishing, to a set of narrower interpretations that would place limits on the exercise of discretion accorded to governmental authorities and other parties.[140] One such narrower interpretation is that hydroelectric development is not an activity that falls within the reference to 'other purposes.'

There are several reasons to prefer an interpretation of 'other purposes' that would not confer open-ended discretion upon governmental authorities and third parties to use surrendered lands for any purpose whatsoever. First, to take again the example of hydroelectric development, the treaty lists the purposes for which the geographic scope of hunting, trapping, and fishing rights can be constrained, namely, 'settlement, mining, lumbering, trading and other purposes.' Specifically excluded from this list is hydroelectric development. Despite the fact that the Province of Ontario was expressly concerned that reserve land not be chosen near locations with hydroelectric potential, its omission from the express list of permitted activity on non-reserve land is significant. Had the drafters of the treaty intended the document to permit the Province of Ontario and other entities to engage in hydroelectric development on waters running through surrendered lands over which the Aboriginal people continue to enjoy hunting, trapping, and fishing rights, the treaty would have been explicit on the subject,[141] especially given that hydroelectric power is mentioned specifically in relation to the location of reserve lands.

One can only speculate about the reasons for its omission from the list of specifically authorized activity. Perhaps the province was of the view that, by virtue of previously enacted legislation, it already possessed the authority to engage in hydroelectric development on waters located on surrendered lands or to delegate such authority to third parties, and therefore viewed it unnecessary to list it in the terms of the treaty. This interpretation is consistent with the province's insistence that there be a clause stipulating that no site suitable for the development of water power exceeding 500 H.P. be included within the boundaries of any reserve. If the province was of the view that it already possessed legislative authority to engage in hydroelectric development, either directly or by delegation, such a clause would protect suitable sites from the possibility of Aboriginal claims based on statutory usufructuary interests in reserve lands.[142] If this is the case, however, the lawful authority to engage in hydroelectric development would stem not from the treaty, but instead from earlier legal entitlements, which would have to be tested against legal requirements for the extinguishment of Aboriginal title. If prior legislation or other legal entitlements did not extinguish Aboriginal title, including the Aboriginal right to enjoyment and use of water on ancestral lands, then the legal authority to use rivers and streams for hydroelectric purposes would be, up until the time of signing, subject to the incidents of Aboriginal title and constitutional principles governing the distribution of legislative authority.[143] Legislation passed subsequent to the signing of the treaty would equally be subject to the principles governing the distribution of legislative authority but also, after 1951 by virtue of the passage of section 88 of the Indian Act, to the terms of the treaty itself.

The essential point, however, is that if hydroelectric development was omitted from the terms of the treaty because the province was of the view that it possessed prior legal authority to engage in hydroelectric development, either directly or by delegation, this would only confirm that the province did not view the treaty as conferring legal authority to engage in such activity. In no way could the treaty be characterized as representing an agreement on the subject of hydroelectric development if the very party that desired to engage in hydroelectric activity did not view that document as authorizing such activity. Had Ontario known that its prior legal authority to engage in hydroelectric development would be subsequently questioned, it may well have approached the treaty negotiations differently and insisted on explicit reference to hydroelectric development. However, the Supreme Court of Canada has declared that treaties are to be interpreted by reference to 'the intention of the parties ... at the time it was concluded.'[144] The benefit of hindsight should not subsequently be used to rewrite the intent of the parties and actual understandings of the legal effect of the treaty.

Second, there is no record of any Aboriginal understandings at the time of signing that the effect of the treaty would be to permit the Province of Ontario or other parties to engage in hydroelectric development on waters running through lands over which Aboriginal people enjoy continued hunting, trapping, and fishing rights. Unlike 'settlement, mining, lumbering, [and] trading,' activities expressly listed in the treaty for which surrendered lands could be used, hydroelectric power came to the area subsequent to the signing of the treaty.[145] Aboriginal peoples living in the area at the time of signing likely had no exposure to or understanding of hydroelectric development. There is no record of any explanation offered of the clause prohibiting the establishment of reserves near sites suitable for hydroelectric development or that the provincial commissioner explained the reasons for the insertion of this clause to Aboriginal signatories. Nor is there any record of any explanation given to Aboriginal signatories that the words 'other purposes' were meant to contemplate future forms of economic development, let alone hydroelectric power. To reiterate Chief Commissioner Duncan Campbell Scott: 'They were to make certain promises and we were to make certain promises, but our purpose and our reasons were alike unknowable. What could they grasp of the pronouncement on the Indian tenure which had been delivered by the law lords of the Crown, what of the elaborate negotiations between a dominion and a province which had made the treaty possible, what of the sense of traditional policy which brooded over the whole? Nothing. So there was no basis for argument.'[146] Given that the Supreme Court of Canada has embraced the proposition that 'Indian treaties must be construed, not according to the technical meaning of their words, but in the sense in which they would naturally be understood by the Indians,'[147] the phrase 'other purposes' should not be interpreted to include activity not comprehended let alone understood by Aboriginal peoples at the time of signing.

Third, and more generally, there is no record of any explanation offered to Aboriginal signatories by the commissioners that either the qualification on hunting, trapping, and fishing rights, or the qualification that such rights are subject to regulation, would confer on governmental authorities the ability to unilaterally restrict the scope of hunting, trapping, and fishing rights. To the contrary, the record is conclusive on the fact that Aboriginal leaders believed that the treaty secured them the right to hunt, trap, and fish on ancestral lands. Protecting Aboriginal ways of life from increased settlement and commercial activity was the very reason Aboriginal peoples in the area sought to enter into a treaty with the Crown. An open-ended interpretation of either of the two qualifications on hunting, trapping, and fishing rights would confer an unbridled authority upon government actors to extinguish precisely that which Aboriginal signatories thought they were protecting.

As stated, the record does indicate that at least some Aboriginal signatories thought that they would have to obey Canadian law,[148] but there is nothing to suggest that they believed that Canadian law would supersede treaty rights to hunt, fish, and trap. In fact, the record suggests that at least some Aboriginal signatories would not have signed the treaty at all had they known that the treaty would be interpreted to permit the province to engage in or allow for economic development on ancestral lands.[149] Other signatories may have signed in any event, but this fact should not support interpreting the terms of the treaty contrary to their actual expectations that it protected hunting, trapping, and fishing rights.[150] Given that treaties are to be interpreted to serve as 'an effective source' of hunting, trapping, and fishing rights,[151] in light of 'the historical context and perception each party might have had as to the nature of the undertaking contained in the document under consideration,'[152] and that 'doubtful expressions [are] to be resolved in favour of the Indians,'[153] some limitations upon the exercise of discretion conferred on governmental authorities ought to be viewed as contained in the terms of the treaty itself. Reference to the landmark case of *Winters* v. *United States* is instructive: 'By a rule of interpretation of agreements and treaties with the Indians, ambiguities occurring will be resolved from the standpoint of the Indians. And the rule certainly will be applied to determine between two inferences, one of which could support the purpose of the agreement and the other impair or defeat it. On account of their relations to the government, it cannot be supposed that the Indians were about to exclude by formal words every inference which might militate against or defeat the declared purpose of themselves and the government.'[154]

In *Horse* v. *R.*,[155] Justice Estey for a unanimous Supreme Court of Canada viewed a similar qualification upon hunting and fishing rights in Treaty 6 as precluding an Aboriginal treaty right, subject to the interests of the property owner and the safety of others, to hunt on privately owned and occupied land, having regard to both the terms of the treaty and the intentions of the parties at the time of signing. *Horse* should not be viewed, however, as support for the proposition that the qualification on hunting, trapping, and fishing rights in Treaty 9 confers open-ended discretion upon government authorities to use surrendered lands for whatever purposes they see fit. In *Horse*, Justice Estey reached his conclusion by relying on extrinsic evidence in relation to Treaties 1, 3, and 4, which in his view suggested that Aboriginal signatories of those treaties understood they did not possess the right to hunt on private, occupied lands. He argued that during the negotiation of Treaty 6, Aboriginal signatories were told that the terms of Treaty 6 were identical to Treaties 1, 3, and 4, and that therefore Treaty 6 did not contemplate a right, subject to the interests of the property owner and the safety of others, to hunt on private, occupied land. Regardless of the actual merits of Justice Estey's argument,[156] its applicability to the issue of the extent of discretion conferred by Treaty 9 on governmental authorities to limit hunting, trapping, and fishing rights is questionable, if only because of the clear indications that Aboriginal signatories did not view Treaty 9 as conferring open-ended discretion upon governmental authorities to restrict the exercise of hunting, trapping, and fishing rights for any purpose. Moreover, *Horse* does not suggest that the similar provision in Treaty 6 confers unbridled authority on governmental authorities to restrict or extinguish rights otherwise provided for in the treaty. The record relied on by the Court in *Horse* speaks only to the narrower issue of the expectations of the parties to Treaty 6 with respect to hunting rights on lands taken up for settlement by private parties.[157] And, as a result of the Court's decision in *Badger*, *Horse* does not stand for the proposition that treaty rights can never be exercised on privately owned land; treaty rights can be exercised on private land that is not being put to a visible, incompatible use.

A final reason for interpreting Treaty 9 as not conferring an open-ended discretion on governmental authorities and other parties to unilaterally restrict the geographic scope of hunting, trapping, and fishing rights lies in the fact that the Supreme Court of Canada has held that the Crown is under a fiduciary obligation in its dealings with Aboriginal peoples. In *Guerin* v. *R.*,[158] the Court held the federal Crown liable for breach of a fiduciary obligation with respect to the leasing of reserve land belonging to the Musqueam Indian Band in British Columbia. The band had surrendered a portion of its land to the Crown to be leased to third parties as a golf club. The Crown in turn leased the land to the third party on terms not as attractive as those the band had been led to believe it would receive upon surrender. In finding for the band, Justice Dickson (as he then was), for a majority of the Court, held the Crown to be under a fiduciary obligation to deal with the surrendered lands for the benefit of the band. Due to the fact that "'the relative legal positions are such that one party is at the mercy of the other's discretion,'" Dickson was of the view that certain obligations attached to the Crown by virtue of its superior position to act in the best interests of the Indian band in its dealings with third parties.[159] Subsequent case law suggests that similar fiduciary obligations attach to the provincial, as well as the federal, Crown.[160]

The legal acknowledgment of a fiduciary obligation on the Crown in its dealings with Aboriginal peoples in general and with surrendered lands in particular has certain ramifications with respect to the constitutional position of Aboriginal peoples asserting treaty rights, a matter to be addressed in the final part of this paper. Its relevance at this juncture is that one interpretation of the text of Treaty 9 places Aboriginal peoples at the mercy of provincial authorities by permitting the province to unilaterally restrict the scope of hunting, trapping, and fishing rights over surrendered land by engaging in activity not contemplated by Aboriginal peoples at the time of signing. The existence of a fiduciary obligation is designed to rein in otherwise unbridled legal authority that ensues to the more powerful party by attaching legal duties on the exercise of that authority. Limitations ought to be placed on provincial authorities in the exercise of the grant of power represented by the second qualification on hunting, trapping, and fishing rights in Treaty 9. The recognition of a fiduciary obligation on the provincial Crown would entail that the type of activity for which lands are taken up not conflict with Aboriginal interests. The exercise of provincial authority in this respect ought to conform to the Crown's fiduciary responsibilities and be in the best interests of the Aboriginal population in the area. In other words, the Crown's fiduciary obligations prevent it from taking lands for 'other purposes' if those purposes conflict with Aboriginal interests.

In summary, there are strong reasons for not interpreting generally the second qualification on the exercise of hunting, trapping, and fishing rights as conferring an unbridled discretion on governmental authorities and other parties to use surrendered lands for any 'purpose' whatsoever, and specifically as conferring the unconstrained authority on the province, either directly or indirectly, to engage in economic development contrary to the interests of Aboriginal people living in the area. As stated, nowhere in the record is there any suggestion that Aboriginal peoples viewed Treaty 9 as permitting the Crown to interfere with hunting, trapping, and fishing rights. The grant of authority to 'take up' lands, either for listed or unlisted purposes, is subject to the Crown's overarching fiduciary obligation to exercise its discretion in accordance with the interests of Aboriginal peoples. Such an obligation entails that its discretion not be used to interfere with hunting, trapping, and fishing rights that can be asserted on surrendered lands. Any ensuing restrictions of the geographic area where Aboriginal people are entitled to hunt, trap, and fish must avoid interfering with the exercise of such rights or, in the alternative, must give top priority to the Aboriginal interests at stake.

(6) Section 35(1) of the Constitution Act, 1982

A final factor in considering the extent to which Treaty 9 authorizes or constrains government or third party economic development within the treaty area is the effect of section 35(1) of the Constitution Act, 1982, which constitutionally recognizes and affirms existing Aboriginal and treaty rights. As a result of the Court's decision in *Badger*, the judiciary is to apply a framework of analysis equivalent to the approach adopted in *R. v. Sparrow*[161] when confronted with an alleged legislative infringement of treaty rights. That is, the judiciary is to regard unextinguished treaty rights as existing in 1982 and thus constitutionally recognized and affirmed by section 35(1) in their original form. Statutes regulating their exercise prior to that time do not delineate their current scope.[162] Legislation interfering with the exercise of those rights would have to be shown to have a valid legislative objective and to infringe the rights as little as possible. Adequate consultation with the Aboriginal peoples whose rights were affected would also be required.[163]

As a result, given that they were not legislatively extinguished prior to 1982,[164] Treaty 9 rights to hunt, trap, and fish on surrendered Aboriginal lands are constitutionally recognized and affirmed by section 35(1). Their scope is not limited by legislation regulating their exercise prior to that time. Therefore, section 35(1) recognizes the right of Aboriginal peoples to assert exclusivity or at least priority of use in the event of conflict with non-Aboriginal hunting, trapping, and fishing; the right to engage in activities reasonably incidental to those pursuits; the right to expect that those pursuits will continue to be successful; and a right approximating a right to water. Moreover, the honour of the Crown and the fiduciary relationship between the Crown and Aboriginal peoples require that valid legislative objectives be met with as little infringement of these treaty rights as possible, and only after consultation with the Aboriginal peoples concerned.[165]

In addition to subjecting legislative infringements of Treaty 9 rights to a justificatory test, section 35(1) may affect the way the treaty itself is interpreted and applied. Section 35(1) recognizes and affirms the treaty rights *'of the Aboriginal peoples,'* not the treaty rights of the Crown. In other words, treaty rights of the Aboriginal peoples are constitutionalized, while the treaty rights of the Crown are not. The *Sparrow* decision held that because Aboriginal rights are constitutional, they take priority over other rights which are not constitutional. Applying that conclusion to Treaty 9 should result in a new perspective on the relative strength of the rights of each party. Earlier in this paper, it was suggested that the fiduciary obligation which the Crown owes to Aboriginal peoples may prevent it from taking lands for 'other purposes' under the hunting, trapping, and fishing rights provision if those purposes conflict with Aboriginal interests.[166] The *Sparrow* decision strengthens this view by reaffirming the fiduciary obligation in the context of section 35(1) and requiring that the rights of the Aboriginal peoples be given priority over other rights. In other words, section 35(1) ought to accord constitutional priority to Treaty 9 hunting, trapping, and fishing rights so that the province cannot restrict the territory to which those rights apply by taking up lands for its own purposes without going through a justificatory test akin to that proposed in *Sparrow* and *Badger*. If this is correct, then even if 'other purposes' include such activities as hydroelectric development, Ontario cannot rely on its right to take up lands to authorize such development without triggering constitutional scrutiny in accordance with the analyses laid down in *Sparrow* and *Badger*.

The effect of constitutional recognition and affirmation of existing Treaty 9 rights by section 35(1) is therefore to make it even more difficult for the province to infringe such rights. Not only does the Ontario legislature have to contend with the terms of the treaty and the distribution of legislative authority, but it now must also meet the justificatory test laid down in *Sparrow* and *Badger*. This test applies to *legislative* infringements of section 35(1) rights, that is, validly enacted federal and possibly provincial statutes and regulations made under statutory authority.[167] *Non-legislative* government infringements of treaty rights, if possible before section 35(1) was enacted in 1982, are no longer permissible because the section has constitutionalized treaty rights, clearly placing them beyond executive infringement. *A fortiori*, private individuals and public corporations cannot infringe existing treaty rights without specific legislative authority, which in the case of treaty rights must be federal authority at least, as a result of section 88 of the Indian Act. Consequently, economic development by government or a third party that infringes treaty rights has to be authorized by specific legislation by the appropriate legislative body even to qualify for the application of the *Sparrow* test. Without that authorization, such development cannot proceed. With it, development can proceed only if the justificatory test in *Sparrow* is met.

The first requirement of that test is proof of a valid legislative objective. Assuming that a court would regard the particular project for economic development to be a valid objective, the next stage of the test would require the government or a relevant third party to prove that the objective has been met with as little negative impact on treaty rights as possible in the circumstances. According to *Sparrow*, 'the way in which a legislative objective is to be attained must uphold the honour of the Crown and must be in keeping with the unique contemporary relationship, grounded in history and policy, between the Crown and Canada's Aboriginal peoples. The extent of legislative or regulatory impact on an existing Aboriginal right may be scrutinized so as to ensure recognition and affirmation.[168] The 'unique contemporary relationship' referred to is fiduciary in nature, by which the government is honour-bound to show sensitivity to and respect for treaty rights.[169] In the context of the Aboriginal fishing rights at issue in *Sparrow*, this meant that the regulations had to give Aboriginal fishing for food, social, and ceremonial purposes priority over non-Aboriginal commercial and sport fishing. In the context of an infringement of a treaty right to hunt, fish, or trap, it means that activities protected by treaty must be given priority over competing non-Aboriginal land use.

Conclusion

By the written terms of Treaty 9, Aboriginal peoples in northern Ontario apparently surrendered certain incidents of Aboriginal title to the Crown in return for reserve land and continued hunting, trapping, and fishing rights over surrendered lands. Continued hunting, trapping, and fishing rights at least entitle Aboriginal peoples to assert exclusivity of use in the event of conflict with non-Aboriginal hunting, trapping, and fishing practices. Hunting, trapping, and fishing rights include not only the right to engage in those specific activities but also the right to engage in activities reasonably incidental to hunting, trapping, and fishing. They include the right to expect that hunting, trapping, and fishing will continue to be successful, measured by reference to the fruits of past practice. Hunting, trapping, and fishing rights protect Aboriginal economic, social, and commercial practices from non-Aboriginal activity and economic development. The right to fish entails a recognition of a right approximating a treaty right to water.

A province is not entitled to pass laws directly in relation to Aboriginal peoples. Prior to 1982, a province was entitled to pass legislation with a valid provincial purpose so long as such legislation did not invade federal jurisdiction by not having uniform territorial application or by impairing the status or capacity of Aboriginal peoples. Parliament has provided in section 88 of the Indian Act that treaty rights are to be immune from provincial law. Any provincial law authorizing or decreeing governmental or third party economic development must therefore not conflict with rights accorded to Aboriginal peoples by virtue of Treaty 9. Governmental or non-Aboriginal initiatives engaged in pursuant to *intra vires* provincial legislation that threaten treaty hunting, trapping, and fishing rights, or threaten activity reasonably incidental to their continued existence and enjoyment on surrendered ancestral lands in the treaty area, must find authorization from the terms of Treaty 9 itself. Otherwise, section 88 of the Indian Act provides that treaty rights are to prevail in the event of conflict with provincial laws of general application.

Treaty 9 does not authorize provincial infringement of hunting, trapping, and fishing rights. Although hunting, trapping, and fishing rights are 'subject to such regulations as may from time to time be made by the Government of the Country,' courts have interpreted this qualification as applying only to Parliament. Although the province is entitled to take up lands 'for settlement, mining, lumbering, trading and other purposes,' it cannot engage in this activity in a manner that threatens continued hunting, trapping, and fishing in the area covered by Treaty 9. Supreme Court of Canada jurisprudence requires that this qualification be interpreted in a manner sensitive to Aboriginal interests and expectations. In this light, some types of economic development may not be included within the general reference to 'other purposes' given the fact that these types of development were unknown to Aboriginal signatories at the time of signing. Even if some types of economic development do fall within 'other purposes' for which lands may be taken up pursuant to Treaty 9, nowhere in the historical record is there any suggestion that Aboriginal peoples viewed Treaty 9 as limiting continued hunting, trapping, and fishing on surrendered ancestral lands. Provincial discretion to use lands for purposes authorized by Treaty 9 is subject to the provincial Crown's overarching fiduciary obligation to act in the best interests of Aboriginal peoples. Such an obligation entails that lands taken up for any purpose, listed or unlisted, not be used in a manner that threatens continued hunting, trapping, and fishing rights of Aboriginal peoples.

Section 35(1) of the Constitution Act, 1982, recognizes and affirms existing treaty rights of the Aboriginal peoples living in the area covered by Treaty 9. According to the *Sparrow* decision, such rights can be infringed only by legislative enactments and regulations which meet certain justificatory standards. Accordingly, governments and third parties cannot undertake economic development in the area which would infringe treaty rights without specific legislative authority to do so. Such legislation would have to be federal due to the fact that treaty rights are shielded from provincial legislation by section 88 of the Indian Act. Moreover, such legislative initiatives would only be valid if it passed the justificatory test established by the Court in *Sparrow* and *Badger*. The party seeking to meet this test would have to prove that the particular proposal for economic development at issue is a valid legislative objective, and that there are no other viable alternatives for meeting that objective without infringing treaty rights. If other alternatives exist, the party in question must pursue them first so that treaty rights are given the priority to which they are entitled under the Constitution.

5
The Meaning of Aboriginal Title

Kent McNeil

Over thirty years have passed since the Supreme Court of Canada decided in *Calder* v. *A.G.B.C.*[1] that the Aboriginal peoples of Canada have a legal right to those ancestral lands where their title has been neither surrendered nor validly extinguished. During that period the courts have had numerous opportunities to clarify the meaning of Aboriginal title, but as we shall see they have failed to do so in a rational and coherent manner. The recent decision of the British Columbia Court of Appeal in *Delgamuukw* v. *The Queen*[2] has simply added to the uncertainty.

This paper will examine two fundamental issues in relation to Aboriginal title which Canadian courts have yet to resolve satisfactorily. The first involves the origin of Aboriginal title, which might be Aboriginal systems of law, occupation of land, or some other source. The second issue, which is closely related to the first, involves the nature and content of Aboriginal title. How is it defined? What are its incidents? Is it all-encompassing, including every possible use and benefit of the land, or is it limited to the traditional uses of the Aboriginal peoples who hold it?

These issues will be analyzed from the perspective of domestic Canadian law, as it has been developed by the courts. While claims to Aboriginal jurisdiction or self-government can be raised in connection with Aboriginal land claims,[3] the relationship between these two types of claims will not be examined here. Nor will international law or the perspectives of the Aboriginal peoples on the legitimacy of European colonization be considered. These broader issues should nonetheless be kept in mind, along with an awareness that the domestic law context examined here is not the only context for analyzing Aboriginal claims.

The Source of Aboriginal Title

Supreme Court of Canada decisions have made clear that Aboriginal title to land existed as a legal right prior to the colonization of North America by Europeans.[4] It was not created by the Royal Proclamation of 1763 or any other executive or legislative act.[5] This apparently means that Aboriginal peoples' rights to their traditional lands are not derived from the legal systems which the Europeans imposed upon them.

However, the Supreme Court has avoided specifying the precise legal origins of Aboriginal title. In an oft-quoted passage in the *Calder* decision, Mr. Justice Judson said: 'the fact is that when the [European] settlers came, the Indians were there, organized in societies and occupying the land as their forefathers had done for centuries. This is what aboriginal title means.'[6]

In *Guerin* v. *The Queen*, Mr. Justice Dickson said that in the *Calder* case the Supreme Court 'recognized aboriginal title as a legal right derived from the Indians' historic occupation and possession of their tribal lands.'[7] He also stated that 'the assumption implicit in *Calder* that Indian title is an independent legal right' is supported by the principle 'that a change in sovereignty over a particular territory does not in general affect the presumptive title of the inhabitants.'[8] Dickson noted that principle had been approved in *Amodu Tijani* v. *Secretary, Southern Nigeria*,[9] where the Judicial Committee of the Privy Council decided that the presumptive title of the African inhabitants of Southern Nigeria was based on their system of customary laws which existed prior to the cession of that territory to Britain.

Implicit in Dickson's approach to Aboriginal title in *Guerin* is a presumption that the Aboriginal peoples of Canada had rights to their lands by virtue of their own laws prior to European colonization. This involves acknowledgment that the Aboriginal peoples had legal systems, which presupposes the existence of governmental structures. This conclusion is consistent with Judson's observation in *Calder* that the Aboriginal peoples were organized in societies. Indeed, in *Baker Lake* v. *Minister of Indian Affairs*,[10] Mr. Justice Mahoney made the existence of an organized society a prerequisite for proof of Aboriginal title. His reason for this requirement is suggested in the following passage: 'there appears no valid reason to demand proof of the existence of a society more elaborately structured than is necessary to demonstrate that there existed among the aborigines a recognition of the claimed rights, sufficiently defined to permit their recognition by the common law upon its advent in the territory.'[11] So for Mahoney, an organized society was apparently necessary for there to be pre-existing rights which could be recognized by the common law after the Crown acquired sovereignty.[12]

If Aboriginal title has its source in the land laws of the Aboriginal peoples prior to European colonization, one would expect that in Canadian courts existence of that title would depend on proof of those laws.[13] However, the Canadian decisions referred to in the preceding paragraphs did not explicitly require proof of Aboriginal law to establish Aboriginal title. In *Calder*, for example, an admission that the Nisga'a Indians had been in possession of their traditional lands at the time the Crown allegedly acquired sovereignty seems to have been sufficient. In *Baker Lake*, proof that the Inuit as an organized society had been in exclusive possession of their lands when sovereignty was asserted by England was also accepted as sufficient to establish their claim to Aboriginal title. The cases therefore reveal that actual proof of an Aboriginal system of land law is not necessary to establish Aboriginal title. Instead, as Madam Justice Wilson repeated in *Roberts* v. *Canada*, Aboriginal title is 'a legal right derived from the Indians' historic occupation and possession of their tribal lands.'[14]

The approach that the courts have taken to the issue of the source of Aboriginal title therefore reveals a logical inconsistency which has not been resolved. If Aboriginal title is based simply on occupation of lands by an organized society at the time the Crown asserted sovereignty, how could it be a pre-existing right? For it to exist as a legal right before the Crown acquired sovereignty, it would need to be based on some system of law, which would have to be Aboriginal, as no other law existed in North America prior to European colonization.[15] But if Aboriginal title originates in Aboriginal systems of law, why is proof of those systems of law not necessary to establish the title? The courts seem to be vacillating between two possible sources of Aboriginal title – Aboriginal occupation and Aboriginal laws – without pronouncing clearly in favour of one or the other.[16]

The issue of the basis of Aboriginal title was revisited recently in the British Columbia Court of Appeal decision in *Delgamuukw* v. *The Queen*.[17] In that case, the Gitksan and Wet'suwet'en peoples sought, among other things, a declaration that their 'ownership of and jurisdiction over [their] Territory existed and continues to exist and has never been lawfully extinguished or abandoned.'[18] As the case involved the most searching examination of Aboriginal title to date in Canada,[19] it is worth spending time to analyze this aspect of each of the four judgments. The two majority judgments were delivered by Justices Macfarlane (Justice Taggart concurring) and Wallace,[20] while Justices Lambert and Hutcheon each delivered minority judgments in which they dissented in part.

On the issue of the source of Aboriginal title, Justice Macfarlane had surprisingly little to say. He repeated Justice Dickson's oft-quoted statement in *Guerin* that Aboriginal land rights arise from 'the Indians' historic occupation and possession of their tribal lands,' concluding from this that 'proof of presence amounting to occupation is a threshold question.'[21] Relying on *Calder*, he said that 'Aboriginal rights arise by operation of law, and do not depend on a grant from the Crown.'[22] He also quoted a passage from Justice Wilson's judgment in *Roberts* which included the statement that 'aboriginal title pre-dated colonization by the British and survived British claims of sovereignty.'[23]

In my view, the most revealing part of Macfarlane's discussion of this issue is his conclusion that 'the common law will give effect to those traditions regarded by an aboriginal society as integral to the distinctive culture, and existing at the date sovereignty was asserted.'[24] So for Macfarlane, in addition to Aboriginal occupation, the existence of an Aboriginal society with a distinctive culture appears to be a requirement for Aboriginal title, similar to Justice Mahoney's requirement of an organized society in *Baker Lake*.[25] However, the traditions which are integral to that culture apparently do not need to amount to laws which have to be proven for Aboriginal title to be established. Instead, as in *Baker Lake*, the test is occupation of specific lands by an Aboriginal society at the time the Crown asserted sovereignty. As we shall see in the second part of this paper, for Macfarlane the traditions are relevant to the content of the Aboriginal title in question rather than to its existence.[26]

Justice Wallace's judgment contains a more detailed analysis of the issue of the source of Aboriginal title. Like Macfarlane, Wallace relied on *Calder* and *Guerin* to conclude that 'aboriginal rights, including aboriginal interests in tribal lands, have as their basis the historic occupation and use of land.'[27] He also relied on *Baker Lake* to hold that the establishment of Aboriginal rights requires proof by the claimants of their occupation of land as an organized society at the time the common law was introduced by the acquisition of sovereignty.[28] In addition, he said the common law requires that 'the practices supporting the rights they claim were integral to the claimants' distinctive and traditional society or culture.'[29]

Of particular interest is Wallace's discussion of the effect of the introduction of the common law on Aboriginal custom. He seems to have rejected any notion that Aboriginal title derives its legal force from the continuation of Aboriginal customary law after the Crown acquired sovereignty by settlement.[30] 'The authorities before this court,' he said, 'make clear that aboriginal rights take their force from the common law.'[31] In his view, Aboriginal customary law was incapable of giving the Aboriginal peoples rights against Europeans. He put it this way:

> Prior to the exercise of sovereignty and the introduction of the common law, the issue of aboriginal 'rights' did not arise. For the aboriginal peoples to have the right, vis-à-vis European settlers, to engage in those traditional practices and uses of land which were integral to their aboriginal society there must be recognition of such a right by those outside the aboriginal community and some mechanism requiring them to respect such a 'right.' An enforceable right, as against European settlers, came only with the

protection which was extended to aboriginal rights by the adjusted common law.[32]

Wallace thus rejected the view that the 'doctrine of continuity' applies broadly to maintain the validity of Aboriginal customary law in settled colonies.[33] He distinguished between customary practices and laws, concluding that, 'while customary practices received the protection of the common law after its introduction into British Columbia, any aboriginal system of customary law did not.'[34] The circumstances of settled colonies like British Columbia which were inhabited by Aboriginal peoples resulted in an adjustment to the common law so that 'it recognized the historical aboriginal presence and title and served to protect aboriginal customs and practices and the traditional relationship the aboriginal people had with the lands they occupied and used.'[35] It was therefore the common law, rather than Aboriginal customary law, which created Aboriginal land rights. In Wallace's words, 'upon the exercise of sovereignty by the Crown, the adjusted common law recognized the aboriginal community's "right" – vis-à-vis the settlers – to engage in those practices and activities associated with the use of the land they occupied which were traditional, integral and distinctive to the aboriginal society and way of life.'[36] For Wallace, then, Aboriginal customs are relevant only to the extent that they determine traditional land use practices which the common law recognizes and converts into rights. They are not themselves the source of Aboriginal title.

Justice Lambert, dissenting in part, took a different approach to the issue of the source of Aboriginal title. Unlike Wallace, he was of the view that the doctrine of continuity applies to a settled colony like British Columbia. He said:

> If sovereignty was asserted by the Crown, and either then or later the Crown adopted the common law as the law of the territory over which sovereignty was claimed, then the common law itself recognized, adopted and affirmed the rights and titles of the indigenous people in relation to land and in relation to their own customs and practices for control of the land and for control of their other rights, except to the extent that their rights were inconsistent with the concept of sovereignty itself, or inconsistent with laws clearly made applicable to the whole territory and all of its inhabitants, or with the principles of fundamental justice. That recognition, adoption and affirmation made those rights themselves part of the common law, carrying with those rights all the remedies and protection of the common law ...

I propose to describe the legal principle which provides for the continuation of indigenous practices, customs and traditions, following British occupation, colonization and settlement, as the common law Doctrine of Continuity.[37]

For Lambert, then, Aboriginal title existed prior to colonization as an entitlement arising from Aboriginal practices, customs, and traditions. Although he referred to it as a 'right,' he cautioned against the use of terminology originating in Western legal thought to describe *sui generis* rights emanating from conceptually different Aboriginal modes of thought. To avoid this problem, he suggested the adoption of 'an approach that tries to characterize aboriginal rights in terms of aboriginal society rather than western society.'[38]

Lambert started with the fact that, prior to European contact, 'the Gitksan and Wet'suwet'en organized their social system in accordance with their own customs, traditions and practices.'[39] Contact did not change that. During the period from contact to the acquisition of British sovereignty, those customs, traditions, and practices continued to apply to the Gitksan and Wet'suwet'en. The common law, which applied to Hudson's Bay traders and other Britons, had no impact on them. Acquisition of sovereignty, however, resulted in a significant change, which Lambert described in the following passage:

> At that time the Gitksan and Wet'suwet'en customs, traditions and practices, to the extent that they related to an integral part of the distinctive culture of the Gitksan and Wet'suwet'en peoples, became incorporated into the common law which became applicable throughout the territory, in so far as it was appropriate. The Gitksan and Wet'suwet'en practices, customs and traditions continued with the same practical results as before, but now they became, in those integral parts of their distinctive culture, a part of the common law and protected by its remedies and its means of enforcement.[40]

So in Lambert's dissenting opinion, Aboriginal rights, including Aboriginal title to land, originate from the practices, customs, and traditions of the particular Aboriginal people who claim the rights. In contrast to Wallace, he did not view the common law as the source of those rights. As the rights already existed, the effect of the introduction of the common law was merely to accord them recognition and additional protection. It did this by incorporating them into the general body of common law which applied throughout the settlement from the time of acquisition of sovereignty by the Crown.[41]

Justice Hutcheon, also dissenting in part, found that the Gitksan and Wet'suwet'en 'were present in parts of the territory for a long, long time prior to sovereignty' and that 'the many villages, lands and fishing sites were used for many purposes including hunting, trapping, fishing, berry-picking and spiritual and cultural reasons.'[42] Given these undisputed facts, he relied on Justice Dickson's judgment in *Guerin* to conclude that 'the common law recognized that "the rights of Indians in the lands they traditionally occupied prior to European colonization both predated and survived the claims to sovereignty."'[43] However, Hutcheon did not clarify the source of those pre-existing rights. He repeated the principle, which Dickson said had been approved by the Judicial Committee of the Privy Council in the *Amodu Tijani* case, 'that a change in sovereignty over a particular territory does not in general affect the presumptive title of the inhabitants,'[44] but did not specify whether the title of the Gitksan and Wet'suwet'en was derived from their own customary laws or from common law acknowledgment that they had rights flowing from occupation of their traditional lands. Hutcheon's decision is therefore consistent with Macfarlane's on this point, but does not shed any new light on the issue.

To sum up, the *Delgamuukw* case does not provide a clear solution to the elusive issue of the source of Aboriginal title. The judgments range from Wallace's, which denies legal force to Aboriginal laws and customs as the source of Aboriginal title, to Lambert's, which incorporates Aboriginal practices, customs, and traditions into the common law through the doctrine of continuity. In between, Macfarlane's majority judgment and Hutcheon's minority opinion attempt to follow earlier Canadian case law without resolving the uncertainty over the relevance of Aboriginal laws and customs to claims to Aboriginal title based on occupation of traditional lands.

The Nature and Content of Aboriginal Title

The nature and content of Aboriginal title obviously depend to a large degree on the source of Aboriginal title. If it is based on Aboriginal laws and customs, one would expect its content to be defined in terms of those laws and customs, which would have to be proved.[45] However, we have seen that so far Canadian courts have generally not required proof of specific Aboriginal laws and customs to establish Aboriginal title, choosing instead to rely on occupation and use of lands by an organized Aboriginal society. We therefore need to assess the implications of this judicial approach in our examination of the nature and content of Aboriginal title, and evaluate the impact of the *Delgamuukw* decision in this context.

The Supreme Court of Canada has so far failed to provide a clear definition of Aboriginal title. This judicial hesitation goes back to the decision of the Judicial Committee of the Privy Council in *St. Catherine's Milling and Lumber Company* v. *The Queen*,[46] the first important case involving Aboriginal land rights in Canada. In that case, the Canadian government, which was aligned with the St. Catherine's Company against the Province of Ontario, argued that Aboriginal title amounted to a complete proprietary interest, limited only by a restriction on alienation other than by surrender to the Crown. Lord Watson, who delivered the judgment, rejected this contention on the ground that it was inconsistent with the terms of the Royal Proclamation issued by George III on October 7, 1763, a few months after the cession of French Canada to Britain at the end of the Seven Years War. According to his Lordship, the possession of the Indian tribes then living under the sovereignty and protection of the British Crown could only be ascribed to the provisions of the Proclamation, the terms of which showed 'that the tenure of the Indians was a personal and usufructuary right, dependent upon the good will of the Sovereign.'[47] While declining to express any opinion on the 'precise quality of the Indian right,' Lord Watson stated their Lordships' view that 'there has been all along vested in the Crown a substantial and paramount estate, underlying the Indian title, which became a plenum dominium whenever that title was surrendered or otherwise extinguished.'[48] The Indian title was nonetheless an 'interest' which formed a 'burden' on the Crown's 'present proprietary estate in the land.'[49]

According to the *St. Catherine's* decision, Aboriginal title is an interest in land which is personal in the sense that it cannot be alienated other than by surrender to the Crown,[50] but is less than a fee simple estate. The Aboriginal people who have the title have a right to occupy and use the land and hold it as against third parties, but their interest is subordinate to the Crown's underlying title.[51] But this description of Aboriginal title was based entirely on an interpretation of the Royal Proclamation which their Lordships regarded as the sole source of Aboriginal land rights.[52] As the Supreme Court of Canada has since told us that the Royal Proclamation is not the *source* of Aboriginal title (a pre-existing right which the Proclamation merely recognized),[53] Lord Watson's description of Aboriginal title should no longer be applicable. To determine the nature and content of Aboriginal title, we therefore have to go behind the Proclamation to see what it recognized.

While acknowledging the limitations of the *St. Catherine's* decision,[54] the Supreme Court of Canada has carefully avoided specifying the nature and content of Aboriginal title. In *Guerin* v. *The Queen*, Justice Dickson, after concluding that the Aboriginal interest cannot be accurately described as a beneficial interest or as a personal, usufructuary right (though each of these descriptions, he said, contains 'a core of truth'), referred to it

as a '*sui generis* interest' which is 'best characterized by its general inalienability [other than by surrender to the Crown], coupled with the fact that
the Crown is under an obligation to deal with the land on the Indians'
behalf when the interest is surrendered.'[55] Because the Aboriginal interest
is unique, Dickson said, descriptions drawn from general property law are
somewhat inappropriate for describing it. Similarly, in *Sparrow* v. *The Queen*
Chief Justice Dickson and Justice La Forest wrote that 'courts must be careful ... to avoid the application of traditional common law concepts of property as they develop their understanding of what the reasons for judgment
in *Guerin* ... referred to as the "*sui generis*" nature of aboriginal rights.'[56]

Classifying Aboriginal title as *sui generis* does not preclude Aboriginal
peoples from having rights of exclusive possession and full use of their traditional lands. While the courts have held that those lands are inalienable
other than by surrender to the Crown as holder of the underlying title,[57]
the Aboriginal peoples may still be entitled to the complete benefit of
them,[58] including both surface and subsurface rights.[59] This should be the
result if Aboriginal title is 'a legal right derived from the Indians' historic
occupation and possession of their tribal lands,' as Dickson said in *Guerin*[60]
and Wilson repeated for the unanimous Court in *Roberts*.[61] This result is
consistent with fundamental common law principles, by which interests
in land ultimately depend on possession, not on the specific uses to which
the land is put.[62] To acquire title to land by adverse possession, for example, a person must possess the land adversely to the dispossessed owner for
the statutory limitation period. At the end of that period, which in some
provinces is as short as ten years, the statute extinguishes the owner's title.
The adverse possessor becomes the owner, not by statutory conveyance,
but simply by being in possession of land to which no one else can show
a better title.[63] In other words, the possession itself is the source of the adverse possessor's title. The use the adverse possessor has made of the land
is relevant as evidence of the possession, but in no way limits the nature
of the adverse possessor's interest once the possession has been established. The type of use necessary to acquire possession depends on the circumstances, including the nature and location of the land, and the
conditions of life, habits, and ideas of the people living there.[64] Thus, in
Red House Farms v. *Catchpole*,[65] the English Court of Appeal held that hunting on a regular basis on unimproved, marshy land sufficed to give the
defendant adverse possession, and therefore title to the land at the end of
the limitation period. There was no question of the defendant's interest
being limited to a mere right to hunt, even though that was the only use
she had made of the land.

Unless some valid reason can be found for not giving the same effect to
possession of lands by Aboriginal peoples,[66] the nature of their interest

should not depend on their uses of the lands at the time of colonization. If their title is derived from their historic possession, then, once that possession has been established by evidence of use as organized societies in accordance with their own ways of life,[67] the title accorded to them by the common law should be for an all-encompassing interest.[68] As we have seen, the reason for describing this interest as *sui generis* rather than as a common law estate such as a fee simple is that Canadian judges have thought it inappropriate to apply 'terminology drawn from general property law' to the 'unique interest' which the Aboriginal peoples have in their lands.[69] But in what sense is the Aboriginal interest unique? It is unique in its origin because it is derived from Aboriginal possession of lands *prior to* acquisition of sovereignty by the Crown. In that sense it is different from a fee simple estate derived from Crown grant or even from adverse possession. Judges also seem to regard it as unique because, unlike a fee simple estate, it cannot be alienated other than by surrender to the Crown.[70] Neither of these unique features, however, has any relation to the nature of the interest which flows from Aboriginal title. It is therefore inappropriate, and highly discriminatory, to limit that interest to Aboriginal uses at the time the Crown acquired sovereignty. It is discriminatory because it means that Aboriginal peoples who may have been in rightful possession of their lands for hundreds or even thousands of years have a lesser interest than a wrongdoer who has acquired a fee simple title by as little as ten years adverse possession.

Canadian courts have nonetheless attempted to limit the interest held by Aboriginal title to Aboriginal uses at the time of acquisition of sovereignty by the Crown. In the *Baker Lake* case, for example, Justice Mahoney said that the common law 'can give effect only to those incidents of that enjoyment [of the Aboriginal peoples of their lands] that were, themselves, given effect by the regime that prevailed before.'[71] He accordingly held that the Aboriginal title of the Inuit plaintiffs in that case was limited to a right to hunt and fish as their ancestors had done.[72] Similarly, in *A.G. for Ontario* v. *Bear Island Foundation*, Justice Steele said that the 'essence of aboriginal rights is the right of Indians to continue to live on the lands as their forefathers lived.'[73] From this he concluded that they could not use the land for any purposes they wished, but only for 'traditional uses for basic survival and personal ornamentation existing as of 1763,' which he took to be the relevant date.[74] However, on appeal the Supreme Court of Canada said that they did not agree with all of Steele's legal findings, casting doubt on the validity of his views on the nature of Aboriginal title.[75]

In the *Delgamuukw* case, the trial judge, Chief Justice McEachern, also took a restrictive view of the nature and content of Aboriginal title. He wrote: 'In my view, the aboriginal rights of the plaintiffs' ancestors included all those sustenance practices and the gathering of all those products of the land and waters of the territory I shall define which they practised and used before exposure to European civilization (or sovereignty) for subsistence or survival, including wood, food and clothing, and for their culture or ornamentation – in short, what their ancestors obtained from the land and waters for their aboriginal life.'[76] On appeal, the judges did not specify the actual content of the Aboriginal title of the Gitksan and Wet'suwet'en, as the parties had mutually agreed to leave that matter to negotiation. The judges did, however, express general opinions on this issue.

Justice Macfarlane said that the 'nature and content of an aboriginal right is determined by asking what the organized aboriginal society regarded as "an integral part of their distinctive culture."'[77] He derived the 'integral part of their distinctive culture' aspect of this test from the *Sparrow* decision, where Chief Justice Dickson and Justice La Forest had said the anthropological evidence suggested that, 'for the Musqueam, the salmon fishery has always constituted an integral part of their distinctive culture.'[78] However, it is not clear that Dickson and La Forest intended that to be a criterion for determining the nature and content of the Musqueam's Aboriginal right to fish.[79] In fact, they avoided the issue of defining the scope of the right and adopted the Court of Appeal's characterization of it as a right to fish for food and social and ceremonial purposes, as that was the way the case had been presented in the courts below.[80]

Macfarlane concluded nonetheless that the 'common law will give effect to those traditions regarded by an aboriginal society as integral to the distinctive culture, and existing at the date sovereignty was asserted.'[81] He went on to observe that

> not all practices in existence in 1846 [which he took as the date of assertion of sovereignty] were necessarily to be regarded as aboriginal rights. To be so regarded those practices must have been integral to the distinctive culture of the aboriginal society from which they are said to have arisen. A modernized form of such a practice would be no less an aboriginal right: see *Sparrow*. A practice which had not been integral to the organized society and its distinctive culture, but which became prevalent as a result of European influences would not qualify for protection as an aboriginal right.[82]

For him, the nature and content of Aboriginal rights are questions of fact which 'may vary from context to context in accordance with distinct patterns of historical occupancy and use of land.'[83] However, for land uses to be regarded as Aboriginal they must have 'formed an integral part of traditional Indian life prior to sovereignty.'[84]

Like Macfarlane, Justice Wallace was of the view that Aboriginal rights are 'site and activity specific and their existence turns on the particular facts of each case.'[85] They 'reflect the traditional practices which were integral to the native society occupying tribal lands when the common law was introduced.'[86] Wallace distinguished between Aboriginal rights which require a historical and cultural dimension going back to the Crown's assertion of sovereignty, and non-Aboriginal rights which all Canadian citizens, including Aboriginal persons, have.[87] 'Engaging in activities,' he said, 'that are different in nature and scope from those integral to aboriginal society and traditional ways of life cannot be said to be the exercise of an aboriginal right.'[88] Relying on *Sparrow*, he also stated that it is crucial 'to distinguish between the evolution or modernization of a right and a modern method of exercising a right. A "modern aboriginal right" is a contradiction in terms. It is the *manner* of exercising the right which may assume a contemporary or modern form.'[89]

Depending on the nature of the traditional practices, in Wallace's view Aboriginal title could amount to extensive interests in land. Commenting on Lord Watson's description of Aboriginal title in the *St. Catherine's* case as 'usufructuary,' he said that that term 'indicates, at least, the approximate bounds of what "aboriginal title" entails; it shows that interests in land and beneficial uses of land are the basic category of what was protected as aboriginal rights. This is a broad category indeed. In respect of land, it may range from an exclusive and plenary beneficial interest over certain parcels of land, to occasional presence for sustenance activities. A host of practices fall within the category including fishing, hunting and gathering.'[90]

Justice Lambert took a significantly different approach to the issue of the nature and content of Aboriginal title. Unlike Macfarlane and Wallace, who regarded Aboriginal title as immutably tied to traditional practices and land uses at the time of assertion of sovereignty, he said that 'aboriginal rights are evolving rights. They are not frozen at the time of sovereignty or at any other time. The evolution which occurred before sovereignty and the evolution which occurred after sovereignty are both relevant to an understanding of the rights.'[91]

Moreover, if the right was a general right of exclusive occupation, possession, use, and enjoyment of land, apparently it would include the right to use the land for whatever purpose the Aboriginal titleholders chose. As an example, Lambert said that a general right of that nature would encompass the taking of game on the land. In that event, the right relied on would be the general right rather than a specific right to take game. Similarly, Lambert suggested, 'a claim may be made that the installation of a sanitary landfill site or a waste recycling depot on an Indian reserve is done in the exercise of an aboriginal right to exclusive occupation, possession, use and enjoyment of the reserve land, and not as a modernization of a more specific aboriginal right to create middens.'[92] However, if the Aboriginal right relied upon was a right to hunt on land where no right of exclusive occupation, possession, use, and enjoyment was claimed, then the right to hunt would be limited in the way it was prior to the assertion of Crown sovereignty.[93] In that case, Lambert said, 'if the aboriginal right was limited to a particular season, and a particular purpose, then the contemporary exercise of that right could be limited also in the same way, even though modern tools could be used in the exercise of the right.'[94] So in Lambert's view, 'a good deal may depend on an accurate characterization of the scope of the right in 1846 [when Crown sovereignty was asserted] in terms of the generality or specificity of the manner in which the right is described, and also in terms of the perspective from which the right is viewed. But it is the evidence with respect to the aboriginal peoples' own description of the right which should control the way it is expressed, not the description selected by the settlers' society to meet the needs of the settlers' society by making all aboriginal rights as narrow as possible.'[95]

Although the manner in which Aboriginal rights may evolve after assertion of sovereignty by the Crown is not entirely clear from Lambert's judgment, it seems that changes may occur as a result of changes in Aboriginal customs, traditions, and practices. In Lambert's view, Aboriginal rights of self-government and self-regulation were not necessarily extinguished by Crown sovereignty. The two could coexist. Subject to some qualifications, the Aboriginal peoples could retain their rights to manage use of the land and resources encompassed by their Aboriginal title and to regulate internal relationships within their own societies through their own customs, traditions, and practices.[96] Changes to those customs, traditions, and practices would evidently result in changes to the Aboriginal rights which flow from them. Describing this process in the context of the *Delgamuukw* case, Lambert said that, subject to overriding change, 'Gitksan and Wet'suwet'en customs, traditions and practices, forming an integral part of their distinctive culture, would continue as part of the common law, and be protected by the common law, up until the present time. Those customs, traditions and practices, so protected, may undergo modifications. They were not frozen in 1846. Those modified forms will receive the same common law protection as the forms which the customs, practices and traditions received in 1846.'[97] So Lambert apparently linked Aboriginal rights of self-government with other Aboriginal rights, providing the Aboriginal peoples with a means to modify their own customs, traditions, and practices in accordance with their own needs after the Crown's assertion of sovereignty.[98]

Justice Hutcheon, in his relatively short judgment, said very little about the nature of Aboriginal title, no doubt because the Court had been asked to leave 'the precise location, scope, content and consequence of the existing aboriginal rights' for negotiation between the parties.[99] He simply listed the incidents of Aboriginal rights that were not in dispute, namely that they are collective, inalienable except to the Crown, and extend to the traditional territory of the particular people who claim them. He thought it unnecessary to classify them as personal or proprietary, finding 'it sufficient to say that aboriginal rights to land are of such a nature as to compete on an equal footing with proprietary interests.'[100]

To sum up the Court of Appeal's decision on the nature and content of Aboriginal title in *Delgamuukw*, there was apparent agreement between Macfarlane and Wallace that the scope of that title is limited to Aboriginal uses of the land which were integral to the distinctive cultures of the Aboriginal peoples at the time the British Crown asserted sovereignty. Hutcheon did not express an opinion on this matter. Lambert alone took an expansive view of Aboriginal title, regarding it to be capable of change, both before and after assertion of sovereignty, in accordance with changes in Aboriginal customs, traditions, and practices.[101]

We have already seen that limiting Aboriginal title to Aboriginal uses of the land at the time the Crown asserted sovereignty does not accord with common law principles, and is in fact discriminatory because it means that the interests of Aboriginal peoples in their traditional lands are less than those of wrongdoers who acquire a title by adverse possession.[102] In my opinion, the majority judgments in *Delgamuukw* used the Supreme Court's characterization of Aboriginal title as *sui generis* in *Guerin* as a way to limit the Aboriginal interest as much as possible. The *Guerin* decision does not support that approach. It is important to remember that *Guerin* involved reserve lands, not lands held by Aboriginal title. Justice Dickson discussed Aboriginal title in his judgment because, in his view, the Indian interest in reserve lands and lands held by Aboriginal title is the same.[103] If Dickson's view on this matter is correct,[104] then Aboriginal title should not be limited to uses integral to Aboriginal societies at the time the Crown acquired sovereignty unless the Indian interest in reserve lands is limited in the same way.

We do not have to look very far to discover that the Indian interest in reserve lands is an all-encompassing interest, subject only to a restriction on alienation other than by surrender to the Crown in whom the legal title is vested.[105] This is clear from federal legislation, enacted under the authority of section 91(24) of the Constitution Act, 1867, which gives Parliament exclusive legislative jurisdiction over 'Indians, and Lands reserved for the Indians.'[106] For example, section 2(j) of the 1927 Indian Act defined 'reserve' as 'any tract or tracts of land set apart by treaty or otherwise for the use or benefit of or granted to a particular band of Indians, of which the legal title is in the Crown, and which remains so set apart and has not been surrendered to the Crown, and includes all the trees, wood, timber, soil, stone, minerals, metals and other valuables thereon or therein.'[107] When the Indian Act was revised in 1951, this definition was amended and the reference to trees, wood, etc., was removed. The amended version, which remains unchanged in the current Indian Act,[108] reads as follows: '"reserve" means a tract of land, the legal title to which is vested in His [now Her] Majesty, that has been set apart by His [Her] Majesty for the use and benefit of a band.'[109] This amendment cannot have been intended to diminish the Indian interest in reserve lands, as that would have infringed their vested rights. While Parliament had the power to do that in 1951,[110] a rule of statutory interpretation directs that statutes are to be construed, as far as possible, so as not to infringe vested rights.[111] As Chief Justice Duff said in *Spooner Oils Ltd.* v. *Turner Valley Gas Conservation Board*, '[a] legislative enactment is not to be read as prejudicially affecting accrued rights, or "an existing status" ... unless the language in which it is expressed requires such a construction ...; the underlying assumption being that, when Parliament intends prejudicially to affect such rights or such a status, it declares its intention expressly, unless, at all events, that intention is plainly manifested by unavoidable inference.'[112] Since the 1951 amendment does not reveal an intention, either expressly or by unavoidable inference, to diminish the Indian interest in reserve lands, that interest must have continued to include 'trees, wood, timber, soil, stone, minerals, metals and other valuables.'[113]

Further evidence of Parliament's position that the Indian interest in reserve lands is not limited to uses integral to Aboriginal societies at the time the Crown asserted sovereignty can be found in the Indian Oil and Gas Act,[114] first enacted in 1974. Section 4(1) of that Act provides in part that 'all oil and gas obtained from Indian lands after April 22, 1977 is subject to the payment to Her Majesty in right of Canada, in trust for the Indian bands concerned, of the royalties prescribed from time to time by the regulations.' Section 2 defines 'Indian lands' in part as 'lands reserved for the Indians, including any interests therein, surrendered in accordance with the Indian Act.' It is evident from these provisions that Parliament regards the Indian interest in reserves as including oil and gas rights, as the Indian bands are entitled to the benefit in the form of royalties of oil and gas obtained from their surrendered reserve lands.[115] Moreover, section 6(2) provides that 'nothing in this Act shall be deemed to abrogate the rights of Indian people or preclude them from negotiating for oil and gas benefits in those areas in which land claims have not been settled.' This suggests that Indian people may also have oil and gas rights in lands where their Aboriginal title has not been surrendered.

Provincial governments obviously have a stake in this matter, as according to the *St. Catherine's* decision, the underlying title to lands which are subject to Aboriginal title is vested in the Crown in right of the province where the lands are located.[116] In *A.-G. for Quebec* v. *A.-G. for Canada*,[117] the Judicial Committee of the Privy Council applied that aspect of the *St. Catherine's* decision to reserve lands in Quebec which had been set apart prior to Confederation. These decisions created a problem of divided jurisdiction and title, as legislative authority over Indian reserves was given to Parliament by section 91(24) of the Constitution Act, 1867, whereas the underlying title to reserve lands was vested in the provincial Crowns due to section 109 of the same Act. To resolve this problem, most of the provinces entered into agreements with the federal government whereby either the underlying title to reserve lands was transferred to the Crown in right of Canada, or the federal government was authorized to dispose of any reserve lands which were surrendered by the Indians for whom they had been set aside.[118] In some cases, those agreements provide that the benefit, or a portion thereof, of minerals found in or under reserve lands shall go to the Indian bands concerned.[119] In other cases, the issue of entitlement to the beneficial interest in minerals on reserves has led to controversy and prolonged discussions between the federal government and the province in question.[120]

A thorough investigation of the nature and content of the Indian interest in reserve lands cannot be undertaken here. However, enough has been said to show that the interest is not limited to uses of the land which were integral to Aboriginal societies at the time the Crown asserted sovereignty. As a general rule, Indian bands are entitled to the entire beneficial interest in their reserve lands for as long as those lands remain part of their reserves. The extent of this entitlement does not seem to depend on the manner in which a reserve was created.[121] The Indian interest in reserves which were created by exempting certain lands from a general surrender of Aboriginal title in a treaty,[122] for example, appears to be the same as the Indian interest in reserves which were set aside by the Crown out of lands which had already been surrendered by a treaty.[123] In the reserves of the former type, Aboriginal title continued, and in some cases expressly included uses of the lands which were not integral to the societies of the Aboriginal peoples who had signed the treaty.[124] In reserves of the latter type, the Indian interest was derived from the setting aside of reserves in accordance with the treaty, and appears to be equally all-encompassing.[125]

As this discussion of the nature and content of Aboriginal title comes to a conclusion, it is apparent that limiting Aboriginal title to uses integral to Aboriginal societies at the time the Crown asserted sovereignty violates fundamental common law principles and conflicts with the judgment of Justice Dickson in the *Guerin* decision. Dickson said that the Indian interest in reserve lands and in Aboriginal title lands is the same. When that holding is combined with the overwhelming weight of authority that the Indian interest in reserve lands is generally all-encompassing, subject only to a restraint on alienation other than by surrender to the Crown, the conclusion that the Aboriginal peoples are entitled to an all-encompassing interest in their Aboriginal title lands, subject to the same restraint on alienation, is unavoidable. Otherwise, Aboriginal societies would have been denied the right to change and adapt to the new conditions which inevitably resulted from the process of colonization.[126] If taken seriously, this would condemn Aboriginal societies to extinction, as cultures which cannot adapt to changing conditions are bound to disappear.[127]

Justice Wallace attempted to deal with this problem in his judgment in *Delgamuukw* by observing that Aboriginal people, in addition to their Aboriginal rights, have had the right to engage in the same activities as everyone else since the Crown's assertion of sovereignty.[128] In relying on their Aboriginal rights, they are not obliged 'to renounce the contemporary world and revert to the life of their ancestors.'[129] They can also engage in other activities 'different in nature and scope from those integral to aboriginal society and traditional ways of life.'[130] Wallace concluded that 'the fact that aboriginal peoples engage in a particular activity does not qualify such activity for the special protection afforded to aboriginal rights. To hold otherwise is to ignore the "aboriginal" dimension of aboriginal rights.'[131]

Wallace is no doubt right that every activity that Aboriginal people engage in cannot be regarded as the exercise of an Aboriginal right. An Aboriginal doctor practising Euro-Canadian medicine in Vancouver, for example, could not necessarily claim an Aboriginal right to do so. The activity does not become Aboriginal just because an Aboriginal person is engaged in it. However, an Aboriginal healer practising traditional medicine may have an Aboriginal right to perform that activity. There must, then, be a connection with an Aboriginal society and culture for an activity to be classified as Aboriginal. The difficult question, of course, is the degree of connection that is required.

The problem with Wallace's approach, then, is not his requirement of a connection with Aboriginal society and culture, but his view, which

Justice Macfarlane shared, that only those activities which were integral to that society and culture prior to the Crown's assertion of sovereignty are protected under the rubric of Aboriginal rights.[132] This places the Aboriginal peoples in an untenable position. To retain their Aboriginal rights, they must attempt to maintain their societies in a precolonial state, which is obviously an impossible task. If they try to adapt to meet the changes in circumstances caused by European colonization, as they must to survive, their activities are no longer 'Aboriginal' and so are not encompassed by their Aboriginal rights. According to Wallace and Macfarlane's approach, then, the Aboriginal peoples are denied the opportunity to develop contemporary ways of life within their own communities on the basis of their Aboriginal rights. If sustained, this approach will probably result in the disappearance of the Aboriginal cultures which make those communities distinct, as the Aboriginal peoples will be obliged to assimilate into the dominant Canadian culture which surrounds them in order to survive.

I am not suggesting that either Wallace or Macfarlane would favour the assimilation of the Aboriginal peoples into Canadian society generally. However, I do think that their views on the nature and content of Aboriginal rights, if adopted by other courts and applied by the federal and provincial governments, would have that result. Admittedly, this might be avoided if those governments negotiate agreements with the Aboriginal peoples based on conceptions of Aboriginal rights which are sufficiently large to enable the Aboriginal peoples to preserve their distinctive cultures. Indeed, Macfarlane expressly favoured a negotiated settlement in the *Delgamuukw* case. Near the end of his judgment, he said: 'The parties have expressed willingness to negotiate their differences. I would encourage such consultation and reconciliation, a process which may provide the only real hope of an early and satisfactory agreement which not only gives effect to the aspirations of the aboriginal peoples but recognizes there are many diverse cultures, communities and interests which must co-exist in Canada. A proper balancing of all those interests is a delicate and crucial matter.'[133] But what incentive is there for governments to reach agreements which give effect to 'the aspirations of the aboriginal peoples' after the courts have reduced the already limited bargaining power of those peoples by embracing a narrow definition of their Aboriginal rights?[134] Court decisions can have a powerful influence on the positions governments adopt at the bargaining table.[135] Moreover, public support for negotiated agreements can also be influenced by judicial pronouncements on the nature of Aboriginal rights. Without judicial support for their rights, the Aboriginal peoples have much less chance of negotiating agreements which will permit their distinctive cultures to flourish and grow rather than wither and die.

Conclusion

We have seen that Canadian courts have failed to specify clearly the origins of Aboriginal title. The *Delgamuukw* decision, like other cases from *Calder* on, wavers between Aboriginal law and occupation of land as possible sources. On balance, however, the judges seem to favour occupation as the source, as Canadian courts generally have not required proof of Aboriginal law as a prerequisite for establishing Aboriginal title. In this respect, I think the judges are on the right track. Aboriginal land law would have been developed to govern internal landholding within the Aboriginal nations themselves. It would have been designed to regulate landholding among the members of each of those nations. It would not serve to determine the land rights of those nations vis-à-vis other nations, especially colonizing European powers. This is not to suggest that Aboriginal law is any less valid than Euro-Canadian law, or that it would not continue to govern landholding among the members of the Aboriginal nations.[136] It is simply a recognition of the inappropriateness of trying to use the internal law of Aboriginal nations to determine their land rights against an external power like the British, and hence the Canadian, Crown.

If occupation of land is taken as the source of the Aboriginal title which Canadian courts have found to exist at common law, then the nature and content of that title should stem from that source. It is in this regard that judicial decisions, in particular the majority judgments in *Delgamuukw*, have gone seriously wrong. As we have seen, in that case Justices Macfarlane and Wallace were of the view that Aboriginal title is limited to Aboriginal uses of the land which were integral to the distinctive cultures of the Aboriginal peoples prior to the Crown's assertion of sovereignty. That approach is discriminatory because it means that the interest of Aboriginal peoples in their lands is less than that of a wrongdoer who acquires title to land by adverse possession. If common law principles relating to occupation of land are applied, the Aboriginal peoples should have an all-encompassing interest, subject only to a restraint on alienation other than by surrender to the Crown.[137] This approach is consistent with Dickson's judgment in *Guerin*, as he said that the Indian interest in Aboriginal title lands and reserve lands is the same, and we have seen that the Indian interest in reserve lands is an all-encompassing interest except for the restraint on alienation.

The most disturbing aspect of Macfarlane and Wallace's approach is that it would prevent Aboriginal societies from adapting their use of land to meet changes caused by European colonization. As they would not have an Aboriginal right to use their ancestral lands for purposes that were not integral to their cultures at the time the Crown acquired sovereignty, they would have to try to maintain their precolonial uses in order to exercise their Aboriginal rights. As other uses of the land would exceed their rights, they would be denied the possibility of developing their communities in contemporary ways on the basis of those rights. As a result, they would probably have to assimilate into Canadian society in order to survive, which would no doubt lead to the destruction of their distinctive cultures.

The better approach, therefore, is to define Aboriginal title as an all-encompassing interest which is not limited to precolonial uses of the land. This approach accords with common law principles, avoids discrimination, and provides the Aboriginal peoples with the opportunity to develop their lands in ways that meet the contemporary needs of their communities. It is an approach which supports the self-sufficiency and growth of those communities and the preservation of Aboriginal cultures. For these reasons, it should be adopted both by the courts and by governments in their negotiations of Aboriginal land claims.

6
Wampum at Niagara: The Royal Proclamation, Canadian Legal History, and Self-Government

John Borrows[1]

The Royal Proclamation of 1763[2] is a 'fundamental document' in First Nations and Canadian legal history.[3] Yet, recent Canadian commentators[4] have often treated the Royal Proclamation of 1763 as a unilateral declaration of the Crown's will in its provisions relating to First Nations.[5] It is time that this misunderstanding was corrected. First Nations were not passive objects, but active participants, in the formulation and ratification of the Royal Proclamation.[6] In the colonial struggle for northern North America, and in the foundational development of principles to guide the relationship between First Nations and the British Crown, First Nations were not dependent victims of a greater power.[7] In these early confrontations with the Crown, First Nations possessed their own power and a range of choices to which they could bring their own considerations and alternatives. First Nations faced a pivotal period of choice and decision-making between 1760 and 1764, after the British had asserted control over the French in North America.[8] The options then chosen are important today because the principles agreed upon form the foundation upon which the present First Nations/Crown relationship rests.

This article will show that the Royal Proclamation is part of a treaty between First Nations and the Crown which stands as a positive guarantee of First Nation self-government.[9] The other part of the treaty is contained in an agreement ratified at Niagara in 1764. Within this treaty are found conditions that underpin the Proclamation and that lie outside of the bare language of the document's words. The portion of the treaty confirmed at Niagara has often been overlooked, with the result that the manuscript of the Proclamation has not been integrated with First Nation understandings of this document. A reconstruction of the events and promises of 1763-4, which takes account of the treaty of Niagara, transforms conventional interpretations of colonialism which allow the Crown to ignore First Nations participation.[10] Through this re-evaluation of early

Canadian legal history, one is led to the conclusion that the Proclamation cannot be interpreted to undermine First Nations rights.[11] As will be illustrated, Proclamation/Treaty of Niagara rights persisted throughout the early colonization of Canada. These Aboriginal rights survived to form and sustain the foundations of the First Nations/Crown relationship, and to inform Canada's subsequent treaty-making history. The approach developed in this paper will provide an example of the partiality of conventional ethnocentric colonial interpretations of Canadian legal history.[12]

Canadian Legal History from a First Nations Perspective

In order to appreciate the meaning that the Royal Proclamation holds for First Nation peoples, one must first understand its historical context.[13] Contextualization of the Proclamation reveals that one cannot interpret its meaning using the written words of the document alone. To interpret the principles of the Proclamation using this procedure would conceal First Nations perspectives and inappropriately privilege one culture's practice over another.[14] First Nations chose to chronicle their perception of the Proclamation through other methods such as contemporaneous speeches, physical symbols, and subsequent conduct. First Nations perspectives about the Proclamation become more conspicuous when reconstructed using these different sources because this method respects the fact that literacy in First Nations was orally based.[15] The compilation of First Nations understanding about the Proclamation from various sources will form the substance of this paper.

Historical Background to the Royal Proclamation and the Treaty of Niagara

The principles of the Proclamation found their genesis in the relationships between First Nations and colonial powers in the decades leading up to the 1760s. The interaction of Native and non-Native people during this period resulted in the formulation of principles to regulate the allocation of land, resources, and jurisdiction between them. These principles were developed through practised experience, war, and negotiation and, as such, were the product of both societies' precepts.

The traditional lifestyle of First Nations around the Great Lakes was altered after their first contact with non-Indigenous people in the early 1600s when the French intruded on Aboriginal territory.[16] The French established Jesuit missions near the shores of the Great Lakes and had contact with First Nations through exploration and trading.[17] At the same time, the Dutch, and later the British, were establishing settlements to the south of the Great Lakes along the Atlantic coast into the Appalachian Mountains.[18] The French and English were each seeking to establish greater control over territories within North America, and they courted First Nation allies to solidify their interests.[19] Conflict between the French and English for the control of trade on the upper Great Lakes eventually led to the Seven Years' War.[20] A large proportion of First Nation people around the Great Lakes, with the notable exception of the Haudenoshonee, supported the French in their fight against the British for control of the region.[21] Despite the loss of the war by their French allies in 1760, First Nation peoples did not consider their sovereignty extinguished by this event. One British colonial official observed this to be the case when he wrote: 'The Six Nations, Western Indians [Anishnabe, etc.] & c. having never been conquered, Either by the English or French, nor subject to the Laws, consider themselves as free people.'[22]

A First Nations perspective reflecting the view that they were not conquered was made by Minavavana, an Ojibwa chief from west of Manitoulin at Michilimackinac. Minavavana declared:

Englishman, although you have conquered the French you have not yet conquered us! We are not your slaves. These lakes, these woods and mountains, were left to us by our ancestors. They are our inheritance; and we will part with them to none. Your nation supposes that we, like the white people, cannot live without bread, and pork and beef! But, you ought to know, that He, the Great Spirit and Master of Life, has provided food for us, in these spacious lakes, and on these woody mountains.

Englishman, our Father, the king of France, employed our young men to make war upon your nation. In this warfare, many of them have been killed; and it is our custom to retaliate, until such time as the spirits of the slain are satisfied. But, the spirits of the slain are to be satisfied in either of two ways; the first is the spilling of the blood of the nation by which they fell; the other, by covering the bodies of the dead, and thus allaying the resentment of their relations. This is done by making presents.

Englishman, your king has never sent us any presents, nor entered into any treaty with us, wherefore he and we are still at war; and, until he does these things, we must consider that we have no other father or friend among the white man, than the king of France ...

You have ventured your life among us, in the expectation that we should not molest you. You do not come armed, with an intention to make war, you come in peace, to trade with us, to supply us with necessities, of which we are in much want. We shall regard you therefore as a brother; and you may sleep tranquilly, without fear of the Chipeways. As a token of our friendship we present you with this pipe, to smoke.[23]

This speech is notable in many respects as a statement of the government to government relationship which First Nation peoples were proposing to the British. Minavavana recounted some of the principles of peace and coexistence being formulated by First Nations. First, it is significant that the Ojibwa stated unequivocally that they were 'not yet conquered.' They considered their allegiance as being to the Great Spirit, and not to any European power. Second, it is important to note that the Ojibwa regarded themselves and the English as being reliant on one another for trade and peace, and therefore their power relationship as being parallel. Finally, the Ojibwa stated that the British had to fulfil certain obligations, such as the giving of gifts, in order to attain even a state of coexistence with them.

In the early stages of First Nation/settler association, the English failed to comprehend some of the diplomatic fundamentals that First Nations required in the definition of their Constitutional relationship. One example of the British failure in this regard concerned the presentation of gifts.[24] The French had followed the diplomatic formalities which formalized First Nation/settler relations and were thus able to maintain peace by supplying gifts to all their First Nation allies. When the British did not meet all the conditions that First Nations established for coexistence, conflict resulted.

Presents were important to First Nations because they were regarded as a necessary part of diplomacy which involved accepting gifts in return for others sharing their lands.[25] The cessation of presents caused some First Nations, led by an Odawa Indian named Pontiac,[26] to resume fighting the British again in 1764.[27] This continued aggression by First Nations against the British illustrates that First Nations used their sovereignty to uphold the official diplomatic conditions they imposed upon the British and to direct the structure of their relationship. The British later instituted the exchange and giving of gifts to First Nations to recognize and affirm their alliance with them.[28]

First Nations/settler policies constructing the foundational principles for their relationship were further developed through Articles of Capitulation drawn up at the end of the Seven Years War. The Articles were framed to insulate First Nations from British interference and they supported First Nations in their view about the unextinguished nature of their sovereignty. Despite the articles apparently being drafted without First Nation input, they reflected First Nations perspectives as much as if First Nations were present and in agreement at the signing because of the relative power possessed by First Nations in 1760.[29]

Article 40, agreed to by British Major-General Amherst and French Lieutenant-Governor the Marquis de Vaudreuil, demonstrates the awareness of both the French and the English that First Nations were autonomous and independent. The article stated: 'The Savages or Indian allies of his most Christian Majesty, shall be maintained in the Lands they inhabit, if they chose to remain there; they shall not be molested on any pretence whatsoever, for having carried arms, and served his most Christian Majesty; they shall have, as well as the French, liberty of religion.'[30] This article verified French and English policy that First Nations should be maintained in their lands and not be molested in the use of their lands. The capitulation agreement represented the promise that First Nations territory was not to be reduced, nor was First Nations sovereignty to be subsumed, by alliance with either the French or the English. Both the French and the English wanted to maintain the cooperation of First Nations because of the military and economic power that First Nations continued to possess. There was a realization that non-interference with First Nations territory and jurisdiction was the best way for the colonies to benefit from the strong influence that First Nations could still exercise over colonial affairs.[31] As a result, until the early 1760s First Nations maintained much of their ability to determine their activities. First Nations control began to change with the introduction of the Royal Proclamation.

The Royal Proclamation

A principal incident concerning First Nation rights after the Articles of Capitulation was the promulgation of the Royal Proclamation of 1763[32] and the associated Treaty of Niagara. Immediately prior to the Proclamation, First Nation land in the Ohio valley, and elsewhere in the West, had been increasingly threatened by European speculation and settlement.[33] As a result of rapid European settlement on the eastern seaboard of the North American continent,[34] First Nation peoples in the southern Great Lakes region began to feel pressures to leave their traditional homelands and resettle west of the Mississippi River.[35] Often, both First Nations and settlers used crass power and force to confront these difficulties.[36] The discontent caused by this conflict necessitated the formulation of principles to mediate First Nation/settler contention.[37] For First Nations, the lamentable alternatives to generating foundational principles of coexistence were resettlement or the defence of their territory with the high cost of persecution and bloodshed. The First Nations of the southern Great Lakes region saw such conflict as antithetical to their interests.[38]

To alleviate conflict, the Royal Proclamation was declared to delineate boundaries and define jurisdictions between First Nations and the Crown.[39] The Proclamation attempted to convince First Nations that the British would respect existing political and territorial jurisdiction by incorporating First Nations understandings of this relationship in the document. The

Proclamation does this by implying that no lands would be taken from First Nation peoples without their consent.[40] However, in order to consolidate the Crown's position in North America, words were also placed in the Proclamation which did not accord with First Nations viewpoints of the parties' relationship to one another and to the land. For example, the British inserted statements in the Proclamation that claimed 'dominion' and 'sovereignty' over the territories that First Nations occupied. In placing these divergent notions within the Proclamation, the British were trying to convince Native people that there was nothing to fear from the colonists, while at the same time trying to increase political and economic power relative to First Nations and other European powers. The British perceptively realized that alleviating First Nations' 'discontent'[41] required that Native people believe that their jurisdiction and territory were protected; however, the British also realized that the colonial enterprise required an expansion of the Crown's sovereignty and dominion over the 'Indian' lands. Thus, while the Proclamation seemingly reinforced First Nation preferences that First Nation territories remain free from European settlement or imposition, it also opened the door to the erosion of these same preferences.

The Proclamation uncomfortably straddled the contradictory aspirations of the Crown and First Nations when its wording recognized Aboriginal rights to land by outlining a policy that was designed to extinguish these rights. These rights and their potential removal were affirmed by three principles or procedures: 1) colonial governments were forbidden to survey or grant any unceded lands; 2) colonial governments were forbidden to allow British subjects to settle on Indian lands or to allow private individuals to purchase them; and 3) there was an official system of public purchases developed in order to extinguish Indian title.[42] In implementing these principles an area of land was designated as First Nation territory. The boundaries were determined by past cessions and existing First Nation possessions.[43] These principles codified pre-existing First Nation/colonial practice and reflected some First Nation preferences in maintaining territorial integrity and decision-making power over their lands.[44] These principles simultaneously worked against First Nation preferences by enabling the Crown to enlarge its powers by creating a process to take land away from First Nations.

The implications of this policy were that First Nations, for the most part, would not be integrated with the European population, as immigration would be directed to the south and the east where First Nations had already ceded their lands.[45] While the Proclamation did make provision for future surrenders of land,[46] the wording of the document made it unclear as to whether First Nations would have the political power required to exercise autonomy through their own sovereignty or under British jurisdiction. The document's equivocation between Aboriginal sovereignty and subordination is evidenced in the Proclamation's description of 'Nations or Tribes with whom we are connected, and who live under our protection.'[47] The status of First Nation/Crown jurisdiction was also confused in the Proclamation by the implication that British civil[48] and criminal[49] jurisdiction would not be administered on First Nation lands, while at the same time the Proclamation allowed for people to be charged with British offences committed in Indian territory.[50] Therefore, the Proclamation illustrates the British government's attempt to exercise sovereignty over First Nations while simultaneously trying to convince First Nations that they would remain separate from European settlers and have their jurisdiction preserved.[51]

The different objectives that First Nations and the Crown had in the formulation of the principles surrounding the Proclamation is the reason for the different visions embedded within its text. Britain was attempting to secure territory and jurisdiction through the Proclamation, while First Nations were concerned with preserving their lands and sovereignty. Paradoxically, at the same time that the Crown was trying to reassure First Nations that their communities would be undisturbed, many First Nations were inviting colonial assistance to gain military and economic advantages. These competing policies between and within the parties' objectives were not resolved in the wording of the Proclamation because the Crown privileged its understanding of how land would be allocated. The effect of this privileging was to limit First Nations' ability to freely determine their land use, despite Aboriginal non-agreement with such a result, as evidenced by the Treaty of Niagara.

The Treaty of Niagara

Since the wording of the Proclamation is unclear about the autonomy and jurisdiction of First Nations, and since the Proclamation was drafted under the control and preference of the colonial power,[52] the spirit and intent of the Royal Proclamation can best be discerned by reference to a treaty with First Nations representatives at Niagara in 1764.[53] At this gathering a nation-to-nation relationship between settler and First Nation peoples was renewed and extended,[54] and the Covenant Chain of Friendship,[55] a multination alliance in which no member gave up their sovereignty,[56] was affirmed. The Royal Proclamation became a treaty[57] at Niagara because it was presented by the colonialists for affirmation, and was accepted by the First Nations.[58] However, when presenting the Proclamation, both parties made representations and promises through methods other than the written word, such as oral statements and belts of wampum.[59] It is significant to note that Sir William Johnson, superintendent of Indian affairs, had earlier agreed to meet with the First Nations and reassert their mutual relationship through requirements prescribed by the Aboriginal peoples,[60] which involved the giving and receiving of wampum belts.[61] Some principles which were implicit in the written version of the Proclamation were made explicit to First Nations in these other communications. For example, First Nation peoples approved terms of the Proclamation which encompassed more than a system of land allotment, including express guarantees of First Nations sovereignty.

In the winter after the Royal Proclamation was issued, First Nation leaders throughout the northeast, mideast, and midwest of North America were invited to attend a conference to be held the following summer to discuss the formation of principles that would govern their relationship with the Crown. The people of the Algonquin and Nipissing nations met with the British superintendent of Indian affairs at Oswegatchie and were persuaded to be messengers in inviting other First Nations to attend a peace council at Niagara in the summer of 1764.[62] Representatives of these two nations travelled throughout the winter of 1763-4 with a printed copy of the Royal Proclamation, and with various strings of wampum, in order to summons the various First Nations to a council with the British.[63]

William Johnson described the purpose of the intended meeting at Niagara as a 'Treaty of Offensive and Defensive Alliance' that would include British promises to 'assure them of a Free Fair & open trade, at the principal Posts, & a free intercourse, & passage into our Country, That we will make no Settlements or Encroachments contrary to Treaty, or without their permission. That we will bring to justice any persons who commit Robberys or Murders on them & that we will protect & aid them against their & our Enemys, & duly observe our Engagements with them.'[64] It is clear that, in conjunction with their issuance of the Proclamation, the British proposed that a treaty be entered into to negotiate and formalize the principles upon which their relationship would be based. The invitation to treaty, with the accompanying promises that were to govern the parties' relationship, demonstrates the intent of the British to enter into momentous negotiations with the First Nations of North America. Johnson further proposed, on behalf of the British, that: 'at this treaty ... we should tie them down (in the Peace) according to their own forms of which they take the most notice, for example by exchanging a very large belt with some remarkable & intelligible figures thereon. Expressive of the occasion which should always be shown to remind them of their promises.'[65] Thus, the treaty at Niagara was to be recorded in the manner that the First Nations were familiar with. Wampum belts were to be exchanged which would communicate the promises exchanged, and which would form the record of the agreement.

The treaty at Niagara was entered into in July and August 1764, and was regarded as 'the most widely representative gathering of American Indians ever assembled,'[66] as approximately two thousand chiefs attended the negotiations.[67] There were over twenty-four Nations gathered[68] with 'representative nations as far east as Nova Scotia, and as far west as Mississippi, and as far north as Hudson Bay.'[69] It is also possible that representatives from even further afield participated in the treaty as some records indicate that the Cree and Lakota (Sioux) nations were also present at this event.[70] It is obvious that a substantial number of First Nations people attended the gathering at Niagara. Aboriginal people throughout the Great Lakes and northern, eastern, and western colonial regions had travelled for weeks and months to attend this meeting.[71]

When everyone was assembled,[72] William Johnson presented 'the terms of what he hoped would prove a Pax Britannica for North America.'[73] Johnson read the terms of the Royal Proclamation to representatives of the nations[74] and a promise of peace was given by Aboriginal representatives and a state of mutual non-interference established.[75] Presents were exchanged to certify the binding nature of the promises being exchanged.[76] Johnson then presented the Covenant Chain and wampum belts and stated:

> Brothers of the Western Nations, Sachems, Chiefs and Warriors;
>
> You have now been here for several days, during which time we have frequently met to renew and Strengthen our Engagements and you have made so many Promises of your Friendship and Attachment to the English that there now remains for us only to exchange the great Belt of the Covenant Chain that we may not forget out mutual Engagements.
>
> I now therefore present you the great Belt by which I bind all your Western Nations together with the English, and I desire that you will take fast hold of the same, and never let it slip, to which end I desire that after you have shewn this Belt to all Nations you will fix one end of it with the Chipeweighs at St. Marys [Michilimackinac] whilst the other end remains at my house, and moreover I desire that you will never listen to any news which comes to any other Quarter. If you do it, it may shake the Belt.[77]

By this speech, and an exchange of presents and wampum, a treaty of alliance and peace was established between the parties. When Johnson had finished speaking, a two-row wampum belt was used by First Nation peoples to reflect their understanding of the treaty of Niagara and the words of the Royal Proclamation.[78]

The two-row wampum belt reflects a diplomatic convention that recognizes interaction and separation of settler and First Nation societies. This agreement was first struck by the Haudonosaunee (Iroquois) upon contact with the Europeans, and the principles it represents were renewed in 1764.[79] The symbolism of the two-row wampum belt has been commented on by a leading Native legal academic, Robert A. Williams, Jr.:

> When the Haudenosaunee first came into contact with the European nations, treaties of peace and friendship were made. Each was symbolized by the Gus-Wen-Tah, or Two Row Wampum. There is a bed of white wampum which symbolizes the purity of the agreement. There are two rows of purple, and those two rows have the spirit of your ancestors and mine. There are three beads of wampum separating the two rows and they symbolize peace, friendship and respect. These two rows will symbolize two paths or two vessels, travelling down the same river together. One, a birch bark canoe, will be for the Indian people, their laws, their customs and their ways. The other, a ship, will be for the white people and theirs laws, their customs, and their ways. We shall each travel the river together, side by side, but in our own boat. Neither of us will try to steer the other's vessel.[80]

The two-row wampum belt illustrates a First Nation/Crown relationship that is founded on peace, friendship, and respect, where each nation will not interfere with the internal affairs of the other. An interpretation of the Proclamation using the Treaty of Niagara discredits the claims of the Crown to exercise sovereignty over First Nations. In fact, Sir William Johnson indicated as much when he commented on a questionable treaty in 1865:

> These people had subscribed to a Treaty with me at Niagara in August last, but by the present Treaty I find, they make expressions of subjection, which must either have arisen from the ignorance of the Interpreter, or from some mistake; for I am well convinced, they never mean or intend anything like it, and that they can not be brought under our laws, for some Centuries, neither have they any word which can convey the most distant idea of subjection, and should it be fully explained to them, and the nature of subordination punishment ettc [sic], defined, it might produce infinite harm ... and I dread its consequences, as I recollect that some attempts towards Sovereignty not long ago, was one of the principal causes of all our troubles.[81]

One can see that Sir William Johnson did not regard the extension of the Royal Proclamation and the Treaty at Niagara as an assertion of sovereignty over the First Nations. Records such as the two-row wampum belt, and statements such as Johnson's, further allow First Nations to assert that their jurisdiction can not be molested or disturbed without Aboriginal consent.

The evidence surrounding the Treaty of Niagara demonstrates that the written text of the Proclamation, while it contains a partial understanding of the agreement at Niagara, does not fully reflect the consensus of the parties.[82] The concepts found in the Proclamation have different meanings when interpreted in accord with the wampum belt. For example, the belt's denotation of each nation pursuing its own path while living beside one another in peace and friendship casts new light on the Proclamation's wording 'the several Nations ... with whom we are connected ... should not be molested or disturbed.' These words, read in conjunction with the two-row wampum, demonstrate that the connection between the nations spoken of in the Proclamation is one that mandates colonial non-interference in the land use and governments of First Nations. Therefore, First Nations regarded the agreement, represented by the Proclamation and the two-row wampum, as one that affirmed their powers of self-determination in, among other things, allocating land. This agreement, at the start of the formal relationship between the British and the First Nations of Canada, demonstrates the foundation-building principles of peace, friendship, and respect agreed to between the parties.

Reading the Proclamation and the Treaty of Niagara Together: Subsequent Understandings

A final point in determining First Nations understandings of the Royal Proclamation involves examining subsequent conduct relative to it. Since First Nations were likely to speak and act in accordance with their understandings of the Proclamation, subsequent conduct illustrates First Nations perspectives towards the Proclamation and demonstrates that Native consent was required to any alteration of First Nation land use and governance.[83] Over the years following the treaty of Niagara, including during the War of 1812, many Aboriginal people around the Great Lakes strengthened their alliance with the British in order to fight against the United States.[84] After the War of 1812, many Aboriginal people who resided in the growing American territories of Michigan, Wisconsin, and Ohio wanted to move from the United States because American policies endangered First Nations.[85] In this period Britain maintained its alliance and friendship with First Nations by making an annual distribution of presents[86] and by encouraging Native peoples residing on lands under American control to take up residence 'under their protection.'[87] In 1828 the British bestowal of presents to First Nations was moved from American-controlled Drummond Island to British-controlled Penetanguishine on Georgian Bay.[88]

Transcripts of a meeting in July 1818 at Drummond Island in Lake Huron to the west of Manitoulin between Anishnabe peoples and representatives of the British Crown contain articulate references to the Treaty of Niagara. An account of the meeting is as follows:

> The Chiefs did de camp, laying down a broad Wampum Belt, made in 1764; one made in 1786; and one marked Lieutenant M'Dowal, Commanding Michilimackinac, with the pipe of peace marked on it.
>
> Orcarta [Anishnabe] speaker
>
> Father, Your children now seated round you, salute you sincerely, they intend to talk to you a great deal, and beg you will listen to them with patience, for they intend to open their hearts to you ...
>
> Holding the Belt of 1764 in his hand he said:
>
> Father, This my ancestors received from our Father, Sir W. Johnson. You sent word to all your red children to assemble at the crooked place (Niagara). They heard your voice – obeyed the message – and the next summer met you at the place. You then laid this belt on a mat, and said – 'Children, you must all touch this Belt of Peace. I touch it myself, that we may all be brethren united, and hope our friendship will never cease. I will call you my children; will send warmth (presents) to your country; and your families shall never be in want. Look towards the rising sun. My Nation is as brilliant as it is, and its word cannot be violated.'
>
> Father, Your words were true – all you promised came to pass. On giving us the Belt of Peace, you said – 'If you should ever require my assistance, send this Belt, and my hand will be immediately stretched forth to assist you.'
>
> Here the speaker laid down the Belt.[89]

This speech is significant because it reveals that some fifty-four years after the treaty of Niagara, First Nations of northern Lake Huron maintained their recollection of the promises made there. In particular, the speaker made specific mention of the mutual obligations of peace and friendship, as found in the wampum belt. When considering these events from a First Nations perspective, it is remarkable to understand that these peoples viewed the Royal Proclamation as a treaty of peace and friendship. When one considers, in addition, that this treaty also contained an obligation for the Crown to sustain the welfare of First Nations, as found in the words 'If you should ever require my assistance, send this Belt, and my hand will be immediately stretched forth to assist you,' then one can better appreciate and perhaps reinterpret[90] the contemporary justification for the fiduciary relationship between First Nations and the Crown.

In 1836 the distribution of presents was moved to Manitoulin Island to promote it as a place for the settlement of the Crown's Aboriginal allies.[91] Observance of First Nations perspectives on the Treaty of Niagara and the Royal Proclamation is evidenced at the Manitoulin Island gatherings. One very strong endorsement of the Treaty of Niagara is found in the Manitoulin Island Treaty of 1836 between the Crown and First Nations of the upper Great Lakes.[92] First Nations present at the negotiations reminded Sir Francis Bond Head, lieutenant-governor of Upper Canada, that their relationship must be defined in terms agreed upon in the two-row wampum belt at the treaty of Niagara.[93] Assickinack, an Odawa chief resident at Manitoulin, gave a recitation and interpretation of the two-row wampum belt and the agreement at Niagara.[94] In his reply, Bond Head noted the principles agreed upon at Niagara by stating: 'Seventy snow seasons have now passed away since we met in council at the crooked place (Niagara) at which time your Great Father, the King and the Indians of North America tied their hands together by the wampum of friendship.'[95] The reminder by First Nations to the Crown of the relationship defined at Niagara, and the reaffirmation of that relationship as being one of solidarity and friendship in a very significant treaty, again suggests that the Treaty of Niagara significantly undermines the claims of British sovereignty over First Nations as found in the Proclamation. This understanding should be kept in mind when interpreting the subsequent treaties in Canada. The agreement at Niagara created specific guarantees to certain rights and, while these guarantees were sometimes made explicit in subsequent acts, they were certainly implied as they were woven through the negotiations, often forming the protocol by which decisions were made.[96]

Aside from preserving the agreement represented by the Royal Proclamation in wampum belts and oral recollections, First Nations also preserved copies of the Proclamation they received in 1764. Copies of the document were often brought forward to colonial officials when First Nations wanted to assert their perspective of what was written in the Proclamation.[97] Evidence of First Nation peoples' use of the Proclamation to convey their understanding of its principles is found in an 1847 colonial report. Commissioners of the colonial government spoke with many First Nation peoples to determine their views on a variety of matters. When views were solicited relative to the Proclamation, the commissioners were referred to the document, and First Nation peoples expressed their understanding of it. The commissioners wrote the following regarding First Nations' understanding: 'The subsequent proclamation of His Majesty George Third, issued in 1763, furnished them with a fresh guarantee for the possession of their hunting grounds and the protection of the crown. This document the Indians look upon as their charter. They have preserved a copy of it to the present time, and have referred to it on several occasions in their representations to government.'[98] This statement illustrates that First Nation peoples possessed copies of the Proclamation and presented the document to other governments to convey their perspective of what it contained. In the particular communications that these officials received, First Nation peoples expressed their conviction that the agreement represented by the Proclamation was their charter.

That the Proclamation represented a charter for First Nations in the definition of their relationship with the Crown was observed by the commissioners' writing in another part of the report:

> This public instrument [the Royal Proclamation] was formally communicated to the Indians of Canada, by the officer who had a few years before been appointed for their special superintendence; and that they have since regarded it as a solemn pledge of the King's protection of their interests, is proved by the claim of the Algonkians and Nippissing Indians, to be maintained in the possession of their remaining hunting grounds on the Ottawa River, which your excellency has referred to the Committee, and in support of which those tribes exhibited an authentic copy of this Royal Proclamation as promulgated to them in 1763 by the Superintendent General.[99]

These statements further reveal that First Nations continued to hold out the document of the Proclamation and the agreement it represented as an affirmation of their rights some eighty years after it was penned. They expected the Crown to protect their interests, and not allow them to be interfered with, especially with regard to their land use and means of livelihood. This demonstrates the strength with which First Nations must have expressed their views that they were to be 'maintained' and 'protected' in their 'interests.'[100] It further illustrates the fact that First Nations had a perspective of the document that contradicts claims to British sovereignty found in the Proclamation.

Conclusion

The promises made at Niagara and echoed in the Royal Proclamation have never been abridged, repealed,[101] or rendered nugatory.[102] Since Aboriginal rights are presumed to continue until the contrary is proven,[103] the supposed 'increasing weight' of colonial history and its disregard of the Treaty of Niagara does not render void the Aboriginal rights under its protection.[104] Furthermore, since the Proclamation is not a 'unilateral declaration of the Crown,'[105] but part of a treaty into which First Nations had considerable input, it therefore must be interpreted as it would be 'naturally understood' by them.[106] A 'natural understanding' of the Proclamation by First Nations prompts an interpretation that includes the promises made at Niagara. These promises are: a respect for the sovereignty of First Nations,[107] the creation of an alliance[108] ('the several Nations ... with whom we are connected'[109]), free and open trade and passage between the Crown and First Nations[110] ('shall not be molested or disturbed'), permission or consent needed for settlement of First Nations territory[111] ('same shall be purchased for use ... at some public meeting or assembly of Indians'), the English provision of presents to First Nations,[112] mutual peace, friendship, and respect[113] ('that the Indians may be convinced of our Justice and determined resolution to remove all reasonable cause of discontent'). The promises made at Niagara, and their solemnization in proclamation and treaty, demonstrate that there was from the outset considerable doubt[114] about the Crown's assertion of sovereignty and legislative power over Aboriginal rights.[115] The securing of these significant promises demonstrates that First Nations treated with the Crown as active and powerful partners in making provisions for the future relationship between the parties.

This article has also provided evidence that the Royal Proclamation of 1763 is not only a 'fundamental document'[116] but, along with the Treaty of Niagara, the most 'fundamental agreement' yet entered into between First Nations and the Crown, and much more than a unilateral declaration of the Crown's will. A significantly large and representative number of First Nations were present at the negotiations, and both parties have bound themselves to adhere to its terms through over 230 years of subsequent treaty-making.[117] From 1764 to 1994, principles derived from the Royal Proclamation have provided the procedural rules which govern the treaty-making enterprise in Canada.[118] As such, the express terms and promises made in the Proclamation and at Niagara may yet be found to form the underlying terms and conditions which should be implied in all subsequent and future treaties. This would provide First Nations treaty law with some universality and consistency which heretofore has been missing from the case-by-case, factually specific, judicial treatment of each agreement. The existence of the promises exchanged at Niagara demonstrates that the obligations undertaken by the Crown in subsequent treaties may be greater than formerly acknowledged. There may be important support at common law for this finding.

Since Canadian Indian treaties have been described as *sui generis*,[119] legal interpretations of treaties can only rely upon analogies to categories of contract and international law.[120] However, despite the potential uncertainty which may surround when to engage such analogies, it has been found that the basic analogy which Canadian jurists rely upon in *sui generis* formulations of First Nations treaties is that of contract.[121] With contract as an analogy, as appropriate, the courts could view contractual doctrines governing the express terms of the Royal Proclamation/Treaty of Niagara as implied terms in later First Nation treaties.

The doctrine that allows for the placement of implied terms into contracts has been summarized in a leading text on contracts as follows:

> The contents of a contract are not necessarily confined to those that appear on its face. The parties may have negotiated against a background of commercial or local usage whose implications they have tacitly assumed, and to concentrate solely on their express language may be to minimise or to distort the extent of the liabilities. Evidence of custom may thus have to be admitted. Additional consequences, moreover, may have been annexed by statute to particular contracts, which will operate despite the parties' ignorance or even contrary to their intention. Finally, the courts may read into a contract some further term which alone makes it effective, and which the parties may be taken to have omitted by pure inadvertence.[122]

Following such a course in First Nations jurisprudence would ensure that the express terms of the Proclamation and the Treaty of Niagara are implied in subsequent treaties between the Crown and First Nations. This would lead to the recognition of national treaty standards to protect the express promises made at Niagara, and would also allow for local variations in treaties as they dealt with local concerns.

For example, it is quite probable that the contents of each treaty signed after the Royal Proclamation/Treaty of Niagara have more to them than appears on their face.[123] The parties negotiated subsequent treaties against a background of Canadian Proclamation/Niagara usage (extending from the Maritimes to the foothills of the Rocky Mountains[124]), the implications of which both parties can be tacitly assumed to accept. The implied conditions each party would assume in subsequent treaties would be the promises spelled out in 1764, or those similar to them renewed at later meetings. As will be recalled, these were promises of a preservation of sovereignty, alliance, trade, consent to land surrender, and affirmations of peace, friendship, and respect. To concentrate solely on the express language of the subsequent treaties, without accounting for these promises, would minimize or distort the extent of the liabilities the Crown undertook in 1763-4. Since the terms of the Niagara agreement were often referred to in later treaties, but did not find their way into the text, evidence of custom may be admitted to demonstrate understanding of sovereignty, alliance, free trade, gift giving, consent to surrender, and peace, friendship, and respect.[125]

The *sui generis* nature of treaty interpretation also increases the potential for additional matters to be annexed by statute to particular treaties. This addition can occur despite the parties' ignorance or even contrary to their intention because the Proclamation has the force of a statute. 'There is a well-established common law principle that instruments issued under the Royal Prerogative in British colonial possessions lacking legislative assemblies have the force of statutes in these areas.'[126] The Royal Proclamation, having the force of statute, would affix the promises made in the Proclamation/Treaty to the subsequent treaties, despite the parties' (usually the Crown's) disregard of the earlier agreement's intention. Thus, the courts may read into subsequent treaties some further specific terms that alone make the promises at Niagara effective.

An approach to treaty interpretation which followed contractual analogies in the manner just outlined would provide a more principled and consistent basis from which to understand these agreements. While the application of these principles would not be determinative because of their *sui generis* nature, they could prove to be very helpful analogies to make treaty interpretation more 'large, liberal and fair.' This would reduce some of the 'patchwork' of treatment now accorded to this area of the law.[127] An interpretation of treaties which recognized the general terms implied from the Treaty of Niagara, while accepting specific express terms in local negotiations, would both acknowledge the differences between the treaties and harmonize rights more equitably among First Nations. The acceptance of both the national and local character of treaties would allow the courts to interpret them according to the particular history, legend, politics, and moral obligations of an area, while also developing principles which would apply on a more global basis.[128]An understanding of First Nations rights as guaranteed by the Royal Proclamation/Treaty of Niagara would overcome much of the ethnocentrism that has informed colonial legal history in Canada. First Nations would then be regarded as active participants in the formulation and ratification of their rights in Canada. This would go a long way to dispelling notions found in Canadian legal and political discourse that regard First Nations as subservient to or dependant upon the Crown in pressing and preserving their rights. In light of the history and subsequent agreements in relation to the Treaty of Niagara, the Royal Proclamation can no longer be interpreted as a unilateral declaration of the Crown. As a result, the Royal Proclamation can no longer be interpreted as a document which undermines First Nations rights. Colonial interpretations of the Royal Proclamation should be recognized for what they are – a discourse that dispossesses First Nations of their rights.

7
Understanding Treaty 6: An Indigenous Perspective

Sharon Venne[1]

Introduction

For an understanding of the relationship between the Treaty Peoples and the Crown of Great Britain and later Canada, one must consider a number of factors beyond the treaty's written text. First, the written text expresses only the government of Canada's view of the treaty relationship: it does not embody the negotiated agreement. Even the written versions of treaties have been subject to considerable interpretation, and they may be scantily supported by reports or other information about the treaty negotiations. Fortunately, Treaty Nations have also kept a record of the treaties in their oral histories, and these can provide another understanding of treaty agreements.

A second factor is critical to understanding treaty relationships: the authority given to the negotiators. Each nation in treaty negotiations delegated certain members of their citizenry to negotiate the treaty, and empowered them to make a certain kind of agreement with negotiators from the other nation. Neither the Crown nor the Indigenous[2] nations gave their negotiators free and unfettered authority to negotiate, although negotiators from both sides may have been uncertain about the mandate of the other nation's negotiators.

The authority structure on the Crown's side is fairly well known. However, on the Indigenous side, the authority, responsibilities, and mandate of negotiators, as well as of Chiefs and other members of society, are not clearly understood. An appreciation of the authority to negotiate treaties on the Indigenous side is essential to understanding the treaty relationship.

This article will discuss these two factors – the oral basis for interpreting the treaties, and the authority vested in Indigenous negotiators – focusing on Cree society and Treaty 6, signed in 1876. The paper looks at the authority structures developed generally by Indigenous peoples and practised in

Cree society. It also examines the international context in which treaties were made. Finally, based on all these factors, the paper looks at the Cree version of Treaty 6, and the Elders' understanding of the treaty's importance for all peoples (Indigenous and non-Indigenous). As the paper draws extensively on oral history taught by Cree Elders, it begins with a discussion of the oral tradition, its context, and its reliability.

Oral History

This is a story about Plains Cree Peoples, their traditional selection of their leadership, and the role of their leadership in entering into Treaty 6 with the British Crown. It is a story about the Cree Peoples' understanding of the promises made in Treaty 6. It is based on what the Elders have passed on in their teachings. In an oral culture, the means of passing on information is via story telling. That is not to say someone makes up a story, but a story is the manner in which the information is told.[3]

When the Elders come together, the stories begin to flow. One Elder alone has many stories, but when a number of Elders are placed in the same room, the stories multiply. One Elder may know part of a story and another will know the rest of the story. Together, the Elders tell the history of the nation. Narrative is a powerful method for teaching many things, including the history of an oral people. The key is to listen and learn.

From early childhood, an Indigenous person learns to listen to the Elders, and eventually listening becomes an acquired skill. It takes a lot of patience to learn to listen. The Elders watch the young people to look for good listeners: it is the good listeners who will learn the stories. When a child is young, he or she is allowed to stay when Elders are speaking, but if the child becomes noisy, then the child must leave the room. If a child wants to learn the stories, then learning to be quiet and listen becomes important. The Elders see which children have the patience to learn.

Storytelling is an art and a skill among the Cree Peoples, as it is for all peoples who use the oral method to convey stories. A skilled storyteller is a master of the language and of the history of the peoples. It is through telling stories that the histories of the peoples, as well as important political, legal, and social values are transmitted.

The Use of Detail

When Elders begin to tell a story, they will describe in great detail the history which gave rise to the story. For example, Elder Charles Blackman of the Cold Lake Reserve begins: 'I'm 68 years old. Of what has been said, I will elaborate some things too, regarding the first signing of Treaty 6. I have heard in many place that I have been, and I've heard a lot the time the Elders assembled at Duck Lake, Saskatchewan. Elders were called up from many parts of the country. The expression the Elders gave then was the same as to what we have been saying.'[4] If the listener wants to verify the words of the Elder, they are made welcome to check with persons who were present at the meeting in Duck Lake, Saskatchewan. Another Elder from the same Cold Lake community, who was interviewed at the same time, said the following about learning the history of the people:

> I have attended quite a few meetings such as All Chiefs' Conferences. The reason why I go to these is I am concerned about the young people and at the same time, trying to understand what the Indian people are doing. And as I have heard what the old people said. The reason I'm saying this is because no matter where you are, a person will always find something that is good, traditions that are good and also find something that could be useful. This is where a young person could get a lot of ideas. But, then again a lot of these people don't attempt to follow these [teachings] ... you must not forget the Elders.[5]

The Elder began his story with the following words:

> He was my close relative. He was my grandfather, this old man Bear. And also Bighead was my grandfather. These were the people I used to hear talked about those things. They would tell these stories to the peoples. When I was small, I was one of those kids that liked to listen to everything. I guess that's why I'm telling you these things and today as we are sitting here ... I would appreciate very much if you could put these interviews out so the people could hear them all over and the things you are doing. Even though I will say we are past over seventy years of age. Still it would nice.

When I was a young child, I remember my grandmother describing a meeting which she attended as a young woman. The meeting was to discuss the land and whether land should be surrendered from the reserve. She told me the exact location of the meeting, pinpointing the hill where the meeting took place. My grandmother told of all the persons present at the meeting, including the clothing the women were wearing, right down to the colour of their head scarves. Her telling of the story occurred about fifty years after the meeting had taken place. She neither read nor wrote, but her mind was strong and sharp.

Why would she spend so much time describing what was said by each person and what kind of clothes they were wearing? That kind of detail gives life to the historical event. The description of people, speeches, and clothing puts breath into the story. It is also a way of verifying the story. These details can be checked by other people present at the meeting.

Recounting the smallest details indicates the memory is accurate. The way of mentally recording that meeting would be critical in later years when issues related to lands were discussed by the citizens of the community. The detail held by my grandmother's mind about the meeting served to ensure that future generations could listen to the story and feel and hear the context and texture of the discussions.

Collective Memory

No one Elder knows the complete story. The information is spread among a wide group of people for a variety of reasons. For one thing, the only one who knows the complete story within one mind is the Creator. No person could ever claim to be the Creator. So, the stories are spread among the people, and only through repeated and continuous contact with Indigenous communities can the complete stories be known. In addition, with stories spread over a number of people, the accuracy of the story is constantly open to review. If one Elder is changing their part of the story, then the parts held by other Elders will not fit together.

To a listener, sometimes the stories do not make sense. Often this is a way the Elders communicate the story: they tell a piece and wait to see if there is interest in the whole story. The story is then like a puzzle. Are the Elders making a puzzle? No, this is only the perception of the listener. The Elder wants the person to want to learn more. There is one piece in this corner, then another piece given at another time. It remains to the listener to put the pieces together and sort out the complete picture. If there are more questions, then the listener must make return visits to the Elders.

Learning is an individual experience and responsibility. One will never find Elders chasing after a listener; that is not their role. Their role is to remember and recount when asked the right question. The key is the question and how to ask it. Sometimes, it is difficult to understand the words of the Elders, but with patience and time, the meaning comes clear. The Elders do not operate like instant pudding. There is no 'add water, mix, and wait five minutes' for the pudding to set. It may take years to understand the lesson being taught. Many people have said that a story told to them made sense only after they heard another component of the story years later.

There are positive benefits to having many Elders keep the stories. The Elders with their age and wisdom have the time and patience to teach. Each Elder keeps the stories like a sacred trust to be handed down to the next generation. It is through continuous contact with the Elder that one will hear the complete story known by that Elder. It is not a process of sitting for one hour or an afternoon. The history of Indigenous peoples is learned over many years, as the depth of an Elder's knowledge is immeasurable.

In approaching Elders, there is a protocol. First, it is customary to ask an Elder to help you. Your request should be accompanied by a gift of tobacco and cloth. Sometimes, the Elder will tell you to see another person they believe to have more information. That is not to say that Elder does not know the subject area, but he or she may feel another is more knowledgable. Patience is important. An Elder does not always answer on the day the question is asked. Sometimes, you are requested to return a few days later. Not only does one learn about listening, but one learns about patience. In her book *Poundmaker,* Norma Sluman writes: 'Poundmaker was surprised with the Treaty Commissioner who was upset that he had been with them four days without an answer to the issue of Treaty making. This was following on his [Poundmaker's] mission to the Blackfoot Confederacy to make peace which took him all winter to negotiate. Four days to him seemed such a short time when discussing the future of his children's children. Time becomes irrelevant when the issues are related to Treaty. Time must be taken to ensure that everything is done right.'[6] If the Elder wants a person to know a story and not just part, they take time so the person remembers it, rather than rushing and letting some parts be forgotten.

The Elders have within their memories a collective history. No one Elder has all the information about a particular event; each has a personal memory which embraces their parents' or grandparents' memory of the details and circumstances of events that took place: 'My grandfather was the one who provided this testimony to me. I am sure that he was telling the truth. If my grandfather was a liar, I am a liar also by stating that what I have stated today.'[7] The stories are solemnly recalled by the Elders, as memory is a gift of the Creator. Many times, the Elders will say that the Creator has given a person a mind to use: do not waste the gift.

When the Elders talk about history, they never refer to non-Indigenous judicial or political considerations. The Elders refer only to the jurisdictions and political rights of our own people. It is from the Elders that we learn how to operate our governments and the standards to which our leaders must aspire in order to maintain a strong Indigenous government. The Elders have been taught about inheritances in the oral traditions. Their knowledge has been discussed, pondered, and reflected upon. The Elders, then, hold the inherited collective body of knowledge that transcends time and space.

The Selection of Chiefs

Some of the most instructional stories told by the Elders concern the position of Chiefs and the way a Chief is to be respected. When speaking of a Chief, the Elders change their tone of voice. They lower their voice to almost a hush, and there is a lot of respect shown even in the mentioning of a Chief's name. The Chief is looked to for guidance and leadership. Many times, people would say that we should talk to the Chief about such and such difficulty or tell the Chief about the good news of such and such. The Chief and the Headmen were placed in positions of honour and respect. Even today, people will refer to a person who is no longer Chief as the 'old Chief,' a place of honour among the peoples.

A Chief was chosen by the people to assume the leadership role. The position was not bestowed lightly by the people. The Chief and Headmen were an extension of the community to be respected and loved by their followers: 'The *okimaw* or leader of a group or band was always well looked after by his followers. They gave him the choicest cuts of their kill, and his larder was supposed to be amply supplied at all times so that he in turn could treat his many visitors to the best.'[8] The selection of a leader was not a competition. There was no such thing as a term of office. By their actions, the people made known their wishes to be led by a certain person. If another person aspired to the position, he would probably move away with some followers and form his own group. The process of leaving to form a new band was lost after the treaty was signed. The government of Canada unilaterally imposed a law against forming new bands. There is now a provision in the Indian Act, as amended by Bill C-31, for forming new bands. This provision has been used twice, when the minister of Indian affairs created the Woodland Cree Band and the Loon River Band in an attempt to undermine the rights of the Lubicon Cree in northern Alberta.

A story circulated in Indigenous country not long ago about a traditional selection process in northern Saskatchewan, where one man wanted to be Chief but was a mean person. In that community's selection process, the supporters of a person go and stand behind their choice. In this particular case, no one stood behind the man, not even his wife. This is one example of the process used to select the best person to be the leader.

A leader held his position as long as he had the respect of the people. If the time came to replace the leader, a person was selected who had been observed by the people for many years.

No matter how brave a man is and no matter how many horses he brings back [from raids], if he has nothing, he can't be a chief. It happened many times that a man would be brave and bring back many horses. But he would trade the horses for clothes and would be too lazy to get hides for a tipi cover and so he could never be chief. When a young man showed [by his deeds] that he would be a chief some day, the old men would go to see him and say, 'Now young man, you are climbing higher and higher and are on the way to become a chief. It is for your own good [that we speak]. It is not an easy thing to be chief. Look at this chief now. He has to have pity on the poor. When he sees a man in difficulty he must try to help in whatever way he can. If a person asks for something in his tipi, he must give it to him willingly and without any bad feeling. We are telling you this now because you will meet these things and you must have a strong heart.'[9]

This was the place of the Chief prior to the signing of the treaties, and remains so to the present day.

At the arrival of the non-Indigenous peoples into Indigenous territories, these Indigenous governmental structures were well established and functioning. The political structure of the Indigenous peoples is best described as a democracy, in the full sense of the word.[10] The leaders were selected by and accountable to the citizens of the communities. No one was excluded from the process. The leader chosen was always the 'bravest' man.[11] Citizens had access to their leaders, and if a leader was not performing as expected, he would be replaced.

Indigenous Peoples Are the Boss of the Chief

In a Cree Indigenous community, the *okimaw* (Chief) and Headmen[12] are only empowered to implement decisions made by their citizens. An individual who is chosen as a Chief or a Headman does not have any prerogative to make unilateral legal or political decisions binding the citizenry without their express consent. The Indigenous peoples who selected the Chief and Headmen are the boss. If the community has previously given direction, then the leaders are obligated to follow that direction. Chiefs cannot change the direction to suit the occasion, and they do not make decision isolated from their people. Community members ensure that they are involved in all decisions given to their leadership. This is not to say that the Chiefs and Headmen are not consulted about the direction of the communities. But the people have the political and legal authority, and the Chiefs carry out decisions, not the reverse. Chiefs should not and cannot order their people to do things in contravention of the peoples' wishes.

In a traditional Indigenous community, selection for a leadership position does not mean an end to the process; it is only the beginning. The leadership is under constant review and scrutiny by the members of the community. If you were to visit a Chief at his or her office or home, you would see community members and other Indigenous peoples arriving from early in the morning to late at night. In an Indigenous community, the Chief is a person to see on all matters, good and bad.

War Chiefs

One of the most interesting facets of the traditional government of the Crees was the role of the War Chief, which was usually different from that of a political leader. The War Chief occupied a very integral role within the community. He was the leader of the soldiers' lodge, which was comprised of young men under his direction:

> The Warrior's lodge was erected in the centre of the camp circle when the band came together in the spring. The societies did not function during the winter, except on those rare occasions when plentiful food and fuel made a large winter encampment possible. Their lodge was an enlarged tipi and was erected by the wives of the Warriors ... The members were seated in the order of their prestige, the place of honour behind the fire being reserved for the Warrior Chief ... This official was chosen by the Warriors; his authority was confined to those activities performed by the Warriors as a group ... The Warrior Chief was distinct from the Chief proper ... he was always one of the boldest and ablest of the fighting men ... When the Cree were gathered in large encampments, individual hunting could not be tolerated lest the game be driven away from the vicinity in a short time. When a herd was sighted, the Warriors went on guard to see that no one disturbed the buffalo before adequate preparations for the hunt were made. When all the hunters were ready, they were allowed to approach the herd slowly until the signal for the charge was made.[13]

The Warriors' tent was always placed behind the political Chief's tipi in the centre of the camp. In times when their enemies were far away, the Chief had undisputed control of the village. The soldiers carried out his edicts without complaint, controlling the hunts, dispensing justice to those who broke the laws, and acting as the police force of the camp.

However, if the village was in danger of attack, the leader of the soldiers' lodge immediately became the War Chief and ruled with complete authority. This custom was rooted in the logic of survival, for the political Chief of a camp was often an old man, interested only in peace and harmony. The delicate balance between the Chief and the leader of the soldiers' lodge was recognized by everyone in the camp, so it was rarely the source of conflict or jealousy. However, as the story of Chief Big Bear reveals, the settlers' government did not understand or choose to recognize the distinction between the two kinds of leadership.

Traditional Chiefs: The Case of Big Bear

The Elders talk about the qualities of Big Bear as a Chief. During his time, he was a well-known medicine man who had great powers. Big Bear also possessed many qualities of a good Chief, including being a great hunter, with proven abilities during times of battle. He was known to be warm-hearted, with a good sense of humour. There are many accounts of his ability to speak in a loud, booming voice for long periods of time.

As was the custom, Big Bear was selected as Chief by consensus in 1865. When Big Bear first assumed the position of Chief, his following was small, but near the end of his life his camp was one of the largest. Big Bear had been groomed for the job: his father had been Chief. As a result, Big Bear had sat in council meetings from a very young age and had listened to the Elders making decisions. He grew up observing the role of the Chief and thus, when selected as Chief, he stepped easily into the position.

Once I went with an Elder to the area known as Sounding Lake, which is in the eastern part of present-day Alberta. The Elder spoke about Big Bear and his ability to lead people. During one huge gathering of over a thousand, Big Bear was the main Chief of the camp and all the other Chiefs deferred to him. There was a dispute over a horse, which could have led to violence in the camp, but Big Bear rode among the fighting men and spoke to them. They stopped their fighting at the request of Big Bear. He was a kind and fair man, which is the reason he receives such respect from the Cree People to this day.

Big Bear did not sign Treaty 6 in 1876 because he was not invited by the representatives of the Crown to the original treaty negotiations in Fort Carlton. Poundmaker was concerned that the old man was not present at the treaty signing: 'Poundmaker was still a young man, not a Chief ... he had nothing like the real influence that the old medicine man Big Bear had with his people. [Big Bear] would see the negotiations in a clear light. It was hard to understand his absence. He had served his people long and faithfully, it was unthinkable that he would knowingly have been absent on this crucial occasion. Big Bear later confirmed this opinion: he had not been notified to attend.'[14] It is easy to see that other leaders among the Cree looked up to Big Bear. He was one Chief among many, but his influence was widespread among the Cree Peoples. Though his failure to attend the treaty negotiations did not stop the other Chiefs from negotiating, clearly the leaders felt Big Bear's presence would have helped the process.

There are a number of reasons for Big Bear's not being invited to the treaty negotiations. First, it seems clear that the government's agents were afraid of his influence. In addition, Big Bear did not subscribe to the Christian faith which was being spread among the Cree at the time, and the priests were active in trying to persuade the Indigenous peoples to accept less in the negotiations. Most importantly for the Cree, Big Bear, not being a signatory to the treaty in 1876, could ensure that the treaty commitments undertaken by the Crown were honoured.

When Big Bear did arrive at the treaty encampment, the treaty was already signed. He was then asked to sign but declined. He was concerned that the Crown would not live up to its obligations, and wanted to see how the treaty would be implemented. Big Bear's people did not sign Treaty 6 until 1884, a full eight years after the initial treaty was negotiated. During that time, he continued to live on the plains, following the buffalo herds and conducting his camp in the manner handed down to him by his ancestors. He watched the implementation of the treaty, keeping in mind that as long as he did not sign, he was a free agent to negotiate his own camp into the treaty. His camp was the largest, with traditional territory extending from north of the North Saskatchewan River down to the American border and beyond. He moved his camp within this territory and refused to share that land with the Crown.

As Big Bear followed the buffalo across the plains, he could see that the Indigenous peoples were beginning to suffer with settlement on reserves. As he saw that the treaty was not being implemented, Big Bear talked with Poundmaker and other Chiefs about the treaty and what could be done to ensure that it was implemented. Discussions were undertaken with the Blackfoot Confederacy. Poundmaker was an adopted son of Crowfoot, so Big Bear sent Poundmaker to the Blackfoot to canvas them on their feelings about the implementation of the treaty. Big Bear had the ability to mobilize the whole of the Indigenous population in what is now Western Canada against the government for their violations of the treaty. It is no wonder the government was afraid of Big Bear.

Initially, Big Bear wanted to settle in the Cypress Hills in the southern part of present-day Alberta and Saskatchewan. But, the government of Canada did not want Big Bear so near the American border. There was concern that Big Bear would lead the Indigenous peoples against the government. As a result of the government of Canada's refusal to recognize Big Bear's request for land in the Cypress Hills, the Chief moved his camp north towards Sounding Lake, south of the present-day town of Provost, Alberta.

At Sounding Lake, Big Bear was the main Chief of the camp. A marker at Sounding Lake commemorating a visit from the governor general of Canada indicates that over 5,000 Cree were camped there. This camp was under the control of one Chief: Big Bear. David G. Mandelbaum describes the meeting structure that would have governed the encampment:

When several bands gathered in large encampments, the Chiefs would meet in one of the Warrior lodges. The hierarchy of rank among the Chiefs would be tacitly recognized or, in any case of doubt, settled by a word or hint from a respected old man. The highest ranking Chief sat directly behind the fire at the back of the lodge, the next highest on either side of him and so around the lodge, with the least esteemed near the door. On such occasions the status accorded to a Chief did not depend on the size of his following, but hinged largely on his war record. His fame as an open-handed person also was considered.[15]

It must have frightened the government to see such a large encampment under the jurisdiction of one Chief. As a result of that meeting, the government told Big Bear's people that they could not have their reserve set aside at Sounding Lake. Once again the followers of Big Bear moved north as winter approached.

Big Bear's people camped near Frog Lake in the winter of 1884, which led to his eventual imprisonment for crimes he did not commit. The colonizer's agents had told Big Bear that at Frog Lake food would be provided to his people. Under the treaty, Indigenous peoples were to be taken care of during times of famine and need. The followers of Big Bear were in need of food. There was not much game, and hunting was poor. The War Chief – not the old Chief – went to the Indian agent and asked for food. It must be stressed that requesting food for his people was an action not lightly taken by a War Chief. The War Chief was a proud man, and it would have been humiliating to request food when the food should have been given under the treaty.

The agent told them that they could have food if they brought wood for the camp. The men, weak from hunger, agreed to gather wood. They chopped and brought the wood but were denied food by the agent. Again, the War Chief requested food for the people, and again he was denied. He then went to his camp and got the men to come and ask for food. Again he asked and was denied. At this time, Big Bear was not present; he was north of the camp hunting for food and did not return until after the events described below.

For the Cree, there is no fourth time to make a request. The War Chief and his men killed the Indian agent and other men at Frog Lake and took the food for the people. For this action of enforcing their treaty right, Big Bear and his people were hunted by the government. They were not captured, even though they were chased by a large force. In the end, Big Bear and his people surrendered to the government forces to save the women and children from further hardship. The War Chief and others were hung at North Battleford, and Big Bear was sent to prison. Big Bear should never have been imprisoned, but the Canadian government would not or could not understand the difference between a Chief and a War Chief.

The Indigenous Peoples' Basis for Treaty-Making

Indigenous Chiefs dealt with the arrival of the non-Indigenous settlers into Indigenous territory in the same manner as they dealt with others entering their jurisdiction. There was a protocol to be followed. The Chiefs had requested that all who came into their territory follow this protocol. Prior to entering into treaty, the Chiefs requested that the Crown and its settlers not enter their territory without concluding an agreement. It was the Indigenous peoples who had the jurisdiction in this area and told the Crown that their jurisdiction must be respected.

A number of significant events occurred prior to the signing of Treaty 6 in 1876. The Indigenous peoples heard that the Hudson's Bay Company had sold lands to the British Crown. The Chiefs could not believe that the trading company could have acquired their lands. In present circumstances, it would be tantamount to Pepsi Cola or another such company gaining title to the lands of another country merely by engaging in trading. The Indigenous peoples never recognized that the company had any jurisdiction over them. Trading beaver pelts was one thing, but having the land given to someone else was quite another.

In order to clarify the situation, the Chiefs sent a message to the representative of the Queen to inform her of the true situation. They stated that the Hudson's Bay Company could not gain control of their lands through its trading activities. These lands belonged to the Indigenous peoples who demanded that the Crown respect their rights before moving into their territory. They wanted the jurisdictional issue settled as soon as possible. They wanted the Crown to determine the exact nature of its agreement with the Hudson's Bay Company, which was undertaken without the consent of Indigenous peoples. They considered such an agreement to be invalid as a means of gaining access to their lands.

All over the West following 1870, Indigenous Peoples prevented surveyors and other people – including the builders of the telegraph – from coming into their territory without a treaty. The Indigenous peoples were protecting their jurisdiction. If the Crown wanted to have access to their territories, the Crown would need an agreement from the Indigenous peoples. This is no different than the request that Chief Sitting Bull of the Sioux People placed before the Cree when the Sioux moved north. The treaty between the Cree and the Sioux remains in force: a number of Sioux communities are spread among the Cree communities within the areas covered by Treaties 4 and 6.

Sharing the land through treaty-making was a known process. The treaty-making process with the British Crown and others followed the Cree laws. The only way to access the territories of the Cree, Assiniboine, Saulteau, and Dene was to enter into a treaty.

The Crown's Obligation to Make Treaties

In 1492, Christopher Columbus arrived on the shores of the Americas to exploit the lands for his own wealth and the wealth of the Spanish Crown. To accomplish this task, Spain, as well as other imperial European nations, tried to divest Indigenous peoples of any international legal status by developing the legal concept of *terra nullius*. According to this myth, the land belongs to no one, and the colonizers could occupy the lands of Indigenous peoples without their consent. 'From this it followed that such territories would vest automatically in the first civilized power which chose to occupy them, regardless of the wishes or resistance of the Indigenous population.'[16] Thus European colonizers established their own framework in law, which allowed them to kill, maim, and dispossess the Indigenous inhabitants of the land.

However, this was not the case in North America, where the British needed the Indigenous peoples as allies against the French. After Britain's war in America against the French and Indigenous nations (1755-63), the British monarch George III reconfirmed boundaries between the colonies and the Indigenous territories in the Royal Proclamation of 1763.[17] Nearly one-third of the text is devoted to British relations with Indigenous nations. The Proclamation recognized Indigenous peoples as 'Nations,' as distinct societies with their own forms of political organization, with whom treaties had to be negotiated. It also enshrined the protection of Indigenous lands by the British Crown, and a process of seeking Indigenous consent to European settlement through treaty-making. Finally, the Royal Proclamation clearly spelled out that Indigenous nations had an inalienable right to their lands.[18]

The Royal Proclamation was never binding upon Indigenous peoples: it bound the British Crown and its colonial agents to follow certain rules in relation to Indigenous peoples and lands. In fact, the Proclamation was a codification of the norms of customary international law for entering into treaties. International law required that a sovereign enter into formal agreements with another people's sovereign prior to entering lands occupied by those peoples.[19] The Royal Proclamation extended this norm of international law to Indigenous peoples in the British colonies in America.

However, because of the doctrine of discovery, treaties with Indigenous nations did not ensure a place for Indigenous peoples within the family of nations under international law. The discovery doctrine allowed competing European powers to define their respective spheres of influence in the colonies. Joseph Story wrote that, in the nineteenth century as a conventional rule, discovery might 'properly govern all the nations which recognised its obligations, but it could have no authority over the Aborigines of America, whether gathered into civilised communities or scattered in hunting tribes of the wilderness.'[20] According to Lindley, discovery was 'adapted to regulate the competition between European Powers themselves, and it had no bearing upon the relations between those Powers and the natives. What the discoverer's State gained was the right, as against other European powers, to take steps which were appropriate to the acquisition of the territory in question. What those steps were would depend on whether there was already a native population in possession of the territory.'[21] Consequently, discovery only gave an inchoate title.

Treaty-making served as a double-edged sword for the colonizing state. In order to claim international legitimacy, the state must be able to claim the land – but through what means? Can a state lay claim to lands through a treaty process with Indigenous peoples while at the same time denying the rights of the Indigenous peoples as international subjects? This is exactly the conundrum that Indigenous peoples have seized upon to nip at the heels of state legitimacy.

In the case of Canada, the British Crown asserted its jurisdiction over the lands of the Indigenous peoples and enacted various proclamations to regulate its agents in their dealings with Indigenous peoples. The Proclamation of 1763 set out the obligations of the Crown of Great Britain and its successor states for the acquisition of the right to enter into Indigenous territory, and it specified the treaty method to be used when dealing with Indigenous peoples.

There is a further amplification of the treaty-making obligation of the British Crown in relation to Indigenous peoples under the Imperial Order in Council of 1870. That law set out the Crown's powers to negotiate treaties with those Indigenous peoples occupying the lands west of the colony of Canada which had been established in the eastern part of Great Turtle Island. The international law norm to enter into treaties was confirmed by a 1975 International Court of Justice (ICJ) which looked at the doctrines of *terra nullius*, discovery, and conquest.[22]

In an advisory opinion, the Court found that *terra nullius*, discovery, and conquest were not legitimate doctrines to assert sovereignty over a territory. The ICJ stated that land occupied by a group of people having some political and social organization was not *terra nullius*. The Court pronounced that the only way for a foreign sovereign to acquire any right to enter into territory that is not *terra nullius* is through an agreement with the original inhabitants who have given their freely informed consent. In coming to this decision, the ICJ reviewed the colonial history of the settlement of the Western Sahara and the ties that existed between Spain and the leaders of the land in question. The ICJ determined that the treaties entered into with the Western Sahara leaders were sufficient to form a legal tie that excluded the states of Morocco and Mauritania from claiming the lands.

The settlement of the Western Sahara took place in the same period that the British Crown entered into Treaty 6. And the International Court of Justice is clear in its 1975 judgment that, at the time Treaty 6 was made, the international community no longer accepted the concept of *terra nullius*: 'Whatever difference of opinion there may have been among jurists, the State practice of the relevant period [at the time of colonization] indicates that territories inhabited by tribes or peoples having a social and political organization were not regarded as *terra nullius*. It shows that in the case of such territories the acquisition of sovereignty was not generally considered as effected unilaterally through "occupation" of *terra nullius* by original title but through agreements concluded with local rulers.'[23]

The only way for the British Crown to have access to the lands of the Indigenous peoples was to enter into agreements with the rulers, in this case Chiefs and Headmen, who were in possession of their lands.

The Process of Making Treaty 6

The Elders relate the history of the treaty commissioner who came to the Chiefs and Headmen to negotiate a treaty. The Chiefs and Headmen did not travel to London, England, or another place to enter into a treaty: it was the Crown and its agents who wanted a peaceful settlement of the territory. In order to accomplish this, they would have to make a treaty with the Indigenous peoples, so the treaty commissioner came to the Chiefs and Headmen. The commissioner requested that, for the future security of settlers, a Peace and Friendship Treaty be entered into with the Cree, Assiniboine, Saulteau, and Dene Peoples in the western part of present-day Canada. Those Indigenous nations formed an alliance and entered into Treaty 6 with the British Crown in 1876, to last as long as the sun shines and the waters flow.

At their meeting with the treaty commissioner, the Indigenous peoples did not immediately agree about the nature of the treaty. 'The Indians[24] also were having meetings for seven days trying to work some arrangement that would be suitable for them. When they were through discussing, the Indians were ready to present their side of the bargain.'[25]

The late Elder Fred Horse spoke often about the treaty, as he was taught by this father, John Horse: 'My father listened to these things. He said that when I was growing up. Many times at night, he would lift the big pipe, light it and proceed to talk to me of these matters ... When the Commissioner arrived, he was not agreed with right away but time and deliberation was made ... The Commissioner stated that the Queen's subjects were being overcrowded where they were and they wanted land so they could make a living.'[26] Elder Toussait Dion, also from the community of Frog

Lake, stated: 'What the old man used to tell me was, he use [sic] to say he was there [at the Treaty signing] himself, when the Queen's representative came to make the negotiations. The Queen, herself, never came across the ocean to negotiate. It was her representatives that came, and this Queen's representative said that the Queen has sent me to come here on her behalf. The old man used to say, there I've heard and listened to the negotiations when the big gathering took place.'[27] The Elders have kept alive the events which occurred at the treaty signing for the younger generations to know their history.

The Chiefs and the treaty commissioner followed both Cree and international laws concerning treaty-making: the two equal parties negotiated in good faith, at arm's length without external pressure, and arrived at a meeting of the minds. Negotiations took place over a number of days: 'The progress of the negotiations was slow because there was a lot of discussion going on, a lot of deliberations took place. And, then, there the Treaty Commissioner made the strong statement. The sun and the water, if these exist, the terms would always be the same. As long as the sun shines and the water flows. [This the father used to say.] Consequently, the negotiators figured that they had finished their business then.'[28] The treaty commissioner accepted that the treaty would be concluded with the smoking of the pipes according to Cree custom:

> [The Chiefs] told the officials that they were using their greatly respected power for a legal transaction [peace pipe]. With the promises made by the Queen, they did not want them to ever come to an end. These promises were made with the smoking of the pipe. [The treaty commissioner's] lips touched the stem of the pipe. This wasn't done ordinarily for no reason. If one puts a pipe stem to his lips, that was a highly honoured agreement ... He smoked the pipe stem ... The Indians didn't use only one pipe either is what my father told me. They sang their sacred songs.[29]

The smoking of the pipes was acceptable for the Cree and the treaty commissioner for the conclusion of the agreement within Cree territory. Smoking the pipe would signify to the Creator the intention of the parties to keep the terms of the agreement in a strong binding manner. The Indigenous peoples wanted this treaty to last as long as the earth would exist; this is the reason they smoked the pipe with the commissioner.

It was more than a pipe ceremony: it was a solemn undertaking by both sides before the Creator that this agreement would last into the future. Often, the Elders speak of a third party at the negotiations. They are speaking of the Creator, who was a witness to the process. In the face of the Creator, it is not possible for the Indigenous peoples to break the agreement undertaken with the Crown's representative. The honour and pride associated with this solemn agreement bind future generations.

Whose Treaty Is It?

When Treaty 6 was entered into in 1876, Canada was a colony of Great Britain. None of the Elders who know the Treaty 6 process acknowledge the state of Canada as being a party to the treaty. Even the written version of Treaty 6 acknowledges that the treaty was entered into with the Queen of England, Scotland, Ireland, and Wales – without mentioning the colony of Canada. Thus, the government of Canada, which is not a party to the treaty, does not have the authority to change the treaty.

In one instance, an Elder questioned the government of Canada's ability to overrule the Chief who had signed the treaty with the Queen: '"As long as the sun walks, as long as the river flows, you will not have liquor," that is what the Commissioner said. Today, even when the Chiefs don't want liquor, it is still legalized. It looks like they don't have any authority at all after the Commissioners had decorated them as Chiefs. So they try to stop the liquor without success. I wonder if the people in Ottawa have overruled the Queen to be able to do that.'[30] The Elder understands that the Chief and the Queen were on the same footing.

The Elders are entirely correct in their understanding of a traditional international treaty. Colonies could not enter into treaties without the authority of the Parliament that created them. Canada did not have the authority to enter into treaties in its own right until the Statute of Westminster was enacted by the British Parliament in 1932. Canada could not become a party to the treaty without the consent of both parties. The Indigenous peoples never gave their consent for Canada to be a party to the treaty, and Canada did not sign Treaty 6.

The signing of the treaty was not a mere formality on the part of the British Crown to save 'the pride' of Indigenous peoples. The Crown had a legal obligation to enter into formal agreements with Indigenous peoples prior to settling on their lands. The signing of a treaty had international legal significance for the colonizer.

The Treaty Chiefs' Authority Regarding the Treaty

The legal and political capacity of the Indigenous peoples to enter into treaty is clear. It flows from the traditional laws which govern the role of the Chiefs and Headmen: 'I always ask the Creator to help our people to help our leadership when they go and speak for us, that they may return safely, and the Creator might look upon them, so that they could be successful in what it is they are trying to do for their people.'[31] The Chiefs were trying to do something for their children's children. The role of the Chiefs and

Headmen was to ensure that the agreement entered into with the British Crown did not destroy their relationship to the land and their citizens.

Treaty 6 begins and ends with a succinct declaration of the authority given to the Chiefs and Headmen by their people to enter into treaty with the Crown. In the preamble to Treaty 6 is the following: 'And whereas the Indians of the said tract, duly convened in council, as aforesaid, and being requested by Her Majesty's said Commissioners to name certain Chiefs and Headmen, who should be authorized on their behalf to conduct such negotiations and sign any Treaty to be founded therein, and to become responsible to Her Majesty for their faithful performance by their respective Bands of such obligations as shall be assumed by them.'[32] At the conclusion of the Treaty 6 document, the Chiefs 'on their own behalf and on behalf of all other Indians inhabiting the tract,'[33] were recognized by the treaty commissioner as having authority to enter into treaty. The treaty process acknowledges and accedes to the jurisdictional authority of the Chiefs and Headmen as the legitimate government of the Indigenous peoples.

The Chiefs and Headmen were accustomed to being recognized as leaders in their interactions with others, including the Hudson's Bay Company. Political alliances were validated by the exchange of gifts. Early in trading relationships, European traders realized that they must give gifts.[34] Trading relations did not change the political authority of the Chiefs and Headmen. The factor at the Hudson's Bay Company trading posts gave presents to the Chiefs as an acknowledgment of their position.

The position of the Chief was also secured and acknowledged by the treaty process. In recognition of the position of the Chiefs and Headmen, the treaty document specifically stated that the Chiefs and Headmen would receive annual payments of money, though a dispute continues to this day as to the amount of monies that were to be received. The Indigenous peoples agreed to share some of the lands with the settlers; in return, there must be a gift. The annuity monies were to ensure that each year the alliance was validated through the gift process.

The Crown's Authority Regarding the Treaty

At the time of treaty-making, the Chiefs did not ask the Crown to submit any documents which demonstrated their authority. The Chiefs and Headmen accepted the commissioner's word that he was the legitimate representative of the Crown: '[Alexander] Morris[35] was well into his speech. The Great Mother in sending him to them was demonstrating her concern for her red children and her desire for them to be happy and secure in the changing times ahead. As he expanded on this theme, many of his listeners were truly moved by this picture of the Queen's great power, compassion and generosity, traits the Crees admired in their own leaders.'[36] Each party accepted the other as equals capable of concluding a binding agreement.

Women's Authority in Relation to the Treaty

There has been much misunderstanding and inaccurate writing about the role of Chiefs and women in the treaty-making process. This is often the result of applying a Eurocentric model to historical material, which fails to recognize and understand the role of the Chief and Headmen in the treaty-signing process. In addition, there is no understanding of the role of the women in Cree society, nor of why Indigenous women did not sign the treaties. It is sometimes assumed that Indigenous women held the same inferior status as non-Indigenous women of the same time period. Nothing could be further from the truth.

One of the strongest teachings of the traditional Elders concerns the women. When the Elders speak about the role of women at the treaty, they talk about the spiritual connection of the women to the land and to treaty-making. The Creator gave women the power to create. The man is the helper to the woman, not the other way around. Women are linked to Mother Earth by their ability to bring forth life. The women sit beside the Creator as a recognition of their role and position.

Once there was a story of a young man who criticized a woman at a meeting. After the meeting was concluded, an old man went to speak to the young man. The old man asked the young man to hold out his hand and make something grow. The young man replied that he could not make something grow in his palm. The old man told him that a woman could make things grow. Until the young man could make something grow in his hand, he should not speak against women.

Because of this spiritual connection with the Creator and Mother Earth, it is the women who own the land. Man can use the land, protect and guard it, but not own it. Women can pass on authority of use to the man, but not the life of the earth. When a man hunts, the women come along and claim the meat. If a woman is the Chief's wife, she distributes the choice meat in the village after the hunt, because the women own the meat and the hide.

To comprehend the role of women is to understand the limits placed upon the Chiefs in the negotiation of the treaty. The Chiefs did not go to the treaty table with unlimited authority to negotiate with the representatives of the Crown. Just as the Queen's commissioner was limited by the Crown's legislative authority, so too were the Chiefs limited.

The Chiefs who entered into treaty only had the authority to share the lands, never to sell or surrender it. One of the reasons women did not take on political roles such as Chief, or participate in the treaty-making process, was to protect their jurisdiction and possessory rights. Women never signed the treaties: they never signed away possession of the lands to the Crown. This is the main reason that the Elders and Chiefs can say with such authority that the land was never sold in the treaty process.

The role of women within Indigenous society also helped the British treaty commissioner, Alexander Morris, conclude Treaty 6. The fact that Great Britain had a Queen made it easier for the Indigenous peoples to accept the request for 'land to be set aside for settlement.' The Queen was a powerful object who wanted to enter into a treaty – a woman who knew the role and importance of the laws of the Creator. When Morris was appealing to the Indigenous peoples to enter into treaty, he spoke of the poverty and starvation of the Queen's people who wanted to farm the lands of the Indigenous peoples. The Queen was appealing on behalf of her children for the use of the land to the depth of the plough. The Queen did not want to own the land, the fish, the animals, the plants, the water, or the birds. Her people had their own animals (cattle, pigs, sheep) and their own birds (chickens, ducks, geese). All these things were to remain under the jurisdiction of the Indigenous peoples as intended by the laws of the Creator. This was acceptable.

Alexander Morris also spoke of the Queen as the 'Great White Mother' who lived across the great waters to the east. He described her as having arms big enough to look after all the Indigenous people who made treaty. Because of the role of women in the Indigenous world, Indigenous people accepted the idea that a woman wanted to make a treaty to share the land with her people. This concept of sharing was acceptable. One of the Elders whose grandfather had been in attendance at the treaty confirmed the story about an Elder who stood up and asked if the Queen had breasts big enough to care for all the Indigenous peoples.[37] Other Elders have repeated the same story, indicating the importance placed upon the role of the Queen in the treaty-making process.

As one Elder stated: 'That is why they were agreeable to treaty because the promises were so good. The government official was always making references to a woman who had sent them. The Indians sympathized with the woman, the Queen, through her representatives.'[38]

The Elders' Version of Treaty 6

The Elders have long disputed many aspects of the government of Canada's version of Treaty 6. The main criticism of the written version has to do with the language used about the lands. The written version contains the wording 'cede, surrender and forever give up title to the lands.' The Elders maintain that these words were not included in the original treaty. The Chiefs and Elders could not have sold the lands to the settlers as they could only share the lands according to the Cree, Saulteau, Assiniboine, and Dene laws.

When the Elders were told of the written words, they had difficulty understanding them. These words do not exist in their languages. The Elders give an account of the original treaty being written on the back of a buffalo hide: 'It will also be written on the raw hide, never to be erased. Once again, the Commissioner said, "these things as it will be written on the hide. What is written on the hide, one will be given to your Chief and one will be kept in England where the Queen is. All the Chiefs in the future when any trouble arises between the white man and you, Indians will be able to see the agreement made today." Today, we find the Treaty is written different as it has been said. The way it was written originally should be the same today.'[39] This hide was hidden from the government's forces during the Poundmaker and Big Bear troubles in 1885. There are Elders within the Treaty 6 area who know about the existence of this hide. At some point in the future, this hide will be produced by the Elders for people to see the actual articles of the treaty.

The following discussion refers to the terms of the treaty as understood by the Elders, without reference to the document claimed by Canada to be the treaty.

Three Things Requested by the Treaty Commissioner
The treaty commissioner requested three things at the time the treaty was signed: use of the land to the depth of the plough for the Queen's subjects to farm, trees to construct houses, and grass for the animals brought by the settlers.

> The Commissioners said he wanted three things. He only wanted the pine to makes houses, grass for his animals and land to the depth of six inches to break and plant crops. Anything underneath remained under the jurisdiction and the property of the Indigenous peoples. The Indian people would never be in want as they had ensured their future good life by sharing their lands. [The Commissioner] stated that he had not bought the water nor the fish in it. All the creatures that flew or walked were the Indian's property ... The Queen had promised that the wealth of the land would be ours.[40]

The treaty rights of the Queen's subjects were that they could live in peace and share the lands of the Indigenous peoples. In return, the Indigenous peoples were to receive certain benefits for as long as the sun shines and the waters flow.

A true test of a person's knowledge of the treaty is to listen to his or her description of how long the treaty is to last. Those who learned their history of the treaty from sources other than the Elders say the treaty will last 'as long as the sun shines, the grass grows and the rivers flow.' In the Cree legal system, it is inaccurate to put the treaty in those terms. First, the Elders would not want to tie the treaty to the grass growing because the medicines for the people came from the lands. Our medicines were not tied to the treaty, as the Elders did not want to give their medicines to the non-Indigenous people. Second, the Elders did not tie the treaty to the rivers flowing because they knew that the rivers could change direction or dry up. What would become of the treaty if the rivers ceased to flow? The correct phrase is as follows: the treaty will last 'as long as the sun shines and the waters flow.' What waters? The water is from a woman, which breaks just before the birth of a child. As long as Indigenous women were giving birth to Indigenous children, there would be a treaty.[41] Therefore 'as long as the sun shines and the waters flow' means that the treaty will last as long as there is life on Mother Earth. The Crown entered into an agreement for the future generations of both parties to the treaty agreement.

The Promises Made to Indigenous Peoples

Health Care

The Chiefs and Headmen successfully negotiated universal health care for all Indigenous peoples within Treaty 6. Treaty 6 is the only numbered treaty that includes a 'medicine chest' provision. The Chiefs knew about the diseases of non-Indigenous people that were destroying their populations, and needed to have the non-Indigenous medicine to fight them. The far-sightedness of the Chiefs and Elders to include health care was a result of their concern for future generations. (The non-Indigenous population of Canada did not have universal health care until the 1960s.)

The leaders did not give up their traditional health care and medicines to the non-Indigenous people in this process. This was a gift from the Creator which they were not prepared to share with non-Indigenous people.

Education

There was also successful negotiation of universal access to education for all Indigenous peoples without discrimination by age or sex. A school house was to be built in each community for all children. The Chiefs and Elders wanted their young people to be able to cope with the newcomers, and believed the most successful way would be for the children to understand their ways: 'In the future and today you Indians see that the white man speaks different languages. At the school, the people could learn the language, so we can speak with the white man.'[42] (In Alberta, universal access to education for the non-Indigenous population was not achieved until the 1920s, a full fifty years after education was guaranteed in the treaty.)

What the Elders and Chiefs did not count on was the forced education of their children into a foreign value system, and the introduction of residential schools where the language and spirituality of the Indigenous peoples were beaten out of them. The successor government of Canada, hand in hand with the Christian churches, began the systematic destruction of the children through the residential school system, in complete violation of this provision of the treaty. 'The Commissioner never mentioned that the children would be taught outside of the reserve.'[43] People resisted this type of education and refused to allow their children to attend such schools – the children were not to be stripped of their identity by church-run schools.

However, the government of Canada used the pass system, introduced in 1886, to force children into the residential schools. With the pass system, Indigenous peoples could not travel outside the reserves to hunt, and starvation became a reality among the people for the first time in their history (the Elders often speak of starvation as coming with the settlers). The people were forced into dependence on the Ottawa-appointed Indian agent for food rations or a pass. If the people refused to send their children to school, there was no food and no pass. It became a choice between allowing the children to starve or sending them to school where they would be fed.

The residential school system was in place until the late 1960s. The destruction of the Indigenous family and community by the residential schools is felt to this day. What culture has been able to withstand a continuing and unrelenting assault upon its weakest members, the children? Canadian society would like to turn a blind eye to this treaty violation, but as long as Indigenous peoples are affected by it, there is a debt owed to Indigenous peoples. Education was a right secured through the treaty process, a right that was consistently violated.

Water

When the treaty was negotiated, the Chiefs and Elders never gave up their rights to water, or to the fish, animals, or other things that lived in the water. 'The water is not what she [The Queen] wants.'[44] Many of the communities within the Treaty 6 area are located on or near a lake. Prior to signing the treaty, Indigenous peoples made a good living from trapping fish and animals that lived in the water. Since the commissioner specifically stated that the Queen did not want the waters or the living things within the waters, the Indigenous peoples could finalize an agreement.

The state of Canada knows the treaty did not deal with water rights. Under Cree, Assiniboine, Saulteau, and Dene laws, the Creator had placed Indigenous peoples upon the back of the turtle who was floating on water (Great Turtle Island). If the people were asked to give up their rights to the water, they would be relinquishing their life. Water rights remain within the jurisdiction of Indigenous peoples, as intended by the Creator who placed Indigenous peoples upon Great Turtle Island.

Fishing, Hunting, and Trapping

Many living things have been placed within the waters by the Creator. From these living things, Indigenous peoples have been able to survive. The commissioner said that 'anything that the Indian uses was to be left alone. The White Man has nothing to do with it. He [the commissioner] only wanted three things.'[45] There would be no need for the settlers to use any of the Indigenous peoples' animals, fish, or birds, as they would bring their own animals like cattle, pigs, sheep, chickens, ducks, and geese. To emphasize that the Indigenous peoples would continue their way of life, the commissioner undertook to provide nets for fishing and ammunition for hunting.

The Elders now question the Natural Resources Transfer Act, whereby the federal government transferred to the provinces all the natural resources – including fish and all other living things – without the consent of Indigenous peoples. They ask how it is that the provinces, which did not exist at the time of the treaty, can make rules and regulations in contravention of the treaty. Why do non-Indigenous people fish and use the resource that belongs to Indigenous peoples? The Creator never placed these things on Great Turtle Island to be used by others.

Police

The commissioner told the Chiefs and Elders that if anyone violated the treaty, there would be somebody who would deal with the violators.

So, the men are going to protect you, pointing to the Northwest Mounted Police who were standing there with their horses. The head of the police commissioners rode a dark horse with gleaming riding gear with his sword almost touching ground level. Grandfather said, In the distant future with the promises made by the Queen and the white man attempts to break them, when the Chief and Council fail to prevent this and the white man goes ahead, this is the one the Chief is to rely on. The fellow can do anything. He was given power and authority by the Queen. He makes his living by risking his death at any time. The Indians are entitled to this man's services. To be of some help to them if necessary. Today, they will not protect us, but they are protecting the white men. They were supposed to protect us, that is what my dad used to tell me, today the police do not protect us.[46]

The only reason the Chiefs and Headmen allowed the Northwest Mounted Police into their territory was so that the police could guard them against violations by the settlers. At one time, a police officer would not come onto the reserve without the authorization of the Chief. Now, the Royal Canadian Mounted Police enter reserve lands at any time. This is a treaty violation because the Chiefs and Headmen never relinquished jurisdiction within reserves to any other government or police force.

Reserves

When the treaty to share some of the land with the Queen's subjects was concluded, the Indigenous peoples said that certain lands would not be shared. These lands would be kept by the Indigenous peoples for the future use of their children's children. These lands became known as reserved lands or reserves. Reserved lands were for Indigenous peoples to live on without interference by the settlers. These were not lands given to the Indigenous peoples by the Crown or the government. The Elders question how the government or the Queen could give them lands when all the lands belonged to them. If the Elders were to agree that the Crown or the government could give lands to the Indigenous peoples, then that would mean the land had been given at some point to the Crown or the government. The Elders and Chiefs could not agree to such an interpretation of the treaty.

At the treaty signing, the Chiefs understood they could reserve as much land as they wanted. 'As long as the sun shines and once you get your reserves, there's no two-legged man that's going to break these reserves. This is what he said. Here on earth no two-legged person that's going to break those reserves once you select the site.'[47] But within years of the treaty signing, surveyors came and set limits on the size of the reserves to 160 acres per person. The people resisted the surveyors. Resistance grew until the uprising in 1885 by Big Bear and Poundmaker's people. However, as a result of the sentencing of Big Bear and Poundmaker to prison, resistance to the surveys decreased. The Elders maintain that the government's setting of a limited number of acres per person is a violation of the treaty.

Mountains

The mountains were not part of the treaty. The Chiefs and Headmen told the treaty commissioner that the mountains were not to be included in the treaty. The commissioner agreed with the Chiefs and Headmen, stating that since the mountains could not be used for agriculture, the Queen was not interested in them. The Elders say the lands that were four days' travel from the foot of the mountains were not included in the treaty.

There is a strong spiritual reason for the mountains to be excluded from the treaty. The pipe bowl is made from rock which comes from the mountains. Anything included in the pipe – the stone, the wood, the medicine, and the fire – was not included in the treaty. The mountains were not included as they were spiritual places of the ancestors where people went to pray and fast. There are places in the mountains where Indigenous peoples go on a yearly basis to participate in various ceremonies. The mountains, the forests, and the medicines were withheld during the negotiation process and are not in the treaty.

Birds

The treaty commissioner assured the Indigenous peoples at the treaty signing that the Queen was not interested in the birds. The Queen's subjects would be bringing their own birds, such as chickens, ducks, and geese. The non-domestic birds would remain within the jurisdiction of Indigenous peoples. When the Canadian government entered into the Migratory Birds Convention Treaty with Mexico and the United States, Indigenous peoples had never agreed that birds could come under the jurisdiction of the state of Canada.

The lakes and rivers used by birds have been increasingly damaged by settlers, harming water fowl and other species. '"Canada" means in Cree a pure state. The old people used this term of how perfect this was one time. Now the white man has greatly destroyed our proud land. Pollution, he has polluted lakes and rivers. He doesn't realize this because he is too busy looking for ways how he could rob the Indians. He has forgotten the promises.'[48] Settlers were to share the lands with Indigenous peoples, not pollute and destroy the lands. The land used to be clean; the Indigenous peoples agreed to share clean land which was to be kept clean. Land and water which is polluted hurts all living things. 'All the creatures that flew or walked were the Indian's property.'[49] The Creator gave the responsibility to Indigenous peoples of caring for their relatives. Indigenous peoples consider themselves to be part of the circle of life that includes the animals, the birds, the fish, and all other living things. These are all interconnected and, thus, all related. Indigenous people cannot carry out their responsibility because of pollution of the water, land, and air. The Elders consider pollution a violation of the treaty.

Social Assistance

At the time of the treaty-making, there was a growing realization that the buffalo herds were being diminished by over-hunting in the south of the territory. Each year fewer buffalo made their way north. The Chiefs and Headmen were concerned about the future without access to a good supply of food. As a result, they requested that a provision be included in the treaty for the distribution of food during times of need. This was the first negotiated agreement that included the provision that people would be taken care of in times of famine.

When the peoples wanted to know how this was going to be accomplished, the commissioner said that the 'Queen's breasts were big enough and could last that long to feed and care for all the Indian peoples. You could never exhaust the supply of them to feed you all. This was the answer the Elder got from the Commissioner.'[50] As the people pressed the commissioner for more information, he said the Queen had long arms which would stretch across the ocean to help care for Indigenous peoples if the need arose in the future. The Elders wanted to ensure that in the future the young people would always be looked after. (The social welfare state did not develop in Canada until the 1930s, a full fifty years after the signing of the treaty.)

One of the Elders, John B. Tootoosis, who was very knowledgable about the treaty, often told the story about starvation. He reminded people never to believe that we were starving at the time of the treaty-making. This was a story made up by the government after the treaty was signed, to try to change the treaty and make Indigenous peoples look weak. But all Indigenous people had to do was go outside their tents. There was food all around them – roots, berries, animals, birds, and fish, in addition to the buffalo. John B. Tootoosis said, 'Never let anyone tell you that we were starving before the treaty. We never knew starvation. After the Treaty things changed and there was starvation because of the rules and regulations passed against us.'[51]

It was as a result of the Indian agent's failure at Frog Lake to provide rations as stipulated in the treaty that Big Bear's Warrior Chief took things into his own hands in order to feed Big Bear's people. When the Indian agent refused to provide rations, even after the people cut wood for him, he and others were killed because they failed to live up to the terms of the treaty.

The worst food was given to the people. As a child, I remember getting hard, dark biscuits (referred to as dog biscuits) from the Indian agent as part of the rations given to Indigenous peoples. As the settlers grew rich and prosperous from the lands of Indigenous peoples, these dog biscuits replaced buffalo, moose, deer, ducks, geese, roots, and berries. In the present day, rations have come to be understood as social assistance. Though many non-Indigenous people protest this 'handout,' the

Indigenous peoples view such assistance as a treaty obligation. It is unfortunate that Indigenous peoples are sometimes made to feel small or worthless for receiving a treaty benefit.

Minerals

As has been discussed earlier, Indigenous peoples agreed to share the topsoil 'to the depth of a plough' (meaning six inches deep). There was no mention in the treaty agreement of the minerals below the six inches. The Elders are quite firm on this point: 'Although the white man is cunning and smart. And these that are under the ground, they've never mentioned them. But the white people had just taken those without the consent of the Indians. They just went ahead and started drilling, which they should not have done.'[52]

The extraction and sale of minerals without the consent of the Indigenous peoples is a violation of the treaty. The Natural Resources Transfer Act, whereby the federal government transferred the minerals to the provinces, further violates the treaty. Indigenous peoples had never given jurisdiction over minerals to the state of Canada, and certainly had not agreed that the provinces, which did not even exist at the time, could benefit from minerals that belong to Indigenous peoples.

The Indian Agent

The Crown was to appoint an Indian agent, paid by the Crown to be a servant to the Indigenous peoples. If the people wanted to send a message or proposal to the Crown, the Indian agent would write and transmit it. The agent was supposed to be the Indigenous peoples' servant, but turned out to be the keeper of the federal system. Gradually, the Indian agent came to run the affairs of the community completely. Chiefs were not allowed to direct their people, and the Indian agent could replace a Chief who did not cooperate with him. The Indian agent determined what cattle, wood, hay, and other items could be sold. Without an agent's permit, Indigenous peoples could not dispose of their goods.

As an employee of the government of Canada, the Indian agent took his direction from the Indian Act and officials in Ottawa. Neither the Indian Act nor the government in Ottawa were part of the treaty, yet Indian agents controlled access to food and rations, and had a great deal of influence. To this day the minister of Indian affairs uses his authority, the Indian Act, and the monies voted from Parliament, to control Indigenous peoples in violation of the treaty.

A Farm Instructor

The Indigenous peoples wanted to learn agriculture, and the Crown promised to appoint a farm instructor. In order to allow Indigenous peoples to become self-sufficient in agriculture, the Crown also promised to supply equipment on a yearly basis. Indigenous peoples became so successful at farming that the government of Canada, pressured by non-Indigenous farmers, restricted the sale of Indigenous produce.[53] This treaty right was violated by the jealousy of non-Indigenous people who did not believe that Indigenous peoples should become successful farmers. The farm instructor had done a good job – too good to allow the treaty right to continue.

Treaty Money

At the signing of the treaty, the commissioner handed out money to the Indigenous peoples. There was no knowledge among the people about the money. The people did not know why they were given money. The Elders asked the reason for the money, the commissioner said the money was a gift from the Queen for entering into the treaty.

The Elders recall that the treaty annuities given initially were $50 for the Chief and $25 for the Headmen, but later were reduced to $25 and $15 respectively. After two years, the payment to the ordinary people dropped from $15 to $5 a year, where it remains to this day. The Indigenous peoples were told that some of these monies would be set aside for them in Ottawa for their future use. 'In the future, schools and hospitals, we could use some of the money; that was cut to be used towards these. That's how I've heard.'[54]

The $5 which is given on treaty day each year in the various communities is seen by the Indigenous peoples as a symbol of the treaty commitment, even though the payment was reduced. The Elders wonder how much money is kept by the government and for what purpose that money is kept. Once in a while an Elder will refer to the money and instruct the Chiefs to inquire as to the amount of money in the trust fund. There has never been an accounting of this fund by the federal trustee.

Citizenship

At the time of the treaty-making, it was a recognized right that Indigenous peoples would control their citizenship: the commissioner asked the Indigenous people to point out their people. The commissioner himself did not place people within the various communities. Over the years, the state of Canada has tried to get Indigenous peoples to relinquish their rights to determine their own citizenship. All kinds of methods have been used to get Indigenous peoples to give up this treaty right. One method recently introduced in Parliament is Bill C-31. Through this legislation, the government of Canada tried to gain control of citizenship.

The legislation was seen by the Chiefs, Headmen, and Elders as a direct attack on fundamental aspects of the treaty. If Indigenous peoples cannot determine who is a citizen within the treaty, the treaty would soon be broken for future generations.

Indigenous Responsibility to the Treaty

Through a non-Indigenous education process that promotes a Eurocentric view of life, the treaty is diminished, and the role of the Indigenous peoples within the treaty is not stressed. Indigenous men and women begin to think that they can live like non-Indigenous people and still maintain the treaty relationship. The identity of Indigenous peoples is destroyed in the process, and the perpetuation of Indigenous identity becomes unimportant. The very important roles of women, men, and children become confused and easily influenced by the non-Indigenous society. In this way, Indigenous children are being taught not to carry on the treaty. It is crucial at this time to put the record on the treaty process in the proper light.

When Elders speak of Indigenous people breaking their own treaty, their interpretation is as follows: We are to coexist and share our rich country with the non-Indigenous people. At the time that the treaty was entered into, it was the understanding of the Elders that we were not to take non-Indigenous people as spouses. When Indigenous men and women take on this partnership with one of another race, that is one of the ways, according to the Elders, in which they are breaking the treaties. It has already happened and continues to happen, as people do not know about the meaning of the agreement entered into with the British Crown.

In addition, women had a very important task to perform in perpetuating, teaching, and instilling cultural values, ways, language, etc., in the children. This responsibility is not to be taken lightly, for it is the women who socialize the children into Indigenous societies by the way they teach them.

Further Lessons from the Elders About the Treaty

There are additional lessons the Elders have given regarding the treaty, as well as prophecies about the future of Indigenous peoples. They were told to me by an Elder, and are recounted here as he told them.[55] The Elder gave permission to tape-record his words. In fact, he wanted this information passed on to the Indigenous peoples. He requested that a book be written, with pictures, to record his teachings, because he feels they might get lost. With the influences upon the young people and the direction present leaders are taking, it is important for this information to reach the wider Indigenous community, for if we do not record it or pass it on, our people will lose it. The teachings are invaluable and need to be reinforced for leaders and Indigenous youth. In fact, from these teachings come the direction, authority, and leadership that Indigenous leaders need to practise and reinforce in order to reaffirm their treaty.

After I approached the Elder with tobacco and flags and he accepted the gifts, he smudged his bundle and then asked, what did I really want to know? At this point, with the Elder's bundle sitting on the table in front of him, with the smudging that had cleansed negative energies, and with the atmosphere of balance and harmony, it did not seem appropriate to ask about treaty. The Elder began to unwrap the blue bundle. Inside the bundle were sacred objects which were as old as the treaty. But they had been kept wrapped for the last twenty-one years, since he last opened the bundle to teach someone else who had been interested in learning about the treaty. He picked up each object and talked about its significance in the treaty process.

After he completed his teachings of the bundle, he left out a set of ten sticks. The ten sticks represented the ten promises which had been given by the commissioners at the signing of the treaty. But he did not go into the teaching at that time. His teachings were as follows:

On Learning

As people, leaders, and learners who want to do what is proper for their people, when you see something that looks appealing to you and you want to learn it, do not copy that teaching or song from anybody, but rather learn it from that teacher. For then you have earned the right to use the teaching, and therefore you also have the responsibility of passing it on. Otherwise it is not yours to pass on, you have only stolen it. If this information is passed on to you, you sit there and learn. Do not rely on anyone else to get the work done for you. You do it yourself.

The Ten Sticks

At the treaty signing, the white man made ten promises stating that they would never be broken as long as the sun shines and the waters flow. The commissioner said that he could never pay for the land. In addition, no two-legged person could ever break those promises. An Elder by the name of Pakan (who was one of the signatories of Treaty 6, and a Chief of the Whitefish Lake Reserve) expressed concern about how Indigenous peoples could preserve the same information. He stated that the white man had a way in which he could preserve his knowledge about the treaties by writing them on paper, and therefore he could retrieve the information whenever he required it, but Indigenous peoples did not have that gift.

He pointed to the land, which was full of buffalo, and at the animals. He stated, 'Our Father gave all that to us. Are you sure that you will fulfil your promises? I will make ten sticks.' He directed the statement to the commissioner, 'You say that no two-legged can break the promises. We will keep the sticks to signify your promises.' As a result, ten sticks were whittled to represent the ten promises made at the treaty signing. Those were the ten sticks that this Elder had been given to preserve – to be taught and honoured by the generations of Indigenous peoples whose forefathers had signed the treaty.

These are the values that the Elder stressed: Believe in the Creator. Practise your spirituality. Be loving, caring, and nurturing. Care for and respect your Elders as you would orphaned children.

Initially, there were pressures from white people to sell the land, but Indian people did not want to sell land. They respected it and therefore could share, but not sell it. The Elders stated that white men can never repay or ever pay in full, the cost of this land. Finally people agreed to lend it out. Land was never sold.

The commissioners stated that soil six fingers deep only, trees for building houses, and grass for their animals, that was what the Queen was asking to use, but they will pay you money, and money will be kept for your use later on. Taxes that the white man pays are supposed to be for your use, yet we do not see it.

The Queen's commissioner made these promises to the people:

As Indians, you will never be sorry. You will never be in want if transaction [treaty] takes place with the Queen. It is your land, your animals, all for your use. Continue to do so and also in the future. No one will ever bother you for they are your animals. Reserves were to have been for Indians. Inside there, no one will bother you. White man cannot walk into your reserve unless by your permission. You will have your law, your rule. Everything will be provided [education]. You will wear clothes like the Queen. If you travel anywhere, you will pay half the fare only. You will never pay for your medical needs. If you agree to transaction, and if riches are found, you will never have to work. You will never starve. My arms [the Queen's] are full enough to look after all Indians.

The treaty talks continued for three days. The Chiefs' words were based on Creation, respect, and use of the pipe. Today we still respect. Where are the white man's promises? Treaties were made between two nations. Now he is pushing us aside. The treaty is still there and the white man owes us a great deal.

Grandfather's Prophecies

When Margaret Quinney was speaking about the treaty as she learnt the story, she started to talk about the prophecies handed down to her.[56] She was told that white men will fill this place. There will be wires everywhere. Religions will be as numerous as branches on a tree. The road will look glittery and will be shortened by the use of vehicles. White man's road will poison your land. The land will be full of poison. Even the food and the water you drink will be impure. White man is killing himself. He is no longer thankful. Instead he wants more, goes everywhere, digs deeper, turns away Indian people from whom he had taken land. Yet he used to depend on them for their livelihood. White man used to sit with us before. Now he discriminates. His bible sat there too! [as part of the treaty process, yet he did not honour the word of God].

He will influence your children by drugs, alcohol, and even with the spoken word. Your grandchildren will not be able to speak their language. White man is never satisfied. He will begin to look to your reserve and will break it up.

The Elder expressed her observations and concerns that leaders of today are lacking in a sense of direction and are not strong enough. Nor do they believe they have their own authority, and therefore they do not stand up to issues they are confronted with, in particular with the white man (the government). That is where they go wrong. They have no concept of the value of the treaty, and are becoming more influenced by today's almighty dollar and other physically gratifying influences which are temporary.

Decisions are made without considering how Indigenous peoples or future generations are affected, as if our cultural and spiritual ways are no longer of any value. Leaders are no longer listening to Elders, nor are they interested in our treaties, or learning the significance of the treaties, but are more interested in keeping up with the dictates of today's influences.

The Elder encouraged treaty work, for it is these teachings and this information that need to be passed on to future generations. Her grandfather taught her everything about the treaty-making process and drilled this information into her, so that somewhere farther down the road, it could be utilized and prove invaluable.

Conclusion

Elders who have been interviewed in both the distant and recent past continue to repeat and validate the same historical information – the same values of respect and sharing, and the same concept and understanding of the treaty as an agreement in which land and resources were never sold, but only loaned. In the Eurocentric academic community, history is validated if two separate sources confirm the same information. The information passed on from the Elders has been validated over and over again. Elders have spoken the truth, for they believe they are governed by a universal principle to do so. It is a part of their spirituality.

In any analysis or teachings of the treaty, it is up to Indigenous peoples to represent themselves, to indicate their understanding from within their cultural and spiritual context. For no one can truly represent an Indigenous person or claim to understand the significance of their treaties unless they have the understanding from within that cultural and spiritual context. It requires a perspective that encompasses the total picture, and an understanding of the cultural values, beliefs, and philosophy that have been practised for many generations – a view from within.

If only one aspect or one perspective of the treaty-making process is represented, how can it be the truth as Indigenous peoples see it? It is like telling a story as two people see it. If one tells only his side of the story, it is only half the truth. If both people tell the story, then we get a more complete truth. If history is to be validated, Indigenous peoples will not only have to represent themselves, but ensure that their story is told, recognized, recorded, and sanctioned.

But Indigenous peoples ourselves have to believe in that story first of all, and practise that belief. We must keep in mind, as we tell our story, that we are of one mind, we are unified. We acknowledge our God-given right and authority as Indigenous nations by understanding, affirming, and practising our rights. This perspective needs to be taught to youth, to Indigenous communities, and, first and foremost, to leaders, in order to regain that right and authority as given by the Creator and as understood, practised, and taught by our spiritual Elders.

It was within the spirituality of Indigenous peoples, their belief and practice of respect, kindness, honesty, and sharing, that the treaty-making process took place. But now it is by the abuse of those same values by the state of Canada that this great country is slowly being destroyed by pollution and other environmental degradation. It is by Indigenous peoples reinforcing and practising these values and spiritual principles that the treaties will be understood and honoured.

Our system of leadership saw the Indigenous peoples through the first five hundred years after Columbus. If the state of Canada wants to claim use of the lands of Indigenous peoples, it must recognize that the traditional governments of the Indigenous peoples are the only governments which lend legitimacy to the state of Canada. The International Court of Justice was very clear in its decision concerning *terra nullius* and the role of treaty-making with Indigenous peoples. Only agreements entered into with the Indigenous peoples of the territory can give any legitimacy to the use and occupancy of the lands. Canada must recognize the position of the traditional governments that entered into treaty with the British

Crown. To discount the legitimate governments of Indigenous peoples is to discount Canada's own legitimacy.

8

Affirming Aboriginal Title: A New Basis for Comprehensive Claims Negotiations

Michael Asch and Norman Zlotkin[1]

Introduction

In 1973, the federal government announced its willingness to negotiate comprehensive claims[2] agreements in those parts of Canada where Aboriginal people[3] had never signed treaties. These regions are primarily in British Columbia, Quebec, Labrador, and the North. Since that time, ten agreements have been concluded,[4] while some fifty more claims remain to be settled.[5] Settlement of comprehensive claims has been very slow and the process cumbersome. Given the current pace of negotiations, it does not seem unreasonable to conclude that the settlement of all outstanding comprehensive claims could take us well into the next century.

A fundamental obstacle to the completion of agreements has been disagreement over whether settlements should contain wording that extinguishes all or part of Aboriginal rights and title. On the one hand, the federal government, following a policy that historically sought the extinguishment of Aboriginal title in treaties and earlier comprehensive agreements, still requires extinguishment as a condition for settling outstanding claims. Conversely, many Aboriginal parties completely reject this condition and refuse to settle when it is included in proposed agreements. Instead, they seek recognition and affirmation of Aboriginal rights and title. Many First Nations leaders and others have suggested repeatedly that a resolution of the extinguishment issue would go a long way towards creating an environment in which settlements surrounding land rights (or comprehensive claims) might be concluded more quickly.

We believe that at the heart of the differences between the Aboriginal peoples' and government's positions are conflicting premises and largely incompatible objectives with regard to extinguishment of Aboriginal title. In the government's view, extinguishment (or a similar concept) is an essential element in resolving outstanding issues; among Aboriginal nations, it is seen as a means for the government to block the resolution of fundamental issues at the negotiating table. We believe an approach that reconciles these differences will go a long way towards resolving the impasse.

The difficulties with the extinguishment provision have been known for years, and we are certainly not the first to seek a means of resolving it. One milestone was the 1985 *Report of the Task Force to Review Comprehensive Claims Policy*[6] (known as the Coolican Report), which proposed three alternatives to 'blanket' or general extinguishment. In a 1986 document entitled *Comprehensive Land Claims Policy*,[7] the federal government adopted the spirit of some of the Task Force proposals as one of its 'acceptable options.'[8] As a result, the federal government may require only a limited rather than a total extinguishment of Aboriginal rights and title. However, this alternative has proved to be no more acceptable to Aboriginal peoples than the blanket extinguishment policy. More recently, in 1995, the Royal Commission on Aboriginal Peoples released a report[9] formally considering alternatives to extinguishment. In the same year, the Ministry of Indian Affairs and Northern Development commissioned Justice Hamilton to review the matter.

While we will detail our reasoning below, we wish to begin by clearly stating that in our view the extinguishment policy is harmful and counterproductive. It constructs a vision of resolving outstanding settlements that runs counter to our understanding of what the purpose of such settlements needs to be if we are to build a new relationship between Aboriginal peoples and Canada. We recommend that federal policy be changed significantly in partnership with Aboriginal people and that, within the context of such a change, the idea of requiring extinguishment be rejected. Instead, the focus of negotiations between the Canadian government and Aboriginal peoples should be on reconciliation based on an affirmation of Aboriginal title and rights, according to the principle of equitable sharing of ownership and jurisdiction.

In this paper, we will describe the history and evolution of the federal policy, and the current state of the extinguishment controversy. We will outline the federal and Aboriginal perspectives on both Aboriginal title and the purposes of negotiations, and then discuss the ethnocentric basis of the federal position and other reasons for rejecting an extinguishment policy. We will propose that comprehensive claims negotiations be based on mutual accommodation and the affirmation of Aboriginal title and, finally, will look briefly at the kind of agreement such negotiations might produce.

The Extinguishment Controversy

In standard legal terminology, the word 'extinguishment' means 'the destruction or cancellation of a right.'[10] In Canadian law, the extinguishment of Aboriginal rights and title has occurred in two ways. The first involves extinguishment by unilateral government action. The second involves extinguishment with the alleged consent of an Aboriginal party.

The notion of extinguishment by unilateral action is based on the presumption that, prior to the passage of the Constitution Act, 1982, Parliamentary acts represented the supreme law of Canada.[11] Therefore, any Aboriginal right derived from the common law could be extinguished unilaterally and without the consent of Aboriginal people where an act of Parliament directly contradicted it.[12] This view was accepted by Canadian courts prior to 1982, which found that extinguishment of Aboriginal title could occur both through legislation explicitly intended for that purpose,[13] and possibly through legislation merely inconsistent with the continued existence of Aboriginal title.[14] In *Calder* v. *Attorney General of British Columbia*, Justice Hall wrote: '[Aboriginal title] being a legal right, it could not thereafter be extinguished except by surrender to the Crown or by competent legislative authority, and then only by specific legislation.'[15] He went on to state: 'It would, accordingly, appear to be beyond question that the onus of proving that the Sovereign intended to extinguish the Indian title lies on the respondent and that intention must be "clear and plain." There is no such proof in the case at bar; no legislation to that effect.'[16] In contrast, Justice Judson rejected the requirement that specific legislation is required to extinguish Aboriginal title unilaterally. He wrote: 'In my opinion, in the present case, the sovereign authority elected to exercise complete dominion over the lands in question, adverse to any right of occupancy which the Nishga Tribe might have had, when, by legislation, it opened up such lands for settlement, subject to the reserves of land set aside for Indian occupation.'[17]

In 1990, the Supreme Court of Canada adopted the 'clear and plain' intention test from Justice Hall's judgment, when it stated in *R.* v. *Sparrow*[18] that 'the Sovereign's intention must be clear and plain if it is to extinguish an aboriginal right.'[19] After the adoption of section 35(1) of the Constitution Act, 1982, recognizing and affirming existing Aboriginal and treaty rights, extinguishment of Aboriginal title without the consent of Aboriginal people was no longer possible in Canadian law.

Extinguishment by alleged consent of an Aboriginal party describes the effect of certain clauses in the written versions of many historic treaties and comprehensive claims agreements.[20] The typical wording is that the Aboriginal parties agree to 'cede, release and surrender to Her Majesty in Right of Canada ... all their aboriginal claims, rights, titles and interest, if any, in and to lands and waters'[21] in return for specific benefits.[22] In this context, extinguishment is said to be based on an express agreement by

Aboriginal people to 'cede' certain rights. Many Aboriginal peoples, including the Cree of James Bay, who signed a comprehensive claim agreement in 1975,[23] strongly deny that they freely agreed to such clauses. Many treaty peoples assert that the extinguishment clause does not represent their understanding of the essential nature of their treaties. However, governments continue to approach comprehensive claims as fundamentally contractual matters, despite the fact that treaties and comprehensive claims agreements now have constitutional status and protection.

There are only a few modern settlements in which the Aboriginal parties have agreed to terms that include the extinguishment provision. The most recent is that of the Inuit in Nunavut.[24] Even in such cases, the view of the Aboriginal signatories is that such an approach is not preferred and that extinguishment was accepted only to facilitate other goals. In many more cases, settlements have not been reached because of the extinguishment requirement. Negotiations with the Dene-Metis of the Northwest Territories took a decade to complete, but the proposed agreement eventually failed, primarily due to the rejection by the Dene-Metis of the extinguishment clause.

The federal government's insistence on this provision has led to internal division among Aboriginal peoples. Some are reluctantly prepared to accept the extinguishment requirement in order to obtain the perceived benefits of an immediate settlement. They believe they need an agreement in order to receive the much-needed economic benefits of settlement and the right to develop and co-manage lands and other resources. Others are unwilling to agree to the extinguishment of their Aboriginal title, which they view as basic to their Aboriginal identity. In the case of the Dene-Metis, just such a split developed, between those who agreed to the proposed settlement[25] and those who rejected it out of hand.[26]

Finally, the federal policy on extinguishment has had a dampening effect on the settlement of specific claims. First Nations in Saskatchewan have been divided over participation in the Treaty Land Entitlement process,[27] developed to settle outstanding land claims based on insufficient land allotments under the treaties. Many First Nations have opposed participation on the basis that they will never agree to the extinguishment of Aboriginal rights, even if it means their nations will not have an expanded reserve land base.

The Federal Perspective

The federal government's understanding of Aboriginal rights and title, accepted without question by Canadian courts, is based on the assumption that the Canadian state holds underlying title to all of Canada. Underlying title refers to more than the ultimate ownership of land; it also includes the jurisdiction to govern the land in question. For the federal government, Aboriginal rights have scope and content only to the extent that they have been recognized and affirmed through court decisions or constitutional amendment. Canadian courts have acknowledged that the Canadian legal system cannot easily accommodate Aboriginal understandings of Aboriginal rights and title.[28] Nonetheless, Canadian law has characterized Aboriginal title as a form of property right which is a burden on underlying Crown title.[29]

In our view, federal policy derives primarily from the lack of specificity about the content of Aboriginal rights in current Canadian case law and, to a lesser extent, within section 35 of the Constitution Act, 1982.[30] Given the failure of constitutional conferences to reach agreement on the meaning of Aboriginal rights, and the rejection of the Charlottetown Accord, section 35 currently does little to define the nature and content of Aboriginal rights.

Federal policy therefore conceptualizes Aboriginal rights and title as uncertain, especially 'with respect to the legal status of lands and resources.'[31] The federal government states that this uncertainty 'has been created by a lack of political agreement with Aboriginal groups'[32] and has resulted in 'a barrier to economic development for all Canadians and has hindered the full participation of Aboriginal peoples in land and resource management.'[33]

The idea that Aboriginal rights are 'undefined' and that their ultimate definition must be a product of judicial interpretation and constitutional amendment in turn rests on an underlying assumption about the relationship of Aboriginal rights and title to the Canadian constitutional and legal framework. The assumption is that this framework is fixed and supreme and that Aboriginal rights and title form a corpus of rights that are already subsumed under its jurisdiction. In this respect, federal policy fits within a definitional framework already established by the Supreme Court of Canada, which stated in *Sparrow:* 'It is worth recalling that while British policy toward the native population was based on respect for their right to occupy their traditional lands, a proposition to which the Royal Proclamation of 1763 bears witness, *there was from the outset never any doubt that sovereignty and legislative power, and indeed the underlying title, to such lands vested in the Crown'*[34] (emphasis added).

Within this framework, Aboriginal rights and title are seen as common law rights that survived the assertion of sovereignty by Britain and later by Canada. As common law rights (until their entrenchment in the Constitution in 1982), Aboriginal rights and title were weaker than the prerogative rights of the Crown and, later, the rights of the British and Canadian Parliaments. Hence, the legitimate expression of Aboriginal rights could not survive in the face of conflicting legislation passed by the appropriate body. Common law Aboriginal rights thus remain largely undefined not merely because Canadian courts have yet to define them but also because the extent to which they were unilaterally extinguished through inconsistent legislation prior to 1982 is still uncertain.[35] Despite the constitutional recognition now given to existing Aboriginal rights, the Supreme Court of Canada has stated that Parliament still has the authority to pass legislation restricting the exercise of Aboriginal rights, provided it can pass the justification test set out in *Sparrow*. In this sense, the Supreme Court of Canada has recognized the continued supremacy of Parliament over Aboriginal rights.[36]

According to federal policy papers, the focus of comprehensive claims settlements is to replace uncertainty with certainty and to resolve debates and legal ambiguities – the central one being the undefined nature of Aboriginal rights. Therefore, one objective of federal policy is to ask Aboriginal groups 'to relinquish undefined Aboriginal rights which they may have with respect to lands or resources, in favour of the rights and other benefits which are written down in the settlement agreement.'[37] The function of the 'relinquishment' clause is to provide 'confirmation from Aboriginal groups that the rights written down in claims settlements are the full extent of their special rights related to the subjects of the agreements.'[38] Such a clause would counteract the possibility that the courts could interpret Aboriginal rights and title more broadly or differently than the rights set out in a comprehensive claims settlement. Were this to happen, the federal concern is that Aboriginal signatories might be in a position to assert both the rights they obtain through a settlement and their Aboriginal rights and title. From the perspective of the federal government, the most certain protection from such a possibility is a clause that requires the Aboriginal parties to surrender certain Aboriginal rights and title to the Crown as a condition of signing settlement agreements.

In sum, the federal government describes the relinquishment clause as part of an instrument whereby Aboriginal groups exchange[39] undefined rights for rights that are defined and certain, with the stated aim of providing Aboriginal parties with significant benefits. In return, the federal government seeks to ensure that the rights provided in the agreements represent the full extent of the rights asserted.[40] Although the federal government does not use the word 'extinguishment' to describe the impact of comprehensive claims agreements on Aboriginal rights and title (and it has modified its previous requirement of blanket extinguishment), it is clear that the result of clauses proposed by the federal government will be at least partial extinguishment of Aboriginal title.[41]

With regard to the scope of comprehensive claims negotiations, the federal government has stated that it is prepared to address a range of issues. These can include 'land selection, self-government, environmental management, resource revenue-sharing, hunting, fishing and trapping rights, and other topics.'[42] However, in the federal government's view, the comprehensive claims process can only advance self-government objectives in limited ways. Negotiations may arrange for Aboriginal representatives on management boards. They may also address the establishment of 'community-based self-government regimes on designated lands.'[43] However, 'any particular approach to community self-government must respect existing constitutional principles and be consistent with government practices.'[44] Further, while self-government discussions are permitted in comprehensive claims negotiations, the terms must remain in accord with 'federal policy on community self-government negotiations.'[45] Finally, although comprehensive claims agreements receive constitutional protection under section 35(3) of the Constitution Act, 1982, self-government arrangements derived from claims settlements 'will not receive constitutional protection until there is a general constitutional amendment to that effect.'[46]

The federal policy on comprehensive claims is intended to provide a positive alternative to litigation. Although Aboriginal groups are free to seek a determination of their common law Aboriginal rights and title through the legal system, this is a lengthy, unpredictable, and expensive process. Delays will hinder economic development for all Canadians and the participation of Aboriginal people in both economic development and management of lands. Litigation is therefore not seen as advantageous to either the federal government or Aboriginal groups.

Aboriginal Perspectives

Aboriginal people overwhelmingly view their rights and title in a framework very different from that articulated in current federal policy. Resolving the extinguishment issue ultimately rests on changes in the thinking that has produced the federal policy provisions for certainty and finality; but first it requires accommodation between two very different conceptual orientations. In this section, we outline our understanding of the framework within which Aboriginal people describe their rights, the objectives of settling outstanding claims, and the impact of the federal extinguishment policy on both.

As viewed by most Aboriginal peoples, Aboriginal title is a very broad concept that encompasses much more than rights to use and occupy ancestral lands. It includes rights to self-government and jurisdictional rights to make laws, rendering it equivalent to the concept of underlying title in Canadian legal theory. Aboriginal people most often speak of

Aboriginal title as something which is given to them by the Creator and is dependent on their relationship with the land. As Aboriginal title flows from the Creator, it is inherent; it is not something granted to Aboriginal people by an alien legal system. Aboriginal people see Aboriginal title as inextricably linked with their identity as Aboriginal people. In their view, the nature of their title is very certain.

Furthermore, Aboriginal people do not conceptualize their Aboriginal rights and title as largely 'undefined,' but rather as well-defined. For instance, Clem Chartier of the Metis National Council stated at the 1983 First Ministers Conference on Aboriginal Rights: 'What we feel is that aboriginal title or aboriginal right is the right to collective ownership of land, water, resources, both renewable and non-renewable. It is a right to self-government, a right to govern yourselves with your own institutions, whichever way you want your institutions to run; the right to language, to culture, the right to basically practise your own religion and customs, the right to hunt, trap and fish and gather are certainly part of that, but it is not all of it.'[47] John Amagoalik, co-chairperson of the Inuit Committee on National Issues, stated: 'Our position is that aboriginal rights, aboriginal title to land, water and sea ice flows from aboriginal rights and all rights to practise our customs and traditions, to retain and develop our languages and cultures, and the rights to self-government, all of these things flow from the fact that we have aboriginal rights ... In our view, aboriginal rights can also be seen as human rights, because these are the things that we need to continue to survive as a distinct people in Canada.'[48]

Other Aboriginal voices express the same perspective. In their view, Aboriginal rights and title are both robust and fundamental. They might best be described as forming the core elements which enable Aboriginal people to define their ways of life and their relationships with others. Aboriginal title, then, is the term Aboriginal people use when speaking English to represent their essential self-definition as autonomous communities. It is a concept that describes the full scope and content of certain fundamental, collective human rights. In short, Aboriginal rights derive from the very existence of Aboriginal people, communities, and nations. It naturally follows that the requirement to extinguish Aboriginal rights and title would be considered abhorrent.

In this frame of reference, Aboriginal rights and title are not conceptualized as requiring either a determination by the Canadian legal system or explicit constitutional recognition to establish the certainty of their scope or content. Rather, Aboriginal rights and title are self-defining and derive from sources external to the Canadian legal system and constitution. Thus, the recognition of Aboriginal rights by section 35 of the Constitution Act,

1982, means only that their full scope and content have now been accepted by Canada. In the Aboriginal view, the goal of settlements could not be
to define rights and overcome ambiguities in Canadian law and constitutional practice. Rather, a central purpose of negotiations is to reach an
agreement about how these rights, already recognized in the Constitution,
are to be implemented by Canada.

Aboriginal peoples overwhelmingly describe negotiations between
themselves and governments as 'treaty-making.' They do not view either
historic or modern treaties as fixed contracts, but rather as a means of
establishing ongoing political and legal relationships between Aboriginal
collectivities and the Crown. In their view, relationships established
through treaties should be based on a mutual recognition and affirmation
of rights and interconnections between both parties. As Alexander
Christmas, president of the Union of Nova Scotia Indians stated: 'In our
view, if future agreements are to provide for coming generations and
reflect our unique constitutional relationship with the Crown, they must
be based on the recognition of our aboriginal and treaty rights, not on
their extinguishment.'[49]

The language often used by Aboriginal persons to express the goal of a
negotiated settlement is 'sharing' with non-Aboriginal people, but it is
sharing based on a clear recognition of the legitimacy of underlying
Aboriginal title. As Professor Leroy Little Bear of the University of Leth-
bridge states:

> The Indian concept of land ownership is certainly not inconsistent with
> the idea of sharing with an alien people. Once the Indians recognized
> them as human beings, they gladly shared with them. They shared with
> Europeans in the same way they shared with the animals and other peo-
> ple. However, sharing here cannot be interpreted as meaning the
> Europeans got the same rights as any other native person, because the
> Europeans were not descendants of the original grantees, or they were not
> parties to the original social contract. Also, sharing certainly cannot be
> interpreted as meaning that one is giving up his rights for all eternity.[50]

Chief Harold Turner of the Swampy Cree Tribal Council indicates that the
concept of sharing is broadly held within Aboriginal communities and was the
basis of Aboriginal negotiations with Canada from the time of the historic
treaties. During the hearings of the Royal Commission on Aboriginal Peoples,
he stated: 'Our ancestors did not sign a real estate deal as you cannot give away
something you do not own. No, the treaties were signed as our symbol of good
faith to share the land. As well, the treaties were not signed to extinguish our
sovereignty and our form of government.'[51] As for the nature of ownership

and underlying title, Professor Little Bear states: '[Living Aboriginal peoples] are not the sole owners under the original grant from the Creator; the land belongs to past generations, to the yet-to-be-born, and to the plants and animals. Has the Crown ever received a surrender of title from these others?'[52]

Clearly, the 'surrender' of Aboriginal rights and title is not on the table for negotiations. What is negotiable is the relationship of these rights and title to Canada. As the Union of British Columbia Indian Chiefs stated in *Treaty-Making and Title: A Non-Extinguishment Alternative for Settling the Land Question in British Columbia*: 'What is negotiable in treaty-making are *the ways in which our Indian Nations will exercise our rights and jurisdiction* – i.e., the manner in which Indian and non-Indian jurisdictions will accommodate each other in B.C.'[53] (emphasis in original). Given this view of the purpose of negotiations, it is clear that a settlement would necessarily include both property and jurisdictional dimensions. Aboriginal people believe the proper scope of negotiations ranges well beyond matters such as land use, land tenure, resource management, and economic benefits. For this reason, Aboriginal parties tend to describe the outcome of successful negotiations as modern treaties rather than land claims settlements.

Aboriginal peoples conceptualize Aboriginal rights and title as the basis for the ethic of 'sharing' and for the ultimate political and economic accommodation between Canada and themselves. Aboriginal title defines, in essence, the core that legitimates the right of Aboriginal communities, peoples, and nations to enter into such fundamental negotiations with Canada.

This legitimacy is often stated in terms that express the essential connection of Aboriginal peoples to their ancestral homelands. As Jim Antoine, member of the legislative assembly of the Northwest Territories and former chief of the Fort Simpson Dene Band stated: 'We are a real part of the land. Our roots are connected into the land. But if you want to extinguish your aboriginal rights and title to it, then you are cutting off those roots, You are cutting us off from the land, and we are floating.'[54] Mr. Antoine went on to explain the consequence of signing an agreement that requires the surrender of Aboriginal rights and title: 'The government then becomes our base, and any time there is a problem with the land, the government has the final say in settling that dispute.'[55]

In other words, the consequence of an extinguishment provision is the replacement of legitimacy based on self-definition by legitimacy as constructed by Canada. Whether the policy is described as 'extinguishment' or 'exchange' does not matter, for what is being required by a 'cession and surrender' provision is the voluntary relinquishment of the self-defined legitimacy of a people, community, or nation. The extinguishment requirement is seen, in effect, as a contemporary means of furthering what was a long-standing overt objective of federal policy: the assimilation of Aboriginal people into the Canadian mainstream.

The sense of injustice about the extinguishment policy can never be erased. Though the numbered treaties use the language of extinguishment, the First Nations who signed them do not see them as extinguishment documents but as agreements with the Crown to establish ongoing political and social relations and to allow European settlement.

In sum, for Aboriginal people, the purpose of negotiations today is the same as it has always been, since the time of the first historic treaty: to shape a relationship between Aboriginal people and the newcomers based upon sharing, to come to an agreement that clarifies not only property relations but also how Aboriginal people and non-Aboriginal people will accommodate each other. The legitimacy of embarking on such a process is seen by Aboriginal people as intimately connected with the existence of Aboriginal rights and title. These rights are not seen as undefined, nor are they seen as needing court decisions or additional constitutional amendment to provide them with substance. Rather, they are self-defined rights that express the core concept about who Aboriginal peoples are, both among themselves and in their relationships to others.

Assessing the Federal Extinguishment Policy

As indicated above, the positions of Aboriginal peoples and the federal government regarding extinguishment are in stark contrast. For the latter, extinguishment is an essential element of any settlement. Without extinguishment, settlements will not significantly advance the government's central reason for resolving Aboriginal claims, that is, to render the rights of Aboriginal peoples certain and well-defined. For the federal government, negotiations that do not ensure extinguishment hardly seem worthwhile. For many Aboriginal peoples, on the other hand, the affirmation of Aboriginal rights and title is essential to improving relations with Canada. Therefore, any settlement that requires extinguishment of Aboriginal rights and title is unacceptable.

While it is possible to conceptualize short-term or limited settlements that avoid the extinguishment issue completely, this is highly unlikely to be helpful in the long term. It is essential that we resolve the extinguishment controversy. In this section, we consider whether the federal or Aboriginal position is most beneficial, not just to the parties themselves but to Canada as a whole. On this basis we assess the federal position and conclude that it should be rejected and that the option to affirm Aboriginal title and rights rather than extinguish them is the best choice.

We see six fundamental reasons for adopting this perspective. The first concerns the concept of certainty which lies at the heart of the government's desire to incorporate extinguishment in any settlement. In our view, an extinguishment clause does not guarantee certainty. It is our opinion that, in fact, a negotiated agreement affirming Aboriginal title can produce a greater degree of certainty than one which extinguishes it.

Extinguishment provisions have not produced certainty, even in modern treaties. The 1975 James Bay and Northern Quebec Agreement[56] was the first settlement reached after the federal government's 1973 announcement that it would negotiate settlements of comprehensive land claims. Virtually since it was ratified, this agreement has led to disagreement and controversy, even though it was drafted by legal experts, contains an extinguishment clause,[57] and is 450 pages long. The twenty-year period since the signing of that agreement has been marked by bitter political struggle and ongoing litigation.[58] Moreover, the extinguishment clause has failed to provide the government of Quebec with the certainty it needed to proceed with further hydroelectric development in northern Quebec.

Even historic treaties with extinguishment clauses have not prevented Aboriginal peoples from questioning governmental jurisdiction to manage Crown lands. In Ontario alone, one may look at the assertions of the Teme-Augama Anishnabay and the Nishnawbe-Aski Nation. In Saskatchewan, Aboriginal people have challenged the province's right to manage timber harvesting in the Meadow Lake area. In addition, experience shows that legislation extinguishing Aboriginal rights will not produce certainty if it leaves an ongoing sense of injustice. The Metis have continued to press their claims, notwithstanding provisions in the Dominion Lands Act purporting to extinguish Metis land rights.[59]

It must also be remembered that the desire for certainty is not limited to the federal government. One cannot overlook the negative impact of uncertainty on Aboriginal communities. Historically, Aboriginal peoples have lacked both the economic and legal means to resolve questions concerning the nature and scope of Aboriginal rights, and thereby protect their rights from encroachment. Aboriginal concerns about certainty are related largely to the manner in which the federal government currently functions. As we discuss in more detail below, the government operates as though certainty exists, notwithstanding its statements in federal policy documents on comprehensive claims.

Thus, certainty is a concern for both parties. As the 1991 report of the tripartite task force composed of the federal government, the government of British Columbia and First Nations states: 'First Nations and the federal and provincial governments share the common objective of achieving certainty in their relationship, particularly concerning the ownership of and jurisdiction over land and resources. Certainty will create levels of confidence and understanding, and facilitate constructive developments in the political, social, and economic fields.'[60]

In our view, a negotiated agreement based on the affirmation of Aboriginal title can produce more certainty than an extinguishment clause which is obtained through unequal bargaining power and does violence to one party's basic sense of identity. An agreement based on affirmation and mutual accommodation can define specific rights between the parties and provide certainty as regards those rights; it can also cover the kinds of matters dealt with in agreements containing extinguishment clauses. For example, it can address in clear and precise terms such matters as lands and resources (including forests, inland waters, offshore waters and resources, minerals and subsurface resources), management regimes, royalties, and compensation. Third-party interests created or recognized by the agreement can be as legally secure and enforceable as they are in regions where there is an agreement with an extinguishment provision.

Moreover, agreements that acknowledge rather than extinguish Aboriginal title will establish ongoing relations between the parties, especially with regard to cooperative decision-making and the resolution of differences. In the long run, Aboriginal parties will be more committed to seeing that such agreements work. Thus, an affirmation approach will create more certainty than agreements requiring extinguishment, because Aboriginal parties are more likely to challenge the latter through litigation due to the ongoing dissatisfaction they create.

A second reason for rejecting the extinguishment requirement is that it is inconsistent with the constitutional recognition and affirmation of existing Aboriginal rights in section 35 of the Constitution Act, 1982 and with the process of elaborating on the rights of Aboriginal peoples through constitutional conferences, as set out in sections 37 and 37.1. This was one reason the Coolican Report recommended that comprehensive claims agreements should recognize and affirm Aboriginal rights.[61] It commented, 'Why would Parliament recognize aboriginal rights in the most important constitutional document of the century, and then extinguish them in the decades that follow?'[62]

A third reason, closely connected to the second, is that the extinguishment policy is also inconsistent with Canada's fiduciary obligation towards Aboriginal peoples. The Supreme Court of Canada set out this fiduciary relationship in *Guerin* v. *The Queen*,[63] where Justice Dickson stated: 'In my view, the nature of Indian title and the framework of the statutory scheme established for disposing of Indian lands places upon the Crown an equitable obligation, enforceable by the courts, to deal with the land for the benefit of the Indians. This obligation does not amount to a trust in the private law sense. It is rather a fiduciary duty. If, however, the Crown breaches this fiduciary duty it will be liable to the Indians in the same way and to the same extent as if such a trust were in effect.'[64] The Court stated that the 'fiduciary relationship between the Crown and the Indians has its roots in the concept of aboriginal, native or Indian title' which is 'inalienable except upon surrender to the Crown,'[65] and that the fiduciary relationship arose through the historical powers and responsibility assumed by the Crown rather than through operation of the Indian Act.[66] The Supreme Court of Canada further stated in *Sparrow:* 'The government has the responsibility to act in a fiduciary capacity with respect to aboriginal peoples. The relationship between the Government and aboriginals is trustlike, rather than adversarial, and contemporary recognition and affirmation of aboriginal rights must be defined in light of this historic relationship.'[67] It is inconsistent with its fiduciary obligations for the Crown to require Aboriginal peoples to surrender their Aboriginal rights in order to enter into agreements dealing with lands and resources. As the Supreme Court stated in *Sparrow:* 'The honour of the Crown is at stake in dealings with Aboriginal peoples. The special trust relationship and the responsibility of the government vis-à-vis aboriginals must be the first consideration in determining whether the legislation or action in question can be justified.'[68]

A fourth reason for rejection is that a policy requiring extinguishment of Aboriginal rights and title may not be consistent with international human rights standards. Extinguishment is inconsistent with Aboriginal land rights recognized in the *Draft Declaration on the Rights of Indigenous Peoples,*[69] including 'the right to the full recognition of their laws, traditions and customs, land tenure systems and institutions for the development and management of resources, and the right to effective measures by States to prevent any interference with, alienation of or encroachment upon these rights.'[70] The *Draft Declaration* states in article 1 that 'Indigenous peoples have the right to the full and effective enjoyment of all the human rights and fundamental freedoms which are recognized in the Charter of the United Nations and in international human rights law.' Other people in Canada are not required to extinguish their human rights in order to participate in the Canadian federation and exercise basic rights. The extinguishment requirement in federal policy can be seen as a violation of international law, including the prohibition against racial discrimination.[71]

A fifth reason to reject the extinguishment requirement is the strong negative impact it has had on the way many Aboriginal peoples conceptualize the nature of their relations with Canada. Extinguishment, or even exchange of fundamental Aboriginal rights for rights derived from another system, seems inconceivable to most Aboriginal people, for this would be antithetical to their reasons for undertaking negotiations. Extinguishment is also inconsistent with the Aboriginal objective of developing relationships with Canada, for it implies that the objective of negotiations is assimilation within Canada rather than developing a solution based on mutual accommodation. Most Aboriginal peoples will never voluntarily complete negotiations where the agreement states that they extinguish, exchange, surrender, cede, or release their Aboriginal rights and title. As Chief Jean-Guy Whiteduck of the Algonquins of Maniwaki stated: 'One of the most frustrating things for First Nations and for our people is the issue of extinguishment of Aboriginal rights ... We think that there is no need for extinguishment. We feel that asking Aboriginal people to extinguish their rights would be equivalent to asking Canadians to give up their Canadian citizenship. Therefore, that is why it is so difficult when it comes to dealing with the comprehensive claim policy for many of our people.'[72]

Finally, the extinguishment policy should be rejected because of the ethnocentric bias upon which it is based. Ethnocentrism can be defined as 'regarding one's own race or cultural group as superior to others.'[73] Such an attitude is central in the government's view that certainty, specificity, and fairness can be achieved exclusively within a frame of reference based on the cultural values of the Canadian legal and political system, without regard to Aboriginal values. At its most basic level, government policy on negotiations and extinguishment derives from the ethnocentric manner in which government envisions its relationship with Aboriginal peoples and asserts underlying title.

Currently, the Crown presumes that it holds underlying title to all of Canada and that Aboriginal title represents, at best, a mere encumbrance on that title. Because of its presumption of title, the Crown assumes that it has legitimate jurisdiction to govern and enforce its laws in all regions, including those in which Aboriginal title has not been extinguished. The federal government has stated this view categorically, for example, in its interpretation of Aboriginal title at trial in *Delgamuukw* v. *Attorney General of British Columbia*. Here, the attorney general of Canada stated: 'Ownership and jurisdiction constitute a claim to sovereignty. If the Plaintiffs ever had sovereignty, it was extinguished completely by the assertion of sovereignty by Great Britain.'[74] Such an assertion is justifiable only when one assumes that a country was uninhabited at the time of first contact or that its inhabitants were too primitive to have underlying title to the lands they occupied.[75] The assumption of Canadian sovereignty is reflected in a number of court decisions, including both *Delgamuukw* and *Sparrow*.

This ethnocentric bias is based on colonial legal precedents, which serve as the basis for many recent court decisions.[76] One aspect of colonial legal theory is the doctrine of discovery, developed by Chief Justice Marshall of the United States Supreme Court in *Johnson* v. *McIntosh*[77] and *Worcester* v. *Georgia*.[78] According to this doctrine, Aboriginal nations had a legally recognized right to occupy their traditional lands. Upon 'discovery' of their lands, however, underlying title went to the discovering state, subject to the Aboriginal right of occupancy.[79] Chief Justice Marshall articulated this position in *Johnson* v. *McIntosh* as follows:

> Those relations which were to exist between the discoverer and the natives, were to be regulated by themselves. The rights thus acquired being exclusive, no other power could interpose between them.
>
> In the establishment of these relations, the rights of the original inhabitants were, in no instance, entirely disregarded; but were, necessarily, to a considerable extent, impaired. *They were admitted to be the rightful occupants of the soil, with a legal as well as a just claim to retain possession of it, and to use it according to their own discretion; but their rights to complete sovereignty, as independent nations, were necessarily diminished, and their power to dispose of the soil, at their own will, to whomsoever they pleased, was denied by the original fundamental principle, that discovery gave exclusive title to those who made it*.[80] (emphasis added)

Government policy is infused with this view of Canadian sovereignty and Aboriginal title. Because the federal government perceives its title as superior to that of Aboriginal peoples, and views existing Aboriginal title as so limited that it provides no effective block to governmental actions,[81] governments generally act as though the existence of Aboriginal rights and title are of no consequence. An examination of the Dene-Metis negotiations illustrates this point. The experience of the Dene-Metis was that, in the period between the signing of an Agreement in Principle and the initialling of the Final Agreement (except for a brief period where an interim land freeze was in place), the federal and territorial governments continued to grant land use permits and other licences to third parties without consulting or acquiring the consent of the Dene-Metis. Indeed, these governments have continued to issue permits and licences in geographical regions where the Dene-Metis refused to sign a final agreement because it contained an extinguishment provision.

In our view, ethnocentrism is a fundamental element of the extinguishment policy. Because government assumes that underlying title vests solely in Canada on the basis of the doctrine of discovery, it assumes that underlying Aboriginal title has already been extinguished. Thus, existing Aboriginal rights and title with respect to land can only refer to rights of use and occupation. Notwithstanding what Aboriginal spokespersons may say about relations between Aboriginal peoples and the Creator through the land, the federal government is unlikely to regard the extinguishment requirement as a matter of profound significance.

Finally, it is worth noting that the Supreme Court of Canada, despite its unquestioning acceptance of Canadian sovereignty, rejected an ethnocentric view of Aboriginal peoples over twenty years ago. In *Calder*, Justice Judson stated: 'The fact is that when the settlers came, the Indians were there, organized in societies and occupying the land as their forefathers had done for centuries. This is what Indian title means.'[82] This view was expressed even more forcefully by Justice Hall in the same case: 'The assessment and interpretation of historical documents and enactments tendered in evidence must be approached in the light of present-day research and knowledge, disregarding ancient concepts formulated when understanding of the customs and cultures of our original people was rudimentary and incomplete and when they were thought to be wholly without cohesion, laws, or culture, in effect a subhuman species.'[83] We recommend that the federal government policy follow the example of the Supreme Court of Canada and consciously reject ethnocentrism. It will then begin to understand the importance of acknowledging in negotiations the profound nature of Aboriginal rights and title to land as these are understood by the Aboriginal parties. This understanding, in itself, should motivate government to move quickly away from advocating extinguishment as an integral part of their policy on comprehensive settlements.

To summarize, there are six reasons why extinguishment should not be a condition for settlement of outstanding comprehensive land questions. First, an extinguishment clause does not provide certainty to either party. Second, the extinguishment requirement is inconsistent with Canada's constitutional obligations. Third, it is also inconsistent with Canada's fiduciary obligations towards Aboriginal peoples. Fourth, the requirement may violate international human rights standards. Fifth, it has a profound negative impact on Aboriginal parties while providing a negligible benefit to the government. Finally, the extinguishment requirement perpetuates the ethnocentric biases of government with respect to the nature of Aboriginal rights and title.

Affirmation and Mutual Accommodation

We stated at the beginning of this paper that the central objective of settling outstanding land questions must be the construction of a better relationship between Aboriginal peoples and Canada. Ideally, this relationship will be founded on principles of justice, mutual respect, and cooperation. It will reject any idea of domination by one party over the other and avoid reasoning based on ethnocentric theories about the nature of Aboriginal society. Instead, it will recognize the unique character of Aboriginal people, communities, and nations and seek reciprocal ways to build community between Aboriginal peoples and Canada.

Theoretically, settlements could be negotiated that avoid either extinguishment or affirmation. However, such an approach would not motivate government to address Aboriginal concepts, given its ethnocentric belief that the Crown holds underlying title to all of Canada and that Aboriginal title is of minor importance. Even in the short term, the only approach that has any hope of achieving the objectives outlined above is one that bases government policy for settling outstanding land questions on the affirmation of Aboriginal rights and title. This approach does more than merely reflect an Aboriginal perspective. We recommend this approach because it also seems to be the one most beneficial to all Canadians. Moreover, in the present political context, such an approach is not unrealistic. As noted above, it is consistent with judicial comments that date back over twenty years. Even more important, it is consistent with the recommendations of reports either commissioned or agreed to by governments within the last decade.

The view that land claims settlements should develop a new relationship incorporating both jurisdictional and ownership components is found in at least two recent reports: the Coolican Report,[84] commissioned by the federal government in the mid-1980s to provide alternatives to the existing comprehensive claims policy; and the 1991 *Report of the British Columbia Task Force*.[85] Under the heading 'New Relationship,' the B.C. Task Force report states: 'As history shows, the relationship between First Nations and the Crown has been a troubled one. This relationship must be cast aside. In its place, a new relationship which recognizes the unique place of aboriginal people and First Nations in Canada must be developed and nurtured. Recognition and respect for First Nations as self-determining and distinct nations with their own spiritual values, histories, languages, territories, political institutions and ways of life must be the hallmark of this new relationship.'[86] The report also states: 'First Nations should not be required to abandon fundamental constitutional rights simply to achieve certainty for others. Certainty can be achieved without extinguishment. The parties must strive to achieve certainty through treaties which state precisely each party's rights, duties, and jurisdiction.'[87]

An approach to negotiations that recognizes underlying Aboriginal title best addresses a reality that, from an non-ethnocentric perspective, is self-evident: that Aboriginal peoples possessed and still possess – at least in areas where there are unresolved land questions – an underlying title that includes both jurisdiction and ownership.[88] To support this view, we offer the following points. First, Aboriginal nations were present in what is now known as Canada prior to the arrival of Europeans and the European assertion of sovereignty. Second, there is an international consensus that the equality of all peoples is a self-evident truth. Third, there is an understanding that has arisen from modern anthropological evidence that a fundamental characteristic of any culture with circumstances similar to those of First Nations five hundred years ago is the existence of a political system and a territory. Indeed, the recognition of a political system and territory accords well with modern anthropological understandings of how cultures have generally operated during the past ten thousand years.[89] Fourth, recognition of Aboriginal territory and political systems accords with United Nations declarations regarding self-determination, to which Canada is a signatory,[90] and which have been utilized by the Supreme Court of Canada.[91] Given that Aboriginal peoples were here at the time of European contact and that their societies contained the same elements as those found in other societies, it follows that Aboriginal nations had rightful jurisdiction and ownership when Europeans first arrived. Consequently, at least with respect to Aboriginal nations negotiating outstanding land questions, Aboriginal title includes an underlying title that contains both ownership and jurisdictional aspects. Negotiations between Aboriginal peoples and governments must therefore address both aspects of Aboriginal title.

In principle, there are two ways of affirming underlying Aboriginal title. The first would involve mutual recognition that each party holds underlying title. This approach was developed in the report of the Royal Commission on Aboriginal Peoples (RCAP) entitled *Partners in Confederation: Aboriginal Peoples, Self-Government, and the Constitution.*[92] The report argues that, through conscious acts as well as the experience of living side by side, colonists and Aboriginal peoples established a new and expanded meaning of the Crown which includes Aboriginal jurisdiction. In other words, there are now three levels of jurisdiction (and therefore underlying title) in Canada: federal, provincial, and Aboriginal.

There is a fundamental problem with the way this concept has been addressed in the RCAP document. A careful reading of the report reveals that in its formulation of 'the Crown,' the Aboriginal party is not an equal partner in Confederation; it is subordinated constitutionally to the provincial and federal Crowns. The Constitution Act, 1867, specifies the legislative jurisdiction of Parliament and the provincial legislative assemblies in great detail, without making any specific reference to the powers of Aboriginal governments. If the approach of the Royal Commission were followed, Aboriginal governments would be left in the difficult position of having to assert their unspecified jurisdiction against the explicit constitutional recognition of the jurisdiction of other levels of government. This would put them at a severe disadvantage were they to seek clarification of their jurisdiction through litigation. It is most probable, therefore, that governments in Canada would continue to act as though they did not need to acknowledge Aboriginal jurisdiction. Furthermore, after the long history of governments ignoring or overriding Aboriginal jurisdiction, it is too much to expect that Aboriginal peoples would accept that they have been incorporated into a single Crown, in a subordinate position, without their express consent.

Moreover, there are serious difficulties with the proposition that each party holds underlying title, even if the proposition is founded on the premise of equality among the parties. It is necessary to ask, What is the legitimate basis upon which Canada can assert underlying title unilaterally, if we recognize the underlying title Aboriginal peoples had and still have? The primary answer would be that Canada's underlying title arises on an ontological basis that is equivalent to the ontological basis on which the underlying title of Aboriginal peoples arises. Such a view could be based on conventions of international law such as 'prescription,' which suggests that a people who have established effective self-government that has been recognized internationally over a long period of time have thereby established a self-evident right to underlying title.[93] However, if applied to Canada, such a proposition maintains the ethnocentric presupposition that Aboriginal rights are inferior to those of European colonists.

The only way to envision a non-Aboriginal self-defined right to underlying title is to assume that there are certain conditions under which such title could legitimately be asserted without developing a relationship with Aboriginal peoples. Contemporary understanding of the nature of colonialism and of conquest makes such a proposition unacceptable. Therefore, negotiations premised on such a proposition would not achieve the fundamental goal of developing a new and just relationship between Aboriginal peoples and Canada.

We have argued that, in principle, the title of Aboriginal peoples is the better title. What, then, are the rights of non-Aboriginal people in Canada? Western political thinking in such situations tends to focus on the issue of who holds underlying title. This may be because in Western political thought the right to govern is often founded on one people establishing a better title than another. Hence, non-Aboriginal individuals as well as governments might be concerned that the assertion of Aboriginal title would delegitimate the state. In our view, however, this would not be the consequence.

As we see it, the recognition of underlying Aboriginal title would move the discussion away from a focus on title and towards the development of political relationships. Aboriginal peoples have, from the time of European contact, promoted a political relationship that is based on sharing and mutual accommodation. This approach is based on the philosophical premise that underlying title was gifted to Aboriginal people by the Creator, but only on the basis that they maintain an ethic of sharing. To reiterate the words of Leroy Little Bear:

> The Indian concept of land ownership is certainly not inconsistent with the idea of sharing with an alien people. Once the Indians recognized them as human beings, they gladly shared with them. They shared with Europeans in the same way they shared with the animals and other people. However, sharing here cannot be interpreted as meaning the Europeans got the same rights as any other native person, because the Europeans were not descendants of the original grantees, or they were not parties to the original social contract. Also, sharing certainly cannot be interpreted as meaning that one is giving up his rights for all eternity.[94]

Therefore, we believe that, even after an acknowledgment that they hold the superior title, Aboriginal peoples would focus negotiations on political relations rather than the unilateral right to govern.

We propose a plan for negotiations that moves the discussion away from rights and title and towards resolving existing issues in a way that builds relationships between peoples. This approach shifts the focus from a contest where the goal of one party is to delegitimate the other, to a cooperative effort where the goal of all parties is to create a mutually legitimating partnership among equals. From the perspective of Western political theory, this approach suggests a compromise – one which focuses not on the strength of a claim, but on the will to work out a practical and lasting accommodation based on sharing.

What might such an agreement look like? It would begin with a recognition and affirmation of the Aboriginal party's Aboriginal title, and an acknowledgment that this includes both ownership and jurisdictional elements. It would use the language of mutual respect and accommodation rather than domination and subservience. From this starting point, the parties would set out detailed provisions regarding jurisdiction, the application of laws, rights to land and resources, protection of third-party interests, co-management regimes, a dispute resolution system, and the many other issues to be covered in a comprehensive claims agreement. The specifics of an agreement would depend on what the parties agree to in negotiations. An agreement need not, and probably could not, address all future questions involving the interpretation of Aboriginal rights. These will continue to be addressed by the courts, political negotiations, and dispute-resolution structures contained in the agreements themselves.

We believe our proposal provides an avenue that would allow us to construct a history of and future for Canada that avoids colonialist assumptions. It suggests that the original inhabitants offered the newcomers a means to build a political relationship with them under the ultimate sponsorship of the Creator. Because the basis for this relationship is between Aboriginal nations and the Creator, it should not and must not be severed. Therefore, extinguishment makes no sense for either Aboriginal people or newcomers, for it would delegitimate us all. Rather, reconciliation, through the development of a political relationship based on equality and on a commitment to address all matters related to ownership and jurisdiction, would provide the means by which newcomers and Aboriginal people could ultimately construct a future based on a shared understanding of Canada.

Conclusion

We are recommending a major shift in government policy on extinguishment. The extinguishment requirement does not work from either a government or Aboriginal standpoint. As a result, many outstanding claims are not being settled. The present approach does damage to Canada's ethical core, for it founds negotiations on the premise that one party is inherently superior to the other. Any option that insists on extinguishment, even in a circumscribed form, will not resolve the impasse in negotiations. However, a policy that affirms Aboriginal title will greatly facilitate settlements.

We also recommend that Canada reconsider the basis upon which it asserts its legitimacy in the face of Aboriginal title. A conceptual framework for settlement which presumes the continued existence of Aboriginal title provides the opportunity to pursue this goal. We argue that without a legitimate Aboriginal title there cannot be a legitimate Canadian state, for without the recognition of Aboriginal title we would have a state based on colonial rationalizations. The model we propose bases the relationship between Aboriginal peoples and Canada on the recognition of a permanent Aboriginal title that sustains all of us. It represents a direction that can ultimately take Canada from a state founded on colonialism, into the twenty-first century as a state with roots going back to time immemorial.

Notes

Introduction

1 For a detailed discussion on this point, see Peter Fitzpatrick, *The Mythology of Modern Law* (London: Routledge 1992).
2 *Calder* v. *A.G. B.C.*, [1973] S.C.R. 313.
3 Ibid., 346.
4 Ibid.

Chapter 1: Culture and Anarchy in Indian Country

1 Matthew Arnold, *Culture and Anarchy*, Samuel Lipman, ed. (New Haven, CT, 1994), 5.
2 William Butler Yeats, 'The Second Coming,' in *Collected Poems* (London, 1950), 211.
3 Marshall McLuhan, *The Gutenburg Galaxy* (Toronto, 1962), 45, quoted in Leroy Vail and Landeg White, *Power and the Praise Poem: Southern African Voices in History* (Charlottesville, 1991), 19.
4 David Olson, *The World on Paper* (Cambridge, 1994), 6.
5 Quoted in ibid.
6 John L. Austin, *How to Do Things with Words* (Cambridge, MA, 1962), 14.
7 Sandy Petrey, *Speech Acts and Literary Theory* (London, 1990), 6.
8 Daniel Kemmis, *Community and the Politics of Place* (Norman, 1990), 3-4.
9 Quoted in D.C. Scott, 'Indian Affairs, 1763-1841,' in Adam Shortt and Arthur G. Doughty, eds., *Canada and Its Provinces*, vol. 4 (Toronto, 1913-14), 699.
10 Ibid., 695-8.
11 Ibid., 724.
12 Ibid., 697.
13 Quoted in D'Arcy McNickle, *Native American Tribalism: Indian Survivals and Renewals* (New York, 1973), 56.
14 Lewis Cass, (1838) 30 *North American Review* 83. Elsewhere in this discussion (which was published as a book entitled *Considerations on the Present State of the Indians and Their Removal to the West of the Mississippi*), this opinion is stated in a variety of different ways, such as that 'the position occupied by the Indians is an anomaly in the political world, and the questions connected with it are eminently practical, depending upon peculiar circumstances, and changing with them.'
15 Scott, 'Indian Affairs, 1867-1912,' in Adam Shortt and Arthur G. Doughty, eds., *Canada and Its Provinces*, vol. 7 (Toronto, 1913-14), 623.
16 Canada. Parliament. *Minutes of the Proceedings and Evidence of the Special Joint Committee of the Senate and the House of Commons Appointed to Examine and Consider the Indian Act* (Ottawa, 1946), 83.
17 William E.H. Stanner, *After the Dreaming* (Sydney, 1969), 44-5.
18 Doug Owram, *Promise of Eden: The Canadian Expansionist Movement and the Idea of the West*, 1856-1900 (Toronto, 1980), 131.

19 Gerald Friesen, *The Canadian Prairies: A History* (Toronto, 1984), 135.
20 Ibid., 136.
21 Quoted in Edmund Oliver, 'The Political History of Saskatchewan and Alberta,' in Adam Shortt and Arthur G. Doughty, eds., *Canada and Its Provinces*, vol. 19 (Toronto, 1913-14), 193-4.
22 Friesen, *The Canadian Prairies*, 137.

Chapter 2: Challenging Assumptions: The Impact of Precedent in Aboriginal Rights Litigation
1 (1982) (U.K.), 1982, c.-11.
2 *Delgamuukw v. British Columbia* (1991), 79 D.L.R. (4th) 185 (B.C.S.C.), affirmed. (1993), 104 D.L.R. (4th) 470 (B.C.C.A.) on appeal to S.C.C.; and *Baker Lake v. Min. of Indian Affairs* (1979), 107 D.L.R. (3d) 513 (F.C.A.).
3 F. Schauer, 'Precedent' (1987) 39 Stanford L.R. 571 at 571.
4 Schauer, 'Precedent,' 576.
5 *Delgamuukw* (1991), 79 D.L.R. (4th) 185 (B.C.S.C.) at 452.
6 Schauer, 'Precedent,' 598.
7 Ibid., 596.
8 J. Eisenhower, 'Four Theories of Precedent and Its Role in Judicial Decisions' (1988) 61 Temple L. Rev. 871 at 876.
9 Schauer, 'Precedent,' 575. For examples of other distinguishing techniques, see L. Alexander, 'Constrained by Precedent' (1989-90) Southern Calif. L. Rev. 1; and K. Abraham, 'Three Fallacies of Interpretation: A Comment on Precedent and Judicial Decision' (1981) 23 Ariz. L. Rev. 771.
10 Dickson C.J. (as he then was), 'The Role and Function of Judges' (1980) 14 L. Soc. Gaz. 138 at 182.
11 M.R. Cohen, 'The Process of Judicial Legislation,' in P. Shuchman, ed., *Cohen and Cohen's Readings in Jurisprudence and Judicial Philosophy* (Toronto: Little, Brown 1979), 242 [hereinafter *Cohen and Cohen*].
12 *Reference Re Farm Products Marketing Act*, [1957] S.C.R. 198 at 212. In this case the Supreme Court of Canada stated that it was not bound by its own decisions in the area of constitutional law. *Binus v. The Queen*, [1967] S.C.R. 594 stated the principle in clear terms suggesting its extension to non-constitutional cases. The ability to overrule decisions of the Privy Council was endorsed in *Reference Re Agricultural Products Marketing Act*, [1978] 2 S.C.R. 1198.
13 J. Murphy and R. Reuter, Stare Decisis *in Commonwealth Appellate Courts* (Toronto: Butterworths 1981), 21-2.
14 See, generally, ibid. at 24-55.
15 *R. v. Simon* (1985), 24 D.L.R. (4th) 392; *R. v. Syliboy*, [1929] 1 D.L.R. 327 (N.S. Co. Ct.).
16 *Simon*, ibid., 400.
17 Quoted in C. Haines, 'General Observations on the Effects of Personal, Political and Economic Influences in the Decisions of Judges,' in Shuchman, *Cohen and Cohen*, 251.
18 Ibid.
19 *Edwards v. A.G. Canada*, [1930] A.C. 123.
20 See, generally, M. Mossman, 'Feminism and Legal Method: The Difference It Makes,' in M.A. Fineman and N.S. Thomadsen, eds., *At the Boundaries of Law: Feminism and Legal Theory* (New York: Routledge 1991), 285.
21 *Edwards, supra* note 19 at 128; and Mossman, ibid., 293-4.
22 M. Moore, 'Precedent, Induction, and Ethical Generalization,' in L. Goldstein, ed., *Precedent in Law* (Oxford: Clarendon Press 1987), 210.
23 K. Llewellyn, *The Case Law System in America*, trans. M. Ansaldi (Chicago: University of Chicago Press 1989), 12.
24 D. Gibson, 'Judges as Legislators: Not Whether But How' (1987) 25 Alta. L. Rev. 249 at 252 [herinafter 'Judges as Legislators'].
25 B. Ziff, *Principles of Property Law* (Toronto: Carswell 1993), 29.
26 *R v. Morin*, [1992] S.C.R. 286 at 295.

27 *Stein v. The 'Kathy K'* (Storm Point), [1976] 2 S.C.R. 802 at 808; *Bank of Montreal v. Bail Ltee,* [1992] 2 S.C.R. 554 at 572.
28 See, generally, P. Wesley-Smith, 'Theories of Adjudication and the Status of *Stare Decisis,'* in Goldstein, *Precedent in Law,* 75-6.
29 Gibson, 'Judges as Legislators,' 253.
30 Ibid., 255.
31 Ibid., 251-3.
32 Ibid., 252.
33 *Johnston v. McIntosh,* 21 U.S. (8 Wheat.) 543 (1823).
34 K. McNeil, *Common Law Aboriginal Title* (Oxford: Clarendon Press 1989), 301.
35 *Johnston, supra* note 33 at 592.
36 Ibid., 588.
37 Ibid.
38 Ibid., 572-3.
39 Ibid.
40 *Worcester v. Georgia,* 6 Pet. (U.S.S.C.) 515 (1832).
41 Ibid., 544. There are numerous academic opinions supporting this analysis. See, for example, McNeil, *supra* note 34 at 245-8; M. Jackson, 'The Articulation of Native Rights in Canadian Law' (1984) 18 U.B.C. L. Rev. 255, and M. Davies, 'Aspects of Aboriginal Rights in International Law,' in B. Morse, ed., *Aboriginal Peoples and the Law* (Ottawa: Carleton University Press 1989), 1.
42 *Calder v. A.G. B.C.* (1973), 34 D.L.R. (3d) 145 (S.C.C.) at 193 per Hall J.
43 B. Slattery, 'Understanding Aboriginal Rights' (1987) 66 Can. Bar Rev. 727 at 730.
44 *St. Catherine's Milling and Lumber Co. v. R.* (1888), 14 App. Cas. 46 at 69 and 52-3.
45 Ibid., 54.
46 Slattery, 'Understanding Aboriginal Rights,' 748.
47 Ibid., 748-9.
48 *Calder, supra* note 42 at 156.
49 Although the concept of contingent rights is less influential in the evolution of Aboriginal title than in the past, it continues to permeate Aboriginal rights discourse in a modified form when combined with the principle that Aboriginal rights can be terminated by government.
50 *Guerin v. R.* (1984), 13 D.L.R. (4th) 321 at 339. The nature of the interest is also characterized by 'its general inalienability, coupled with the fact that the Crown is under an obligation to deal with the land on the Indians' behalf when the interest is surrendered. Any description which goes beyond these two features is both unnecessary and potentially misleading.'
51 See, for example, *Calder, supra* note 42, per Hall J. and *Delgamuukw* (B.C.C.A.), *supra* note 2, per Lambert J.
52 *Guerin, supra* note 50.
53 *R. v. Sparrow* (1990), 70 D.L.R. (4th) 385 (S.C.C.) at 398. In *Sparrow* the Supreme Court has indicated that the judiciary is to interpret these rights in a manner 'sensitive to the aboriginal perspective of the meaning of the rights at stake' and in a flexible manner that 'allows their exercise in a contemporary manner.' These directives combined with the *sui generis* nature of Aboriginal title provide the basis for a progressive court to reject the prevalent notion in Aboriginal title litigation that Aboriginal rights are only those rights exercised at the date sovereignty was asserted which survived free from substantial alteration. A rejection of the frozen rights analysis could shift the onus to the Crown to prove that certain rights should not be included in the bundle or that certain practices are not 'Aboriginal' once Aboriginal occupation is established.
54 *Delgamuukw* (B.C.S.C.), *supra* note 5 at 284.
55 Ibid., 437 and 415.
56 *Re Southern Rhodesia,* [1919] A.C. 211 at 233-4.
57 *Delgamuukw* (B.C.S.C.), supra note 5 at 447.
58 Ibid., 374.
59 Ibid., 434.

60 Ibid., 453.
61 Constitution Act, 1867, reprinted in 1985 R.S.C., app. I.
62 *Delgamuukw* (B.C.S.C.), *supra* note 5 at 453.
63 *Delgamuukw* (1993), 104 D.L.R. (4th) 470 (B.C.C.A.) at 641.
64 *Campbell v. Hall* (1774), 1 Cowp 204, 98 E.R. 1045 (K.B.).
65 *Mabo v. Queensland* (1992), 107 A.L.R. 1 (Aust. H.C.).
66 *Delgamuukw* (B.C.C.A.), *supra* note 63.
67 Ibid., 650.
68 Ibid.
69 Ibid., 631.
70 Others have interpreted the case to support time immemorial analysis. See, generally, Slattery, *supra* note 43.
71 *Supra* note 2 at 651.
72 Ibid., 653.
73 Ibid., 718.
74 Ibid., 719.
75 Ibid., 673.
76 Ibid., 672.
77 Ibid., 715.
78 Ibid., 716-17.
79 Ibid., 679-89.
80 *Mabo, supra* note 65.
81 M. Asch and C. Bell, 'Definition and Interpretation of Fact in Canadian Aboriginal Title Litigation: An Analysis of *Delgamuukw*' (1994) 19 Queens L.J. 503.
82 Ibid.
83 *Baker Lake v. Min. of Indian Affairs* (1979), 107 D.L.R. (3d) 513 (F.C.A.).
84 Quoted in *Delgamuukw* (B.C.S.C.), *supra* note 5 at 410.
85 Re *Southern Rhodesia, supra* note 56 at 214.
86 Ibid., 233-4; quoted in *Delgamuukw* (B.C.S.C.), *supra* note 5 at 226.
87 *Calvin's Case* (1608), 7 Co. Rep. 1a, 2 State Tr. 559, Moore KB 790, Jenk 306, 77 E.R. 377 at 398.
88 St. George Tucker, *Blackstone's Commentaries* (Philadelphia: William Young Birch and Abraham Small 1803), 107-8.
89 See, for example, Alfred Haddon who says in 1898: 'In a general survey of mankind we find that there are peoples in all stages of culture,' and, 'if, then, we examine a people that has for a long time remained isolated from contact with other peoples, we shall find that in most instances it is a backward people, and otherwise what we call a savage one.' Alfred C. Haddon, *The Study of Man* (London: John Murray 1898), xx-xxi.
90 *Baker Lake, supra* note 83.
91 Ibid., 42.
92 Ibid.
93 Ibid.
94 Ibid.
95 Ibid.
96 Ibid., 42f.
97 Ibid., 43.
98 Ibid., 43.
99 Ibid., 49.
100 Ibid., 16.
101 Ibid., 17f.
102 Ibid., 44.
103 Slattery, 'Understanding Aboriginal Rights,' *supra* note 43 at 759.
104 *Sparrow, supra* note 53 at 452.
105 M. Asch and P. Macklem, 'Aboriginal Rights and Canadian Sovereignty: An Essay on *R. v. Sparrow*' (1991) 29 Alta. L. Rev. 2.
106 *Delgamuukw* (B.C.C.A.), *supra* note 63 at 37.

107 Ibid., 104.
108 Ibid., 153.
109 Ibid., 163.
110 Ibid., at 67, 68 per Macfarlane J.; at 97 per Wallace J.; at 134f. per Lambert J.
111 Ibid., at 21, 38, 44 per Macfarlane J.; at 99 per Wallace J.
112 Ibid., 211.
113 Ibid., 259.
114 Ibid., at 242 per Lambert J.; at 268 per Hutcheon J.
115 Ibid., 134f.
116 Ibid., 135.
117 Ibid., 240.
118 Ibid., at 241 per Lambert J.; at 268 per Hutcheon J.
119 Ibid., 58.
120 Ibid., 94, 114.
121 Ibid., at 49, 43, 44 per Macfarlane J.; at 93, 115-16, 119 per Wallace J.
122 Ibid., 114.
123 Ibid. These include: 1) the 'ontological argument' (at 40, 43-4 per Macfarlane J.; at 93 per Wallace J.); 2) the argument that such a discussion was beyond the authority of a municipal court (at 68 per Macfarlane J.; at 93 per Wallace J.); 3) the acquisition of sovereignty by 'peaceful annexation' (at 93, 102 per Wallace J.); 4) the view, following *Mabo*, that it is not possible to make a decision 'that would fracture the law' (at 96 per Wallace J.); 5) the argument that the plaintiffs had a society too primitive for Britain to recognize its sovereignty (at 103, 103f per Wallace J.); 6) that sovereignty was established because there was no armed resistance (at 163 per Lambert J.).
124 *Re Southern Rhodesia, supra* note 56.
125 *Delgamuukw* (B.C.S.C.), *supra* note 5 at 103.
126 From *The Advocate-General of Bengal v. Dossee* cited in ibid., per Wallace J.
127 Ibid., 103f.
128 B. Malinowski, *Argonauts of the Western Pacific* (New York: E.P. Dutton 1961 [1922]), 25.
129 B. Malinowski, 'The Rationalization of Anthropology and Administration' *Africa 3* (1930): 414-15.
130 M. Fortes, 'Social Anthropology at Cambridge Since 1900' (1953), reprinted in R. Darnell, ed., *Readings in the History of Anthropology* (New York: Harper and Row 1974), 432.
131 Ibid., 437.
132 *Delgamuukw* (B.C.S.C.), *supra* note 5 at 441. The evidence to support this postulate is found mainly in McEachern's 'Reasons for Judgment,' particularly where he says, 'I do not accept the ancestors "on the ground" behaved as they did because of "institutions." Rather I find they more likely acted as they did because of survival instincts which varied from village to village.' As is well known in the social sciences, 'instinct' is a basic characteristic of group organization based on biological factors, and 'institution' a basic characteristic of group organization based on social ones. Therefore, this statement infers the possibility that people may live in groups, but still not live in a society.
133 Evidence for the postulate that societies can exist that are not organized is found in the manner by which the courts, including Justice Mahoney himself, have interpreted the provision in *Baker Lake* that requires Aboriginal litigants to demonstrate 'proof that the Plaintiffs and their ancestors were members of an organized society' (*Baker Lake, supra* note 83 at 42). Evidence for the postulate regarding the presumption that societies may be organized only with respect to some aspects of social life is derived from decisions such as *Baker Lake* where Mahoney J. held that all the society of the Inuit could do is 'hunt and fish and survive' (ibid., 43) and his noting of the absence of other institutions, most notably political ones (ibid., 16). Evidence is also provided by McEchearn's assertion cited above that he is 'quite unable to say that there was much in the way of precontact social organization among the Gitksan and Wet'suwet'en' (*Delgamuukw* (B.C.S.C.), *supra* note 5 at 456).
134 This view, as discussed above, is exemplified in a number of places in the trial judgments in both *Baker Lake* and *Delgamuukw* (see, for example *Delgamuukw* (B.C.S.C.), *supra* note

5 at 449 and 452), as well as Mahoney's assertions respecting the lack of a political organization among the Inuit. It is stated in principle by Justice Lambert where he says it is
possible to find a society so primitive as to 'not be regarded as an organized self-regulating society' *(Delgamuukw* (B.C.C.A.), *supra* note 63 at 163).

135 Given the nature of the plaintiffs' case, there was little discussion in *Baker Lake* respecting this question, but support for the proposition is implicit in Mahoney's reasoning.
However, there is abundant evidence to support this conclusion from the various judgments in *Delgamuukw*. For example, both McEachern and Macfarlane believe that the evidence supported the view that the societies of the Gitksan and Wet'suwet'en in the period
prior to the assertion of British sovereignty had practices that could be defined as 'use and
occupancy' of land as much as 'ownership.'

136 M. Harris, *Culture, People, Nature*, 2nd ed. (New York: Thomas Crowell 1975 [1971]).

137 L. Mair, *An Introduction to Social Anthropology* (London: Oxford University Press, 1965).

138 Dr. Harris comes from the cultural anthropological tradition. This tradition, as he sees it,
adheres to a contemporary form of evolutionary theory. It is, however, a form which
eschews the kinds of ethnocentric assumption that were characteristic of the nineteenth
century form described above. Dr. Mair comes from the social anthropology tradition.
This tradition is organized on the premise that primacy is to be given to contemporary
societies rather than to evolution and sees itself as a form of comparative sociology.

139 Mair, *An Introduction to Social Anthropology*, 1.

140 Harris, *Culture, People, Nature*, 482.

141 Ibid., 105f.

142 Mair, *An Introduction to Social Anthropology*, 10.

143 Ibid., 112.

144 Ibid., 139.

145 Harris, *Culture, People, Nature*, 113.

146 Ibid., 292-9.

147 Ibid., 295.

148 Mair, *An Introduction to Social Anthropology*, 143.

149 Ibid., 142-52.

150 Harris, *Culture, People, Nature*, 290.

151 Ibid., 290.

152 Ibid.

153 Ibid.

154 Mair, *An Introduction to Social Anthropology*, 111.

155 M. Asch, 'Wildlife: Defining the Animals the Dene Hunt and the Settlement of Aboriginal
Rights Claims' (1989) 15:2 Can. Public Policy 205 at 217.

156 Ibid.

157 Interest in the topic arises virtually at the beginning of modern anthropological thought
(see L.H. Morgan, *Ancient Society* [New York: World Publishing 1877] and H.S. Maine,
Ancient Law [London: John Murray 1861]).

158 M. Asch, 'Wildlife,' 217.

159 Mair, *An Introduction to Social Anthropology*, 153.

160 Harris, *Culture, People, Nature*, 292. These are the only kinds of societies about which it
has been hypothesized that there is no individual ownership of any property.

161 However, as I stated above, the concepts of 'ownership' and 'jurisdiction' regarding land
are often conflated in anthropological discourse. Therefore, the division I am making
here may be somewhat artificial, as the properties of 'ownership' described by both Harris
and Mair are to be attributed equally to both 'ownership' and 'jurisdiction.'

162 Mair, *An Introduction to Social Anthropology*, 153, and Harris, *Culture, People, Nature*, 292.

163 This conclusion is self-evident in the discussion by Mair. However, it is not in the discussion by Harris. Nonetheless, Harris suggests that even societies such as what he terms
'simple hunter-gatherers' contain the 'prevalence of communal ownership of land'
(*Culture, People, Nature*, 292). I presume that in this discussion 'communal' means
'belonging to the society as a whole and not divisible on the basis of small units within
the society.' It is a premise which is not generally accepted. Most anthropologists would

argue that ownership of land in all societies is likely divisible into smaller units (ibid.).
164 Mair, *An Introduction to Social Anthropology*, 152-9.
165 Harris defines 'emics,' which is a specialized term within anthropology, as: 'Descriptions or judgments concerning behaviour, customs, beliefs, values, and so on, held by members of a societal group as culturally appropriate and valid' (*Culture, People, Nature*, 483).
166 Ibid., 290.
167 Mair, *An Introduction to Social Anthropology*, 152-8.
168 Ibid., 156.
169 Ibid., 153.
170 Ibid., 137.
171 Harris, *Culture, People, Nature*, 290.
172 Anthropological evidence indicates that this principle also applies to the question of whether the landowner can alienate his or her land through 'sale' to another party.
173 The 'Persons' case: *Edwards v. A.G. Canada*, [1929] 3 W.W.R. 479.
174 *Brown v. Board of Education*, 374 U.S. 483 (1954).
175 *Calder, supra* note 42 at 169f.
176 Asch and Bell, 'Definition and Interpretation,' *supra* note 81.
177 Quoted in *Delgamuukw* (B.C.C.A.), *supra* note at 147.
178 M. Asch, 'Aboriginal Self-Government and the Construction of Canadian Constitutional Identity' (1992) 30:2 Alta. L. Rev. 465.
179 *Edwards, supra* note 173.
180 *Dred Scott v. John F.A. Stanford*, 18 Howard 393.

Chapter 3: Re-examining Culturally Appropriate Models in Criminal Justice Applications

1 For a more detailed discussion on violence against Native women including recommendations for alternative responses, see my contribution 'Violence in Aboriginal Communities,' in *The Path to Healing* (Ottawa: Royal Commission on Aboriginal Peoples 1993), 72-89.
2 *Report of the Aboriginal Justice Inquiry of Manitoba*, vol. 1 (Government of Manitoba 1991), 265. See also chapters 2, 10, and 13 [hereinafter referred to as *Report of the AJI (Manitoba)*].
3 Ibid., 266.
4 Ibid., 323.
5 *Robert Hart, Beginning a Long Journey: A Review of Projects Funded by the Family Violence Prevention Division, Health Canada, Regarding Violence in Aboriginal Families* (Ottawa: Health and Welfare Canada, April 1996), 7 [hereinafter referred to as the *Hart Report*]. This is a draft document being circulated for discussion prior to its release.
6 The history of Canada is a history of the colonization of Aboriginal peoples. Franz Fanon (*The Wretched of the Earth*, 1963) and Albert Memmi (*The Colonizer and the Colonized*, 1957) have convincingly shown that colonization is a pervasive structural and psychological relationship between the colonizer and the colonized and is ultimately reflected in the dominant institutions, policies, histories, and literatures of occupying powers. Since the 1970s, Native writers and educators, including myself, have articulated this colonial experience, and in the last decade or so, a growing number of other scholars from various disciplines and backgrounds have also begun to document Native/white relations from the context of colonization.
7 For further discussion on the social and academic consequences of 'typologizing' Native cultures, see my essay 'Three Conventional Approaches to Native People in Society and in Literature' (published as a pamphlet by Saskatoon: Saskatchewan Library Association 1984). See also my book on stereotypes in the school system, *Defeathering the Indian* (Agincourt, ON: Book Society of Canada 1975).
8 Len Sawatsky, 'Self-Determination and the Criminal Justice System,' in Diane Engelstad and John Bird, eds., *Nation to Nation: Aboriginal Sovereignty and the Future of Canada* (Toronto: Anansi 1992), 88-97.
9 Ibid., 231n.
10 *Hart Report*, see especially pages 2 and 8-13.

11 Sawatsky, 'Self-Determination,' 92-3.

12 Indeed, if the overriding Native objective was communal harmony no matter what, then why are 49.5 per cent of Aboriginal peoples (James S. Frideres, *Native People in Canada: Contemporary Conflicts*, 4th ed. [Scarborough, ON: Prentice-Hall 1993]) living in urban centres? Studies show that one of the biggest reasons Native women leave their communities and move to urban centres is to escape violence.

13 For a more detailed discussion on the 'heroification' of and 'undifferentiated sympathy' for sexual offenders within minority groups, see my article 'Racism/Sexism and Its Effects on Native Women,' in *Public Concerns on Human Rights* (Winnipeg: Canadian Human Rights Commission 1990), 30-9.

14 Concerning 'wanton leniency' in the criminal justice system's response to sexual offenders, see my article 'Violence in Aboriginal Communities,' *supra* note 1 at 76-83.

15 Native lawyer Theresa Nahanee has spoken to the issue of individual/collective rights in relation to Native women's fight for sexual equality in a paper presented to the National Association of Women and the Law in Vancouver, 1993. Joyce Green has also discussed these issues in 'Constitutionalizing the Patriarchy: Aboriginal Women and Aboriginal Government,' *Constitutional Forum* 4:4 (1993): 114.

16 See *Report of the AJI (Manitoba)*, 496.

17 *Hart Report*, 9.

18 I find Hart's report very troubling on a number of grounds. It appears that federal funding now requires Native projects, in this case violence prevention projects, to meet 'culturally appropriate' qualifications. But who defines and sets the cultural standards? This leads to a related issue: Hart claims he has 'incorporated' the views of his reviewers, most of whom are institution based. Much to my dismay, he lists me as one of his reviewers. Hart and I had one rushed telephone conversation in which I directed him to my article on violence in Aboriginal communities (*supra* note 1), the findings of which clearly contradict Hart's methodology (i.e., charting) and proposals (i.e., keeping abusers at home).

19 It is well known that recidivism of sexual offenders is very high, and as yet there are no substantive studies as to the success of Native mediation programs in 'rehabilitating' offenders. As well-publicized community reports have shown, sexual violence in Native communities continues to remain a staggering problem.

20 See, for example, Linda Ledray, *Recovering from Rape* (New York: Henry Holt 1986).

21 Most community and organizational submissions to provincial and national studies on Aboriginal peoples (e.g., the Aboriginal Justice Inquiry, the Royal Commission on Aboriginal Peoples, and now the *Hart Report* from Health and Welfare Canada) have included much rhetoric on 'healing' victims, but the direction suggested is always in tandem to offenders. It should be noted, however, that the study on violence against northern Ontario's Native women by the Ontario Native Women's Association, *Breaking Free: A Proposal for Change to Aboriginal Family Violence* (Thunder Bay: Ontario Native Women's Association 1989), and the submission by the Indigenous Women's Collective of Manitoba to the Royal Commission stress safety first for women.

22 See, for example, E. Bass and L. Davis, *The Courage to Heal* (New York: Harper and Row 1988).

23 In both white and Native communities, sexual violence within families is disturbingly high. See, for example, *Each Small Step*, an anthology of writing by and for women who are childhood sexual abuse survivors (prepared by the Women's Post-Treatment Centre of Winnipeg 1991); Rita Gunn and Candice Minch, Sexual Assault (Winnipeg: University of Manitoba Press 1988); Ontario Native Women's Association, *Breaking Free: A Proposal for Change to Aboriginal Family Violence*; Anastasia M. Shkilnyk, *A Poison Stronger than Love* (New Haven: Yale University Press 1985).

24 The disintegrating effects on families, loss of Aboriginal languages, and child abuse in residential schools are well documented. See, for example, Celia Haig-Brown, *Resistance and Renewal: Surviving the Indian Residential School* (Vancouver: Tillacum Library 1988). On the 'sixties scoop' of Native children, see Patrick Johnston, *Native Children and the Child Welfare System* (Canadian Council on Social Development and James Lorrimer 1983). See also Judge E.C. Kimelman, *Group Home Review: Review Committee on Indian and Metis*

Adoptions and Placements (Province of Manitoba 1983), and *Children First: Our Responsibility, Report of the First Nation's Child and Family Task Force* (Province of Manitoba 1993).

25 I grew up in a Metis community in northeastern Alberta, and our first language was Plains Cree. I conferred with Mercedez Cardinal Rizzoli about this word; Ms. Rizzoli has taught Cree and grew up in a community close to mine.

26 Again, if I may draw on my cultural background: one of the most memorable characteristics of my community was its appreciation of personality; individuality and independence were definitely valued and encouraged, and such valuation of the human personality was not seen as any devaluation of community caring and responsibility.

27 Anthony F. Wallace, *The Death and Rebirth of the Seneca* (New York: Vintage Books 1969), 28.

28 See, for example, Bruce G. Trigger, *The Children of Aataentsic: A History of the Huron People to 1660* (Montreal: McGill-Queen's University Press 1976).

29 See A. Irving Hallowell, *The Ojibway of Berens River, Manitoba*, Jennifer S.H. Brown, ed. (Harcourt Brace Jovanovich College Publishers 1992).

30 With the exception of Ruth Landes, *The Ojibwe Woman* (New York: Columbia University Press 1938).

31 Research methodologies by early anthropologists are discussed in 'Images of Women' by Katherine Weist, and in 'The Shackles of Tradition' by Alice Kehoe, both in Patricia Albers and Beatrice Medicine, eds., *The Hidden Half: Studies of Plains Indian Women* (Lanham and New York: University Press of America 1983). For early European fur trader views on sexuality and gender roles, see Sylvia Van Kirk, *Many Tender Ties* (1980).

32 James Axtell, *The Invasion Within* (Oxford: Oxford University Press 1985), 306-27.

33 Ibid., 310.

34 Ibid.

35 Ibid.

36 Robert and Pat Ritzenthaler, *The Woodland Indians of the Western Great Lakes*, rev. ed. (Milwaukee Public Museum 1983); see also works by Jennifer S.H. Brown, Bruce Trigger, Anthony F. Wallace, Francis Jennings, Albers and Medicine, and William A. Haviland, among others.

37 Sawatsky, 'Self-Determination,' 93.

38 My phrase 'abandoning the oppressed to the oppressed' means exactly that: mainstream society is abandoning Native victims of Native violence. Native men who assault are the oppressed who, in turn, become the oppressors within their communities.

39 LaRocque, 'Violence in Aboriginal Communities,' 79-89.

40 There are numerous books and resources available on this issue. See Lenore Tarr, *Too Scared to Cry* (New York: Basic Books 1990); Charles L. Whitfield, *Healing the Child Within* (Deerfield Beach, FL: Health Communications 1987); Susan Brownmiller, *Against Our Will* (New York: Bantam 1975). For an international perspective see Diana E.H. Russell and N. Van de Ven, *Crimes Against Women: Proceedings of the International Tribunal* (East Palo Alto: Frog in the Well Press 1984).

41 Thomas Berger, *Northern Frontier, Northern Homeland: The Report of the Mackenzie Valley Pipeline Inquiry*, vol. 1 (Ottawa: Supply and Services Canada 1977), 93-9. By associating Native culture so inextricably with 'traditional' uses of land, Berger may have unwittingly advanced corporate lawyers' arguments of 'no culture, no land.'

42 Among the more astounding decisions on land rights is Chief Justice McEachern's 1991 ruling (B.C. Supreme Court) against the Gitksan and Wet'suwet'en on the basis of eighteenth-century prejudices. For other contemporary examples of judicial bias on land rights, see Peter Kulchyski, *Unjust Relations: Aboriginal Rights in Canadian Courts* (Toronto: Oxford University Press 1994). On equally medieval rulings regarding sexual assault, see Margo Nightingale, 'Judicial Attitudes and Differential Treatment: Native Women in Sexual Assault Cases' (1991) 23:1 Ottawa L. Rev. 71-98.

43 One of the earlier texts on European theory and law regarding Aboriginal land rights is by Peter A. Cumming and Neil H. Mickenberg, *Native Rights in Canada* (Toronto: General Publishing Company 1980). See also Menno Boldt and J. Anthony Long, eds., *The Quest for Justice* (Toronto: University of Toronto Press 1985).

44 The study of Aboriginal rights is a field on its own. Among the many works are: Michael Asch, *Home and Native Land: Aboriginal Rights and the Canadian Constitution* (Toronto: Methuen 1984); Bruce Clark, *Native Liberty, Crown Sovereignty* (Montreal: McGill-Queen's University Press 1990); Bradford Morse, ed., *Aboriginal Peoples and the Law* (Ottawa: Carleton University Press 1985); Brian Slattery, 'Understanding Aboriginal Rights' (1987) 66 Can. Bar Rev.; Jack Woodward, *Native Law* (Toronto: Carswell 1989).

45 Joyce Green, 'Constitutionalising the Patriarchy' (*supra* note 15); see also 'Women Confront Mercredi,' *Winnipeg Free Press*, 14 March 1992; Native Women's Association of Canada, *An Aboriginal Charter of Rights and Freedoms: A Discussion Paper* (April 1992).

46 The Canadian academy (and society) have been slow to dismantle and abandon the Euro-Canadian myth of 'Civilization' inevitably conquering 'Savagery.' My early discussion of this can be found in my unpublished M.A. thesis, 'White Control of Indian Education,' University of Manitoba 1978; I have subsequently dealt with this theme more extensively in a number of unpublished and published works.

47 In response to my article, 'Violence in Aboriginal Communities,' a young woman wrote this letter to me in June 1994.

48 In a number of previous works I have called attention to problems inherent in the overemphasis on culture and its association with a static past: *Defeathering the Indian*, and 'Three Conventional Approaches' (*supra* note 7); an autobiographical essay, 'Tides, Towns and Trains,' in Joan Turner, ed., *Living the Changes* (Winnipeg: University of Manitoba Press 1990); 'Racism/Sexism and Its Effects on Native Women' (1990); and the article on violence in the Royal Commission on Aboriginal Peoples collection (*supra* note 1).

49 Margo Nightingale, 'Judicial Attitudes,' (*supra* note 42), 92-4.

50 I have been directed to an unpublished work by Theresa Nahanee, 'Sex and Race in Inuit Rape Cases: Judicial Discretion and the Charter' (1992). Unfortunately, I have not been able to get a copy of this.

51 Diane Bell, 'Considering Gender: Are Human Rights for Women Too?' an unpublished paper presented at the International Conference on Human Rights in Cross-Cultural Perspectives, College of Law, University of Saskatchewan (1989), 5.

52 LaRocque, 'Violence in Aboriginal Communities,' 76 and 79.

53 Metis analyst Howard Adams first called attention to the 'ossification of Native society' in *Prison of Grass* (Saskatoon: Fifth House Publishers 1975), Chapter 5.

54 A well-worn Hollywood tradition, one might add. See Daniel Francis, *The Imaginary Indian* (Vancouver: Arsenal Pulp Press 1992); Robert Berkhofer, *The White Man's Indian* (New York: Random House 1979); and Emma LaRocque, *Defeathering the Indian* (*supra* note 7).

55 Sawatsky et al. claim that the existing justice system is 'retributive.' I am arguing that it is wantonly lenient in cases of sexual violence.

56 For an absorbing discussion on international human rights vis-à-vis women's rights, see Diane Bell, 'Considering Gender,' (*supra* note 51).

57 See, for example, Frideres, *Native Peoples in Canada* (*supra* note 12); Geoffrey York, The Dispossessed: Life and Death in Native Canada (London: Vintage U.K. 1990); Royal Commission on Aboriginal Peoples, *Choosing Life: Special Report on Suicide Among Aboriginal People* (1995); *Report of the AJI (Manitoba)* (*supra* note 2); etc.

58 Throughout the 1980s and 1990s, the press has reported on northern concerns regarding judicial leniency with violent criminals, particularly with regard to keeping them in the communities. Similar concerns have been expressed by national and provincial Native women's organizations. For incarcerated women's concerns, see Fran Sugar and Lana Fox, *Survey of Federally Sentenced Aboriginal Women* (Ottawa: Native Women's Association of Canada 1990).

59 Gail Stacey-Moore, 'In Our Own Voice: Aboriginal Women Demand Justice,' *Herizons* vol. 6 no. 4 (1993): 23.

60 Joyce Green, 'A Comprehensive Analysis of the Charlottetown Accord' *The Womanist* 3 (1982); 'Sexual Equality and Indian Government: An Analysis of Bill C-31 Amendments to the Indian Act,' *Native Studies Review* 1 (1985); others are listed above and below.

61 Joyce Green, 'Constitutionalising the Patriarchy,' 111 (*supra* note 15).

62 Ibid., 118.
63 Bell, 'Considering Gender,' 6 (*supra* note 51).
64 Ibid.
65 Joyce Green, 'Democracy, Gender and Aboriginal Rights-Talk,' (Unpublished, November 1993), 15.

Chapter 4: The Impact of Treaty 9 on Natural Resource Development in Northern Ontario

1 I am grateful to Michael Asch, John Borrows, and Kent McNeil for their helpful comments on previous drafts of this paper.
2 By 'natural resource exploration and development activity' I mean to refer to an array of non-Aboriginal activity that seeks to extract and exploit natural, mineral, and forestry resources as well as hydroelectric potential.
3 But see Claudia Notzke, *Aboriginal Peoples and Natural Resources in Canada* (North York: Captus 1994).
4 The following analysis does not address the legal validity of Treaty 9; I assume that the treaty is legally binding on the parties and express no opinion on its legal validity. Four points, however, should be noted in passing. First, the Rupert's Land Order required Canada to negotiate land claims with the Aboriginal inhabitants of Rupert's Land, in consultation with the British government, and required that Canada 'make adequate provision for the protection of the Indian tribes whose interests and well-being are involved in the transfer' (R.S.C. 1985, App. II, No. 9, 2). The Rupert's Land Order may have placed conditions precedent on the validity of Treaty 9.
   Second, a court will declare a contract to be unconscionable where a stronger party uses its superior bargaining power to extract a bargain from a party in a weaker position, and where the bargain is substantially unfair. See *Lloyd's Bank Ltd. v. Bundy* (1974), 3 All E.R. 757. Canadian courts have set aside a transaction as unconscionable where a party with superior bargaining power failed to explain the ramifications of a transaction fully to the weaker party, or to advise the weaker party to obtain independent legal advice, and thereby gained an unfair advantage. See *Black v. Wilcox* (1976), 12 O.R. (2d) 759 (Ont. C.A.); *Morrison v. Coast Finance Ltd.* (1965), 55 D.L.R. (2d) 711 (B.C.C.A.); *Towers v. Affleck*, [1974] 1 W.W.R. 714 (B.C.S.C.); *Buchanan v. Canadian Imperial Bank of Commerce* (1980), 125 D.L.R. (3d) 394 (B.C.C.A.); *Royal Bank of Canada v. Heinz* (1978), 88 D.L.R. (3d) 428 (Ont. H.C.); and *Harry v. Kreutziger* (1978), 95 D.L.R. (3d) 231 (B.C.C.A.).
   Third, a court will intervene in cases where one party in a position of trust and confidence has used its superior power in an unconscionable way to induce the weaker party to enter into a contract. See *Earl of Aylesford v. Morris* (1873), 8 Ch. App. 484. See also *Vanzant v. Coates* (1917), 39 D.L.R. 484 (Ont. C.A.); and *Brydon v. Hawkins*, [1948] 3 D.L.R. 252 (Ont. H.C.).
   Fourth, under the principle of *non est factum*, a party is entitled to avoid a written contract where that party can prove that the contract is fundamentally different than what the party thought it signed: see *Taylor v. Strong* (1979), 24 O.R. (2d) 614 (Ont. H.C.).
   Some, if not all, of the above grounds may be subject to a number of potential Crown defences, including time limits pursuant to the Crown Liability Act, R.S.C. 1970, c. C-38 and the Limitations Act, R.S.O. 1980, c. 240, and the defences of laches and estoppel. This paper expresses no opinion on the availability of these aforementioned defences. For a rejection of the defence of laches and Crown reliance on time limits in a different context, see *Guerin v. R.* (1984), 13 D.L.R. (4th) 321 (S.C.C.), per Dickson J. (as he then was).
5 James Morrison, *Treaty Research Report: Treaty Nine (1905-1906): The James Bay Treaty* (Ottawa: Treaties and Historical Research Centre 1986), 73.
6 *Nowegijick v. The Queen* (1983), 144 D.L.R. (3d) 193 (S.C.C.).
7 *Jones v. Meehan*, 175 U.S. 1 (1899).
8 *R. v. Badger*, [1996] S.C.J. No. 39 at 10.
9 *R. v. Horse* (1988), 47 D.L.R. (4th) 526 (S.C.C.) at 537.
10 *R. v. Sioui* (1990), 70 D.L.R. (4th) 427 (S.C.C.) at 445.
11 Ibid.

12 Ibid., 446.
13 See *R. v. Badger*, *supra* note 8; *Mitchell v. Peguis Indian Band* (1990), 71 D.L.R. (4th) 193 (S.C.C.); *R. v. Horseman*, [1990] 1 S.C.R. 901; *R. v. Sioui*, ibid.; *Simon v. The Queen* (1985), 24 D.L.R. (4th) 390 (S.C.C.).
14 *Simon v. The Queen*, ibid.
15 Ibid., 402.
16 Ibid., 403.
17 Ibid.
18 *R. v. Sioui*, *supra* note 10.
19 Ibid., 432.
20 Ibid., 435.
21 Ibid., 435 and 460.
22 Ibid., 462.
23 *R. v. Badger*, *supra* note 8 at 13.
24 Ibid., 12.
25 For a similar approach, see *R. v. Cooper* (1969), 1 D.L.R. (3d) 113 (B.C.S.C.) at 115 ('the document embodying this larcenous arrangement must have been drawn by or on behalf of the Hudson's Bay Company (the signing Chiefs being unable to write) and so any ambiguity must be construed in favour of the exploited Chiefs'); and *R. v. White and Bob* (1965), 50 D.L.R. (2d) 613 (B.C.C.A.) at 659 ('the word as used in the section should ... be given its widest meaning in favour of the Indians'). See also *Winters v. United States*, 207 U.S. 564 at 576-7 (1908); *Arizona v. California*, 373 U.S. 546 at 597-8 (1963). But see *Howard v. The Queen* (1994), 115 D.L.R. (4th) 312 (S.C.C.) at 317, per Gonthier J. for the Court ('the 1923 Treaty does not raise the same concerns as treaties signed in the more distant past or in more remote territories where one can legitimately question the understanding of the Indian parties').
26 Louis Espagnol to James Phipps (in French), 15 December 1884. Public Archives of Canada (PAC), Record Group 10 (RG 10), vol. 2289, file 57, 641. Chief Louis Espagnol reiterated his request seventeen years later in a letter to Samuel Stewart of the Indian Department: Memorandum, 22 August 1901, PAC RG 10, vol. 3033 , file 235, 225-1.
27 J.A. Macrae to Clifford Sifton, 3 June 1901, PAC, RG 10, vol. 3033, file 235, 225-1.
28 Petition of Osnaburgh Indians, 12 December 1901, PAC, RG 10, vol. 3033, file 235, 225-1.
29 Ibid.
30 William Nichols to J.D. MacLean, 24 July 1902, PAC, RG 10, vol. 3033, file 235, 225-1. See also letter from Port Arthur Indian Agent J.F. Hodder to J.D. MacLean, 6 December 1902, PAC, RG 10, vol. 3033, file 235, 225-1 ('each summer for a number of years I have been asked by Indians from the north if there was any talk of a Treaty'), and memorandum by Parry Sound Indian Superintendent W.B. Maclean, 28 January 1903, PAC, RG 10, vol. 3033, file 235, 225-1 (reporting there to be 'about 400 Indians residing around Lake Abbittibi who desired to enter into a Treaty with the Crown' and 'a considerable number ... in the vicinity of Lake Matawagamingue'); letter from Rat Portage Indian Agent R.S. McKenzie to J.D. MacLean, 22 June 1904, PAC, RG 10, vol. 3033, file 235, 225-1 ('some of the Indians near Assniburgh and Cate Lake ... are very desirous to come into Treaty'); North Temiskaming Indian Agent Adam Burwash letter to J.D. MacLean, 21 June 1906, PAC, RG 10, vol. 3033, file 235, 225-1 (Abitibie Aboriginal leaders wish to talk about 'having a treaty, securing a Reserve, [and] prevent liquor being brought to Abitibie'); Long Point Aboriginal people petition, 20 June 1906, PAC, RG 10, vol. 3033, file 235, 225-1 ('well, father, I am coming to ask you to give us land to make a living on. We are not asking land, only for the sake of asking it, we want you to give us land so that we may farm and make a living with').
See also Chief James Stoney petition to Department of Indian Affairs, 29 July 1915, PAC, RG 10, vol. 3033, file 235, 225-1 ('our hunting grounds in this northern climate are very poor, and we would be very pleased to be able to join in any of these Treaties, now that the Hudson's Bay is being approached by railways and white men are coming into this northern country we will be driven from our land'). See, generally, John Long, *Treaty No.*

9: *The Indian Petitions*, 1889-1927 (Cobalt, ON: Highway Book Shop 1978) [hereinafter *Indian Petitions*]. See also John Long, 'Treaty No. 9 and Fur Trade Company Families: Northeastern Ontario's Halfbreeds, Indians, Petitioners and Métis,' in J. Peterson and J.S.H. Brown, eds., *The New Peoples: Being and Becoming Métis in North America* (Winnipeg: University of Manitoba Press 1985), 137-63.

31 Jabez Williams to Alex Matheson, 12 June 1902, HBC Arch., B155/b/2, as quoted in Morrison, *Treaty Research Report*, 17 (*supra* note 5).

32 Ibid.

33 See text accompanying note 26 above.

34 James Phipps to superintendent-general of Indian affairs, 5 February 1885, PAC, RG 10, vol. 2289, file 57, 641, as quoted in Morrison, *Treaty Research Report*, 2-3 (*supra* note 5).

35 Ontario, Legislative Assembly, Sessional Papers, 53 Vic. (1890), No. 87, p. 85, *Northerly and Westerly Ontario, Borron's Reports* 1880-92 (Toronto: Queen's Printer 1892), 15.

36 Long, *Indian Petitions*, 5 (*supra* note 30).

37 Report of J.P. Donnelly, Indian Agent at Port Arthur, Canada, Parliament, House of Commons, *Sessional Papers* 57 Vic. (1894), No. 14, 12, as cited in Morrison, *Treaty Research Report*, 11 (*supra* note 5).

38 *Borron's Report, 1890*, 88 (*supra* note 35).

39 Ibid.

40 Borron's sentiment in this regard ought to be contrasted with his views on public ownership of provincial waterfalls and waterpowers. In his 1888 *Report on the Lakes and Rivers, Water and Water-Powers of the Province of Ontario* (published separately in Toronto in 1891), Borron recommended 'that in all future sales of land the water, whether of lakes or rivers (with the exception of that which may be required for domestic and sanitary purposes), should be reserved to the Crown as trustee for the benefit of the people of the Province generally. And that the waterpowers should not be sold, but leased for a term of years, the rent charged varying according to circumstances.' The province ultimately responded with the Waterpower Reservation Act, 61 Vict. c. 8, reserving the province's major waterpowers to the Crown. For discussion, see H.V. Nelles, *The Politics of Development: Forests, Mines and Hydro-Electric Power in Ontario, 1849-1941* (Hamden: Archon Books 1974), 36-47.

41 In *Indian Petitions*, 3 (*supra* note 30), Long summarizes the activity as follows:
    Men of the Geological Survey of Canada had criss-crossed the area – especially in the period before 1891, after which Ontario established its own Bureau of Mines. Thus, Dr. Robert Bell explored the Kenogami River in 1871, the Mattagami and Moose Rivers in 1875. A.S. Cochrane travelled the Abitibi River in 1877, A.P. Low and G.A. Young the Missinaibi River in 1896. Low had surveyed the Severn River in 1886 and Bell the Attawapiskat in the same year. In 1901, Dowling explored the Ekwan River; two years later McInnes ... went down the Winisk River. When 'Niven's Line,' the boundary between the Districts of Nipissing and Algoma (running straight north from Georgian Bay to James Bay) was surveyed in the 1890s, traces of gold were discovered. Indeed, the Treaty 9 Commissioners wrote: 'As we ascended the Abitibi evidences of approaching civilization and of the activity in railway construction and surveying ... were constantly met with. Surveying parties of the Transcontinental railway, the Temiskaming and Northern Ontario railway and Ontario Township surveyors were constantly met with.'
    Long, quoting 'Treaty Commissioners Report,' *James Bay Treaty* (Ottawa: Queen's Printer 1964, reprint of 1931 edition), 10 [hereinafter *James Bay Treaty*].

42 Long, *Indian Petitions*, iv.

43 Department of Indian Affairs, *Annual Report*, 1904-5, Ottawa, xviii.

44 Frank Pedley to Clifford Sifton, 10 June 1904, PAC, RG 10, vol. 3033, file 235, 225-1.

45 Frank Pedley to Aubrey White, 23 June 1904, PAC, RG 10, vol. 3033, file 235, 225-1.

46 Frank Pedley to Wilfrid Laurier, 'In re James Bay Treaty,' 27 April 1905, PAC, RG 10, vol. 3033, file 235, 225-1.

47 Ibid.

48 An unreported decision of the Privy Council, embodied in an Imperial Order in Council

made 11 August 1884.
49 *St. Catherine's Milling and Lumber Co. v. R.* (1888), 14 App. Cas. 46 (P.C.).
50 1891, 54-55 Vic., c. 5.
51 1891, 54-55 Vic., c. 3.
52 *James Bay Treaty*, 26 (*supra* note 41).
53 52 & 53 Vic., c.28 (U.K.).
54 Morrison, *Treaty Research Report*, 23 (*supra* note 5).
55 *Ontario Mining Co. v. Seybold*, [1903] A.C. 399 (P.C.).
56 Agreement between E.L. Newcombe and Edward Blake, 7 July 1902, Ontario, Legislative Assembly, 'The James Bay Treaty: Treaty Number Nine,' *Sessional Papers* (1908), no. 71, 6.
57 J.A. McKenna to Clifford Sifton, 22 February 1902, PAC, RG 10, vol. 3033, file 235, 225-1.
58 *Sessional Papers*, vol. 40, part 9, Fourth Session of Eleventh Legislature of the Province of Ontario (1908), letter, 30 April 1904.
59 See letter, Aubrey White to Frank Pedley, 30 May 1904, in Ontario, Legislative Assembly, *Sessional Papers* 1908, No. 71.
60 Frank Pedley to Aubrey White, 23 June 1901, PAC, RG 10, vol. 3033, file 225-1.
61 Frank Pedley to J.J. Foy, 8 May 1905, PAC, RG 10, vol. 3033, file 235, 225-1.
62 A.J. Matheson to Frank Pedley, 1 June 1905, PAC, RG 10, vol. 3033, file 235, 225-1.
63 Frank Pedley to A.J. Matheson, 1 June 1905, PAC, RG 10, vol. 3033, file 235, 225-1.
64 A.J. Matheson to Frank Pedley, 23 June 1905, PAC, RG 10, vol. 3033, file 235, 225-1.
65 Frank Pedley to superintendent-general of Indian affairs, 26 June 1905, PAC, RG 10, vol. 3033, file 235, 225-1.
66 PAC, RG 2, file 1231 D no. 1222.
67 Morrison interview with Robert Laurence, as quoted in Morrison, Treaty Research Report, 56 (*supra* note 5).
68 Letters of 4 June and 5 August 1921, PAC, RG 10, vol. 7835, file 30065-3 vol. 1, as quoted in Morrison, *Treaty Research Report*, 56 (*supra* note 5).
69 Long, *Indian Petitions*, 4 (*supra* note 30).
70 *James Bay Treaty* (*supra* note 41).
71 Ibid.
72 Ibid.
73 Ibid.
74 Ibid.
75 Ibid., 10-11.
76 See text accompanying notes 26-32 above.
77 Duncan Campbell Scott, 'The Last of the Indian Treaties,' *Scribner's Magazine*, November 1906, 578.
78 *James Bay Treaty*, 4-5 (*supra* note 41).
79 Ibid.
80 Scott, 'The Last of the Indian Treaties,' 578.
81 Duncan Campbell Scott, Journal, *James Bay Treaty*, 5.
82 Ibid.
83 Ibid., 6.
84 Morrison, *Treaty Research Report*, 45 (*supra* note 5), quoting *James Bay Treaty*, 10-11, 17 (*supra* note 41).
85 Morrison, *Treaty Research Report*, 49.
86 Interview of Robert Laurence taped by James Morrison in Sault Ste. Marie, Ontario, 17 March 1974, as cited in Morrison, *Treaty Research Report*, 47-48.
87 Interview of James Wesley, Kashechewan, October 1972, taped and transcribed by Arthur Cheechoo, as cited in Morrison, Treaty Research Report, 48.
88 James Wesley interview, as quoted in Morrison, *Treaty Research Report*, 53.
89 Paul Driben and Robert Trudeau, *When Freedom Is Lost: The Dark Side of the Relationship Between Government and the Fort Hope Band* (Toronto: University of Toronto Press 1983), 19.
90 Ojibway-Cree Cultural Centre, *Nishnawbe-Aski Nation: A History of the Cree and Ojibway of Northern Ontario* (Timmins: Ojibway-Cree Cultural Centre 1986), as quoted in Long, '"No Basis for Argument": The Signing of Treaty Nine in Northern Ontario, 1905-1906' (1989)

5 Native Studies Rev. 19 at 37.

91 Ibid., 40.

92 Ibid., 35-6.

93 *James Bay Treaty*, 6 (*supra* note 41).

94 Long, '"No Basis for Argument,"' 36. For an overview of Aboriginal and governmental understandings of the 1930 treaty adhesion signing, see John S. Long, 'Removing the Burden: Treaty Making at Winisk, 1930' (10 November 1990), unpublished manuscript on file with author.

95 See text accompanying notes 84-8 above.

96 Morrison, *Treaty Research Report*, 17.

97 Ibid., 49.

98 *Simon v. The Queen, supra* note 13.

99 Ibid.

100 In *R. v. Horseman, supra* note 13, the Supreme Court of Canada held that Treaty 8 hunting rights were designed to protect Aboriginal economies and commercial practices from non-Aboriginal intrusion. As stated by Justice Cory: 'An examination of the historical background leading to the negotiations for Treaty 8 *and the other numbered treaties* leads inevitably to the conclusion that the hunting rights reserved by the Treaty included hunting for commercial purposes. The Indians wished to protect the hunting rights which they possessed before the Treaty came into effect and the Federal Government wished to protect the native economy which was based upon those hunting rights' (emphasis added).

101 See, generally, Michael C. Blumm, 'Native Fishing Rights and Environmental Protection in North America and New Zealand: A Comparative Analysis of Profits A Prendre and Habitat Servitudes' (1990) 4 Canterbury L. Rev. 211. For a similar view with respect to the terms of the Comprehensive Land Agreement in Principle between Canada and the Dene Nation and the Metis Association of the Northern Territories (Ottawa, DIAND 1988), see Michael Asch, 'Wildlife: Defining the Animals, the Dene Hunt, and the Settlement of Aboriginal Rights Claims' (1989) 15:2 Can. Public Policy 205; see also Peter Usher, 'Property Rights, the Basis of Wildlife Management,' in *Proceedings of National and Regional Interests in the North* (Canadian Arctic Resources Committee 1984), 389.

102 The treaty right to water is implied from the recognition of a right to fish. It should be noted, however, that even in the absence of express language supporting such an inference, it would still be open to claim the existence of such a right. In *R. v. Taylor and Williams* (1981), 34 O.R. (2d) 360, the Ontario Court of Appeal, on the basis of oral promises, implied into a treaty entered into by the Crown and six chiefs of the Chippewa Nation a treaty right to hunt, despite the fact that the written text of the treaty said nothing at all about hunting rights.

103 A.S. Williams to Scott, 27 July 1920, PAC, RG 10, vol. 3660, file 9755-4, as quoted in Richard H. Bartlett, 'Hydroelectric Power and Indian Water Rights on the Prairies' (1989) 14 Prairie Forum 177, 183.

104 *Winters v. United States*, 207 U.S. 564 (1908). See also *Arizona v. California*, 373 U.S. 546 (1963).

105 See *United States v. Adair*, 723 F. 2d 1394 (9th Cir. 1983), cert. refused 104 S. Ct. 3526. For more discussion, see Bartlett, 'Hydroelectric Power,' 181-3 (*supra* note 103).

106 Ibid.

107 Bartlett, 'Hydroelectric Power,' 183-4.

108 (1989), 57 D.L.R. (4th) 161 (B.C.C.A.).

109 Ibid.

110 *Simon v. The Queen, supra* note 13 at 171.

111 Ibid.

112 [1973] 6 W.W.R. 97 (N.W.T.S.C.).

113 Ibid. Morrow J.'s judgment was reversed by the Northwest Territories Court of Appeal ((1975), 63 D.L.R. (3d) 1), on the narrow ground that a caveat could not be registered against unpatented Crown lands. The Supreme Court of Canada ([1977] 2 S.C.R. 628) upheld the Court of Appeal on this point. Neither appellate judgment addressed the

validity or effect of the two treaties. For an extensive analysis of 'blanket extinguishment,' see Royal Commission on Aboriginal Peoples, *Treaty Making in the Spirit of Co-existence: An Alternative to Extinguishment* (Ottawa: Minister of Supply and Services 1995).

114 *R. v. Badger, supra* note 8 at 20.

115 See Kent McNeil, 'The Meaning of Aboriginal Title,' in this collection.

116 See, for example, *Pawis v. R.* (1980), 102 D.L.R. (3d) 602 (F.C.T.D.) (Robinson-Huron Treaty 'tantamount to a contract).' This approach ought to be contrasted to an earlier view that treaties were simply political arrangements unenforceable in a court of law. See *R. v. Syliboy,* [1929] 1 D.L.R. 307 (N.S. Co. Ct.). For commentary on these two approaches, see Patrick Macklem, 'First Nations Self-Government and the Borders of the Canadian Legal Imagination' (1991) 36 McGill L.J. 382 at 425-45.

117 (U.K.), 30 & 31 Vict., c. 3.

118 See, for example, *R. v. Derriksan* (1976), 71 D.L.R. (3d) 159 (S.C.C.) (federal law regulating Aboriginal rights held *intra vires*); and *R. v. George* (1966), 55 D.L.R. (2d) 386 (federal law regulating treaty rights held *intra vires*).

119 See, for example, *R. v. Sutherland* (1980), 113 D.L.R. (3d) 374.

120 *R. v. Badger, supra* note 8 at 17.

121 *Kruger and Manuel v. R.* (1977), 75 D.L.R. (3d) 434 (S.C.C.).

122 Ibid.

123 *Four B Manufacturing v. United Garment Workers of America* (1979), 102 D.L.R. (3d) 385 (S.C.C.).

124 See, for example, *Hodge v. The Queen* (1883), 9 App. Cas. 117 at 130 ('subjects which in one aspect and for one purpose fall within section 92, may in another aspect and for another purpose fall within section 91').

125 See, for example, *R. v. White and Bob* (1965), 50 D.L.R. (2d) 613 (B.C.C.A.), affirmed 52 D.L.R. (2d) 481n (S.C.C.), where Davey J.A. (at 618), stated:

> Legislation that abrogates or abridges the hunting rights reserved to Indians under the treaties and agreements by which they sold their ancient territories to the Crown and to the Hudson's Bay Company for white settlement is, in my respectful opinion, legislation in relation to Indians because it deals with rights peculiar to them ... In my opinion, their peculiar rights of hunting and fishing over their ancient hunting grounds arising under agreements by which they collectively sold their ancient lands are Indian affairs over which Parliament has exclusive legislative authority, and only Parliament can derogate from those rights.'

This view may well represent an outgrowth of the 'enclave theory' in which Indian reserves were seen as exclusive enclaves of federal jurisdiction, subsequently rejected by the Supreme Court of Canada in *Cardinal v. A.G. Alberta* (1974), 40 D.L.R. (3d) 553 (S.C.C.).

126 R.S.C. 1985, c. I-5.

127 *Derrickson v. Derrickson* (1986), 26 D.L.R. (4th) 175 (S.C.C.); *Dick v. The Queen* (1985), 23 D.L.R. (4th) 33 (S.C.C.).

128 See, for example, *Bank of Montreal v. Hall* (1990), 65 D.L.R. (4th) 361 (S.C.C.); and *Multiple Access v. McCutcheon* (1982), 138 D.L.R. (3d) 1 (S.C.C.).

129 See, for example, *R. v. Sioui and R. v. Simon, supra* note 13; *R. v. White and Bob* (1966), 52 D.L.R. (2d) 481n (S.C.C.).

130 For more discussion, see Bruce Ryder, 'The Demise and Rise of the Classical Paradigm in Canadian Federalism: Promoting Autonomy for the Provinces and First Nations' (1991) 36 McGill L.J. 308.

131 See, for example, *Saanichton Marine v. Claxton, supra* note 108, where Hinkson J.A. held that: 'There is no question that if the license of occupation derogates from the treaty right of the Indians, it is of no force and effect. The province cannot act to contravene the treaty rights of Indians, nor can it authorize others to do so.'

132 (1987), 84 D.L.R. (4th) 377 (Ont. Dist. Ct.).

133 Ibid., 385.

134 [1981] 3 C.N.L.R. 45 (Ont. Dist. Ct.).

135 Ibid., 48.

136 *R. v. Badger, supra* note 8 at 18.
137 This assumption ought to be read in light of the evidence outlined earlier suggesting that it is highly unlikely that Aboriginal signatories understood the treaty to involve an absolute surrender to the Crown of rights with respect to land. See text accompanying notes 111-14 above.
138 See *St. Catherine's Milling and Lumber Co. v. R., supra* note 49 and text accompanying notes 48-54 above.
139 *Nowegijick v. The Queen, supra* note 6.
140 While earlier lower court jurisprudence has suggested that the qualification on hunting, trapping, and fishing rights should not be subject to the *ejusdem generis* rule (see *R. v. Smith*, [1935] 3 D.L.R. 703, and *R. v. Mirasty*, [1942] 1 W.W.R. 343), holdings that implicitly admit of more than one potential interpretation of the qualification, are dated in light of subsequent Supreme Court of Canada judgments on the legal principles of treaty interpretation referred to in part 1 of this paper. Whether to invoke the *ejusdem generis* rule, which would limit the types of activity contemplated by the words 'other purposes' to activities that are of the same genus as those that are explicitly listed, or whether to invoke any other canon of interpretation, is a question that must be asked in light of this case law.
141 For a similar conclusion with respect to the phrase 'the government of Canada,' see *R. v. Batisse, supra* note 132; and *Cheechoo* v. *R., supra* note 134, and text accompanying notes 132-6.
142 Indian Act, R.S.C. 1985, c. I-5.
143 See text accompanying note 21 above.
144 *R. v. Sioui, supra* note 10.
145 See text accompanying notes 67-9 above and, generally, Nelles, *The Politics of Development, supra* note 40.
146 Scott, 'The Last of the Indian Treaties,' *supra* note 77.
147 *Nowegijick v. The Queen, supra* note 6, quoting with approval *Jones v. Meecham, supra* note 7.
148 See text accompanying notes 92-4.
149 See text accompanying notes 89-90.
150 For a similar conclusion respecting Treaties 8 and 11, see *Re Paulette, supra* note 112, where Justice Morrow stated: 'It is almost unbelievable that the Government party could have ever returned from their efforts with any impression but that they had given an assurance in perpetuity to the Indians in the Territories that their traditional use of the lands was not affected.'
151 *Simon v. The Queen, supra* note 13.
152 *R. v. Sioui, supra* note 10.
153 *Nowegijick v. The Queen, supra* note 6.
154 207 U.S. 564 at 576-7 (1908).
155 *Horse v. R., supra* note 9.
156 Even if Aboriginal signatories were told that the terms of Treaty 6 were identical to the other treaties, one cannot conclude from this that they necessarily understood that those other treaties precluded the right to hunt on private lands subject to actual competing interests of the property owners and the safety of others, let alone that they understood Treaty 6 to preclude such a right. For further commentary, see Macklem, 'First Nations Self-Government,' 438-40 (*supra* note 116). See also John Leonard Taylor, 'Two Views on the Meaning of Treaties Six and Seven,' in Richard Price, ed., *The Spirit of the Alberta Indian Treaties* (Edmonton: Pica Pica 1987), 9-45.
157 For the view that Treaty 9 does not preclude hunting on private lands for which a timber licence had been issued but where no lumbering activity was occurring, see *R. v. Weesk*, [1986] 2 C.N.L.R. 158 (Ont. Dist. Ct.) at 163 ('the mere existence of a timber licence alone is not sufficient to bring it within the scope of an activity'). See also *R. v. Bartleman* (1984), 12 D.L.R. (4th) 73 (B.C.C.A.); *R. v. Badger*, note 8 above.
158 (1984), 13 D.L.R. (4th) 321 (S.C.C.).
159 Quoting Ernest Weinrib, 'The Fiduciary Obligation' (1975), 25 U.T.L.J. 1 at 7.
160 See Chief Justice Dickson's concurring judgment in *Mitchell and Milton Management Ltd.*

v. Peguis Indian Band (1990), 71 D.L.R. (4th) 193 (S.C.C.). ('from the aboriginal perspective, any federal-provincial divisions that the Crown has imposed on itself are internal to itself and do not alter the basic structure of Sovereign-Indian relations'). See, generally, Peter Hutchins et al., 'When Do Fiduciary Obligations to Aboriginal People Arise?' (1995) 59 Sask. L. Rev. 97; Leonard Rotman, 'Provincial Fiduciary Obligations to First Nations: The Nexus Between Governmental Power and Responsibility' (1994) 32 Osgoode Hall L.J. 735.

161 [1990] 1 S.C.R. 1075.

162 See *R. v. Potts*, [1992] 1 C.N.L.R. 142 (Alta. Prov. Ct.); *R. v. Daniels*, [1990] 1 C.N.L.R. 108 (Man. Q.B.), notice of appeal filed (Man. C.A.); *R. v. Flett* (1989), 60 Man. R. 294 (Q.B.), leave to appeal denied [1991] 1 C.N.L.R. 140 (Man. C.A.); *R. v. Arcand* (1989), 65 Alta. L.R. (2d) 326 (Q.B.); *R. v. Agawa* (1988), 53 D.L.R. (4th) 101 (Ont. C.A.). Compare *R. v. Sutherland and Napash*, [1984] 4 C.N.L.R. 133 (Ont. Prov. Ct.).

163 See *R. v. Jones* (1993), 14 O.R. (3d) 421 (Prov. Div.); *R. v. Bombay*, [1993] 1 C.N.L.R. 92 (Ont. C.A.); *R. v. Jackson*, [1992] 4 C.N.L.R. 121 (Ont. C.A.). An alternative approach would be for the Court to view treaty rights as absolute, i.e., not subject to legislative interference under any circumstances. Compare Russel Lawrence Barsh and James Youngblood Henderson, *The Road: Indian Tribes and Political Liberty* (Berkeley: University of California Press 1980), 285 ('unless that original consent expressly included some right in the United States to act without constraint, the presumption should be that any alteration of tribes' circumstances requires their fresh consent').

164 For a similar conclusion regarding rights under the 1850 Robinson-Huron Treaty, see *R. v. Agawa* (1988), 53 D.L.R. (4th) 101.

165 See *R. v. Nikal*, [1991] 1 C.N.L.R. 62 (B.C.S.C.); *R. v. Robinson*, [1991] 4 C.N.L.R. 125 (B.C. Prov. Ct.); *R. v. Jack*, [1992] 1 C.N.L.R. 122 (B.C.S.C.); *R. v. Joseph*, [1992] 2 C.N.L.R. 128 (Yukon Terr. Ct.); and *R. v. Sampson*, [1992] 3 C.N.L.R. 146 (B.C.S.C.), all involving an Aboriginal right to fish and the application of federal legislation.

166 See text accompanying notes 158-60 above.

167 *R. v. Sparrow*, [1990] 1 S.C.R. 1075, esp. 1108-9.

168 Ibid., 1110.

169 Ibid., 1108, 1119.

Chapter 5: The Meaning of Aboriginal Title

1 *Calder v. A.G.B.C.*, [1973] S.C.R. 313 at 328.

2 *Delgamuukw v. The Queen* (1993), 104 D.L.R. (4th) 470 (B.C.C.A.).

3 Ibid.

4 *Guerin v. The Queen*, [1984] 2 S.C.R. 335 at 376-9 per Dickson J.; *Roberts v. Canada*, [1989] 1 S.C.R. 322 at 340.

5 *Guerin v. The Queen*, [1984] 2 S.C.R. 335 at 379 per Dickson J.

6 *Calder*, supra note 1 at 328.

7 *Guerin*, supra note 4 at 376.

8 Ibid., 378.

9 *Amodu Tijani v. Secretary, Southern Nigeria*, [1921] 2 A.C. 399.

10 *Baker Lake v. Min. of Indian Affairs*, [1980] 1 F.C. 518 at 557.

11 Ibid., 559.

12 This interpretation is supported by the following statement by Lambert J. (dissenting on other grounds) in *Delgamuukw* (B.C.C.A.), supra note 2 at 630: 'The reason why there must be an organized society is that it is only in such a society that the practices of the people reveal that there are recognized rights which underlie the practices.'

13 In common law courts, laws of Aboriginal peoples are generally treated as factual matters requiring evidentiary proof: see *Angu v. Attah* (1916), P.C. Gold Coast 1874-1928 43 at 44; *Effuah Amissah v. Effuah Krabah* (1936), 2 W.A.C.A. 30 at 31; *Re Bed of Wanganui River*, [1955] N.Z.L.R. 419 at 432.

14 *Roberts*, supra note 4 at 340. Wilson J. was relying on the *Calder* decision, as Dickson J. had done in *Guerin* (supra note 4).

15 For legal positivists, the existence of laws is a prerequisite for the existence of legal rights.

A classic statement of this view appears in Jeremy Bentham, 'Pannomial Fragments,' in Mary Peter Mack, ed., *A Bentham Reader* (New York: Pegasus 1969), 257: 'Rights are, then, the fruits of the law, and of the law alone. There are no rights without law – no rights contrary to the law – no rights anterior to the law.' While natural law theorists postulate the existence of rights outside any body of positive law (e.g., see, generally, John Finnis, *Natural Law and Natural Rights* ([Oxford: Clarendon Press 1980]), the Supreme Court of Canada does not seem to have had natural rights in mind when it has described Aboriginal title as a pre-existing legal right. Dickson J.'s reliance on *Amodu Tijani* in particular in the *Guerin* case reveals that he was referring instead to rights which existed under Aboriginal systems of law.

16 For further discussion, see Kent McNeil, *Common Law Aboriginal Title* (Oxford: Clarendon Press 1989), 274-90.

17 *Delgamuukw* (B.C.C.A.), *supra* note 2.

18 Statement of Claim, as quoted ibid., 483.

19 The trial alone took 374 days, and the reported judgment is 456 pages long: *Delgamuukw v. British Columbia* (1991), 79 D.L.R. (4th) 185 (B.C.S.C.). For commentary on the trial judgment, which will not be discussed directly here as we are going to focus on the judgments given in the Court of Appeal, see Frank Cassidy, ed., *Aboriginal Title in British Columbia: Delgamuukw v. The Queen* (Lantzville, BC: Oolichan Books 1992).

20 Macfarlane's judgment can be regarded as the majority judgment because Wallace, while writing a judgment of his own, stated in it that he agreed with Macfarlane's 'reasons and the conclusions' he had reached: *Delgamuukw* (B.C.C.A.), *supra* note 2 at 549.

21 Ibid., 492.

22 Ibid.

23 Ibid., 493, quoting *Roberts*, *supra* note 4 at 340.

24 Ibid., 492.

25 See also ibid., 497, where Macfarlane J. said that Mahoney's requirements illustrate 'the established common law approach to the proof of an aboriginal right.'

26 In his 'summary,' Macfarlane concluded that 'the Gitksan and Wet'suet'en people had an organized society ... [with] traditions, rules and regulations' (ibid., 545). He also concluded that 'the use and occupation of land and certain products of the lands and water were integral to that society' (ibid., 543). However, he did not give a precise definition of their Aboriginal land rights, stating that the characteristics of those rights 'may vary depending upon the particular context in which the rights are said to exist, and having regard to specific fact situations' (ibid., 542). By mutual agreement of the parties, the actual content of the Aboriginal title of the Gitksan and Wet'suwet'en was left for negotiation instead (ibid., at 725 per Lambert J.).

27 Ibid., 571.

28 Ibid., 575, 579.

29 Ibid., 579.

30 Wallace classified British Columbia as settled in accordance with the standard British colonial law distinction between colonies the Crown acquired by settlement and colonies it acquired by conquest or cession: on this distinction, see McNeil, *Common Law Aboriginal Title*, *supra* note 16 at 108-33.

31 *Delgamuukw* (B.C.C.A.), *supra* note 2 at 570.

32 Ibid.

33 Ibid., 569-70. On this doctrine, see Brian Slattery, *The Land Rights of Indigenous Canadian Peoples* (Saskatoon: University of Saskatchewan Native Law Centre 1979), 50-9.

34 *Delgamuukw* (B.C.C.A.), *supra* note 2 at 577.

35 Ibid., 568.

36 Ibid., 570.

37 Ibid., 641.

38 Ibid., 644.

39 Ibid., 655.

40 Ibid., 655-6. Note that Lambert placed three limitations on this incorporation into the common law of Gitksan and Wet'suwet'en practices, customs, and traditions. First, it

applies only to those practices, customs, and traditions which are 'an integral part of their distinctive culture,' a phrase Lambert used 'to describe the differentiation between a practice, custom or tradition that is sufficiently significant and fundamental to the culture and social organization of a particular group of aboriginal people as to command recognition as an aboriginal right, on the one hand, and a practice or habit that was merely an incident in the lives of the people in this group, on the other' (ibid., 646-7). Secondly, if there was a conflict between Gitksan and Wet'suwet'en customary law and federal law (after section 35(1) of the Constitution Act, 1982, came into force), the federal law might prevail, depending on the application of the justification test set out in *Sparrow v. The Queen*, [1990] 1 S.C.R. 1075 (ibid., 656). Thirdly, 'upon the assertion of sovereignty the laws and customs of the Gitksan and Wet'suwet'en in relation to affairs external to the Gitksan and Wet'suwet'en peoples were abrogated' (ibid., 657).

41 Lambert's views on the source of Aboriginal title are very similar to the views of the majority of the High Court of Australia in *Mabo v. Queensland* [No. 2] (1992) 175 C.L.R. 1. While an analysis of that important decision is outside the scope of this paper, it is worth noting that the divergence of opinion between the majority there and the majority of the British Columbia Court of Appeal in *Delgamuukw* adds to the uncertainty over Aboriginal title in former British settlements.

42 *Delgamuukw* (B.C.C.A.), *supra* note 2 at 750.

43 Ibid., quoting *Guerin, supra* note 4 at 377-8.

44 Ibid., 751, quoting *Guerin* at 378.

45 That was one approach Brennan J. took in *Mabo, supra* note 41 at 58: 'Native title has its origin in and is given its content by the traditional laws acknowledged by and the traditional customs observed by the indigenous inhabitants of a territory. The nature and incidents of native title must be ascertained as a matter of fact by reference to those laws and customs.' However, Brennan also said that, where an Indigenous community is in exclusive possession of land, their communal title amounts to ownership, even if the customary law rights of individuals within the community are usufructuary in nature. In his words, 'The ownership of land within a territory in the exclusive occupation of a people must be vested in that people: land is susceptible of ownership, and there are no other owners' (ibid., 51).

46 *St. Catherine's Milling and Lumber Co. v. The Queen* (1888), 14 App. Cas. 46.

47 Ibid., 54.

48 Ibid., 55.

49 Ibid., 58.

50 See *A.-G. of Quebec v. A.-G. of Canada*, [1921] 1 A.C. 401 at 408; *Guerin, supra* note 4 at 382 per Dickson J.; *Canadian Pacific v. Paul*, [1988] 2 S.C.R. 654 at 677.

51 For critiques of the 'good will of the Sovereign' and 'underlying title' aspects of the decision, see Kent McNeil, 'The Temagami Indian Land Claim: Loosening the Judicial Strait-Jacket,' in Matt Bray and Ashley Thomson, eds., *Temagami: A Debate on Wilderness* (Toronto: Dundurn Press 1990), 200-5; and Patrick Macklem, 'First Nations Self-Government and the Borders of the Canadian Legal Imagination,' (1991) 36 McGill L.J. 382 at 395-414, respectively.

52 See *Delgamuukw* (B.C.C.A.), *supra* note 2 at 625 per Lambert J.

53 See *Calder, supra* note 1 at 328, 375-6, 390, 394; *Guerin, supra* note 4 at 377-8; *Roberts, supra* note 4 at 340.

54 In *Calder* at 328, Judson J. said that Lord Watson's 'personal and usufructuary right' description 'does not help one in the solution of this problem' (of determining what Indian title means).

55 *Guerin, supra* note 4 at 382.

56 *Sparrow, supra* note 40 at 1112.

57 For a critical analysis of this limitation on Aboriginal title, see McNeil, *Common Law Aboriginal Title, supra* note 16 at 221-35.

58 In *Mabo, supra* note 41 at 217, the High Court declared that the Meriam people on whose behalf the claim had been brought were 'entitled as against the whole world to possession, occupation, use and enjoyment' of the land they held by virtue of their native title.

The court relied in part on *Amodu Tijani*, *supra* note 9 at 409-10, where the Judicial Committee of the Privy Council said that native title might be extensive enough to reduce the 'radical right' of the Crown to 'comparatively limited rights of administrative interference.' In both those cases the Crown's underlying title was not regarded as incompatible with an all-encompassing interest held by the Aboriginal peoples.

59 For American cases supporting this conclusion, see *U.S. v. Paine Lumber*, 206 U.S. 467 (1907); *U.S. v. Shoshone Tribe*, 304 U.S. 111 (1938), esp. 116-17; *U.S. v. Klamath and Moadoc Tribes*, 304 U.S. 119 (1938) at 122-3. See also the long list of authorities in McNeil, *Common Law Aboriginal Title*, *supra* note 16 at 256n.51.

60 *Guerin*, *supra* note 4 at 376.

61 *Roberts*, *supra* note 4 at 340.

62 See McNeil, *Common Law Aboriginal Title*, *supra* note 16 at 6-78.

63 See *Tichborne v. Weir* (1892), 67 L.T. 735; *Re Atkinson and Horsell's Contract*, [1912] 2 Ch. 1 at 9, 17; *Fairweather v. St. Marylebone Pty.*, [1963] A.C. 510, esp. 535.

64 See *Lord Advocate v. Lord Lovat* (1880), 5 App. Cas. 273 at 288; *Kirby v. Cowderoy*, [1912] A.C. 599 at 603; *Cadija Umma v. S. Don Manis Appu*, [1939] A.C. 136 at 141-2.

65 *Red House Farms v. Catchpole* (1976), 244 E.G. 295 (leave to appeal to the House of Lords refused). See also *Curzon v. Lomax* (1803), 170 E.R. 737; *Harper v. Charlesworth* (1825), 107 E.R. 1174 at 1177-8.

66 The kind of justifications given during the colonial period for not according Aboriginal peoples land rights equivalent to those of Europeans were self-serving and discriminatory, and, according to *Mabo*, *supra* note 41, are therefore unacceptable today: see esp. at 38-43 per Brennan J. For example, Aboriginal peoples were regarded as 'heathens' and 'savages' who were too 'primitive' to own lands: see Wilcomb E. Washburn, 'The Moral and Legal Justifications for Dispossessing the Indians,' in James Morton Smith, ed., *Seventeenth Century America: Essays in Colonial History* (Chapel Hill: University of North Carolina Press 1959), 15; Geoffrey S. Lester, 'Primitivism versus Civilization: A Basic Question in the Law of Aboriginal Rights to Land,' in Carol Brice-Bennett, ed., *Our Footprints are Everywhere: Inuit Land Use and Occupancy in Labrador* (Ottawa: Labrador Inuit Association 1977), 351; Robert A. Williams, Jr., *The American Indian in Western Legal Thought: The Discourses of Conquest* (New York: Oxford University Press 1990).

67 In *Baker Lake*, *supra* note 10, Mahoney J. found that Inuit land use at the time of colonization amounted to possession. In *Mitchel v. U.S.*, 9 Pet. 711 (1835) at 746, Baldwin J., delivering the unanimous judgment of the United States Supreme Court, said Indian possession 'was considered with reference to their habits and modes of life; their hunting-grounds were as much in their actual possession as the cleared fields of the whites; and their rights to its exclusive enjoyment were as much respected, until they abandoned them, made a cession to the government, or an authorized sale to individuals.' See also *U.S. v. Santa Fe Pacific Railroad*, 314 U.S. 339 (1941) at 345.

68 In *Calder*, *supra* note 1 at 368, 375, Hall J. (dissenting on other grounds) said that the Nisga'a Indians were *prima facie* 'the owners of the lands that have been in their possession since time immemorial' because 'possession is of itself [at common law] proof of ownership.' Hall did not, however, specify the nature of the interest the Nisga'as had, as their counsel, who were not claiming a fee simple, did not ask for a definition of the interest (see ibid., 352-3, 410). Hall's view, which is amply supported by authority (see McNeil, *Common Law Aboriginal Title*, *supra* note 16 at 6-78), that possession is proof of ownership, was applied by Morrow J. in *Re Paulette* (1973), 42 D.L.R. (3d) 8 at 28 (reversed on other grounds (1975), 63 D.L.R. (3d) 1, [1977] 2 S.C.R. 628). Ownership, of course, is the most extensive right a person or persons can have to a thing.

69 *Guerin*, *supra* note 4 at 382 per Dickson J. See text accompanying notes 55-6.

70 Note, however, that the common law has acknowledged the existence of inalienable fee simple estates (see McNeil, *Common Law Aboriginal Title*, *supra* note 16 at 233).

71 *Baker Laker, supra* note 10 at 559.
72 For a critical assessment of this aspect of the decision, see McNeil, *Common Law Aboriginal Title, supra* note 16 at 282-4.
73 *A.G. Ontario v. Bear Island Foundation,* [1985] 1 C.N.L.R. 1 (Ont. S.C.) at 34.
74 Ibid., 34, 39. Steele adopted 1763 as the relevant date because he applied the Royal Proclamation of that year. His views on Aboriginal title were influenced by the Judicial Committee of the Privy Council's interpretation of the Proclamation in the *St. Catherine's* decision, *supra* note 46 (see ibid., 26-8), and are open to the same criticisms as that decision.
75 [1991] 2 S.C.R. 570 at 575.
76 *Delgamuukw* (B.C.S.C.), *supra* note 19 at 458.
77 *Delgamuukw* (B.C.C.A.), *supra* note 2 at 492.
78 *Sparrow, supra* note 40 at 1099.
79 In their discussion of the existence of the right, Dickson and La Forest said: 'The evidence reveals that the Musqueam have lived in the area as an organized society long before the coming of European settlers, and that the taking of salmon was an integral part of their lives and remains so to this day' (ibid., 1094). On the next page, in a longer passage that deserves to be quoted in full, they gave their reasons for concluding that the Musqueam had an Aboriginal right to fish:

> While the trial for the violation of a penal prohibition may not be the most appropriate setting in which to determine the existence of an aboriginal right, and the evidence was not extensive, the correctness of the finding of fact of the trial judge 'that Mr. Sparrow was fishing in ancient tribal territory where his ancestors had fished from time immemorial in that part of the mouth of the Fraser River for salmon' is supported by the evidence and was not contested. The existence of the right, the Court of Appeal tells us, was 'not the subject of serious dispute.' It is not surprising, then, that, taken with the other circumstances, that court should find at p. 320, that 'the judgment appealed from was wrong in ... failing to hold that Sparrow at the relevant time was exercising an existing aboriginal right.'

While Dickson and La Forest said that the evidence of continuity of the right was 'scanty' for one period, they decided not to disturb the Court of Appeal's finding on this issue of the right's existence.

80 Ibid., 1101.
81 *Delgamuukw* (B.C.C.A.), *supra* note 2 at 492.
82 Ibid., 493-4.
83 Ibid., 496.
84 Ibid., 497. On the same page, Macfarlane concluded: 'Thus, native title does not have a single, generic form encompassing all activities. Its content is determined by traditional aboriginal enjoyment.'
85 Ibid., 572, citing *Kruger and Manuel v. The Queen,* [1978] 1 S.C.R. 104 at 109.
86 Ibid., 571.
87 Ibid., 571, 575.
88 Ibid., 575.
89 Ibid., 574.
90 Ibid., 573.
91 Ibid., 648.
92 Ibid., 648.
93 Recall that Lambert regarded Aboriginal rights as originating in Aboriginal practices, customs, and traditions which continued as legal rights after the assertion of Crown sovereignty due to the doctrine of continuity. See text accompanying notes 37-41.
94 Ibid. See also p. 659, where Lambert gave another example:

> If the aboriginal right, in 1846, was a right to take all the fish that the holders of the right wanted to take, subject to the needs of conservation, then the aboriginal right in 1993 is a right to take all the fish that the holders of the right want to take, subject again only to the needs of conservation. So fish could be caught for sale, and the money used to put a roof over the rightholders' heads and hamburger on their tables. But if the aboriginal right was a right to take only so many fish as the fisher and his

or her individual dependants would eat in the course of a season, then perhaps the modern version of the right as so defined would be limited to permitting the rightholder to catch only so many fish as would be eaten within his or her family over the course of the season.

95 Ibid., 659-60, relying on *Sparrow, supra* note 40 at 1112.

96 Ibid., 726-31.

97 Ibid., 657. Support for Lambert's view that Aboriginal customs were not frozen at the time of assertion of sovereignty by the Crown can be found in the 1919 decision of the Judicial Committee of the Privy Council in *Hineiti Rirerire Arani v. Public Trustee*, [1840-1932] N.Z.P.C.C. 1 at 6:

It may well be that ... the Maoris as a race may have some internal power of self-government enabling the tribe or tribes by common consent to modify their customs, and that the custom of such a race is not to be put on a level with the custom of an English borough or other local area which must stand as it always has stood, seeing that there is no quasi-legislative internal authority which can modify it.

98 This linkage is apparent as well in Lambert's discussion of section 35 of the Constitution Act, 1982. Referring to that section, he said (*Delgamuukw* (B.C.C.A.), *supra* note 2 at 645):

Its purpose must have been to secure to Indian people, without any further erosion, a modern unfolding of the rights flowing from the fact that, before the settlers with their new sovereignty arrived, the Indians occupied the land, possessed its resources, and used and enjoyed both the land and the resources through a social system which they controlled through their own institutions. That modern unfolding must come not only in legal rights, but, more importantly, in the reflection of those rights in a social organization and in an economic structure which will permit the Indian peoples to manage their affairs with both some independence from the remainder of Canadian society and also with honourable interdependence between all parts of the Canadian social fabric.

99 Ibid., 749.

100 Ibid., 756. Note that Macfarlane, Wallace, and Lambert were also of the opinion that it was unnecessary, and even futile, to try to classify Aboriginal title as personal or proprietary, given the fact that it is *sui generis* (ibid., 510-11, 573, 649-50).

101 Note that the British Columbia Court of Appeal handed down seven other decisions, all of them involving Aboriginal hunting and fishing rights, at the same time as the *Delgamuukw* decision. Three of those decisions involved the scope of Aboriginal fishing rights, and in each case the majority, consisting of Macfarlane, Taggart, and Wallace JJ., decided that those rights do not include a right to engage in commercial fishing activities (see *R. v. Gladstone*, [1993] 4 C.N.L.R. 75; *R. v. N.T.C. Smokehouse Ltd.*, [1993] 4 C.N.L.R. 158; *R. v. Vanderpeet*, [1993] 4 C.N.L.R. 221). Consistent with his expansive view of Aboriginal rights, Lambert J. dissented in each of those cases. Hutcheon J. dissented in *Vanderpeet* on the ground that the accused's ancestors, the Sto:lo people, began to trade in fish in commercial quantities in the period between European contact and assertion of sovereignty; for him, this commercial activity was part of the Aboriginal right because it was being exercised at the relevant date when sovereignty was asserted. On the scope of Aboriginal rights to fish, at least, Hutcheon therefore appears to stand between the majority on the one hand and Lambert on the other. While a detailed examination of these cases might cast further light on the views of the judges of the Court of Appeal on Aboriginal title, it would take us beyond the scope of our present inquiry. In particular, it would necessitate a discussion of the connection between Aboriginal title to land and Aboriginal rights to engage in activities such as hunting and fishing. As this book was going to press, the Supreme Court of Canada handed down its decisions in the *Gladstone*, [1996] S.C.J. No. 79; *N.T.C. Smokehouse*, [1996] S.C.J. No. 78; and *Van der Peet*, [1996] S.C.J. No. 77, appeals, as well as in two other relevant cases, *R. v. Adams*, [1996] S.C.J. No. 87, and *R. v. Coté*, [1996] S.C.J. No. 93. As it would be impossible to incorporate a discussion of those decisions into this paper without very substantial revisions, analysis of those decisions is best left for another time.

102 Note that in British Columbia, where the *Delgamuukw* case arose, acquisition of title by adverse possession was generally abolished by the Limitations Act, S.B.C. 1975, c.37, now

R.S.B.C. 1979, c.236, s.12. However, section 14(5) provides that 'Nothing in this Act interferes with any right or title to land acquired by adverse possession before July 1, 1975.' Moreover, title to land can be acquired by adverse possession in other provinces in Canada.

103 *Guerin, supra* note 4 at 379, where Dickson said: 'It does not matter, in my opinion, that the present case is concerned with the interest of an Indian band in a reserve rather than with unrecognized aboriginal title in traditional tribal lands. The Indian interest in the land is the same in both cases.'

104 Note that Dickson's equation of the Indian interest in reserve and Aboriginal title lands has been questioned. See Richard Bartlett, 'You Can't Trust the Crown. The Fiduciary Obligation of the Crown to the Indians: *Guerin v. The Queen*' (1985) 49 Sask. L. Rev. 367; Henri Brun, 'La Possession et la réglementation des droits miniers, forestiers et de réversion dans les réserves indiennes du Québec' (1985) 30 McGill L.J. 415; McNeil, *Common Law Aboriginal Title, supra* note 16 at 287.

105 The fact that the Crown has the legal title does not prevent the Aboriginal interest from being all-encompassing, in the same way as the equitable title of a beneficiary under a trust can be all-encompassing even though the legal title is vested in the trustee.

106 30 & 31 Vict., c. 3 (U.K.), s. 91(24).

107 R.S.C. 1927, c. s. 2(j).

108 R.S.C. 1985, c. I-5, s. 2(1).

109 S.C. 1951, c.29, s. 2(1)(o).

110 That power has since been restricted by section 35(1) of the Constitution Act, 1982, enacted as Schedule B to the Canada Act 1982 (U.K.) 1982, c.11 (see *Sparrow, supra* note 40).

111 See P. St. J. Langan, *Maxwell on the Interpretation of Statutes*, 12th ed. (London: Sweet & Maxwell 1976), 251-6; S.G.G. Edgar, *Craies on Statute Law*, 7th ed. (London: Sweet & Maxwell 1971), 118-21; Elmer A. Driedger, *Construction of Statutes*, 2nd ed. (Toronto: Butterworths 1983), 183-5. Also relevant is 'the valuable rule never to enact under guise of definition' (Edgar, 213).

112 [1933] S.C.R. 629 at 638. For other authorities and further discussion of the application of this rule of statutory interpretation to the land rights of indigenous peoples, see Kent McNeil, 'Racial Discrimination and Unilateral Extinguishment of Native Title' (1996), 1 A.I.L.R. 181, esp. 183-90, 200-3.

113 Those things were probably originally included in the definition of 'reserve' as a precautionary measure which was no longer regarded as necessary in 1951. In *Apsassin v. Canada*, [1988] 1 C.N.L.R. 73 (F.C.T.D.), affirmed [1993] 2 C.N.L.R. 20 (F.C.A.), reversed [1995] 4 S.C.R. 344, (S.C.C.), Addy J. commented on the 1927 definition, at [1988] 1 C.N.L.R. 109: 'The inclusion of these objects in the term "reserve" might have been deemed preferable as the Indians do not have a title to the reserve but merely a usufructuary interest in it and there does not exist in such a case a common law rule which, as in the case of an absolute title, provides that all of these are necessarily included in a fee simple unless specifically excepted.' Addy J. clearly thought that the Indian interest in reserves includes the benefit of all the things listed in the 1927 definition. Moreover, the Supreme Court of Canada in *Apsassin* affirmed that this interest includes mineral rights.

114 R.S.C. 1985, c.I-7.

115 Indian entitlement to the benefit of oil and gas on reserve lands did not originate with the Indian Oil and Gas Act: for example, see *Apsassin, supra* note 113. That case involved a surrender to the Crown of mineral rights, including oil and gas, on reserve lands in northeastern British Columbia in the 1940s, which was held to impose a fiduciary duty on the Crown.

116 *St. Catherines, supra*, note 46.

117 [1921] 1 A.C. 401.

118 See Peter A. Cumming and Neil H. Mickenberg, eds., *Native Rights in Canada*, 2nd ed. (Toronto: General Publishing Co. 1972), 227-33.

119 For example, see An Act for the Settlement of Certain Questions Between the Governments of Canada and Ontario Respecting Indian Reserve Lands, S.C. 1924, c.48; An Act

to Confirm an Agreement Between the Government of Canada and the Government of the Province of New Brunswick Respecting Indian Reserves, S.C. 1959, c.47.

120 See discussions of the situation in British Columbia in Cumming and Mickenberg, *Native Rights in Canada, supra* note 118 at 229, and N.D. Banks, 'Indian Resource Rights and Constitutional Enactments in Western Canada, 1871-1930,' in Louis A. Knafla, ed., *Law and Justice in a New Land* (Toronto: Carswell 1986), 148-51. Note that the controversy has generally been over entitlement to the benefit of such things as mineral rights *after* the reserve lands have been surrendered to the Crown; there has been little doubt that the Indian interest includes the entire benefit (with the possible exception of precious metals in some cases) of reserve lands *prior* to any surrender. This is apparent not only from the definition of 'reserve' in the Indian Act, but from other provisions of that statute as well (e.g., see R.S.C. 1985, c.I-5, ss. 20, 71, 93).

121 It may, however, depend to some extent on the specific terms of federal-provincial agreements over Indian reserves (see *supra* note 120).

122 See the Robinson-Superior and Robinson-Huron treaties, 1850, in Alexander Morris, *The Treaties of Canada with the Indians of Manitoba and the North-West Territories* (Toronto: Belfords, Clarke and Co. 1880; reprinted Toronto: Coles Publishing Company 1979), 302-4, 305-9.

123 For example, see Treaties 3 (1873) and 4 (1874), ibid., 320-7, 330-5.

124 The Robinson-Superior Treaty (ibid., 302-4) provided for a general surrender

> save and except the reservations set forth in the schedule hereunto annexed, which reservations shall be held and occupied by the said Chiefs and their tribes in common, for the purposes of residence and cultivation, – and should the said Chiefs and their respective tribes at any time desire to dispose of any mineral or other valuable productions upon the said reservations, the same will be at their request sold by order of the Superintendent-General of the Indian Department for the time being, for their sole use and benefit, and to the best advantage.

An equivalent provision appears in the Robinson-Huron Treaty (ibid., 305-9). Moreover, an examination of William Robinson's Report on the Robinson-Huron Treaty (ibid., 17-21), reveals that the consideration which Robinson offered in exchange for surrender of the Aboriginal title over the lands which were not exempted as reserves was based on past and potential future revenues from mining, which the government at the time regarded as virtually the sole economic value of the surrendered lands (see Kent McNeil, 'The High Cost of Accepting Benefits from the Crown: A Comment on the Temagami Indian Land Case,' [1992] 1 C.N.L.R. 40 at 66-7).

125 See Treaties 3 and 4 *(supra* note 123), both of which provide that the reserves of land, *'or any interest or right therein or appurtenant thereto,* may be sold, leased or otherwise disposed of by the said Government *for the use and benefit of the said Indians,* with the consent of the Indians *entitled thereto* first had and obtained' (my emphasis).

126 As Professor Brian Slattery has pointed out in his article, 'Understanding Aboriginal Rights' (1987) 66 Can. Bar Rev. 727 at 747, the Crown could never have intended to deny them that right:

> it would have been contrary to imperial interests in America to confine native land uses to those existing at the time of contact. The European fur trade, which was central to the development of Canada, depended on the activities of native hunters and trappers whose practices had changed considerably since pre-European times. When colonial officials, in other contexts, urged certain native groups to 'abandon their wandering ways' and to take up farming, they were not sanctioning an unlawful user of the land.

127 See Hugh Brody, *Maps and Dreams: Indians and the British Columbia Frontier* (Harmondsworth, UK: Penguin 1983), 21-30, 85-6, 247, relied on by Slattery, 'Understanding Aboriginal Rights,' *supra* note 126 at 747, on the same point.

128 He was addressing the plaintiffs' assertion 'that aboriginal rights must be permitted to evolve to maintain contemporary relevance to the needs of the holders as those needs change in accord with the changes in overall society' *(Delgamuukw* (B.C.C.A.), *supra* note 2 at 574).

129 Ibid., quoting the plaintiffs' argument.
130 Ibid., 575.
131 Ibid.
132 I regard this as a 'frozen rights' view of Aboriginal rights, despite Wallace J.'s purported rejection of that view in *Vanderpeet*, (B.C.C.A.), *supra* note 101 at 241-2. As he had done in *Delgamuukw*, in *Vanderpeet* he 'distinguished the evolution of an Aboriginal right from the modern manner of exercising a traditional right': ibid., 242. In his view, the right was not frozen, even though its nature and scope could not be altered by evolution after colonization, because the manner of exercising it could take a modern form. With respect, I think Wallace was simply trying to avoid the apparent inconsistency between his narrow approach to Aboriginal rights and the Supreme Court's rejection of the frozen rights approach in *Sparrow*, *supra* note 40 at 1093, where Dickson C.J. and La Forest J. said in reference to section 35(1) of the Constitution Act, 1982:
> ... the phrase 'existing aboriginal rights' must be interpreted flexibly so as to permit their evolution over time. To use Professor Slattery's expression, in 'Understanding Aboriginal Rights,' *supra* at 782, the word 'existing' suggests that those rights are 'affirmed in a contemporary form rather than in their primeval simplicity and vigour.' Clearly, then, an approach to the constitutional guarantee in s.35(1) which would incorporate 'frozen rights' must be rejected.

Instead of citing this general rejection of the frozen rights approach by the Supreme Court, Wallace quoted the following passage at page 1091 of the *Sparrow* judgment: 'Further, an existing aboriginal right cannot be read so as to incorporate the specific manner in which it was regulated before 1982. The notion of freezing existing rights would incorporate into the Constitution a crazy patchwork of regulations.' In my view, the latter passage illustrates one application of the more general rejection of the frozen rights approach in the former passage. Unlike Wallace, I do not think the Supreme Court meant to limit its rejection of that approach to the narrow context of the manner in which an Aboriginal right is exercised. (Compare the decision of the Supreme Court of Canada in *Van der Peet* (S.C.C.), *supra* note 101, which was handed down too recently to be discussed in this paper.)
133 *Delgamuukw* (B.C.C.A.), *supra* note 2 at 547.
134 On the power imbalance between Aboriginal peoples and governments in the negotiation of comprehensive land claims, see Andrea McCallum, 'Alternative Dispute Resolution in Aboriginal Land Claims,' LL.M. thesis, Osgoode Hall Law School, 1993.
135 The decision of the Supreme Court in *Calder*, *supra* note 1, in fact *brought* the federal government to the bargaining table, as for almost fifty years prior to that Canada had been unwilling to negotiate comprehensive land claims.
136 See Slattery, 'Understanding Aboriginal Rights,' *supra* note 126 at 745.
137 For further development of this approach, see McNeil, *Common Law Aboriginal Title*, *supra* note 16, where I argued that Aboriginal title amounts to a fee simple interest in land. But whether it is actually classified as a fee simple or described by some other term, the point is that it is equivalent to a fee simple in the sense that it encompasses rights to the entire use and benefit of the land.

Chapter 6: Wampum at Niagara: The Royal Proclamation, Canadian Legal History, and Self-Government

1 I would like to thank Joel Bakan, Nitya Iyer, Patrick Macklem, and Kent McNeil for their helpful comments. This article is a revised version of an essay that appeared in (1994) 28 U.B.C. L. Rev. 1.
2 R.S.C. 1985, App. II, No. 1 [hereinafter Royal Proclamation].
3 Hall J. in *Calder v. A.G. B.C.* (1973), 34 D.L.R. (3d) 145 (S.C.C.) at 203.
4 Most academic commentary on the Proclamation, despite extensive documentary research, remains largely silent on the question of whether the formation of the Proclamation included First Nations participation. See Jack Stagg, *Anglo-Indian Relations in North America to 1763 and an Analysis of the Royal Proclamation of 7 October 1763* (Ottawa: Research Branch, Indian and Northern Affairs 1981); Brian Slattery, *The Legal Status and*

Land Rights of Indigenous Canadian Peoples, as Affected by the Crown's Acquisition of the Territories (Saskatoon, SK: Native Law Centre 1979); Kent McNeil, *Common Law Aboriginal Title* (Oxford: Clarendon Press 1989); Geoffrey Lester, *The Territorial Rights of the Inuit of the Canadian North-West Territories: A Legal Argument* (LL.M. Thesis, York University 1984); Kenneth Narvey, 'The Royal Proclamation of 7 October 1763: The Common Law and Native Rights to Land Within the Territory Granted to the Hudson's Bay Company' (1974) 38 Sask. L. Rev. 123; William Pentney, 'The Rights of Aboriginal Peoples of Canada and the Constitution Act 1982: Part I, The Interpretive Prism of Section 25' (1988) 22 U.B.C. L. Rev. 207. Despite the thoroughness of these authors in uncovering colonial understandings relative to the Proclamation, First Nations' perspectives remain, for the most part, untouched.

5 'The Royal Proclamation of 1763 was entirely unilateral and was not, and cannot be described, as a treaty': *R. v. George* (1966), 55 D.L.R. (2d) 386 (S.C.C.). For a similar finding, see *R. v. Tennisco* (1982), 131 D.L.R. (3d) 96 (Ont. H.C.J.) at 104.

6 Native society has long been written about from a Western perspective ...

> These accounts have often portrayed us in a way that does not capture the active and transformative role that we have played when reacting to settler institutions. We were not passive objects of colonial policy, but were active agents and creators of our own history.

John Borrows, 'A Genealogy of Law: Inherent Sovereignty and First Nations Self-Government' (1992) 29 Osgoode Hall L.J. 291 at 297-98.

7 J.R. Miller, 'Owen Glendower, Hotspur and Canadian Indian Policy,' in J.R. Miller, ed., *Sweet Promises: A Reader on Indian-White Relations in Canada* (Toronto: University of Toronto Press 1991) at 323.

8 The power that First Nations wielded in this period is echoed in *R. v. Sioui* (1990), 70 D.L.R. (4th) 427 at 448 by Lamer J. of the Supreme Court of Canada: 'We can conclude from the historical documents that both Great Britain and France felt that the Indian nations had sufficient independence and played a large enough role in North America for it to be good policy to maintain relations with them very close to those maintained between sovereign nations.'

9 If the rights guaranteed by the Royal Proclamation (as described in this article) are found not to be extinguished, then one could argue that the rights therein are 'existing' rights protected by section 35(1) of the Constitution, and are not to be impinged upon by the Crown. Section 35 (1) states: 'The existing aboriginal and treaty rights of the aboriginal peoples of Canada are hereby recognized and affirmed.' Constitution Act, 1982, being Schedule B to the Canada Act 1982 (U.K.) 1982, c. 11, s. 35.

10 The conventional colonial interpretation of the Royal Proclamation is described in *R. v. Tennisco, supra* note 5 at 104-5, per Griffiths J.:

> The Provincial court judge found as a fact, however, that the Proclamation was communicated to, accepted by, and relied upon by the Algonquins after it was proclaimed. Counsel for the respondent submits that when the Royal Proclamation was communicated to the Algonquin Nation by the Crown's representative, Sir William Johnson, and the Algonquins thereinafter accepted the Proclamation by adhering to its terms and procedure, then such acceptance converted the Proclamation into a treaty ... In my view, the fact that the Indians accepted the Royal Proclamation in the sense that they complied with it and respected its Provisions, does not constitute the Proclamation a treaty. The Proclamation remained a unilateral act of the Crown, offering rights and protections dependent upon the goodwill of the Crown.

11 If the Royal Proclamation was 'reassessed in the light of contemporary concepts of equality of peoples, the need for interpreting the historical record would be substantially reduced but not eliminated. Ibid., 548. For a detailed discussion of how interpretations with their basis as the Equality of Peoples can make a difference in overcoming ethnocentric assumptions see Patrick Macklem, 'Distributing Sovereignty: Indian Nations and Equality of Peoples' (1993) 45 Stanford L. Rev. 1311.

12 Colonial interpretations of Canadian legal history are often formed through the 'enth-

nocentric bent' of Canada's institutions. For an example of this in the courts see Michael Asch and Catherine Bell, 'Definition and Interpretation of Fact in Canadian Aboriginal Title Litigation' (1993) 19 Queen's L.J. 503.

13 For one such contextualized treatment of the Proclamation see *Calder, supra* note 3 at 203 per Hall J.:

> The Proclamation was an Executive Order having the force and effect of an Act of Parliament and was described by Gwynne, J. in St. Catherine's Milling case at p. 652 as the 'Indian Bill of Rights': see also Campbell v. Hall. Its force as a statute is analogous to the status of Magna Carta which has always been considered to be the law throughout the Empire. It was a law which followed the flag as England assumed jurisdiction over newly-discovered or acquired lands or territories.

14 For a discussion of the importance of not applying one culture's standard to judge another see D. Bates and F. Plog, *Cultural Anthropology*, 3rd ed. (New York: McGraw-Hill 1990), see especially chapter 1.

15 For an introduction to the sophistication of oral literacy in First Nations, see Penny Petrone, *Native Literature in Canada: From the Oral Tradition to the Present* (Toronto: Oxford University Press 1990).

16 Hurons who lived in present-day Simcoe County, Ontario, in the 1600s had 'first direct contact ... in 1609, while a formal alliance was completed between them seven years later': Bruce G. Trigger, *The Children of Aataentsic: A History of the Huron People to 1660*, 2 vols. (Kingston/Montreal: McGill-Queen's University Press 1976).

17 For primary documentation of this period see Rueben Thwaites, *The Jesuit Relations and Allied Document*, 73 Vols. (New York: Pagent Books 1959). For a good overview of the French colonial relationship with First Nations see Cornelius Jaenen, *Friend and Foe: Aspects of French-Amerindian Cultural Contact in the Sixteenth and Seventeenth Centuries* (Toronto: McClelland and Stewart 1976).

18 For a good critical historical description of this period see Francis Jennings, *The Invasion of America: Indians, Colonialism, and the Cant of Conquest* (New York: W.W. Norton 1975), particularly chapters 5 and 6.

19 The description of the British efforts and alliance in this period has been described by Justice Lamer in *Sioui, supra* note 8 at 450: 'The British Crown recognized that the Indians had certain ownership rights over their land, it sought to establish trade with them which would rise above the level of exploitation and give them a fair return. It also *allowed them autonomy in their internal affairs*, intervening in this area as little as possible' (emphasis mine). For a general historical survey of First Nations alliances with the French and English in this period see Olive Patricia Dickason, *Canada's First Nations: A History of Founding Peoples from Earliest Times* (Toronto: McClelland and Stewart 1992), especially 'Part 2: The Outside World Intrudes.'

20 J.R. Miller, *Skyscrapers Hide the Heavens: A History of Indian-White Relations in Canada* (Toronto: University of Toronto Press 1989), 59-80. The Seven Years War was known in America as the French and Indian War and was known to First Nations as the Beaver War.

21 First Nations generally supported the French because they were territorially less intrusive than the British. The French primarily had only trade routes and forts in First Nation country. This was more palatable to First Nations than were the British encroachments because the British had large settlements on the eastern seaboard which displaced thousands of First Nation peoples from their lands. As Miller, ibid., 68, has confirmed: 'To many Indian nations the French were the merchants and soldiers who did not want to take possession of their lands, but merely trade for fruits of the forest; the British, though some of them were merchants, were also largely agricultural settlers who inexorably dispossessed the original inhabitants with their expanding farm settlements.'

22 William Johnson to the Lords of Trade, 8 October 1764 in E. B. O'Callaghan, ed., *Documents Relative to the Colonial History of the State of New York*, vol. 7 (Albany: Weed, Parsons and Co. 1856), 665 [hereafter Colonial History of New York].

23 Quoted in Wilbur R. Jacobs, *Wilderness Politics and Indian Gifts: The Northern Colonial Frontier, 1748-1763* (Lincoln: University of Nebraska Press 1966), 75.

24 Not all English people in North America in the 1760s misunderstood First Nation diplo-

macy. Colonial officials such as William Johnson and George Croghan understood that First Nations would not accept the cessation of presents. However, after the Beaver War, they were subordinates to General Jeffrey Amherst who did not appreciate the First Nations' power and sovereignty. Since Amherst set colonial policy, his notions temporarily determined the British response to First Nations' exigencies. See Richard White, *The Middle Ground: Indians, Empires and Republics in the Great Lakes Region, 1650-1815* (Cambridge: Cambridge University Press 1991), 256-68.

25 See Bruce M. White, 'A Skilled Game of Exchange: Ojibway Fur Trade Protocol' (1987) *Minnesota History* 229.

26 Pontiac's discontent was expressed as follows: 'And as for these English, – these dogs dressed in red, who have come to rob you of your hunting grounds, and drive away the game, – you must lift the hatchet and drive them away. Wipe them from the face of the earth, and thus you will win my favour back again, and once more be happy and prosperous. The children of your great father, the King of France, are not like the English.' Miller, *Skyscrapers Hide the Heavens*, 74.

27 'Although many historians would refer to the bloody and unsuccessful uprising as the Conspiracy of Pontiac, it was only another angry response by hunter-gatherers to the encroachments of farmers' (ibid.).

28 See, generally, Wilbur R. Jacobs, *Diplomacy and Indian Gifts: Anglo-French Rivalry Along the Ohio and Northwest Frontiers, 1748-1763* (Stanford: Stanford University Press 1950).

29 The Supreme Court of Canada recently recognized this fact in *Sioui, supra* note 8 at 488: 'The mother countries did everything in their power to secure the alliance of each Indian nation and to encourage nations allied with the enemy to change sides. When these efforts met with success, they were incorporated in treaties of alliance or neutrality. This clearly indicates that the Indian nations were regarded in their relations with the European nations which occupied North America as independent nations.'

30 James Sullivan, ed., *The Papers of William Johnson*, vol. 3 (Albany: New York University State Press 1921-1962), 457.

31 The power which First Nations could wield against the French and the English was one of the reasons the colonial powers did not interfere with the Indians. As Lamer J. stated in *Sioui, supra* note 8 at 450:

> One of the extracts from Knox's work which I cited above reports that the Canadians and the French soldiers who surrendered asked to be protected from Indians on the way back to their parishes. Another passage from Knox ... relates that the Canadians were terrified at the idea of seeing Sir William Johnson's Indians coming among them. This proves that in the minds of the local population the Indians represented a real and disturbing threat. The fact that England was also aware of the danger the colonies and their inhabitants might run if the Indians withdrew their cooperation is echoed in the following documents.

32 Royal Proclamation, *supra* note 2.

33 In particular, a company called the Ohio Company had been formed to profit from the speculation on over half a million acres in the Ohio valley. See Miller, *Skyscrapers Hide the Heavens*, 69. See also Brian Slattery, 'The Hidden Constitution: Aboriginal Land Rights in Canada' (1984) 32 American J. Comp. L. 361 at 369 [hereinafter 'The Hidden Constitution'].

34 Peter Schmalz, *The History of the Saugeen Indians* (Ottawa: Ontario Historical Society 1977), 15-16.

35 See John Borrows, *A Genealogy of Law: Inherent Sovereignty and First Nations Self-Government* (LL.M. Thesis, University of Toronto 1991 [unpublished]), 42-82.

36 For descriptions of war and conflict between First Nations and settlers in North America, see, generally, R.A. Goldstein, *French-Iroquois Diplomatic and Military Relations, 1609-1701* (The Hague: Mouton 1969); F.W. Rowe, *Extinction: The Beothucks of Newfoundland* (Toronto: McGraw-Hill Ryerson 1977); S.F. Wise, 'The American Revolution and Indian History,' in J.S. Moir, ed., *Character and Circumstance: Essays in Honour of Donald Grant Creighton* (Toronto: Macmillan 1970); Robert Allen Wooster, *The Military and the United States Indian Policy, 1865-1903* (New Haven: Yale University Press 1988).

37 See, generally, Bruce Clark, Native Liberty, *Crown Sovereignty: The Existing Right of Aboriginal Self-Government in Canada* (Montreal/Kingston: McGill-Queen's University Press 1991). See also Richard White, *The Middle Ground*, 223-365 (*supra* note 24).

38 Chief Pontiac stated to other First Nation peoples in a formal council-of-war on 23 May 1763: 'My brothers! I begin to grow tired of this bad meat which is upon our lands. I begin to see that this is not your case, for instead of assisting us in our war with the English, you are actually assisting them. I have already told you, and I now tell you again, that when I undertook this war, it was only your interest that I sought, that I knew what I am about. This year they [the English] must all perish.' Quoted in Penny Petrone, *First Peoples, First Voices* (Toronto: University of Toronto Press 1983), 29.

39 The Royal Proclamation followed an earlier proclamation of 1761 that recognized First Nations as allies holding both 'possessions' and 'rights' which were to be supported and protected by the British. The Proclamation of 1761 states:

> Whereas the peace and security of Our Colonies and Plantations upon the Continent of North America does greatly depend upon the Amity and Alliance of the several Nations or Tribes of Indians bordering upon said Colonies ... We therefore taking this matter into Our Royal Consideration, as also the fatal Effects which would attend a discontent amongst the Indians in the present situation of affairs, and being determined upon all occasions to support and protect the said Indians in their just Rights and Possessions and to keep inviolable the Treaties and Compacts which have been entered into with them, Do hereby strictly enjoin and command that neither yourself nor any Lieutenant Governor ... pass any Grant or Grants to any persons whatever of any lands within or adjacent to the Territories possessed or occupied by the said Indians or the Property Possession of which has at any time been reserved to or claimed by them.

Quoted in Peter A. Cumming and Neil H. Mickenberg, *Native Rights in Canada*, 2nd ed. (Toronto: Indian-Eskimo Association/General Publishing 1972), 285.

40 The principle of First Nation consent being recognized by the British in this period is found in a letter from the Secretary of State, Lord Egremont, to George III, 5 May, 1763:

> Tho' ... it may become necessary to erect some forts in the Indian Country, with their CONSENT yet his Majesty's Justice and Moderation inclines Him to adopt the more eligible Method of conciliating the Minds of the Indians by the Mildness of his Government, by protecting their Persons and Property and securing to them all the Possessions, Rights and Privileges they have hitherto enjoyed, and are entitled to, most cautiously guarding against any Invasion or Occupation of their Hunting Lands, the Possession of which is to be acquired by fair Purchase only.

Adam Shortt & Arthur G. Doughty, eds., *Documents Relating to the Constitutional History of Canada 1759-1791* (Ottawa: Public Archives of Canada 1918), 128-9.

41 An illustration of the level of hostility, and the desire on the part of both parties to remove enmity between them, is found in the following anecdote, recorded by an nineteenth-century Ojibwa writer:

> For two years after the ending of Pontiac's war, the fear of Indian hostility was still so great that the British traders dared not extend their operations to the more remote villages of the Ojibways, and La Pointe, during this time, was destitute of a resident trader. To remedy this great evil, which the Indians, having become accustomed to the commodities of the whites, felt acutely, Ma-mong-e-sa-da, the war chief of this village, with a party of his fellows, was deputed to go to Sir Wm. Johnson, to ask that a trader might be sent to reside among them. He is said to have been well received by their British father, who presented him with a broad wampum belt of peace, and gorget. The belt was composed of white and blue beads, denoting purity and the clear blue sky, and this act settled the foundation of a lasting good-will, and was the commencement of an active communication between the British and the Ojibways of Lake Superior.

Quoted in William W. Warren, *History of the Ojibway Indians* (St. Paul, MN: Minnesota Historical Society 1885) reprinted (Minneapolis, MN: Ross & Haines 1957), 218-19.

42 Slattery, 'The Hidden Constitution,' 369 (*supra* note 33).

43 Ibid.

44 The principles of the Proclamation reproduced the official protocol demanded by First Nations in diplomatic relations with colonial officials. In the words of Francis Jennings, 'treaty protocol was of Indian manufacture' (*The Invasion of America, supra* note 18, 123). For a further description of First Nation requirements in early North American diplomacy, see, generally, Francis Jennings et al., eds., *The History and Culture of Iroquois Diplomacy* (Syracuse, NY: Syracuse University Press 1985).

45 Slattery, 'The Hidden Constitution' (*supra* note 33).

46 Royal Proclamation, *supra* note 2: 'But that, if at any time Any of the said Indian lands reserved to the said Indians should be inclined to dispose of the said Lands, the same shall be purchased solely for Us, solely in our Name, at some public Meeting or Assembly of said Indians.'

47 Ibid.

48 That such provisions were intended to take the lands reserved to Indians out of British civil governmental jurisdiction is evidenced in a letter from the Lords of Trade to Sir William Johnson, the Northern Superintendent of Indian Affairs, 11 July 1766: 'The subject matter of the several letters we have received from you has reference to the whole state of that Interior Part of His Majesty's Dominions in America which is by the Royal Proclamation of October 7, 1763, precluded from settlement and taken out of the jurisdiction of the civil Governments.' Quoted in Kenneth M. Narvey, 'The Royal Proclamation,' 135 (*supra* note 4).

49 Royal Proclamation, *supra* note 2:
 And we do further expressly enjoin and require all Officers whatever, as well Military as Those employed in the Management and Direction of Indian Affairs within the Territories reserved as aforesaid for the Use of said Indians, to seize and apprehend all Persons whatever, who, standing charged with Treasons, Misprisons or Treason, Murders, or other Felonies and Misdemeanors, shall fly from Justice and take Refuge in said territory, and to send them under a proper Guard to the Colony where the Crime was committed of which they stand accused, in order to take Trial for the same.

50 Ibid.

51 When the Proclamation was enacted, the Lords of Trade in England decided that 'no particular form of Civil Government' would be established in the areas that were reserved for Indians (Lords of Trade to the King, 8 June 1763, quoted in Narvey, 'The Royal Proclamation,' 134 (*supra* note 4)). While the Proclamation purported to reserve these lands under English sovereignty, the fact that civil government was not imposed coincided with First Nations' perceptions that they were to continue to be self-governing with respect to activities of hunting, fishing, etc., on the lands reserved to them.

52 The doctrines of the common law that allow contrast and difference to be respected talk about interpreting evidence in a manner which is sensitive to a First Nations perspective. Such doctrines declare that 'Indian treaties should be given a fair, large and liberal construction in favour of the Indians ... [and] doubtful expressions resolved in the favour of the Indians ... [Moreover] treaties should construed not according to the technical meaning of their words, but in the sense they would naturally be understood by the Indians.' *Simon v. The Queen* (1985), 24 D.L.R. (4th) 390 at 435. See also *Jones v. Meehan* (1899), 175 U.S. 1 at 10-11; *Nowegijick v. The Queen* (1983), 144 D.L.R. (3d) 193 at 198; *Sioui, supra* note 7, 453. These cases suggest that events involving First Nations should be interpreted in a generous way to preserve their understanding of the incident. If there is doubt about which parties' perspective should prevail in the event of contrasting interpretations, the recognition of the power imbalance in the parties' relationship suggests that doubtful expressions should be resolved in favour of the Indians.

53 Donald Braider, *The Niagara* (New York: Holt, Rinehart and Winston 1972) at 137.

54 O'Callaghan, *Colonial History of New York*, 648 (*supra* note 22).

55 See Paul Williams, *The Chain* (LL.M. Thesis, York University [unpublished] 1982) for a description of the Covenant Chain of Friendship.

56 Francis Jennings, 'Iroquois Alliance in American History,' in Francis Jennings et al., *The History and Culture of Iroquois Diplomacy*, 37-9 (*supra* note 44).

57 One can read about the colonial government's reasons for entering into the treaty from

the pen of the British leader who represented the Crown. British motivation sprang from the need to secure an alliance of friendship because of the power advantage First Nations possessed. Sir William Johnson stated:

> They [the Indians] apprehend that we design to enslave them ... if we conquer their prejudices by our generosity they will lay aside their Jealousy's, & we may rest in security. This is much cheaper than any other plan, and more certain of success. Our extensive Frontier renders it necessary if we will provide for their security ... [in the last campaign] they saw themselves able to effect what was looked upon by many of our Prejudiced politicians here as utterly impossible ... The Indians all know we cannot be a Match for them in the midst of an extended woody Country.

Quoted in O'Callaghan, *Colonial History of New York*, 649 (*supra* note 22). First Nations expressed a similar fear of war with the English. See Alexander Henry, *Travels and Adventures in Canada and the Indian Territories between the years 1760-1776* (Toronto: Morang 1901) at 157-70.

58 O'Callaghan, *Colonial History of New York*, 648.

59 For example, one of the remembered promises the British made to First Nations which did not find its way into the Proclamation is stated by Andrew J. Blackbird, *History of the Ottawa and Chippewa Indians of Michigan* (Ypsilanti, MI: Ypsilanti Job Printing House 1887), 8:

> That was the time the British government made such extraordinary promises to the Ottawa tribe of Indians, at the same time thanking them for their humane action upon those remnants of the massacre. She promised them that her long arms will perpetually extend around them from generation to generation, or as long as there should be rolling sun. They should receive gifts from her sovereign in the shape of goods, provisions, firearms, ammunition, and intoxicating liquors! Her sovereign's beneficent arm should even be extended unto the dogs belonging to the Ottawa tribe of Indians ... and when you get up in the morning, look to the east, you will see that the sun, as it will peep through the earth, will be as red as my coat, to remind you why I am likened unto the sun, and my promises will be as perpetual as the rolling sun.

60 General Gage wrote to the Earl of Halifax on 13 April 1764 regarding the anticipated treaty of Niagara:

> After concerting with Sir Wm. Johnson the proper measures to be taken in order to conclude a peace with the Indians of that district, I have wrote [sic] to Major Gladwin, that if he finds them sincerely disposed to peace, in the spring, he would give notice to the Chiefs of the several Nations to repair to Niagara by the end of June, where Sir Wm. Johnson would meet them in order to complete the work of peace according to their own forms and ceremonies.

Quoted in O'Callaghan, *Colonial History of New York*, 78.

61 First Nations had stated to colonial officials: 'Know that our words are of no weight unless accompanied by wampum' (ibid., vol. 9, 604).

62 Williams, *The Chain*, 76.

63 Public Archives of Canada (PAC), Sulpician Documents, M. 1644, No. 70.

64 C. Flick, ed., *The Papers of Sir William Johnson*, vol. 4 (Albany, NY: The University of the State of New York 1925), 328.

65 Ibid., 329.

66 Braider, *The Niagara*, 137.

67 William G. Godfrey, *Pursuit of Profit and Preferment in Colonial North America: John Bradstreet's Quest* (Waterloo: Wilfrid Laurier University Press 1982), 197.

68 Representatives of the following Nations were in attendance: Western Confederacy – Algonquins, Chippewas, Crees, Foxes, Hurons, Menominees, Nipissings, Odawas, Sacs, Toughkamiwons, and Winnebagoes; Iroquois Confederacy – Cannesandagas, Caughnawagas, Cayugas, Conoys, Mohawks, Mohicans, Nanticokes, Oniedas, Onondagas, and Senecas: Flick, *The Papers of Sir William Johnson*, vol. 2, 278-281, 481, 511-514. It is also believed that representatives of the Lakota, MicMac and Pawnee Confederacies were in attendance.

69 Williams, *The Chain*, 79.

70 Ibid.

71 Henry, *Travels and Adventures*, 157-174 (*supra* note 57).

72 In attendance at the treaty, among many others, were 'deputys from almost every nation to the Westward viz Hurons, Ottawaes, Chippawaes, Meynomineys or Folles avoins, Foxes, Sakis, Puans, etc. with some from the north side of Lake Superior and the neighbourhood of Hudson's Bay.' The Delawares and Shawnees were not in attendance at the treaty (O'Callaghan, *Colonial History of New York*, 648).

73 G. Johnson to T. Faye, 16 March 1764, quoted in Flick, *The Papers of Sir William Johnson*, 487.

74 Warren, an Ojibwa writer, records that 'twenty-two different tribes were represented' at the council at Niagara (*History of the Ojibway Indians*, 219).

75 Braider, *The Niagara*, 137.

76 Williams, *The Chain*, 82, records: 'The expenditures for the provisions and presents at Niagara were enormous for that day and age.' Johnson's papers list:

Expense of provisions for Indians only ... £25,000 New York Currency.

Besides the Presents ... £38,000 Sterling.

77 Flick, *The Papers of Sir William Johnson*, 309-10.

78 Public Archives of Canada, Record Group 10 (PAC, RG 10), vol. 391, Head to Glenelg, 20 August 1836 (see references to Assikinack's speech). See also J.B Assikinack, 'Memories of the Covenant Chain,' PAC, RG 10, vol. 613 21/10/1851, 440-443.

79 F.W. Major, *Manitoulin: Isle of the Ottawas* (Gore Bay: Recorder Press 1974), 11-15 ('An Indian Council').

80 Robert A. Williams, Jr., 'The Algebra of Federal Indian Law: The Hard Trail of Decolonizing and Americanizing the White Man's Indian Jurisprudence' (1986) Wisconsin L. Rev. 219 at 291.

81 Williams, *The Chain*, 83, quoting Sir William Johnson.

82 The Proclamation contains principles that do not find place in the two-row wampum. An example of a principle which finds place in the Proclamation which does not find reference in the two-row wampum is 'the several ... Tribes of Indians ... who live under our Protection' (Royal Proclamation, *supra* note 2).

83 The 1790s contain an example that confirms the parties' subsequent understanding of the Proclamation, despite the continuing double-talk over who had ultimate sovereignty over the land. Guy Carleton, governor general of Upper and Lower Canada and commanding chief of the Crown's North American forces, told the First Nations in 1791:

The King's rights with respect to your territory were against the nations of Europe; these he resigned to the States. But the King never had any rights against you but to such parts of the country as had been fairly ceded by yourselves with your own free consent by public convention and sale. How then can it be said that he gave away your lands?

So careful was the King of your interests, so fully sensible of your rights, that he would not suffer even his own people to buy your lands, without being sure of your free consent, and of ample justice being done you.

Guy Carleton, 1791, *Simcoe Papers, Letterbook 17, 1791*, Ontario Archives, quoted in Clark, *Native Liberty, Crown Sovereignty*, 80.

84 Ibid.

85 Plans were initiated to forcibly remove all Aboriginal peoples to the west of the Mississippi River: see Francis Paul Prucha, *American Indian Policy in the Formative Years* (Lincoln: University of Nebraska Press 1970), 226-9 and 242-8. Removal was threatened not only because of a desire for land for settlement but also because First Nations had fought against the United States. One historian has noted: 'The Americans had no love for the Indians of this region, who had supported the British in the recent conflict. They made no secret of their feelings, promising future confiscation of lands held by these tribes' (J.R. Wrightman, *Forever on the Fringe: Six Studies in the Development of Manitoulin Island* [Toronto: University of Toronto Press 1982], 10). See also 'Tenure of Land,' *Journal of the Legislative Assembly of the Province of Canada* 1847, App. T. No. 95.

86   Robert Surtees, *Indian Land Cessions in Ontario, 1763-1862: The Evolution of a System* (Ph.D. Thesis, Carleton University 1983 [unpublished]), 87.

87   Anna Brownell Jameson, *Winter Studies and Summer Rambles in Canada* (Toronto: McLelland and Stewart 1965), 147-54.

88   Major, *Manitoulin*, 17-18. Testimony of these people is recorded in A.C. Osborne, 'The Migrations of Voyageurs from Drummond Island to Penetangiushene in 1828' (1901) 3 *Ontario Historical Association*, 123-66.

89   Capt. Thomas G. Anderson, 'Report on the Affairs of the Indians of Canada, Section III' Appendix No. 95 in App. T of the *Journals of the Legislative Assembly of Canada*, vol. 6 (1818).

90   The reinterpretation of the fiduciary responsibility on the part of the Crown may shift from being based in the exercise of the Crown's discretion on First Nations' behalf (*Guerin v. The Queen* (1985), 13 D.L.R. (4th) 321 (S.C.C.)) to being the result of promises made when the relationship between the parties was established. This is a healthier basis for the relationship because it does not convey a hierarchical confederation of unequal powers but a parallel alliance of mutual support between nations.

91   Colborne to Glenleg, 22 January 1836, PAC, RG 10, vol. 389.

92   For a detailed study of this treaty, see John Borrows, 'Negotiating Treaties and Land Claims: The Impact of Diversity Within First Nations Property Interests' (1993) 12 *Windsor Yearbook on Access to Justice* 179.

93   Bond Head said of First Nations' use of wampum:
     > The most solemn form in which the Indian pledges his word is by the delivery of a wampum belt of shells, and when the purport of the symbol is declared, it is remembered and handed down from Father to Son with an accuracy and retention of meaning which is quite extraordinary ...
     >   The wampum thus given [at Niagara] has thus been preserved, and are [sic] now entrusted to the great orator Sigonat, who was present at the Council I attended on the Manitoulin Island in Lake Huron, and in every sense these Hieroglyphics are moral affidavits of the by-gone transactions to which they relate. On our part, little or nothing documentary exists.

     Correspondence Respecting Indians Between the Provincial Secretary of State and the Governors of British North America (London: Queen's Printer 1837), 128.

94   Williams, *The Chain*, 87.

95   Canada, *Indian Treaties and Surrenders, from 1680-1890* (Ottawa: Printer to the Queen's Most Excellent Majesty 1891-1912 [Toronto: Coles 1971]), 112.

96   For example, Thomas G. Anderson, superintendent of the Indian Department at Island in 1945, records what he had been told about the wampum belts and the Treaty at Niagara:
     > The Indians have no record of past events; all they know of the original engagements between the Government and themselves, as far as I am acquainted, is by tradition, except for two memoranda (wampum) which they hold; the one being a pledge of perpetual friendship between the N.A. Indians, and the British Nations, and was delivered to the Tribes as a Council convened for the purpose, by Sir William Johnson, at Niagara in 1764 ... on the other wampum belt is marked at one end a hieroglyphic denoting Quebec on this continent, on the other, is a ship with its bow towards Quebec; betwixt those two objects are wove 24 Indians, one holding the cable of the vessel with the left hand; one holding the cable of the vessel with his right, and so on, until the figure on the extreme left rests his foot on the land at Quebec. Their traditional account of this is, that at the time that it was delivered to them (1764) Sir William promised, in the name of the Government, that those Tribes should continue to receive presents so long as the Sun would shine ... and if ever the ship came across the Great salt lake without a full cargo, these tribes should pull lustily at the cable until they brought her over full of presents.

     Indian Department, *Report of Indian Affairs* (1845), 269.

97   An example of a First Nation person revealing this perspective in the 1840s comes from an Algonquin chief residing south of the Ottawa River: 'Our father, Sir William Johnson,

gave our ancestors a writing on parchment, we still hold. This document tells us that we shall never be destroyed on our hunting grounds ... that we could not make away with these to strangers.' Chief Greg Sazarin, '220 Years of Broken Promises,' in Boyce Richardson, ed., *Drumbeat: Anger and Renewal in Indian Country* (Toronto: Summerhill Press 1989), 182.

98 Thomas G. Anderson, Report of Indian Affairs (1845).

99 Ibid.

100 One must be careful not to interpret the Proclamation's references as only applying to the protection of hunting grounds and land. While these statements do reflect First Nations' concern for the protection of their subsistence economy on their land, it must be remembered that land and jurisdiction over land were inseparable. The right to hunt necessarily includes the right to self-government. As the Supreme Court of Canada stated in *Simon v. The Queen, supra* note 52, 406: 'It should be clarified at this point that the right to hunt, to be effective must embody those activities reasonably incidental to the act of hunting itself.' When one understands the nature of hunting in an Aboriginal community, one realizes that decision-making and government are 'reasonably incidental' and essential to the use and protection of this resource. See Hugh Brody, *Maps and Dreams: Indians and the British Columbia Frontier* (Vancouver: Douglas and McIntyre 1981), 34-71.

101 *R. v. McMaster (Lady)*, [1926] Ex.C.R., 4 C.N.L.C. 359; *Campbell v. Hall* (1774), 1 Cowp. 204.

102 Bruce Clark, Native Liberty, *Crown Sovereignty*, 86.

103 *Calder, supra* note 3, 208.

104 Bob Freedman, 'The Space for Aboriginal Self-Government in British Columbia: The Effect of the Decision of British Columbia Court of Appeal in Delgamuukw' (1994) 28 U.B.C. L. Rev. 49 at 70-3; Joseph Singer, 'Well Settled? The Increasing Weight of History in American Land Claims' (1994) 28 Georgia L. Rev.; John Lowndes, 'Aboriginal Title: Extinguishment by the Increasing Weight of History' (1994) 42 Buffalo L. Rev.; Kent McNeil, 'The High Cost of Accepting Benefits From the Crown: A Comment on the Temagami Indian Land Case,' [1992] 1 C.N.L.R. 14.

105 *George and Tennisco, supra* note 5.

106 Since the Treaty of Niagara was written by colonial officials according to the 'modes and forms of creating the various technical estates known to their law, and assisted by an interpreter employed by themselves ... the treaty must be construed, not according to technical meaning of its words to learned lawyers, but in the sense in which they would naturally be understood by the Indians.' See *Jones, supra* note 52, followed in *Sioui, supra* note 8, 453.

107 Flick, *The Papers of Sir William Johnson*.

108 Ibid.

109 The references in brackets in this sentence are from the wording of the Royal Proclamation, *supra* note 2.

110 Ibid.

111 Ibid.

112 Compare speech of Orcarta, quoted in Cptn. Anderson, '*Report on the Affairs of the Indians, supra* note 89, and recollection of Anderson, Report of Indian Affairs, *supra* note 96.

113 Flick, *The Papers of Sir William Johnson*; two-row wampum in Williams, *The Chain*.

114 Chief Justice Dickson's reasoning regarding the Proclamation failed to scrutinize the questionable supposition that the British presence in Canada undermined First Nation land use and sovereignty. Dickson wrote: 'It is worth recalling that while British policy towards the native population was based on respect for their right to occupy their traditional lands, a proposition to which the Royal Proclamation of 1763 bears witness, there was from the outset never any doubt that sovereignty and legislative power, and indeed the underlying title to such lands vested in the Crown.' *R. v. Sparrow* (1990), 70 D.L.R. (4th) 385 (S.C.C.) at 404.

115 For additional evidence from legal history on this point, see Hamar Foster, 'Forgotten Arguments: Aboriginal Title and Sovereignty in Canada Jurisdiction Act Cases' (1992) 21 Man. L.J. 343. Jurisprudential evidence of this point is found in Brian Slattery, 'Aboriginal

Sovereignty and Imperial Claims' (1991) 29 Osgoode Hall L.J. 681.
116 *Supra* note 3.
117 See Canada, Indian Treaties and Surrenders, 3 vols. (Toronto: Coles 1971).
118 For example, the Supreme Court of Canada has recognized that the procedures to be followed in First Nations land surrender have their origins in the Royal Proclamation, see *St. Ann's Island Shooting & Fishing Club Ltd. v. R.*, [1950] S.C.R. 211 [Exch.].
119 Literally translated, it means 'of its own kind or class.' *Black's Law Dictionary*, 5th ed. (St. Paul, MN: West Publishing Company 1979), 1286.
120 Peter Hutchins, 'International Law and Domestic Aboriginal Litigation,' in *Aboriginal Rights and International Law: Proceedings of the 1993 Conference of the Canadian Council on International Law* (Ottawa: Canadian Council on International Law 1993), 11.
121 See Sebastien Grammond, 'Aboriginal Treaties and Canadian Law' (1994) 20 Queen's L.J. 57 at 60.
122 M.P. Furmston, ed., *Cheshire, Fifott and Furmston's Law of Contract* (London: Butterworth's 1986), 116-17.
123 A lone note of caution in proceeding with extrinsic evidence in treaty interpretation is expressed in *Sioui, supra* note 8:

> As this court has recently noted in R. v. Horse (1988), 39 C.C.C. (3d) 97 at 108, extrinsic evidence is not to be used as an aid to interpreting a treaty in the absence of ambiguity or where the result would be to alter its terms by adding words to or subtracting words from the written agreement ... However, a more flexible approach is necessary as the question of the existence of a treaty within the meaning of s. 88 of the Indian Act is generally bound up with the circumstances existing when the document was prepared.
>
> The impact of the call for the restricted use of extrinsic evidence may be reduced by the approach in the *Sioui* case itself. Lamer J., despite the restrictive finding of *Horse*, was generally willing to find ambiguity in the treaty in dispute which allowed him to examine extrinsic evidence.

124 There is an argument about whether British Columbia is included in this agreement, though the First Nations were not personally represented at the Treaty of Niagara. 1) The terms of the Proclamation are prospective and declaratory; the Proclamation/Treaty was regarded as a line of policy meant to follow the flag of England and would therefore apply to British Columbia when the Crown met with First Nations there: *Calder, supra* note 3, 205. 2) The words of the Proclamation show that the framers were well aware that there was territory to the west of the sources of the rivers which ran from the west and northwest: ibid. Therefore, the Proclamation/Treaty covered British Columbia First Nations at the 1764 agreement. 3) When the First Nations of British Columbia heard of the Proclamation, they acceded to it and agreed to abide by its terms. See the expression of British Columbia First Nations in the British Columbia Commission Appointed to Enquire into the Conditions of Indians of the North-West Coast, *Papers Relating to the Commission* (Victoria: Government Printer 1888). Many of the expressions of First Nations leaders were for a treaty process similar to that started under the procedures of the Royal Proclamation.
125 Most treaty negotiations in Canadian history have reference to these terms in their oral documentation, though these promises often do not find their way into the text.
126 David Elliot, 'Aboriginal Title,' in Bradford Morse, ed., *Aboriginal Peoples and the Law: Indian, Metis and Inuit Rights in Canada* (Ottawa: Carleton University Press 1989), 56.
127 The Supreme Court of Canada sought to reduce some of the inconsistencies between First Nations rights in different areas in the *Sparrow* case, *supra* note 114 at 396-7. The court's concern with harmonizing rights between First Nations could be applied with similar reasons in this area of the law.
128 This would overcome Dickson J.'s concern expressed in *Kruger v. R.* (1978), 75 D.L.R. (3d) 434 at 437 (S.C.C.): 'Claims to Aboriginal title are woven with history, legend, politics and moral obligations. If the claim of any Band in respect of any particular land is to be decided as a justiciable issue and not a political issue, it should be so concluded on the facts pertinent to that Band and to that land, and not on any global basis.' The evidence

presented in this paper suggests that the resolution of justiciable issues related to treaties should involve both the particular history of the local band and the Crown, as well as the global nature of the promises agreed to at Niagara.

Chapter 7: Understanding Treaty 6: An Indigenous Perspective

1 This essay was written with the permission of the Elders who were kind enough to share their knowledge and time with the author over a period of years. There is still much to be learned from the Elders. The information in this essay is only a portion of the knowledge of the Elders on this issue. Days have passed as the Elders spoke about matters related to the treaty. This essay merely exposes the 'box': we see the box, we know its size and shape, and now we must learn its contents. A glimpse has been provided. Learning is an individual obligation but a collective responsibility.

2 In this document, I am using the term 'Indigenous peoples' as it best describes the relationship of the people to the lands. Indigenous peoples came from these lands. The Elders say that the Creator placed Indigenous peoples on Great Turtle Island. Indigenous peoples did not travel from any place to get to these territories. Increasingly, at the international level, the acceptable term is Indigenous rather than Native, Aboriginal, Indian, or savage.

3 See H. Elizabeth Dallam, who argues in her article, 'The Growing Voice of Indigenous peoples: Their Use of Storytelling and Rights Discourse to Transform Multilateral Development Bank Policies' (1991) 8 Ariz. J. Int'l. & Comp. L. 117, that the use of narrative discourse is a powerful tool for transforming legal thinking: 'The very telling of stories is an expression of power' (121).

4 Elder Charles Blackman, Cold Lake Reserve, Treaty 6 territory. Interviewed 14 May 1974. Mr. Blackman is now in his eighties and alive at the time of this writing. He is a well-known Elder within Treaty 6 territory.

5 Elder Alexander Mechewais, Cold Lake Reserve, Treaty 6 territory. Interviewed 18 February 1974. These interviews were obtained from the office of Specific Claims and Research, Winterburn, Alberta.

6 Norma Sluman, *Poundmaker* (Toronto: Ryerson Press 1967), 14.

7 Elder Henry Gadwa, Long Lake Reserve, Treaty 6 territory. Interviewed 1989.

8 Joseph F. Dion, *My Tribe the Crees* (Calgary: Glenbow-Alberta Institute 1979), 8.

9 Elder Fineday quoted in David G. Mandelbaum, *The Plains Cree: An Ethnographic, Historical and Comparative Study* (Regina: University of Regina, Canadian Plains Research Centre 1979), 106.

10 *Black's Law Dictionary*, 5th ed. (St. Paul, MN: West Publishing Company 1979), defines 'democracy' as that form of government in which the sovereign power resides in, and is exercised by, the whole body of free citizens directly or indirectly through a system of representation, as distinguished from a monarchy, aristocracy, or oligarchy.

11 The Cree adjective which has been translated into English as 'bravest' cannot be exactly translated, although 'bravest' best approximates the Cree meaning.

12 Under the customary law of the Cree, each family within the community selects their own spokesperson, known as a Headman. Decisions are transmitted from the family to the community via the Headman. At the council meetings, the Headman speaks for the family, but only on the areas about which decisions have already been made. If a Headman needs to consult the family, he communicates that to the meeting. After meetings, a Headman reports to the family as to results of the meeting. The advent of the Indian Act, which stated that there can be only one councillor per one hundred people, played havoc with the traditional system. Families were forced by circumstance to join together for the purposes of representation. This was not always productive.

13 Mandelbaum, *The Plains Cree*, 113-15 n. 8.

14 Norma Sluman and Jean Goodwill, *John B. Tootoosis* (Winnipeg: Pemmican 1984), 49 n. 5.

15 Mandelbaum, *The Plains Cree*, 108 n. 9.

16 Gordon Bennett, *Aboriginal Rights in International Law* (London: Royal Anthropological Institute of Great Britain and Ireland 1978), 5.

17 The British Crown issued the Royal Proclamation of 1763 to set out the obligations of the

British Crown vis-à-vis Indigenous peoples, and the process of gaining access to their lands, which required the fully informed consent of Indigenous peoples. 'As reflected in the Proclamation of 1763, this imperial discourse accepted the necessity of peaceful purchase of frontier Indian lands under strict imperial supervision in order to avoid costly, needless wars. Despite this programmatic approach to Indian Affairs, imperial policy ultimately rested on the ancient legitimating formulation of the superior rights of Christian Europeans in lands held by the normatively divergent, non-Christian peoples': Robert A. Williams, Jr., *The American Indian in Western Legal Thought: The Discourses of Conquest* (Oxford: Oxford University Press 1990), 229.

18 The Proclamation says in part:

> And whereas it is just and reasonable, and essential to our Interest, and the Security of our Colonies, that the several Nations or Tribes of Indians with whom We are connected, and who live under our Protection, should not be molested or disturbed in the Possession of such Parts of Our Dominions and Territories as, not having been ceded to or purchased by Us, are reserved to them, or any of them, as their Hunting Grounds; We do therefore, with the Advice of our Privy Council, declare it to be our Royal Will and Pleasure, that no Governor or Commander in Chief in any of our Colonies of Quebec, East Florida, or West Florida, do presume, upon any Pretence whatever, to grant Warrants of Survey, or pass any Patents for Lands beyond the Bounds of their respective Governments, as described in their Commissions.

19 Mark F. Lindley, *The Acquisition and Government of Backward Territory in International Law: Being a Treatise on the Law and Practice Relating to Colonial Expansion* (New York: Negro Universities Press 1926), 307.

20 Joseph Story, *Commentaries on the Constitution of the United States with a Preliminary Review of the Constitutional History of the Colonies and States Before the Adoption of Constitution*, vol. 1 (New York: Da Capo Press 1833, reprint 1970), 6.

21 M.F. Lindley, *The Acquisition and Government of Backward Territory in International Law: Being a Treatise on the Law and Practice Relating to Colonial Expansion* (New York: Negro Universities Press 1926, reprint 1969), 26-7.

22 International Court of Justice, *Western Sahara: Advisory Opinion of 16 October 1975* (The Hague, Netherlands: ICJ Reports 1975), 6.

23 Ibid., 39.

24 The word for 'the Cree People' has been loosely translated to the term 'Indian.' The Cree word used translates literally to 'people.' In this document, I am using the term 'Indigenous peoples,' as it better describes the peoples' relationship to this territory. But in these interviews, undertaken over twenty years ago, the translation from Cree to English was 'Indian.' The texts of the interviews have not been changed, hence the article moves between the terms 'Indigenous' and the translator's original 'Indian.'

25 Elder Fred Horse, Frog Lake Reserve, Treaty 6 territory. Notes of an interview done with Rick Lightning. The interview took place in 1973 when Fred Horse was sixty-four years old. The old man passed to the spirit world in the spring of 1989 at the age of eighty. At many meetings held on the treaty, Elder Fred Horse would often bring the Union Jack – a gift given by the treaty commissioner at the time of the treaty signing.

26 The 'big pipe' that Elder Fred Horse refers to is the original pipe used at the treaty signing. This pipe has been carefully kept and handed down to different keepers over the years since the treaty signing in 1876. With this pipe the stories of the signing are also handed down. The pipe is kept by a citizen of the Frog Lake Reserve within the Treaty 6 territory. There are special ceremonies attached to the keeping of the pipe and its use.

27 Elder Toussait Dion, Frog Lake Reserve, Treaty 6 territory. He was interviewed in 1974 at the age of seventy-five years. The record of his interview is in the office of Treaty and Aboriginal Rights, Winterburn, Alberta. He was born on 11 August 1899 and would have grown up listening to the Elders who were present at the treaty signing in 1876. He clearly states who gave him the information about the treaty (his uncle).

28 Ibid.

29 Elder Fred Horse.

30 Elder John Buffalo, Ermineskin Reserve, Treaty 6 territory. Interviewed 18 April 1975, for

an Indian history film project. A record of the interview is in the office of Treaty and Aboriginal Rights, Winterburn, Alberta.

31 Elder Marie Smallface, Beaver Lake Reserve, Treaty 6 territory. Taken from a transcript of an Elders' meeting held in Saddle Lake in October 1983.

32 Extract from Treaty 6 document in Alexander Morris, *The Treaties of Canada with the Indians of Manitoba and the Northwest Territories Including the Negotiations on Which They Were Based, and Other Information Relating Thereto* (1862, reprint Toronto: Coles Publishing 1979), 351.

33 Ibid., 355.

34 G.T. Hunt, *Wars of the Iroquois: A Study in Inter-Tribal Trade Relations* (Madison: University of Wisconsin Press 1960), 20.

35 Alexander Morris was the lieutenant-governor of Manitoba who was asked by the Crown to negotiate Treaty 6 in 1876. He travelled to Fort Carlton and Fort Pitt in the summer of 1876 to meet with the chiefs in council.

36 Sluman and Goodwill, *John B. Tootoosis*, 13 n. 5.

37 Elder Margaret Quinney, Frog Lake Reserve, Treaty 6 territory. Interviewed at her home in the spring of 1993. Her grandfather, Simon Gadwa, and Fred Horse's father were present at the signing of the treaty. 'My grandfather used to tell us quite a bit of the time of the treaties. And I've listened to these stories closely enough to remember them what he used to say ... I used to listen to my grandfathers with great interest, of what he used to tell us.'

38 Elder Charles Blackman.

39 Elder Fred Horse.

40 Ibid.

41 Elder Margaret Quinney.

42 Elder Fred Horse.

43 Ibid.

44 Ibid.

45 Ibid.

46 Ibid.

47 Elder Capoyapit, Joseph Bighead Reserve, Treaty 6 territory. Interviewed 1989.

48 Elder Margaret Quinney.

49 Elder Fred Horse.

50 Elder Lazarus Roan, Small Boy's Camp. At the time of the interview on 30 March 1974, he was seventy years old. His father and two of his uncles were present at the signing. 'My father Shortback and his uncles Rabbit Eye and Policeman ... This is what they used to tell us when the Treaty was signed.'

51 Elder John B. Tootoosis, Poundmaker Reserve, Treaty 6 territory. This Elder dedicated his life to the teachings of the treaty and working for the protection of the treaty. He passed on to the spirit world in February 1989. The General Assembly of the United Nations passed a resolution in May 1989 to study the place within international law of Indigenous treaties signed with governments. It was this Elder's lifelong work to ensure that the treaties would be recognized as international agreements which are binding on the state of Canada.

52 Elder James Cannepotatoe, Onion Lake Reserve, Treaty 6 territory. Interviewed in the spring of 1992 at his home in Onion Lake.

53 There is a recent book written on this subject: Sarah Carter's *Lost Harvests: Prairie Indian Reserve Farms and Government Policy* (Montreal/Kingston: McGill-Queen's University Press 1990). Ms. Carter catalogues the actions by the federal government against Indigenous peoples in their attempt to become self-sufficient.

54 Elder Charles Blackman.

55 Elder James Cannepotatoe. The subsequent information in this section is told in the words of the Elder. The Elder passed on to the Spirit World in August 1996. His teachings remain with his students, who have the responsibility to carry on his work.

56 The teachings in this section are given in the words of Elder Margaret Quinney.

Chapter 8: Affirming Aboriginal Title: A New Basis for Comprehensive Claims Negotiations

1 The authors contributed equally to the preparation and writing of this paper. The names are listed in alphabetical order.

2 The use of the word 'claims' to describe the process of settlement suggests that Aboriginal parties are negotiating 'claims' against the established jurisdiction and ownership of government parties. A more neutral phrase to describe this process is 'the land question.' While we prefer the latter phrase in general, we have decided, given that the focus of this paper is on federal policy, that the terms 'claims' and 'comprehensive claims' are more appropriate.

3 In this paper, we will generally use the term 'Aboriginal people' or 'peoples.' We intend it to encompass Aboriginal people, peoples, communities, and/or nations, as is relevant. We are not differentiating between the rights of Indians, Inuit, and Metis; the term 'Aboriginal' is intended to include them all. Generally, we do not use the term 'First Nations' as it is sometimes unclear whether this term refers to First Nations as represented by the Assembly of First Nations or all Aboriginal nations. When we refer to First Nations, we are referring specifically to those nations that are considered Indian nations and are eligible for membership in the Assembly of First Nations.

4 James Bay and Northern Quebec Agreement (1975); Northeastern Quebec Agreement (1978); Inuvialuit Final Agreement (1984); Gwich'in Agreement (1992); Nunavut Land Claims Agreement (1993); Sahtu Dene and Metis Agreement (1993); and four Yukon First Nation final agreements.

5 R. Howard, 'Native Standoffs Heat Up B.C. Talks,' *Globe and Mail* (13 September 1995), p. A1. This article states there are 44 outstanding comprehensive claims in British Columbia.

6 Canada, Task Force to Review Comprehensive Claims Policy, *Living Treaties: Lasting Agreements: Report of the Task Force to Review Comprehensive Claims Policy* (Ottawa: Department of Indian Affairs and Northern Development 1985) [hereinafter *Coolican Report*].

7 Canada, Department of Indian Affairs and Northern Development, *Comprehensive Land Claims Policy* (Ottawa: Supply and Services Canada 1986) [hereinafter *1986 Federal Policy*]. A 1993 paper, *Federal Policy for the Settlement of Native Claims*, Department of Indian Affairs and Northern Development (March 1993) [hereinafter *1993 Federal Policy*] is basically a restatement of the 1986 policy paper.

8 *1986 Federal Policy*, 12.

9 Royal Commission on Aboriginal Peoples, *Treaty Making in the Spirit of Coexistence: An Alternative to Extinguishment* (Ottawa: Supply and Services Canada 1993).

10 *Black's Law Dictionary*, 6th ed. (St. Paul, MN: West Publishing Company 1990), 584.

11 *R. v. Derriksan*, [1976] 6 W.W.R. 480, 71 D.L.R. (3d) 159, 31 C.C.C. (2d) 575, 16 N.R. 321, [1977] C.N.L.B. (No. 1) 3 (S.C.C.) (Aboriginal fishing rights); *Sikyea v. R.*, [1964] S.C.R. 642, 50 D.L.R. (2d) 80, [1965] 2 C.C.C. 129, 44 C.R. 266, 49 W.W.R. 306 (treaty hunting rights); *R. v. George*, [1966] S.C.R. 267, 55 D.L.R. (2d) 386, [1966] 3 C.C.C. 137 (treaty hunting rights).

12 The legitimacy of unilateral extinguishment is a particularly critical issue for those Metis who were offered 'scrip' (rights to acquire land) under statutory regimes claiming to grant lands to the Metis in connection with extinguishment of Metis title.

13 *Calder v. A.G. B.C.*, [1973] S.C.R. 313, [1973] 4 W.W.R. 1, 34 D.L.R. (3d) 145 (S.C.C.), per Hall J. [hereinafter cited to D.L.R.].

14 Ibid., per Judson J.

15 Ibid., 208.

16 Ibid., 210.

17 Ibid., 167.

18 *R. v. Sparrow*, [1990] 1 S.C.R. 1076, 70 D.L.R (4th) 385, [1990] 3 C.N.L.R. 160, [1990] 4 W.W.R. 410, 46 B.C.L.R. (2d) 1, 56 C.C.C. (3d) 263, 111 N.R. 241 [hereinafter cited to D.L.R.].

19 Ibid., 401.

20 The term 'comprehensive claims' originates with the federal government. The federal comprehensive claims policy is intended to deal with 'continuing Aboriginal rights and

title which have not been dealt with by treaty or other legal means' (*1993 Federal Policy*, 1). The policy's stated goal is to clarify the land and resource rights of Aboriginal peoples, governments, and the private sector. The federal government sees the claims process as consisting of negotiations between Aboriginal peoples and relevant governments.

21 Dene-Metis Agreement in Principle, section 3.1.9.

22 Similar words appear in the written versions of all treaties signed between 1867 and 1982.

23 *The James Bay and Northern Quebec Agreement* (Quebec: Editeur officiel du Québec 1976).

24 Nunavut Land Claims Agreement (1993).

25 Sahtu Dene and Metis Agreement (1993).

26 *1993 Federal Policy*, 14.

27 For a description of the Treaty Land Entitlement process in Saskatchewan, see Office of the Treaty Commissioner (Cliff Wright), *Report and Recommendations on Treaty Land Entitlement* (Saskatoon 1990).

28 See, for example, *Calder* v. *A.G.B.C.*, *supra* note 13, 175, in which Hall J. quotes Lord Haldane in *Amodu Tijani v. Secretary, Southern Nigeria*, [1921] 2 A.C. 399 at 402: 'Their Lordships make the preliminary observation that in interpreting the native title to land, not only in Southern Nigeria, but other parts of the British Empire, much caution is essential. *There is a tendency, operating at times unconsciously, to render that title conceptually in terms which are appropriate only to systems which have grown up under English law. But this tendency has to be held in check closely*' (emphasis in original).
See also *Sparrow*, *supra* note 18, 411.

29 *Guerin v. The Queen* (1984), 13 D.L.R. (4th) 321 at 339 per Dickson J., [1984] 2 S.C.R. 335, 55 N.R. 161, [1984] 6 W.W.R. 481, [1985] 1 C.N.L.R. 120, 36 R.P.R. 1, 20 E.T.R. 6 [hereinafter cited to D.L.R.]; *Delgamuukw v. B.C.*, [1993] 5 W.W.R. 97, [1993] 5 C.N.L.R. 1, 104 D.L.R. (4th) 470 (B.C.C.A.)

30 *1993 Federal Policy*, 2.

31 Ibid., 5.

32 Ibid.

33 Ibid.

34 *R. v. Sparrow*, *supra* note 18, 404.

35 In *Calder v. A.G. B.C.*, *supra* note 13, the six members of the Supreme Court who addressed the issue of Aboriginal title were split evenly on the issue of whether Aboriginal title in British Columbia had been extinguished by colonial legislation prior to British Columbia's entry into Confederation. This issue is again before the Supreme Court in *Delgamuukw v. B.C.*, *supra* note 29.

36 See Michael Asch and Patrick Macklem, 'Aboriginal Rights and Canadian Sovereignty: An Essay on *R. v. Sparrow*' (1991) 29 Alta. L. Rev. 498.

37 *1993 Federal Policy*, 9.

38 Ibid.

39 Ibid., i.

40 Ibid., 9.

41 *1986 Federal Policy*, 12. The Agreement in Principle between the Nisga'a and the federal and British Columbia governments represents a recent application of this approach. The agreement does not formally call for extinguishment and it does recognize Nisga'a Aboriginal title. Should similar language survive in the final agreement, the approach does indicate a change in federal policy away from extinguishment. However, the approach remains consistent with federal policy on certainty in that the parties agree that the agreement defines these rights completely. In particular it states: 'The Final Agreement will constitute the full and final settlement, and will exhaustively set forth the aboriginal title, rights and interests within Canada of the Nisga'a Nation and its people in respect of the Nisga'a Nation's rights recognized and affirmed by section 35 ... in and to Nisga'a lands and other lands and resources in Canada, and the scope and geographical extent of all treaty rights of the Nisga'a Nation, including all jurisdictions, powers, rights, and obligations of Nisga'a government' (*Nisga'a Treaty Negotiations: Agreement in Principle* [issued jointly by the Government of Canada, the Province of British Columbia, and the Nisga'a Tribal Council, 15 February 1996], 8).

Given the actual terms of the settlement, this agreement effectively extinguishes Nisga'a Aboriginal and treaty rights with respect to fundamental matters concerning jurisdiction and power, as well as ownership. Furthermore, given that the agreement is said to exhaustively set forth rights and obligations, the approach also precludes flexibility in fulfilling treaty and Aboriginal rights relationships as circumstances change.

42 *1986 Federal Policy*, 11.

43 Ibid., 18.

44 Ibid., 17-18.

45 *1993 Federal Policy*, 9.

46 Ibid. The recent Agreement in Principle between the Nisga'a, the federal government, and British Columbia does include constitutional protection for the form of self-government negotiated. However, the powers of a Nisga'a government to have legislative authority that supersedes that of the federal Parliament or the legislature of British Columbia is restricted to such matters as 'laws in respect of the administration, management and operation of Nisga'a government' (*Nisga'a Treaty Negotiations: Agreement in Principle*, Nisga'a Government, sections 28 and 29), a certain corpus of 'laws to preserve, promote and develop Nisga'a culture and language' (section 30), and 'laws in respect of Nisga'a Lands and assets' (section 31). In most other respects, Nisga'a laws will prevail, except that 'in the event of a conflict between Nisga'a laws ... and federal or provincial laws of general application, federal or provincial laws will prevail to the extent of the conflict' (sections 32, 36, 37, 38, 40, 43, 64). Hence, the provisions remain generally consistent with the 1993 federal claims policy. Nonetheless, in that the agreement affords constitutional protection for some form of self-government without requiring a general constitutional amendment regarding self-government, it does represent a change in federal policy.

47 *Canada, First Ministers' Conference on Aboriginal Constitutional Matters: Unofficial and Unverified Verbatim Transcript*, vol. 1 (Ottawa, 15 March 1983), 134.

48 Ibid., 130.

49 Transcripts of the Public Hearings of the Royal Commission on Aboriginal Peoples, Eskasoni, Nova Scotia, 6 May 1992, 162.

50 L. Little Bear, 'Aboriginal Rights and the Canadian "Grundnorm,"' in J.R. Ponting, ed., *Arduous Journey: Canadian Indians and Decolonization* (Toronto: McClelland and Stewart 1986), 246.

51 Transcripts of the Public Hearings of the Royal Commission on Aboriginal Peoples, The Pas, Manitoba, 20 May 1992, 252.

52 Little Bear, 'Aboriginal Rights,' 247.

53 Union of British Columbia Indian Chiefs, *Treaty-Making and Title: A Non-Extinguishment Alternative for Settling the Land Question in British Columbia*, Discussion Paper no. 1 (1989), 23.

54 Transcripts of the Public Hearings of the Royal Commission on Aboriginal Peoples, Fort Simpson, Northwest Territories, 26 May 1992, 3.

55 Ibid.

56 The James Bay and Northern Quebec Agreement.

57 James Bay and Northern Quebec Native Claims Settlement Act, S.C. 1976-7, c. 32, s. 3(3).

58 See, generally, W. Moss, 'The Implementation of the James Bay and Northern Quebec Agreement' in B.W. Morse, ed., *Aboriginal Peoples and the Law: Indian, Metis and Inuit Rights in Canada* (Ottawa: Carleton University Press 1985), 684. Reported decisions include *Quebec (A.G.) v. Canada* (N.E.B.), [1994] 3 C.N.L.R. 49 (S.C.C.); *Eastmain Band v. Canada*, [1993] 3 C.N.L.R. 55 (F.C.A.); *Cree Regional Authority v. Canada*, [1991] 3 F.C. 533; *sub nom Quebec (A.G.) v. Cree Regional Authority*, [1991] 3 C.N.L.R. 82 (C.A.); *Hydro-Quebec v. Canada (A.G.) and Coon Come*, [1991] 3 C.N.L.R. 40 (Que. G.A.); *La Commission Scolaire Kativik v. Procureur Général du Québec*, [1982] 4 C.N.L.R. 54 (Que. S.C.); *Naskapis de Schefferville Band v. Procureur Général du Québec*, [1982] 4 C.N.L.R. 82 (Que. S.C.)

59 Although the Metis were not given constitutional recognition at Confederation in 1867, their role in Canada's formation cannot be ignored. In 1869, the Metis formed a provisional government under the presidency of Louis Riel, which negotiated Manitoba's

entry into Confederation on terms designed to protect the political, cultural, and land rights of the Metis. Through the Manitoba Act, 1870, the federal government put into effect several key demands of the Metis. Manitoba was admitted as a province into Confederation and given representation in Parliament. French language rights were guaranteed. The federal government set aside 1.4 million acres of land for the children of the Metis toward the extinguishment of their share of 'Indian title.' Subsequently the Dominion Lands Act extended scrip to Metis adults in Manitoba and the Northwest Territories (Saskatchewan and Alberta). See, generally, Paul L.A.H. Chartrand, *Manitoba's Metis Settlement Scheme of 1879* (Saskatoon: University of Saskatchewan Native Law Centre 1991).

60 *Report of the British Columbia Claims Task Force* (28 June 1991), 28.
61 *Coolican Report*, 43.
62 Ibid., 41.
63 *Guerin v. The Queen, supra* note 29.
64 Ibid., 337.
65 Ibid.
66 Ibid.
67 *R. v. Sparrow, supra* note 18, 408.
68 Ibid., 413.
69 [1994] 1 C.N.L.R. 40. *The Draft Declaration* has not yet been approved by the United Nations General Assembly.
70 Ibid., art. 26.
71 The prohibition against racial discrimination is found, inter alia, in the *Draft Declaration*, ibid., art. 2; the *International Covenant on Civil and Political Rights* (1966), art. 2, and the *International Covenant on Economic, Social and Cultural Rights* (1966).
72 Transcripts of the public hearings of the Royal Commission on Aboriginal Peoples, Maniwaki, Quebec, 2 December 1992, 27-8.
73 *Webster's Tenth New Collegiate Dictionary* (Springfield, MA: Merriam-Webster 1995), 285.
74 Attorney General of Canada, *Statement of the Attorney General of Canada's Position on Extinguishment, Diminution or Abandonment of Aboriginal Rights in the Claim Area*, December 1989, 2.
75 Michael Asch, 'Aboriginal Self-Government and the Construction of Canadian Constitutional Identity' (1992) 30 Alta. L. Rev. 465.
76 Michael Asch, 'Errors in *Delgamuukw*: An Anthropological Perspective,' in F. Cassidy, ed., *Aboriginal Title in British Columbia*: Delgamuukw v. The Queen (Vancouver: Oolichan Books and The Institute for Research on Public Policy 1992), 221.
77 21 U.S. (8 Wheat.) 240 (1823).
78 31 U.S. (6 Pet.) 350 (1832).
79 P.A. Cumming and N.H. Mickenberg, eds., *Native Rights in Canada*, 2nd ed. (Toronto: Indian-Eskimo Association of Canada and General Publishing 1972), 18.
80 *Johnson v. McIntosh, supra* note 77, 253-4.
81 A full discussion of whether the Crown, by Canadian law, has a title superior to that of Aboriginal peoples and, equally important, what its lawful obligations are regardless of the strength of its title, is beyond the scope of this paper.
82 *Calder v. A.G. B.C., supra* note 13, 156.
83 Ibid., 169.
84 *Coolican Report* (*supra* note 6).
85 *Report of the British Columbia Claims Task Force* (*supra* note 60).
86 Ibid., 17.
87 Ibid., 29.
88 It seems incumbent upon those who wish to challenge this assertion to explain why First Nations were different than other non-European nations in this respect, to the extent that the mere arrival and claim of sovereignty by a European nation would be sufficient to establish a self-evident underlying title in that European nation.
89 See C. Bell and M. Asch 'Challenging Assumptions: The Impact of Precedent in Aboriginal Rights Litigation,' in this volume.

90 *United Nations, International Covenant on Civil and Political Rights* (1966) and International Covenant on Economic, Social and Cultural Rights (1966).
91 See P. Hogg, *Constitutional Law of Canada*, 3rd ed. (Toronto: Carswell 1992), 822-4.
92 Royal Commission on Aboriginal Peoples, *Partners in Confederation: Aboriginal Peoples, Self-Government, and the Constitution* (Ottawa: Supply and Services Canada 1993).
93 See, generally, B. Slattery, 'Aboriginal Sovereignty and Imperial Claims' (1991) 29 Osgoode Hall L.J. 681.
94 L. Little Bear, 'Aboriginal Rights,' 246.

Contributors

Michael Asch is a professor in the Department of Anthropology at the University of Alberta.

Catherine Bell is an associate professor in the Faculty of Law at the University of Alberta.

John Borrows is an associate professor in the Faculty of Law at the University of British Columbia, where he is also the Director of First Nations Legal Studies.

J. Edward Chamberlin is a professor of English and Comparative Literature at the University of Toronto.

Emma LaRocque, a Plains Cree Metis, is a writer, poet, historian, and social and literary critic; she is also a professor in the Department of Native Studies at the University of Manitoba.

Patrick Macklem is an associate professor in the Faculty of Law at the University of Toronto.

Kent McNeil is an associate professor in Osgoode Hall Law School at York University.

Sharon Venne is by marriage a citizen of the Blood Tribe and was originally a member of Muskeg Lake Band of Treaty 6. A graduate of the University of Victoria Law School, she recently received her Masters in Law from the University of Alberta after spending fifteen years at the United Nations advocating the rights of Indigenous Peoples.

Norman Zlotkin is an associate professor in the College of Law at the University of Saskatchewan.

Index

Set in Stone by Chris Munro

Printed and bound in Canada by Friesens

Copy-editor: Pat Feindel

Proofreader: Judy Phillips

Indexer: Annette Lorek